POLITICS AND POWER
Who Should Rule

Politics
and Power
WHO SHOULD RULE

EDITED AND SELECTED WITH INTRODUCTIONS
by Terry Hoy

G. P. PUTNAM'S SONS
NEW YORK

CONTENTS

INTRODUCTION

Political scientists are generally agreed that the exercise of power is the central focus and substance of political behavior. "When we speak of power, we mean man's control over the minds and actions of other men. By political power we refer to the mutual relations of control among the leaders of public authority and between the latter and the people at large."[1] Viewed in another way, politics as power consists fundamentally of relationships of superordination and subordination, of dominance and submission, of the governors and the governed.[2] Politics has been defined "as a study of the act of control, or as the act of human or social control."[3] In a similar vein, Harold Lasswell defines the study of politics as the study of the "influence and the influential."[4]

Inherent in common definitions of political power is the related concept of political rulership which may be characterized as institutionalized political power. This may be a vast complicated design, as in modern constitutional regimes, or it may involve an arrangement within a simple hierarchy, as in autocratic regimes or totalitarian dictatorships. But whether the design is complicated or simple, the structure of such a government forms a pattern composed of institutions identified as parts of a whole. In a more general sense, then, government may be defined as an institutionalized pattern of stabilized power or rule.[5]

What is unique in rulership, however, is the claim of legitimacy. While power, in itself, is the mere capacity of influence or control of the actions of others, rulership embodies a moral claim or justification

[1] Hans Morgenthau, *Politics Among Nations* (New York: Alfred Knopf, 1960), p. 28.

[2] V. O. Key, *Politics, Parties, and Pressure Groups* (New York: Thomas Crowell Company, 1964), p. 3.

[3] George E. G. Catlin, *A Study of the Principles of Politics* (New York: Macmillan, 1930), pp. 68–69.

[4] Harold Lasswell, *Politics: Who Gets What, When and How* (New York: Meridian Books, 1958), p. 13.

[5] See Carl Friedrich, *Man and His Government* (New York: McGraw Hill, N.J., 1963), pp. 180–82.

of the *right* to rule. As Robert Dahl puts it : "Leaders in a political system try to insure that whenever governmental means are used to deal with conflict, the decisions arrived at are widely accepted not solely from fear of violence, punishment or coercion, but also from a belief that it is morally right and proper to do so."[6] Rulership, in this respect, embodies what Charles Merriam refers to as the "credenda of power"; the reasons which oblige the intellect to give assent to the continuance of authority.[7] The concept of legitimacy, it is well to emphasize, should not be confused with legality, which, as Carl Friedrich notes, is only one particular instance of legitimacy: whether a rule is in accordance with positive law. The central question of legitimacy, however, is whether actions of the ruler are in accordance with generally accepted values and beliefs in respect to why some men have the right to command and others the duty to obey.[8]

The concept of legitimacy, as the moral justification for political rule, constitutes a prominent theme in the history of Western political thought. Various views of legitimacy cannot be neatly arranged into types or categories since there is a great deal of overlapping, variation and many subtypes. But it is possible to discern several broad patterns or tendencies. One general conception, given classic expression in Plato's *Republic,* is that political rulership must be exercised by men of exceptional wisdom and knowledge : the philosopher-kings. This view is based on the assumption that virtue is knowledge, and that there is an objective good which can be known by rational, logical investigation. From this it follows that the man who knows—the philosopher, scholar or scientist—ought to have the decisive power in government. The broad mass of the people, by contrast, are ignorant and incompetent. Politicians, Plato believed, are the special curse of democracy, practicing the ignoble art of pandering to the "great beast."

A second general category, prominent in sixteenth-century European history, is founded on the belief that political rule receives its justification from divine sanction which requires neither legal nor rational justification. Those who rule must be seen as the embodiment of qualities which set them apart from ordinary men, possessing superhuman or supernatural powers. This conception of legitimacy includes the principle of theocratic government expressed in the theory and

---

[6] Robert Dahl, *Modern Political Analysis* (Englewood Cliffs, Prentice-Hall, 1963), p. 19.

[7] Charles Merriam, *Political Power* (New York: Collier Books, 1964), p. 118.

[8] See Friedrich, *op. cit.,* p. 234.

practice of Calvinism, and in the theory of the divine right of kings, well illustrated by the views of James I.

A third category, made famous by Machiavelli's *Prince,* embodies a concept of political leadership in which political power becomes an end in itself, divorced from questions of ethics, morality or religion. The political leader, accordingly, must be a man who has qualities necessary for the attainment of power: courage, audacity and fore-sight; skill in the techniques and strategies of warfare and diplomacy; the willingness to resort to whatever means (fair or foul) are necessary to attain political power. Carlyle's hero-theory of history may also be included within this classification. Contemptuous of popular demo-cracy as the rule of mediocrity and incompetence, Carlyle advocated the dominance of power by the heroic leader whose distinctive quality is the capacity for bold audacious actions based on an intuitive, rather than a philosophical, grasp of historical reality.

A fourth position, the democratic concept of political rule, finds its classic expression in the writings of John Locke and Jean-Jacques Rousseau. Locke's *Two Treatises of Government* is the major source of the democratic concept that the purpose of government is the pro-tection of individual natural rights, and that political rule must be based on the principle of consent and majority rule. Rousseau's con-tribution stems from the concept of the General Will, a moral con-sensus of the common good which all individuals have participated in creating. The General Will, Rousseau maintained, is the source of all law and the standard of what is just and unjust within the political community. American democracy has been greatly influenced by the tradition of John Locke, but the political philosophy of the American Constitution owes much to the influence of Montesquieu, who stressed the importance of the principle of separation of powers as a means of prevention of the dangers of abuse of political power. A basic feature of American political evolution has centered on the tension between liberty and authority, and the problem of reconciliation of majority rule and minority rights. This problem is well illustrated in the con-trasting emphasis one finds in the views of Thomas Jefferson and James Madison. Jefferson expressed a confident optimism in majority rule as the basic principle of representative government; Madison voiced alarm at the dangers of majority tyranny as the result of factional combinations and believed that the essence of representative government resides in providing means for controlling and restraining the effects of faction. Jefferson and Madison thus expressed two aspects of constitutional democracy: the belief that government must conform to the will of the people and also the belief that government must be subject to limits and restraints in order to protect the people against the dangers of arbitrary political power.

A fifth conception of political rule stems from the conservative reaction to the principles of liberal democracy of Locke and Rousseau. This reaction was given its most eloquent expression by Edmund Burke. As an approach to defining the grounds of political rule, Burke emphasized the authority of tradition and custom, in contrast to the rule of numbers or electoral decisions. Prescription, he contended, is the most solid of all titles, creating a presumption in favor of any settled scheme of government against any untried schemes or innovations. A nation is an ideal of continuity, which is not the momentary choice of one day or one set of people but the deliberate election of ages and generations; a constitution made up of peculiar circumstances and occasions, moral, civil and social habitudes, which disclose themselves only in a long period of time. Coupled with Burke's emphasis on the authority of tradition is his view that those who are the owners of property are the repositories of vested wisdom and experience and thus have the qualities of prudential judgment and wisdom necessary for the exercise of political leadership.

A sixth category derives from the view that elites are inevitable features of social organization and the historical process; this is a view that has been given its most influential expression in the sociological theories of Gaetano Mosca, Robert Michels and Vilfredo Pareto. The dominance of political power by elites, according to Pareto, is an inevitable feature of historical experience; and the art of government, he believes, depends upon the exercise of deceit and violence. Pareto's elitist doctrine is presented as a scientific theory rather than as a value judgment. But from the view that elites are *inevitable* features of social organization, it is an easy transition to the view that, therefore, such elites have qualities or abilities that give them the *right* to rule. Pareto's theory, for this reason, has been characterized as a modernized version of Machiavelli's *Prince*.

Modern Fascism and Communism are two variants of twentieth-century totalitarianism. They both repudiate parliamentary democracy and place an emphasis upon the natural necessity or inevitability of elites or heroic individuals. But political leadership is seen as the bearer or representative of a larger collective will or entity. Fascist doctrine embodies a conception of political rule which has antecedents in the tradition of Machiavelli's *Prince* and Carlyle. What is unique in Fascism, however, is the emphasis upon the heroic leader as the expression of a collective will embodied in the "racial folk" (the characteristic feature of Nazism) or as the embodiment of the all-powerful state (the central doctrine of Italian Fascism). The Marxist concept of leadership embodies an emphasis upon the unique political role of the working class as the vehicle for revolutionary change and transformation. But Marxism also involves an elitist aspect in the emphasis upon the indispensable role of a revolutionary intelligentsia as the "vanguard of the proletariat," educating the workers in socialist ideology and providing the party discipline and organization necessary to the seizure and consolidation of power.

Although some of the traditional claims to legitimacy, such as the theory of the divine right of kings and the principle of theocracy, are primarily of historical interest, others are still very much a part of the ideological fabric of modern political institutions. Modern democracy rests upon the foundations of legitimacy derived from classical figures such as John Locke, Jean-Jacques Rousseau, Thomas Jefferson and James Madison. The Marxist concept of legitimacy underlies ideological principles of leadership in the Soviet Union, China and other Communist countries. The appeal to the authority of tradition, as formulated by Edmund Burke, has strongly influenced the views of contemporary conservative spokesmen in democratic countries. Fascist conceptions of political rule did not die with Hitler and Mussolini, and its ideas continue to find adherents and exponents in most Western nations. The tradition of Machiavelli has exercised strong influence upon modern exponents of "power politics," and the elitist doctrines of Pareto have had an important influence upon modern developments in sociological and political analysis.

It is hoped, then, that the readings from classical sources presented in this volume will acquaint the reader with conceptions of political rule that are of basic importance. Familiarity with them aids our understanding of Western history; their relevance to problems of modern government sheds light on the political problems of our own time.

1

PLATO
The Rule of the Wise

The conception of political rulership presented in Plato's *Republic* should be seen against the background of the Greek city-states at a time when political strife was in the process of degeneration—warfare among the city-states; civil strife and party factionalism from within. Coming to manhood within this context, it is not surprising that Plato (427–347 B.C.) should have been disillusioned with the political institutions of Greece, as well as being profoundly shocked by the condemnation of his great teacher and master, Socrates, by the Athenian courts. These developments, it can be assumed, deflected him from any intention he may have had of entering public life and influenced his conviction that philosophical knowledge and speculation must be applied to problems of political rule. Between 388 and 369 B.C., Plato founded a school of philosophy called the Academy, and it was about this time that he published his greatest work, the dialogue called the *Republic*, which expressed one of the aims of the Academy: the production of a science of politics necessary to reform the Greek world.

The *Republic* provides a classic statement of the theory that political power should be exercised by individuals of exceptional wisdom and knowledge. This view results from the basic premise of the *Republic*—the general harmony of society requires a cooperative relationship in which each individual performs a specialized function in accordance with his natural fitness and abilities. This principle of specialization of labor divides the citizens into three classes: (1) producers; (2) soldiers; (3) rulers, or the philosopher-kings.

The function of rulership is not simply one of a number of technical crafts such as farming or shoemaking; it is founded upon a more all-encompassing wisdom and knowledge of an objective good which can be apprehended only by the gifted few: those with exceptional mental and physical endowments, trained for the duties of statesmanship by a state-controlled program of higher education. Since political rule must be based on the knowledge of eternal, unchangeable truths, accessible only to the philosopher, Plato gave no place to the role of public opinion. He was convinced that the peculiar malaise of city-state democracy stemmed from the incompetence of politicians, party strife and factionalism.

Plato's theory of rulership, it should be obvious, constitutes a serious challenge to democratic principles; it is a common view that the *Republic* is an ideological support for totalitarian tyranny at worst, or an enlightened despotism at best. The democratic concept of political rule, it is contended, cannot be grounded on the assumption of an eternal, unchanging objective good, accessible only to the gifted few, but upon the recognition of the tentative, hypothetical character of political goals and values. Political rule, for this reason, must be based on the principle of free discussion and debate by all citizens; the acceptance of majority decisions; the full play of public opinion and partisan controversy. What is lacking in Plato's theory is a recognition that all men, and not just a few, have the capacity for participation in the responsibilities of political rule. Nor does the political theory of the *Republic* recognize a central emphasis of constitutional democracy: the belief that government must be subject to institutional restraints and the rule of law as a means of preventing the abuse of power by political leadership.

The view that Plato's theory is an ideological basis for totalitarianism, fundamentally inimical to the spirit and substance of democracy, has not gone without challenge.[1] Plato's theory of rulership, in its central emphasis upon the appeal to reason, justice and the common good, cannot be equated with totalitarian political systems in which naked power, force and compulsion are the established canons of political rule. It can be argued, in fact, that Plato's theory embodies principles and values which are central to the heritage of Western democracy. For democracy is not a radical skepticism or relativism but a commitment to basic moral principles which transcend the interests of particular individuals or popular majorities. The democratic principle of equality, for example, stems from the Christian-Stoic concept of higher law: the view that all men are equal, not in physical endowments or abilities, but in the rational capacity to distinguish right from wrong and to lend the life of virtue. Men submit to majority rule not because of its numerical superiority but because of the belief that the process of reasoned debate and discussion can lead to the realization of justice and the common good. Democratic theory is an emphasis that wisdom is available to all men and not just a few, and in this respect it departs from the assumption of Plato's theory. But it is possible to contend, nonetheless, that Platonism belongs to the higher-law

---

[1] For a symposium of conflicting views on this question see Thomas Thorson, ed., *Plato : Totalitarian or Democrat?* (Englewood Cliffs, N.J.: Prentice–Hall, 1963).

tradition which, through the later Christian-Stoic modifications, provides a major contribution to the moral foundations of Western democracy.*

Let me begin by reminding you that we found our way hither in the search after justice and injustice.

True, he replied; but what of that?

I was only going to ask whether, if we have discovered them, we are to require that the just man should in nothing fail of absolute justice; or may we be satisfied with an approximation, and the attainment in him of a higher degree of justice than is to be found in other men?

The approximation will be enough.

We are enquiring into the nature of absolute justice and into the character of the perfectly just, and into injustice and the perfectly unjust, that we might have an ideal. We were to look at these in order that we might judge of our own happiness and unhappiness according to the standard which they exhibited and the degree in which we resembled them, but not with any view of showing that they could exist in fact.

True, he said.

Would a painter be any the worse because, after having delineated with consummate art an ideal of a perfectly beautiful man, he was unable to show that any such man could ever have existed?

He would be none the worse.

Well, and were we not creating an ideal of a perfect State?

To be sure.

And is our theory a worse theory because we are unable to prove the possibility of a city being ordered in the manner described?

Surely not, he replied.

That is the truth, I said. But if, at your request, I am to try and show how and under what conditions the possibility is highest, I must ask you, having this in view, to repeat your former admissions.

What admissions?

I want to know whether ideals are ever fully realised in language? Does not the word express more than the fact, and must not the actual, whatever a man may think, always, in the nature of things, fall short of the truth? What do you say?

* The selection is taken from Books V, VI and VII of Plato's *Republic*, trans. by B. Jowett.

I agree.

Then you must not insist on my proving that the actual State will in every respect coincide with the ideal: if we are only able to discover how a city may be governed nearly as we proposed, you will admit that we have discovered the possibility which you demand; and will be contented. I am sure that I should be contented—will not you?

Yes, I will.

Let me next endeavour to show what is that fault in States which is the cause of their present maladministration, and what is the least change which will enable a State to pass into the truer form, and let the change, if possible, be of one thing only, or if not, of two; at any rate, let the changes be as few and slight as possible.

Certainly, he replied.

I think, I said, that there might be a reform of the State if only one change were made, which is not a slight or easy though still a possible one.

What is it? he said.

Now then, I said, I go to meet that which I liken to the greatest of the waves; yet shall the word be spoken, even though the wave break and drown me in laughter and dishonour; and do you mark my words.

Proceed.

I said : *Until philosophers are kings, or the kings and princes of this world have the spirit and power of philosophy, and political greatness and wisdom meet in one, and those commoner natures who pursue either to the exclusion of the other are compelled to stand aside, cities will never have rest from their evils,—no, nor the human race, as I believe,—and then only will this our State have a possibility of life and behold the light of day....*

Inasmuch as philosophers only are able to grasp the eternal and unchangeable, and those who wander in the region of the many and variable are not philosophers, I must ask you which of the two classes should be the rulers of our State?

And how can we rightly answer that question?

Whichever of the two are best able to guard the laws and institutions of our State—let them be our guardians.

Very good.

Neither, I said, can there be any question that the guardian who is to keep anything should have eyes rather than no eyes?

There can be no question of that.

And are not those who are verily and indeed wanting in the knowledge of the true being of each thing, and who have in their souls no clear pattern, and are unable as with a painter's eye to look at the absolute truth and to that original to repair, and having perfect vision of the other world to order the laws about beauty, goodness, justice in this, if not already ordered, and to guard and preserve the order of them—are not such persons, I ask, simply blind?

Truly, he replied, they are much in that condition.

And shall they be our guardians when there are others who, besides being their equals in experience and falling short of them in no particular of virtue, also know the very truth of each thing?

There can be no reason, he said, for rejecting those who have this greatest of all great qualities; they must always have the first place unless they fail in some other respect.

Suppose then, I said, that we determine how far they can unite this and the other excellences.

By all means.

In the first place, as we began by observing, the nature of the philosopher has to be ascertained. We must come to an understanding about him, and, when we have done so, then, if I am not mistaken, we shall also acknowledge that such an union of qualities is possible, and that those in whom they are united, and those only, should be rulers in the State.

What do you mean?

Let us suppose that philosophical minds always love knowledge of a sort which shows them the eternal nature not varying from generation and corruption.

Agreed.

And further, I said, let us agree that they are lovers of all true being; there is no part whether greater or less, or more or less honourable, which they are willing to renounce; as we said before of the lover and the man of ambition.

True.

And if they are to be what we were describing, is there not another quality which they should also possess?

What quality?

Truthfulness: they will never intentionally receive into their mind falsehood, which is their detestation, and they will love the truth.

Yes, that may be safely affirmed of them.

"May be," my friend, I replied, is not the word; say rather, "must be affirmed": for he whose nature is amorous of anything cannot help loving all that belongs or is akin to the object of his affections.

Right, he said.

And is there anything more akin to wisdom than truth?

How can there be?

Can the same nature be a lover of wisdom and a lover of falsehood? Never.

The true lover of learning then must from his earliest youth, as far as in him lies, desire all truth?

Assuredly.

But then again, as we know by experience, he whose desires are strong in one direction will have them weaker in others; they will be like a stream which has been drawn off into another channel.

True.

He whose desires are drawn towards knowledge in every form will be absorbed in the pleasures of the soul, and will hardly feel bodily pleasure—I mean, if he be a true philosopher and not a sham one.

That is most certain.

Such an one is sure to be temperate and the reverse of covetous; for the motives which make another man desirous of having and spending have no place in his character.

Very true.

Another criterion of the philosophical nature has also to be considered.

What is that?

There should be no secret corner of illiberality; nothing can be more antagonistic than meanness to a soul which is ever longing after the whole of things both divine and human.

Most true, he replied.

Then how can he who has magnificence of mind and is the spectator of all time and all existence, think much of human life?

He cannot.

Or can such an one account death fearful?

No indeed.

Then the cowardly and mean nature has no part in true philosophy?

Certainly not.

Or again: can he who is harmoniously constituted, who is not covetous or mean, or a boaster, or a coward—can he, I say, ever be unjust or hard in his dealings?

Impossible.

Then you will soon observe whether a man is just and gentle, or rude and unsociable; these are the signs which distinguish even in youth the philosophical nature from the unphilosophical.

True.

There is another point which should be remarked.

What point?

Whether he has or has not a pleasure in learning; for no one will love that which gives him pain, and in which after much toil he makes little progress.

Certainly not.

And again, if he is forgetful and retains nothing of what he learns, will he not be an empty vessel?

That is certain.

Labouring in vain, he must end in hating himself and his fruitless occupation?

Yes.

Then a soul which forgets cannot be ranked among genuine philosophic natures; we must insist that the philosopher should have a good memory?

Certainly.

And once more, the inharmonious and unseemly nature can only tend to disproportion?

Undoubtedly.

And do you consider truth to be akin to proportion or to disproportion?

To proportion.

Then, besides other qualities, we must try to find a naturally well-proportioned and gracious mind, which will move spontaneously towards the true being of everything.

Certainly.

Well, and do not all these qualities, which we have been enumerating, go together, and are they not, in a manner, necessary to a soul, which is to have a full and perfect participation of being?

They are absolutely necessary, he replied.

And must not that be a blameless study which he only can pursue who has the gift of a good memory, and is quick to learn,—noble, gracious, the friend of truth, justice, courage, temperance, who are his kindred?

The god of jealousy himself, he said, could find no fault with such a study.

And to men like him, I said, when perfected by years and education, and to these only you will entrust the State.

Here Adeimantus interposed and said: To these statements, Socrates, no one can offer a reply; but when you talk in this way, a strange feeling passes over the minds of your hearers: They fancy that they are led astray a little at each step in the argument, owing to their own want of skill in asking and answering questions; these littles accumulate, and at the end of the discussion they are found to have sustained a mighty overthrow and all their former notions appear to be turned upside down. And as unskilful players of draughts are at last shut up by their more skilful adversaries and have no piece to move, so they too find themselves shut up at last; for they have nothing to say in this new game of which words are the counters; and yet all the time they are in the right. The observation is suggested to me by what is now occurring. For any one of us might say, that although in words he is not able to meet you at each step of the argument, he sees as a fact that the votaries of philosophy, when they carry on the study, not only in youth as a part of education, but as the pursuit of their maturer years, most of them become strange monsters, not to say utter rogues, and that those who may be considered the best of them are made useless to the world by the very study which you extol.

Well, and do you think that those who say so are wrong?

I cannot tell, he replied; but I should like to know what is your opinion.

Hear my answer; I am of opinion that they are quite right.

Then how can you be justified in saying that cities will not cease from evil until philosophers rule in them, when philosophers are acknowledged by us to be of no use to them?

You ask a question, I said, to which a reply can only be given in a parable.

Yes, Socrates; and that is a way of speaking to which you are not at all accustomed, I suppose.

I perceive, I said, that you are vastly amused at having plunged me into such a hopeless discussion; but now hear the parable, and then you will be still more amused at the meagreness of my imagination: for the manner in which the best men are treated in their own States is so grievous that no single thing on earth is comparable to it; and therefore, if I am to plead their cause, I must have recourse to fiction, and put together a figure made up of many things, like the fabulous union of goats and stags which are found in pictures. Imagine then a fleet or a ship in which there is a captain who is taller and stronger than any of the crew, but he is a little deaf and has a similar infirmity in sight, and his knowledge of navigation is not much better. The sailors are quarrelling with one another about the steering—every one is of opinion that he has a right to steer, though he has never learned the art of navigation and cannot tell who taught him or when he learned, and will further assert that it cannot be taught, and they are ready to cut in pieces any one who says the contrary. They throng about the captain, begging and praying him to commit the helm to them; and if at any time they do not prevail, but others are preferred to them, they kill the others or throw them overboard, and having first chained up the noble captain's senses with drink or some narcotic drug, they mutiny and take possession of the ship and make free with the stores; thus, eating and drinking, they proceed on their voyage in such a manner as might be expected of them. Him who is their partisan and cleverly aids them in their plot for getting the ship out of the captain's hands into their own whether by force or persuasion, they compliment with the name of sailor, pilot, able seaman, and abuse the other sort of man, whom they call a good-for-nothing; but that the true pilot must pay attention to the year and seasons and sky and stars and winds, and whatever else belongs to his art, if he intends to be really qualified for the command of a ship, and that he must and will be the steerer, whether other people like or not— the possibility of this union of authority with the steerer's art has never seriously entered into their thoughts or been made part of their calling. Now in vessels which are in a state of mutiny and by sailors who are mutineers, how will the true pilot be regarded? Will he not be called by them a prater, a star-gazer, a good-for-nothing?

Of course, said Adeimantus.

Then you will hardly need, I said, to hear the interpretation of the figure, which describes the true philosopher in his relation to the State; for you understand already.

Certainly.

Then suppose you now take this parable to the gentleman who is surprised at finding that philosophers have no honour in their cities; explain it to him and try to convince him that their having honour would be far more extraordinary.

I will.

Say to him, that, in deeming the best votaries of philosophy to be useless to the rest of the world, he is right; but also tell him to attribute their uselessness to the fault of those who will not use them, and not to themselves. The pilot should not humbly beg the sailors to be commanded by him—that is not the order of nature; neither are "the wise to go to the doors of the rich"—the ingenious author of this saying told a lie—but the truth is, that, when a man is ill, whether he be rich or poor, to the physician he must go, and he who wants to be governed, to him who is able to govern. The ruler who is good for anything ought not to beg his subjects to be ruled by him; although the present governors of mankind are of a different stamp; they may be justly compared to the mutinous sailors, and the true helmsmen to those who are called by them good-for-nothings and star-gazers.

Precisely so, he said.

For these reasons, and among men like these, philosophy, the noblest pursuit of all, is not likely to be much esteemed by those of the opposite faction; not that the greatest and most lasting injury is done to her by her opponents, but by her own professing followers, the same of whom you suppose the accuser to say, that the greater number of them are arrant rogues, and the best are useless; in which opinion I agreed.

Yes.

And the reason why the good are useless has now been explained?

True.

Then shall we proceed to show that the corruption of the majority is also unavoidable, and that this is not to be laid to the charge of philosophy any more than the other?

By all means.

And let us ask and answer in turn, first going back to the description of the gentle and noble nature. Truth, as you will remember, was his leader, whom he followed always and in all things; failing in this, he was an impostor, and had no part or lot in true philosophy.

Yes, that was said.

Well, and is not this one quality, to mention no others, greatly at variance with present notions of him?

Certainly, he said.

And have we not a right to say in his defence, that the true lover of knowledge is always striving after being—that is his nature; he will not rest in the multiplicity of individuals which is an appearance only, but will go on—the keen edge will not be blunted, nor the force of his desire abate until he have attained the knowledge of the true nature of every essence by a sympathetic and kindred power in the soul, and by that power drawing near and mingling and becoming incorporate with very being, having begotten mind and truth, he will have knowledge and will live and grow truly, and then, and not till then, will he cease from his travail.

Nothing, he said, can be more just than such a description of him.

And will the love of a lie be any part of a philosopher's nature? Will he not utterly hate a lie?

He will.

And when truth is the captain, we cannot suspect any evil of the band which he leads?

Impossible.

Justice and health of mind will be of the company, and temperance will follow after?

True, he replied.

Neither is there any reason why I should again set in array the philosopher's virtues, as you will doubtless remember that courage, magnificence, apprehension, memory, were his natural gifts. And you objected that, although no one could deny what I then said, still, if you leave words and look at facts, the persons who are thus described are some of them manifestly useless, and the greater number utterly depraved; we were then led to enquire into the grounds of these accusations, and have now arrived at the point of asking why are the majority bad, which question of necessity brought us back to the examination and definition of the true philosopher.

Exactly.

And we have next to consider the corruptions of the philosophic nature, why so many are spoiled and so few escape spoiling—I am speaking of those who were said to be useless but not wicked—and, when we have done with them, we will speak of the imitators of philosophy, what manner of men are they who aspire after a profession which is above them and of which they are unworthy, and then, by their manifold inconsistencies, bring upon philosophy, and upon all philosophers, that universal reprobation of which we speak.

What are these corruptions? he said.

I will see if I can explain them to you. Every one will admit that a nature having in perfection all the qualities which we required in a philosopher, is a rare plant which is seldom seen among men.

Rare indeed.

And what numberless and powerful causes tend to destroy these rare natures!

What causes?

In the first place there are their own virtues, their courage, temperance, and the rest of them, every one of which praiseworthy qualities (and this is a most singular circumstance) destroys and distracts from philosophy the soul which is the possessor of them.

That is very singular, he replied.

Then there are all the ordinary goods of life—beauty, wealth, strength, rank, and great connections in the State—you understand the sort of things—these also have a corrupting and distracting effect.

I understand; but I should like to know more precisely what you mean about them.

Grasp the truth as a whole, I said, and in the right way; you will then have no difficulty in apprehending the preceding remarks, and they will no longer appear strange to you.

And how am I to do so? he asked.

Why, I said, we know that all germs or seeds, whether vegetable or animal, when they fail to meet with proper nutriment or climate or soil, in proportion to their vigour, are all the more sensitive to the want of a suitable environment, for evil is a greater enemy to what is good than what is not.

Very true.

There is reason in supposing that the finest natures, when under alien conditions, receive more injury than the inferior, because the contrast is greater.

Certainly.

And may we not say, Adeimantus, that the most gifted minds, when they are ill-educated, become pre-eminently bad? Do not great crimes and the spirit of pure evil spring out of a fulness of nature ruined by education rather than from any inferiority, whereas weak natures are scarcely capable of any very great good or very great evil?

There I think that you are right.

And our philosopher follows the same analogy—he is like a plant which, having proper nurture, must necessarily grow and mature into all virtue, but, if sown and planted in an alien soil, becomes the most noxious of all weeds, unless he be preserved by some divine power. Do you really think, as people so often say, that our youth are corrupted by Sophists, or that private teachers of the art corrupt them in any degree worth speaking of? Are not the public who says these things the greatest of all Sophists? And do they not educate to perfection young and old, men and women alike, and fashion them after their own hearts?

When is this accomplished? he said.

When they meet together, and the world sits down at an assembly, or in a court of law, or a theatre, or a camp, or in any other popular resort, and there is a great uproar, and they praise some things which are being said or done, and blame other things, equally exaggerating both, shouting and clapping their hands, and the echo of the rocks and the place in which they are assembled redoubles the sound of the praise or blame—at such a time will not a young man's heart, as they say, leap within him? Will any private training enable him to stand firm against the overwhelming flood of popular opinion? or will he be carried away by the stream? Will he not have the notions of good and evil which the public in general have—he will do as they do, and as they are, such will he be?

Yes, Socrates; necessity will compel him.

And yet, I said, there is a still greater necessity, which has not been mentioned.

What is that?

The gentle force of attainder or confiscation or death, which, as you are aware, these new Sophists and educators, who are the public, apply when their words are powerless.

Indeed they do; and in right good earnest.

Now what opinion of any other Sophist, or of any private person, can be expected to overcome in such an unequal contest?

None, he replied.

No, indeed, I said, even to make the attempt is a great piece of folly; there neither is, nor has been, nor is ever likely to be, any different type of character which has had no other training in virtue but that which is supplied by public opinion—I speak, my friend, of human virtue only; what is more than human, as the proverb says, is not included: for I would not have you ignorant that, in the present evil state of governments, whatever is saved and comes to good is saved by the power of God, as we may truly say.

I quite assent, he replied.

Then let me crave your assent also to a further observation.

What are you going to say?

Why, that all those mercenary individuals, whom the many call Sophists and whom they deem to be their adversaries, do, in fact, teach nothing but the opinion of the many, that is to say, the opinions of their assemblies: and this is their wisdom. I might compare them to a man who should study the tempers and desires of a mighty strong beast who is fed by him—he would learn how to approach and handle him, also at what times and from what causes he is dangerous or the reverse, and what is the meaning of his several cries, and by what sounds, when another utters them, he is soothed or infuriated; and you may suppose further, that when, by continually attending upon him, he has become perfect in all this, he calls his knowledge wisdom, and makes of it a system or art, which he proceeds to teach, although he has no real notion of what he means by the principles or passions of which he is speaking, but calls this honourable and that dishonourable, or good or evil, or just or unjust, all in accordance with the tastes and tempers of the great brute. Good he pronounces to be that in which the beast delights and evil to be that which he dislikes; and he can give no other account of them except that the just and noble are the necessary, having never himself seen, and having no power of explaining to others the nature of either, or the difference between them, which is immense. By heaven, would not such a one be a rare educator?

Indeed, he would.

And in what way does he who thinks that wisdom is the discernment of the tempers and tastes of the motley multitude, whether in painting or music, or, finally, in politics, differ from him whom I have been describing? For when a man consorts with the many, and exhibits to them his poem or other work of art or the service which he has done the State, making them his judges when he is not obliged, the so-called necessity of Diomed will oblige him to produce whatever they praise. And yet the reasons are utterly ludicrous which they give in confirmation of their own notions about the honourable and good. Did you ever hear any of them which were not?

No, nor am I likely to hear.

You recognise the truth of what I have been saying? Then let me ask you to consider further whether the world will ever be induced to believe in the existence of absolute beauty rather than of the many beautiful, or of the absolute in each kind rather than of the many in each kind?

Certainly not.

Then the world cannot possibly be a philosopher?

Impossible.

And therefore philosophers must inevitably fall under the censure of the world?

They must.

And of individuals who consort with the mob and seek to please them?

That is evident.

Then, do you see any way in which the philosopher can be preserved in his calling to the end? and remember what we were saying of him, that he was to have quickness and memory and courage and magnificence—these were admitted by us to be the true philosopher's gifts.

Yes.

Will not such an one from his early childhood be in all things first among all, especially if his bodily endowments are like his mental ones?

Certainly, he said.

And his friends and fellow-citizens will want to use him as he gets older for their own purposes?

No question.

Falling at his feet, they will make requests to him and do him honour and flatter him, because they want to get into their hands now the power which he will one day possess.

That often happens, he said.

And what will a man such as he is be likely to do under such circumstances, especially if he be a citizen of a great city, rich and noble, and a tall proper youth? Will he not be full of boundless aspirations, and fancy himself able to manage the affairs of Hellenes and of barbarians, and having got such notions into his head will he not dilate and elevate himself in the fulness of vain pomp and senseless pride?

To be sure he will.

Now, when he is in this state of mind, if some one gently comes to him and tells him that he is a fool and must get understanding, which can only be got by slaving for it, do you think that, under such adverse circumstances, he will be easily induced to listen?

Far otherwise.

And even if there be some one who through inherent goodness or natural reasonableness has had his eyes opened a little and is humbled and taken captive by philosophy, how will his friends behave when they think that they are likely to lose the advantage which they were hoping to reap from his companionship? Will they not do and say anything to prevent him from yielding to his better nature and to render his teacher powerless, using to this end private intrigues as well as public prosecutions?

There can be no doubt of it.

And how can one who is thus circumstanced ever become a philosopher?

Impossible.

Then were we not right in saying that even the very qualities which make a man a philosopher may, if he be ill-educated, divert him from philosophy, no less than riches and their accompaniments and the other so-called goods of life?

We were quite right.

Thus, my excellent friend, is brought about all that ruin and failure which I have been describing of the natures best adapted to the best of all pursuits; they are natures which we maintain to be rare at any time; this being the class out of which come the men who are the authors of the greatest evil to States and individuals; and also of the greatest good when the tide carries them in that direction; but a small man never was the doer of any great thing either to individuals or to States.

That is most true, he said.

And so philosophy is left desolate, with her marriage rite incomplete: for her own have fallen away and forsaken her, and while they are leading a false and unbecoming life, other unworthy persons, seeing that she has no kinsmen to be her protectors, enter in and dishonour her; and fasten upon her the reproaches which, as you say, her reprovers utter, who affirm of her votaries that some are good for nothing, and that the greater number deserve the severest punishment.

That is certainly what people say.

Yes; and what else would you expect, I said, when you think of the puny creatures who, seeing this land open to them—a land well stocked with fair names and showy titles—like prisoners running out of prison into a sanctuary, take a leap out of their trades into philosophy; those who do so being probably the cleverest hands at their own miserable crafts? For, although philosophy be in this evil case, still there remains a dignity about her which is not to be found in the arts. And many are thus attracted by her whose natures are imperfect and whose souls are maimed and disfigured by their meannesses, as their bodies are by their trades and crafts. Is not this unavoidable?

Yes.

Are they not exactly like a bald little tinker who has just got out of durance and comes into a fortune; he takes a bath and puts on a new coat, and is decked out as a bridegroom going to marry his master's daughter, who is left poor and desolate?

A most exact parallel.

What will be the issue of such marriages? Will they not be vile and bastard?

There can be no question of it.

And when persons who are unworthy of education approach philosophy and make an alliance with her who is a rank above them, what sort of ideas and opinions are likely to be generated? Will they not be sophisms captivating to the ear, having nothing in them genuine, or worthy of or akin to true wisdom?

No doubt, he said.

Then, Adeimantus, I said, the worthy disciples of philosophy will be but a small remnant: perchance some noble and well-educated person, detained by exile in her service, who in the absence of corrupting influences remains devoted to her; or some lofty soul born in a mean city, the politics of which he contemns and neglects; and there may be a gifted few who leave the arts, which they justly despise, and come to her;—or peradventure there are some who are restrained by our friend Theages' bridle; for everything in the life of Theages conspired to divert him from philosophy; but ill-health kept him away from politics. My own case of the internal sign is hardly worth mentioning, for rarely, if ever, has such a monitor been given to any other man. Those who belong to this small class have tasted how sweet and blessed a possession philosophy is, and have also seen enough of the madness of the multitude; and they know that no politican is honest, nor is there any champion of justice at whose side they may fight and be saved. Such an one may be compared to a man who has fallen among wild beasts—he will not join in the wickedness of his fellows, but neither is he able singly to resist all their fierce natures, and therefore seeing that he would be of no use to the State or to his friends, and reflecting that he would have to throw away his life without doing any good either to himself or others, he holds his peace, and goes his own way. He is like one who, in the storm of dust and sleet which the driving wind hurries along, retires under the shelter of a wall; and seeing the rest of mankind full of wickedness, he is content, if only he can live his own life and be pure from evil or unrighteousness, and depart in peace and good-will, with bright hopes.

Yes, he said, and he will have done a great work before he departs.

A great work—yes; but not the greatest, unless he find a State suitable to him; for in a State which is suitable to him, he will have a larger growth and be the saviour of his country, as well as of himself.

The causes why philosophy is in such an evil name have now been sufficiently explained: the injustice of the charges against her has been shown—is there anything more which you wish to say?

Nothing more on that subject, he replied; but I should like to know which of the governments now existing is in your opinion the one adapted to her.

Not any of them, I said; and that is precisely the accusation which I bring against them—not one of them is worthy of the philosophic nature, and hence that nature is warped and estranged;—as the exotic seed which is sown in a foreign land becomes denaturalized, and is wont to be overpowered and to lose itself in the new soil, even so this growth of philosophy, instead of persisting, degenerates and receives another character. But if philosophy ever finds in the State that perfection which she herself is, then will be seen that she is in truth divine, and that all other things, whether natures of men or institutions, are but human;—and now, I know that you are going to ask, what that State is.

No, he said; there you are wrong, for I was going to ask another question—whether it is the State of which we are the founders and inventors, or some other?

Yes, I replied, ours in most respects; but you may remember my saying before, that some living authority would always be required in the State having the same idea of the constitution which guided you when as legislator you were laying down the laws.

That was said, he replied.

Yes, but not in a satisfactory manner; you frightened us by interposing objections, which certainly showed that the discussion would be long and difficult; and what still remains is the reverse of easy.

What is there remaining?

The question how the study of philosophy may be so ordered as not to be the ruin of the State: All great attempts are attended with risk; "hard is the good," as men say.

Still, he said, let the point be cleared up, and the enquiry will then be complete.

I shall not be hindered, I said, by any want of will, but, if at all, by a want of power: my zeal you may see for yourselves; and please to remark in what I am about to say how boldly and unhesitatingly I declare that States should pursue philosophy, not as they do now, but in a different spirit.

In what manner?

At present, I said, the students of philosophy are quite young; beginning when they are hardly past childhood, they devote only the time saved from moneymaking and housekeeping to such pursuits; and even those of them who are reputed to have most of the philosophic spirit, when they come within sight of the great difficulty of the subject, I mean dialectic, take themselves off. In after life when invited by some one else, they may, perhaps, go and hear a lecture, and about this they make much ado, for philosophy is not considered by them to be their proper business: at last, when they grow old, in most cases they are extinguished more truly than Heracleitus' sun, inasmuch as they never light up again.[2]

But what ought to be their course?

Just the opposite. In childhood and youth their study, and what philosophy they learn, should be suited to their tender years: during this period while they are growing up towards manhood, the chief and special care should be given to their bodies that they may have them to use in the service of philosophy; as life advances and the intellect begins to mature, let them increase the gymnastics of the soul; but when the strength of our citizens fails and is past civil and military duties, then let them range at will and engage in no serious labour, as we intend them to live happily here, and to crown this life with a similar happiness in another.

How truly in earnest you are, Socrates! he said; I am sure of that; and yet most of your hearers, if I am not mistaken, are likely to be still more earnest in their opposition to you, and will never be convinced; Thrasymachus least of all.

Do not make a quarrel, I said, between Thrasymachus and me, who have recently become friends, although, indeed, we were never enemies; for I shall go on striving to the utmost until I either convert him and other men, or do something which may profit them against the day when they live again, and hold the like discourse in another state of existence.

You are speaking of a time which is not very near.

Rather, I replied, of a time which is as nothing in comparison with eternity. Nevertheless, I do not wonder that the many refuse to believe;

[2] Heracleitus said that the sun was extinguished every evening and relighted every morning.

for they have never seen that of which we are now speaking realised;
they have seen only a conventional imitation of philosophy, consisting
of words artificially brought together, not like these of ours having a
natural unity. But a human being who in word and work is perfectly
moulded, as far as he can be, into the proportion and likeness of
virtue—such a man ruling in a city which bears the same image, they
have never yet seen, neither one nor many of them—do you think that
they ever did?

No indeed.

No, my friend, and they have seldom, if ever, heard free and noble
sentiments; such as men utter when they are earnestly and by every
means in their power seeking after truth for the sake of knowledge,
while they look coldly on the subtleties of controversy, of which the
end is opinion and strife, whether they meet with them in the courts
of law or in society.

They are strangers, he said, to the words of which you speak.

And this was what we foresaw, and this was the reason why truth
forced us to admit, not without fear and hesitation, that neither cities
nor States nor individuals will ever attain perfection until the small
class of philosophers whom we termed useless but not corrupt are
providentially compelled, whether they will or not, to take care of the
State, and until a like necessity be laid on the State to obey them; or
until kings, or if not kings, the sons of kings or princes, are divinely
inspired with a true love of true philosophy. That either or both of
these alternatives are impossible, I see no reason to affirm: if they
were so, we might indeed be justly ridiculed as dreamers and vision-
aries. Am I not right?

Quite right.

If then, in the countless ages of the past, or at the present hour in
some foreign clime which is far away and beyond our ken, the perfected philosopher is or has been or hereafter shall be compelled by a
superior power to have the charge of the State, we are ready to assert
to the death, that this our constitution has been, and is—yea, and will
be whenever the Muse of Philosophy is queen. There is no impossibility in all this; that there is a difficulty, we acknowledge ourselves.

My opinion agrees with yours, he said.

But do you mean to say that this is not the opinion of the multitude?

I should imagine not, he replied.

O my friend, I said, do not attack the multitude: they will change
their minds, if, not in an aggressive spirit, but gently and with the

view of soothing them and removing their dislike of over-education, you show them your philosophers as they really are and describe as you were just now doing their character and profession, and then mankind will see that he of whom you are speaking is not such as they supposed—if they view him in this new light, they will surely change their notion of him, and answer in another strain. Who can be at enmity with one who loves them, who that is himself gentle and free from envy will be jealous of one in whom there is no jealousy? Nay, let me answer for you, that in a few this harsh temper may be found but not in the majority of mankind.

I quite agree with you, he said.

And do you not also think, as I do, that the harsh feeling which the many entertain towards philosophy originates in the pretenders, who rush in uninvited, and are always abusing them, and finding fault with them, who make persons instead of things the theme of their conversation? and nothing can be more unbecoming in philosophers than this.

It is most unbecoming.

For he, Adeimantus, whose mind is fixed upon true being, has surely no time to look down upon the affairs of earth, or to be filled with malice and envy, contending against men; his eye is ever directed towards things fixed and immutable, which he sees neither injuring nor injured by one another, but all in order moving according to reason; these he imitates, and to these he will, as far as he can, conform himself. Can a man help imitating that with which he holds reverential converse?

Impossible.

And the philosopher holding converse with the divine order, becomes orderly and divine, as far as the nature of man allows; but like every one else, he will suffer from detraction.

Of course.

And if a necessity be laid upon him of fashioning, not only himself, but human nature generally, whether in States or individuals, into that which he beholds elsewhere, will he, think you, be an unskilful artificer of justice, temperance, and every civil virtue?

Anything but unskilful.

And if the world perceives that what we are saying about him is the truth, will they be angry with philosophy? Will they disbelieve us, when we tell them that no State can be happy which is not designed by artists who imitate the heavenly pattern?

They will not be angry if they understand, he said. But how will they draw out the plan of which you are speaking?

They will begin by taking the State and the manners of men, from which, as from a tablet, they will rub out the picture, and leave a clean surface. This is no easy task. But whether easy or not, herein will lie the difference between them and every other legislator,—they will have nothing to do either with individual or State, and will inscribe no laws, until they have either found, or themselves made, a clean surface.

They will be very right, he said.

Having effected this, they will proceed to trace an outline of the constitution?

No doubt.

And when they are filling in the work, as I conceive, they will often turn their eyes upwards and downwards: I mean that they will first look at absolute justice and beauty and temperance, and again at the human copy; and will mingle and temper the various elements of life into the image of a man; and thus they will conceive according to that other image, which, when existing among men, Homer calls the form and likeness of God.

Very true, he said.

And one feature they will erase, and another they will put in, until they have made the ways of men, as far as possible, agreeable to the ways of God?

Indeed, he said, in no way could they make a fairer picture.

And now, I said, are we beginning to persuade those whom you described as rushing at us with might and main, that the painter of constitutions is such an one as we are praising; at whom they were so very indignant because to his hands we committed the State; and are they growing a little calmer at what they have just heard?

Much calmer, if there is any sense in them.

Why, where can they still find any ground for objection? Will they doubt that the philosopher is a lover of truth and being?

They would not be so unreasonable.

Or that his nature, being such as we have delineated, is akin to the highest good?

Neither can they doubt this.

But again, will they tell us that such a nature, placed under favourable circumstances, will not be perfectly good and wise if any ever was? Or will they prefer those whom we have rejected?

Surely not.

Then will they still be angry at our saying, that, until philosophers bear rule, States and individuals will have no rest from evil, nor will this our imaginary State ever be realised?

I think that they will be less angry.

Shall we assume that they are not only less angry but quite gentle, and that they have been converted and for very shame, if for no other reason, cannot refuse to come to terms?

By all means, he said.

Then let us suppose that the reconciliation has been effected. Will any one deny the other point, that there may be sons of kings or princes who are by nature philosophers?

Surely no man, he said.

And when they have come into being will any one say that they must of necessity be destroyed; that they can hardly be saved is not denied even by us; but that in the whole course of ages no single one of them can escape—who will venture to affirm this?

Who indeed!

But, said I, one is enough; let there be one man who has a city obedient to his will, and he might bring into existence the ideal polity about which the world is so incredulous.

Yes, one is enough.

The ruler may impose the laws and institutions which we have been describing, and the citizens may possibly be willing to obey them?

Certainly.

And that others should approve, of what we approve, is no miracle or impossibility?

I think not.

But we have sufficiently shown, in what has preceded, that all this, if only possible, is assuredly for the best.

We have.

And now we say not only that our laws, if they could be enacted, would be for the best, but also that the enactment of them, though difficult, is not impossible. . . .

And now, I said, let me show in a figure how far our nature is enlightened or unenlightened:—Behold! human beings living in an underground den, which has a mouth open towards the light and reaching all along the den; here they have been from their childhood, and have their legs and necks chained so that they cannot move, and can only see before them, being prevented by the chains from turning round their heads. Above and behind them a fire is blazing at a distance, and between the fire and the prisoners there is a raised way; and you will see, if you look, a low wall built along the way, like the screen which marionette players have in front of them, over which they show the puppets.

I see.

And do you see, I said, men passing along the wall carrying all sorts of vessels, and statues and figures of animals made of wood and stone and various materials, which appear over the wall? Some of them are talking, others silent.

You have shown me a strange image, and they are strange prisoners.

Like ourselves, I replied; and they see only their own shadows, or the shadows of one another, which the fire throws on the opposite wall of the cave?

True, he said; how could they see anything but the shadows if they were never allowed to move their heads?

And of the objects which are being carried in like manner they would only see the shadows?

Yes, he said.

And if they were able to converse with one another, would they not suppose that they were naming what was actually before them?

Very true.

And suppose further that the prison had an echo which came from the other side, would they not be sure to fancy when one of the passers-by spoke that the voice which they heard came from the passing shadow?

No question, he replied.

To them, I said, the truth would be literally nothing but the shadows of the images.

That is certain.

And now look again, and see what will naturally follow if the prisoners are released and disabused of their error. At first, when any of them is liberated and compelled suddenly to stand up and turn his neck round and walk and look towards the light, he will suffer sharp pains; the glare will distress him, and he will be unable to see the realities of which in his former state he had seen the shadows; and then conceive some one saying to him, that what he saw before was an illusion, but that now, when he is approaching nearer to being and his eye is turned towards more real existence, he has a clearer vision,—what will be his reply? And you may further imagine that his instructor is pointing to the objects as they pass and requiring him to name them,—will he not be perplexed? Will he not fancy that the shadows which he formerly saw are truer than the objects which are now shown to him?

Far truer.

And if he is compelled to look straight at the light, will he not have a pain in his eyes which will make him turn away to take refuge in the objects of vision which he can see, and which he will conceive to be in reality clearer than the things which are now being shown to him?

True, he said.

And suppose once more, that he is reluctantly dragged up a steep and rugged ascent, and held fast until he is forced into the presence of the sun himself, is he not likely to be pained and irritated? When he approaches the light his eyes will be dazzled, and he will not be able to see anything at all of what are now called realities.

Not all in a moment, he said.

He will require to grow accustomed to the sight of the upper world. And first he will see the shadows best, next the reflections of men and other objects in the water, and then the objects themselves; then he will gaze upon the light of the moon and the stars and the spangled heaven; and he will see the sky and the stars by night better than the sun or the light of the sun by day?

Certainly.

Last of all he will be able to see the sun, and not mere reflections of him in the water, but he will see him in his own proper place, and not in another; and he will contemplate him as he is.

Certainly.

He will then proceed to argue that this is he who gives the season and the years, and is the guardian of all that is in the visible world, and in a certain way the cause of all things which he and his fellows have been accustomed to behold?

Clearly, he said, he would first see the sun and then reason about him.

And when he remembered his old habitation, and the wisdom of the den and his fellow-prisoners, do you not suppose that he would felicitate himself on the change and pity them?

Certainly, he would.

And if they were in the habit of conferring honours among themselves on those who were quickest to observe the passing shadows and to remark which of them went before, and which followed after, and which were together; and who were therefore best able to draw conclusions as to the future, do you think that he would care for such honours and glories, or envy the possessors of them? Would he not say with Homer, "Better to be the poor servant of a poor master," and to endure anything, rather than think as they do and live after their manner?

Yes, he said, I think that he would rather suffer anything than entertain these false notions and live in this miserable manner.

Imagine once more, I said, such a one coming suddenly out of the sun to be replaced in his old situation; would he not be certain to have his eyes full of darkness?

To be sure, he said.

And if there were a contest, and he had to compete in measuring the shadows with the prisoners who had never moved out of the den, while his sight was still weak, and before his eyes had become steady (and the time which would be needed to acquire this new habit of sight might be very considerable), would he not be ridiculous? Men would say of him that up he went and down he came without his eyes; and that it was better not even to think of ascending; and if any one tried to loose another and lead him up to the light, let them only catch the offender, and they would put him to death.

No question, he said.

This entire allegory, I said, you may now append, dear Glaucon, to the previous argument; the prison-house is the world of sight, the light of the fire is the sun, and you will not misapprehend me if you interpret the journey upwards to be the ascent of the soul into the intellectual world according to my poor belief, which, at your desire, I have expressed—whether rightly or wrongly God knows. But, whether true or false, my opinion is that in the world of knowledge the idea of good appears last of all, and is seen only with an effort; and, when seen, is also inferred to be the universal author of all things beautiful and right, parent of light and of the lord of light in this visible world, and the immediate source of reason and truth in the intellectual; and that this is the power upon which he who would act rationally either in public or private life must have his eye fixed.

I agree, he said, as far as I am able to understand you.

Moreover, I said, you must not wonder that those who attain to this beatific vision are unwilling to descend to human affairs; for their souls are ever hastening into the upper world where they desire to dwell; which desire of theirs is very natural, if our allegory may be trusted.

Yes, very natural.

And is there anything surprising in one who passes from divine contemplations to the evil state of man, misbehaving himself in a ridiculous manner; if, while his eyes are blinking and before he has become accustomed to the surrounding darkness, he is compelled to fight in courts of law, or in other places, about the images or the shadows of images of justice, and is endeavouring to meet the conceptions of those who have never yet seen absolute justice?

Anything but surprising, he replied.

Any one who has common sense will remember that the bewilderments of the eyes are of two kinds, and arise from two causes, either from coming out of the light or from going into the light, which is true of the mind's eye, quite as much as of the bodily eye; and he who remembers this when he sees any one whose vision is perplexed and weak, will not be too ready to laugh; he will first ask whether that soul of man has come out of the brighter life, and is unable to see because unaccustomed to the dark, or having turned from darkness to the day is dazzled by excess of light. And he will count the one happy in his condition and state of being, and he will pity the other; or, if he have a mind to laugh at the soul which comes from below into the light, there will be more reason in this than in the laugh which greets him who returns from above out of the light into the den.

That, he said, is a very just distinction.

But then, if I am right, certain professors of education must be wrong when they say that they can put a knowledge into the soul which was not there before, like sight into blind eyes.

They undoubtedly say this, he replied.

Whereas, our argument shows that the power and capacity of learning exists in the soul already; and that just as the eye was unable to turn from darkness to light without the whole body, so too the instrument of knowledge can only by the movement of the whole soul be turned from the world of becoming into that of being, and learn by degrees to endure the sight of being, and of the brightest and best of being, or in other words, of the good.

Very true.

And must there not be some art which will effect conversion in the easiest and quickest manner; not implanting the faculty of sight, for that exists already, but has been turned in the wrong direction, and is looking away from the truth?

Yes, he said, such an art may be presumed.

And whereas the other so-called virtues of the soul seem to be akin to bodily qualities, for even when they are not originally innate they can be implanted later by habit and exercise, the virtue of wisdom more than anything else contains a divine element which always remains, and by this conversion is rendered useful and profitable; or, on the other hand, hurtful and useless. Did you never observe the narrow intelligence flashing from the keen eye of a clever rogue—how eager he is, how clearly his paltry soul sees the way to his end; he is the reverse of blind, but his keen eyesight is forced into the service of evil, and he is mischievous in proportion to his cleverness?

Very true, he said.

But what if there had been a circumcision of such natures in the days of their youth; and they had been severed from those sensual pleasures, such as eating and drinking, which, like leaden weights, were attached to them at their birth, and which drag them down and turn the vision of their souls upon the things that are below—if, I say, they had been released from these impediments and turned in the opposite direction, the very same faculty in them would have seen the truth as keenly as they see what their eyes are turned to now.

Very likely.

Yes, I said; and there is another thing which is likely, or rather a necessary inference from what has preceded, that neither the uneducated and uninformed of the truth, nor yet those who never make an end of their education, will be able ministers of State; not the former, because they have no single aim of duty which is the rule of all their actions, private as well as public; nor the latter, because they will not act at all except upon compulsion, fancying that they are already dwelling apart in the islands of the blest.

Very true, he replied.

Then, I said, the business of us who are the founders of the State will be to compel the best minds to attain that knowledge which we have already shown to be the greatest of all—they must continue to ascend until they arrive at the good; but when they have ascended and seen enough we must not allow them to do as they do now.

What do you mean?

I mean that they remain in the upper world: but this must not be allowed; they must be made to descend again among the prisoners in the den, and partake of their labours and honours, whether they are worth having or not.

But is not this unjust? he said; ought we to give them a worse life, when they might have a better?

You have again forgotten, my friend, I said, the intention of the legislator, who did not aim at making any one class in the State happy above the rest; the happiness was to be in the whole State, and he held the citizens together by persuasion and necessity, making them benefactors of the State, and therefore benefactors of one another; to this end he created them, not to please themselves, but to be his instruments in binding up the State.

True, he said, I had forgotten.

Observe, Glaucon, that there will be no injustice in compelling our philosophers to have a care and providence of others; we shall explain to them that in other States, men of their class are not obliged to share in the toils of politics: and this is reasonable, for they grow up at their own sweet will, and the government would rather not have them. Being self-taught, they cannot be expected to show any gratitude for a culture which they have never received. But we have brought you into the world to be rulers of the hive, kings of yourselves and of the other citizens, and have educated you far better and more perfectly than they have been educated, and you are better able to share in the double duty. Wherefore each of you, when his turn comes, must go down to the general underground abode, and get the habit of seeing in the dark. When you have acquired the habit, you will see ten thousand times better than the inhabitants of the den, and you will know what the several images are, and what they represent, because you have seen the beautiful and just and good in their truth. And thus our State, which is also yours, will be a reality, and not a dream only, and will be administered in a spirit unlike that of other States, in which men fight with one another about shadows only and are distracted in the struggle for power, which in their eyes is a great good. Whereas the truth is that the State in which the rulers are most reluctant to govern is always the best and most quietly governed, and the State in which they are most eager, the worst.

Quite true, he replied.

And will our pupils, when they hear this, refuse to take their turn at the toils of State, when they are allowed to spend the greater part of their time with one another in the heavenly light?

Impossible, he answered; for they are just men, and the commands which we impose upon them are just; there can be no doubt that every one of them will take office as a stern necessity, and not after the fashion of our present rulers of State. . . .

2

CALVIN

The Principle of Theocracy

Theocracy, as a conception of political rule, embodies an alliance between church and state in which dominant power is exercised by the leadership of the church. Within Western political thought, the principle of theocracy has been given its most notable expression in the theory and practice of Calvinism, best illustrated in the Geneva city-state and the early Puritan commonwealth of Massachusetts Bay.

The doctrine of predestination, as the basic theological postulate of Calvinism, decrees that certain individuals are preordained to salvation and others to eternal damnation. This assumed the necessity of a spiritual aristocracy, as God's saints on earth, entrusted with the duty of bringing the redeemed to light. Within the organization of the church, the interpretation of scripture, as John Calvin (1509–1567) viewed it, must be confined to appropriate officers who are not to be considered agents of the community but instruments of the word of God. Although Calvin's theory implied a formal separation between the functions of the church and the state, he emphasized the necessary role of the government as an instrument for maintenance of the purity of Christian doctrine and for the punishment of heresy. Secular rulers and magistrates, just as church leaders, are invested with divine authority, the vice-regents of God on earth. In recognizing the power of secular authority, Calvin's theology is not an explicit advocacy of theocracy. In actual practice, however, political power gravitated toward the members of the clergy. In the Geneva church, for example, the government came to be administered by the clergy in which civil and spiritual jurisdiction were combined. Laws were prepared by the clergy, and a Consistory, composed of twelve clergymen and twelve laymen (elders), made the final decisions on the law and its enforcement. In the Puritan colony of Massachusetts Bay, theocratic rule was maintained by the predominant position of the clergy in public affairs; the requirement of religious qualifications for voting and office-

holding; and the employment of the civil arm of the state for the enforcement of church law.

It should be emphasized, however, that Calvinist theology, despite its
generally authoritarian political implications, embodied the germs of
democratic development, particularly in the context of the American environment. The congregational idea of the church bound together by a
covenant laid the foundations for the contract theory of government
which found expression in New England sources such as the Mayflower
Compact and the Fundamental Orders of Connecticut. As opponents of
Stuart absolutism in Britain, Puritans were supporters of the principle of
constitutional and limited government. The Protestant principle of individual conscience as the ultimate judge of right and wrong became a
potential basis for opposition to arbitrary state power and authority. The
localistic tendencies of the church in New England, along with the role of
the town meeting in determination of local political policy, also contributed to the growth of democratic influences. Thus tendencies within
Calvinism itself, combined with the effects of the American environment,
moderated and eventually broke down the authoritarian structure of
Puritan theocracy.

The chief expression of the Calvinist concept of political rulership
appears in the *Institutes of the Christian Religion*. This work is, of course,
primarily a famous classic in Protestant theology rather than a treatise in
political theory. But within Calvinism, politics appears as a topic or province of theology, and Calvin was deeply aware of the way in which the
fluctuating policies of rulership affect the reforms of the church. The final
chapter of the *Institutes* deals specifically with the question of civil
government. It was written during a period when the Reformation was
being characterized by opponents as a movement of political subversion,
and Calvin undoubtedly felt the need for stating a positive conception of
politics as a part of his defense of the Reformation.*

ETERNAL ELECTION, BY WHICH GOD HAS PREDESTINED SOME TO SALVATION, OTHERS TO DESTRUCTION

*(Importance of the doctrine of predestination excludes both
presumption and reticence in speaking of it, 1–4).*

*1. Necessity and beneficial effect of the doctrine of election:
danger of curiosity.*

* The selection is taken from John Calvin, *Institutes of the Christian Religion*,
Vol. 2, Chs. XXI, XX, John T. McNeill, ed., trans. by Ford Lewis Battles
(Philadelphia: The Westminster Press, 1960), pp. 920–21; 930–32; 1485–93;
1509–21. Used by permission.

In actual fact, the covenant of life is not preached equally among all men, and among those to whom it is preached, it does not gain the same acceptance either constantly or in equal degree. In this diversity the wonderful depth of God's judgment is made known. For there is no doubt that this variety also serves the decision of God's eternal election. If it is plain that it comes to pass by God's bidding that salvation is freely offered to some while others are barred from access to it, at once great and difficult questions spring up, explicable only when reverent minds regard as settled what they may suitably hold concerning election and predestination. A baffling question this seems to many. For they think nothing more inconsistent than that out of the common multitude of men some should be predestined to salvation, others to destruction. But how mistakenly they entangle themselves will become clear in the following discussion. Besides, in the very darkness that frightens them not only is the usefulness of this doctrine made known but also its very sweet fruit. We shall never be clearly persuaded, as we ought to be, that our salvation flows from the wellspring of God's free mercy until we come to know his eternal election, which illumines God's grace by this contrast: that he does not indiscriminately adopt all into the hope of salvation but gives to some what he denies to others. . . .

3. The election of individuals as actual election.

Although it is now sufficiently clear that God by his secret plan freely chooses whom he pleases, rejecting others, still his free election has been only half explained until we come to individual persons, to whom God not only offers salvation but so assigns it that the certainty of its effect is not in suspense or doubt. These are reckoned among the unique offspring mentioned by Paul [cf. Rom. 9:8; Gal. 3:16 ff.]. The adoption was put in Abraham's hands. Nevertheless, because many of his descendants were cut off as rotten members, we must, in order that election may be effectual and truly enduring, ascend to the Head in whom the Heavenly Father has gathered his elect together, and has joined them to himself by an indissoluble bond. So, indeed, God's generous favor, which he has denied to others, has been displayed in the adoption of the race of Abraham; yet in the members of Christ a far more excellent power of grace appears, for, engrafted to their Head, they are never cut off from salvation. Therefore Paul skillfully argues . . . that where God has made a covenant of eternal life and calls any people to himself, a special mode of election is employed for a part of them, so that he does not with indiscriminate grace effectually elect all [Rom. 9:13]. The statement "I have loved Jacob" [Mal. 1:2] applies to the whole offspring of the patriarch, whom the prophet there contrasts to the posterity of Esau. Still this does not gainsay the fact that there was set before us in the person of one man an example of election that cannot fail to accomplish its purpose. Paul with good reason notes that they are called the "remnant" [Rom. 9:27; 11:5; cf. Isa. 10:22–23]. For experience shows that of the great multitude many fall away and disappear, so that often only a slight portion remains.

It is easy to explain why the general election of a people is not always firm and effectual: to those with whom God makes a covenant, he does not at once give the spirit of regeneration that would enable them to persevere in the covenant to the very end. Rather, the outward change, without the working of inner grace, which might have availed to keep them, is intermediate between the rejection of mankind and the election of a meager number of the godly. The whole people of Israel has been called "the inheritance of God" [Deut. 32:9; I Kings 8:51; Ps. 28:9; 33:12; etc.], yet many of them were foreigners. But because God has not pointlessly covenanted that he would become their Father and Redeemer, he sees to his freely given favor rather than to the many who treacherously desert him. Even through them his truth was not set aside, for where he preserved some remnant for himself, it appeared that his calling was "without repentance" [Rom. 11 : 29]. For the fact that God was continually gathering his church from Abraham's children rather than from profane nations had its reason in his covenant, which, when violated by that multitude, he confined to a few that it might not utterly cease. In short, that adoption of Abraham's seed in common was a visible image of the greater benefit that God bestowed on some out of the many. This is why Paul so carefully distinguishes the children of Abraham according to the flesh from the spiritual children who have been called after the example of Isaac [Gal. 4 : 28]. Not that it was a vain and unprofitable thing simply to be a child of Abraham; such could not be said without dishonoring the covenant! No, God's unchangeable plan, by which he predestined for himself those whom he willed, was in fact intrinsically effectual unto salvation for these spiritual offspring alone. But I advise my readers not to take a prejudiced position on either side until, when the passages of Scripture have been adduced, it shall be clear what opinion ought to be held.

Summary survey of the doctrine of election.

As Scripture, then, clearly shows, we say that God once established by his eternal and unchangeable plan those whom he long before determined once for all to receive into salvation, and those whom, on the other hand, he would devote to destruction. We assert that, with respect to the elect, this plan was founded upon his freely given mercy, without regard to human worth; but by his just and irreprehensible but incomprehensible judgment he has barred the door of life to those whom he has given over to damnation. Now among the elect we regard the call as a testimony of election. Then we hold justification another sign of its manifestation, until they come into the glory in which the fulfillment of that election lies. But as the Lord seals his elect by call and justification, so, by shutting off the reprobate from knowledge of his name or from the sanctification of his Spirit, he, as it were, reveals by these marks what sort of judgment awaits them. Here I shall pass over many fictions that stupid men have invented to overthrow predestination. They need no refutation, for as soon as they are brought forth they abundantly prove their own falsity. I shall pause only over those which either are being argued by the learned or may raise difficulty for the simple, or which impiety speciously sets forth in order to assail God's righteousness. . . .

CIVIL GOVERNMENT

(How civil and spiritual government are related, 1–2)

1. Differences between spiritual and civil government.

Now, since we have established above that man is under a twofold government, and since we have elsewhere discussed at sufficient length the kind that resides in the soul or inner man and pertains to eternal life, this is the place to say something also about the other kind which pertains only to the establishment of civil justice and outward morality.

For although this topic seems by nature alien to the spiritual doctrine of faith which I have undertaken to discuss, what follows will show that I am right in joining them, in fact, that necessity compels me to do so. This is especially true since, from one side, insane and barbarous men furiously strive to overturn this divinely established order; while, on the other side, the flatterers of princes, immoderately praising their power, do not hesitate to set them against the rule of license shout and boast: after we have died through Christ to the elements of this world [Col. 2:20], are transported to God's Kingdom, ingly God has provided in this respect for mankind, that greater zeal for piety may flourish in us to attest our gratefulness.

First, before we enter into the matter itself, we must keep in mind that distinction which we previously laid down so that we do not (as commonly happens) unwisely mingle these two, which have a completely different nature. For certain men, when they hear that the gospel promises a freedom that acknowledges no king and no magistrate among men, but looks to Christ alone, think that they cannot benefit by their freedom so long as they see any power set up over them. They therefore think that nothing will be safe unless the whole world is reshaped to a new form, where there are neither courts, nor laws, nor magistrates, nor anything which in their opinion restricts their freedom. But whoever knows how to distinguish between body and soul, between this present fleeting life and that future eternal life, will without difficulty know that Christ's spiritual Kingdom and the civil jurisdiction are things completely distinct. Since, then, it is a Jewish vanity to seek and enclose Christ's Kingdom within the elements of this world, let us rather ponder that what Scripture clearly teaches is a spiritual fruit, which we gather from Christ's grace; and let us remember to keep within its own limits all that freedom which is promised and offered to us in him. For why is it that the same apostle who bids us stand and not submit to the "yoke of bondage" [Gal. 5:1] elsewhere forbids slaves to be anxious about their state [I Cor. 7:21], unless it be that spiritual freedom can perfectly well exist along with civil bondage? These statements of his must also be taken in the same sense: In the Kingdom of God "there is neither Jew nor Greek, neither male nor female, neither slave nor free" [Gal. 3:28, Vg.; order changed]. And again, "there is not Jew nor Greek, uncircumcised and circumcised, barbarian, Scythian, slave, freeman; but Christ is all in all" [Col. 3:11 p.]. By these statements he means that it makes no difference what your condition among men may be or under what nation's laws you live, since the Kingdom of Christ does not at all consist in these things.

2. The two "governments" are not antithetical.

Yet this distinction does not lead us to consider the whole nature of government a thing polluted, which has nothing to do with Christian men. That is what, indeed, certain fanatics who delight in unbridled

God himself. Unless both these evils are checked, purity of faith will perish. Besides, it is of no slight importance to us to know how lov- and sit among heavenly beings, it is a thing unworthy of us and set far beneath our excellence to be occupied with those vile and worldly cares which have to do with business foreign to a Christian man. To what purpose, they ask, are there laws without trials and tribunals? But what has a Christian man to do with trials themselves? Indeed, if it is not lawful to kill, why do we have laws and trials? But as we have just now pointed out that this kind of government is distinct from that spiritual and inward Kingdom of Christ, so we must know that they are not at variance. For spiritual government, indeed, is already initiating in us upon earth certain beginnings of the Heavenly Kingdom, and in this mortal and fleeting life affords a certain forecast of an immortal and incorruptible blessedness. Yet civil government has as its appointed end, so long as we live among men, to cherish and protect the outward worship of God, to defend sound doctrine of piety and the position of the church, to adjust our life to the society of men, to form our social behavior to civil righteousness, to reconcile us with one another, and to promote general peace and tranquillity. All of this I admit to be superfluous, if God's Kingdom, such as it is now among us, wipes out the present life. But if it is God's will that we go as pilgrims upon the earth while we aspire to the true fatherland, and if the pilgrimage requires such helps, those who take these from man deprive him of his very humanity. Our adversaries claim that there ought to be such great perfection in the church of God that its govern- ment should suffice for law. But they stupidly imagine such a perfec- tion as can never be found in a community of men. For since the insolence of evil men is so great, their wickedness so stubborn, that it can scarcely be restrained by extremely severe laws, what do we expect them to do if they see that their depravity can go scot-free— when no power can force them to cease from doing evil?

(Necessity and divine sanction of civil government, 3–7)

3. *The chief tasks and burdens of civil government.*

But there will be a more appropriate place to speak of the practice of civil government. Now we only wish it to be understood that to think of doing away with it is outrageous barbarity. Its function among men is no less than that of bread, water, sun, and air; indeed, its place of honor is far more excellent. For it does not merely see to it, as all these serve to do, that men breathe, eat, drink, and are kept warm, even though it surely embraces all these activities when it provides for their living together. It does not, I repeat, look to this only, but also prevents idolatory, sacrilege against God's name, blasphemies against his truth, and other public offenses against religion from arising and spreading among the people; it prevents the public peace from being disturbed; it provides that each man may keep his property safe and sound; that men may carry on blameless intercourse among themselves; that honesty and modesty may be preserved among men. In short, it provides that a public manifestation of religion may exist among Christians, and that humanity be maintained among men.

Let no man be disturbed that I now commit to civil government the duty of rightly establishing religion, which I seem above to have put outside of human decision. For, when I approve of a civil administration that aims to prevent the true religion which is contained in God's law from being openly and with public sacrilege violated and defiled with impunity, I do not here, any more than before, allow men to make laws according to their own decision concerning religion and the worship of God.

But my readers, assisted by the very clarity of the arrangement, will better understand what is to be thought of the whole subject of civil government if we discuss its parts separately. These are three: the magistrate, who is the protector and guardian of the laws; the laws, according to which he governs; the people, who are governed by the laws and obey the magistrate.

Let us, then, first look at the office of the magistrate, noting whether it is a lawful calling approved of God; the nature of the office; the extent of its power; then, with what laws a Christian government ought to be governed; and finally, how the laws benefit the people, and what obedience is owed to the magistrate.

4. The magistracy is ordained by God.

The Lord has not only testified that the office of magistrate is approved by and acceptable to him, but he also sets out its dignity with the most honorable titles and marvelously commends it to us. To mention a few: Since those who serve as magistrate are called "gods" [Ex. 88:8, Vg.; Ps. 82:1, 6], let no one think that their being so-called is of slight importance. For it signifies that they have a mandate from God, have been invested with divine authority, and are wholly God's representatives, in a manner, acting as his vice-regents. This is no subtlety of mine, but Christ's explanation. "If Scripture," he says,

"called them gods to whom the word of God came..." [John 10:35].
What is this, except that God has entrusted to them the business of
serving him in their office, and (as Moses and Jehoshaphat said to the
judges whom they appointed in every city of Judah) of exercising
judgment not for man but for god [Deut. 1:16–17; II Chron. 19:6]?
To the same purpose is what God's wisdom affirms through Solomon's
mouth, that it is his doing "that kings reign, and counselors decree
what is just, that princes exercise dominion, and all benevolent judges
of the earth" [Prov. 8:14–16]. This amounts to the same thing as to
say: it has not come about by human perversity that the authority
over all things on earth is in the hands of kings and other rulers, but
by divine providence and holy ordinance. For God was pleased so to
rule the affairs of men, inasmuch as he is present with them and also
presides over the making of laws and the exercising of equity in courts
of justice. Paul also plainly teaches this when he lists "ruling" among
God's gifts [Rom. 12:8, KJV or RV], which, variously distributed
according to the diversity of grace, ought to be used by Christ's servants for the upbuilding of the church. For even though Paul is there
speaking specifically of a council of sober men, who were appointed in
the primitive church to preside over the ordering of public discipline
(which office is called in the letter to the Corinthians, "governments"
[I Cor. 12:28], yet because we see the civil power serving the same
end, there is no doubt that he commends to us every kind of just rule.

But Paul speaks much more clearly when he undertakes a just discussion of this matter. For he states both that power is an ordinance
of God [Rom. 13:2], and that there are no powers except those
ordained by God [Rom. 13:1]. Further, that princes are ministers of
God, for those doing good unto praise; for those doing evil, avengers
unto wrath [Rom. 13:3–4]. To this may be added the examples of
holy men, of whom some possessed kingdoms, as David, Josiah, and
Hezekiah; others, lordships, as Joseph and Daniel; others, civil rule
among a free people, as Moses, Joshua, and the judges. The Lord has
declared his approval of their offices. Accordingly, no one ought to
doubt that civil authority is a calling, not only holy and lawful before
God, but also the most sacred and by far the most honorable of all
callings in the whole life of mortal men.

5. *Against the "Christian" denial or rejection of magistracy.*

Those who desire to usher in anarchy object that, although in
antiquity kings and judges ruled over ignorant folk, yet that servile

kind of governing is wholly incompatible today with the perfection which Christ brought with his gospel. In this they betray not only their ignorance but devilish arrogance, when they claim a perfection of which not even a hundredth part is seen in them. But whatever kind of men they may be, the refutation is easy. For where David urges all kings and rulers to kiss the Son of God [Ps. 2:12], he does not bid them lay aside their authority and retire to private life, but submit to Christ the power with which they have been invested, that he alone may tower over all. Similarly, Isaiah, when he promises that kings shall be foster fathers of the church, and queens its nurses [Isa. 49:23], does not deprive them of their honor. Rather, by a noble title he makes them defenders of God's pious worshipers; for that prophecy looks to the coming of Christ. I knowingly pass over very many passages which occur frequently, and especially in the psalms, in which the right of rulers is asserted for them all [Ps. 21; 22; 45; 72; 89; 110; 132]. But most notable of all is the passage of Paul where, admonishing Timothy that prayers be offered for kings in public assembly, he immediately adds the reason: "That we may lead a peaceful life under them with all godliness and honesty" [I Tim. 2:2]. By these words he entrusts the condition of the church to their protection and care.

6. Magistrates should be faithful as God's deputies.

This consideration ought continually to occupy the magistrates themselves, since it can greatly spur them to exercise their office and bring them remarkable comfort to mitigate the difficulties of their task, which are indeed many and burdensome. For what great zeal for uprightness, for prudence, gentleness, self-control, and for innocence ought to be required of themselves by those who know that they have been ordained ministers of divine justice? How will they have the brazenness to admit injustice to their judgment seat, which they are told is the throne of the living God? How will they have the boldness to pronounce an unjust sentence, by that mouth which they know has been appointed an instrument of divine truth? With what conscience will they sign wicked decrees by that hand which they know has been appointed to record the acts of God? To sum up, if they remember that they are vicars of God, they should watch with all care, earnestness, and diligence, to represent in themselves to men some image of divine providence, protection, goodness, benevolence, and justice. And they should perpetually set before themselves the thought that "if all are cursed who carry out in deceit the work of God's vengeance"

[Jer. 48:10 p.], much more gravely cursed are they who deceitfully conduct themselves in a righteous calling. Therefore, when Moses and Jehoshaphat wished to urge their judges to their duty, they had nothing more effective to persuade them than what we have previously mentioned [Deut. 1:16]: "Consider what you do, for you exercise judgment not for man but for the Lord; since he is beside you in giving judgment. Now then, let the fear of the Lord be upon you. Take heed what you do, for there is no perversity with the Lord our God" [II Chron. 19:6–7 p.]. And in another place it is said: "God stood in the assembly of the gods, and holds judgment in the midst of the gods" [Ps. 82:1]. This is to hearten them for their task when they learn that they are deputies of God, to whom they must hereafter render account of the administration of their charge. And this admonition deserves to have great weight with them. For if they commit some fault, they are not only wrongdoers to men whom they wickedly trouble, but are also insulting toward God himself, whose most holy judgments they defile [cf. Isa. 3:14–15]. Again, they have the means to comfort themselves greatly when they ponder in themselves that they are occupied not with profane affairs or those alien to a servant of God, but with a most holy office, since they are serving as God's deputies.

7. *The coercive character of magistracy does not hinder its recognition.*

Those who, unmoved by so many testimonies of Scripture, dare rail against this holy ministry as a thing abhorrent to Christian religion and piety—what else do they do but revile God himself, whose ministry cannot be reproached without dishonor to himself? And these folk do not just reject the magistrates, but cast off God that he may not reign over them. For if the Lord truly said this of the people of Israel because they refused Samuel's rule [I Sam. 8:7], why will it less truly be said today of these who let themselves rage against all governments ordained by God? The Lord said to his disciples that the kings of the Gentiles exercise lordship over Gentiles, but it is not so among the disciples, where he who is first ought to become the least [Luke 22:25–26]; by this saying, they tell us, all Christians are forbidden to take kingdoms or governments. O skillful interpreters! There arose a contention among the disciples over which one would excel the others. To silence this vain ambition, the Lord taught them that their ministry is not like kingdoms, in which one is pre-eminent above the rest. What dishonor, I ask you, does this comparison do to kingly dignity? Indeed, what does it prove at all, except that the kingly office is not the ministry of an apostle? Moreover, among magistrates themselves, although there is a variety of forms, there is no difference in this respect, that we must regard all of them as ordained of God. For Paul also lumps them all together when he says that there is no power except from God [Rom. 13:1]. And that which is the least pleasant of all has been especially commended above the rest, that is, the power of one. This, because it brings with it the common bondage of all (except that one man to whose will it subjects all things), in ancient times could not be acceptable to heroic and nobler natures. But to forestall their unjust judgments, Scripture expressly affirms that it is the providence of God's wisdom that kings reign [cf. Prov. 8:15], and particularly commands us to honor the king [Prov. 24:21; I Peter 2:17]. . . .

(Obedience, with reverence, due even unjust rulers, 22–29)

22. Deference.

The first duty of subjects toward their magistrates is to think most honorably of their office, which they recognize as a jurisdiction bestowed by God, and on that account to esteem and reverence them as ministers and representatives of God. For you may find some who very respectfully yield themselves to their magistrates and desire somebody whom they can obey, because they know that such is expedient for public welfare; nevertheless, they regard magistrates only as a kind of necessary evil. But Peter requires something more of us when he commands that the king be honored [I Peter 2:17]; as does Solomon when he teaches that God and king are to be feared [Prov. 24:21]. For Peter, in the word "to honor" includes a sincere and candid opinion of the king. Solomon, yoking the king with God, shows that the king is full of a holy reverence and dignity. There is also that famous saying in Paul: that we should obey "not only because of wrath, but because of conscience" [Rom. 13:5, cf. Vg.]. By this he means that subjects should be led not by fear alone of princes and rulers to remain in subjection under them (as they commonly yield to an armed enemy who sees that vengeance is promptly taken if they resist), but because they are showing obedience to God himself when they give it to them; since the rulers' power is from God.

I am not discussing the men themselves, as if a mask of dignity covered foolishness, or sloth, or cruelty, as well as wicked morals full of infamous deeds, and thus acquired for vices the praise of virtues; but I say that the order itself is worthy of such honor and reverence that those who are rulers are esteemed among us, and receive reverence out of respect for their lordship.

23. Obedience.

From this also something else follows: that, with hearts inclined to reverence their rulers, the subjects should prove their obedience toward them, whether by obeying their proclamations, or by paying taxes, or by undertaking public offices and burdens which pertain to the common defense, or by executing any other commands of theirs. "Let every soul," says Paul, "be subject to the higher powers ... For he who resists authority, resists what God has ordained" [Rom. 13:1–2, Vg.]. "Remind them," he writes to Titus, "to be subject to principalities and powers, to obey magistrates, to be ready for every good work" [Titus 3:1, cf. Vg.]. And Peter says, "Be subject to every human creature (or rather, as I translate it, ordinance) for the Lord's sake, whether it be to the king, as supreme, or unto governors who are sent through him to punish evildoers, but to praise doers of good" [I Peter 2:13–14]. Now, in order that they may prove that they are not pretending subjection, but are sincerely and heartily subjects, Paul adds that they should commend to God the safety and prosperity of those under whom they live. "I urge," he says, "that supplications, prayers, intercessions, and thanksgivings be made for all men, for kings, and all that are in authority, that we may lead a quiet and peaceable life, with all godliness and honesty" [I Tim. 2:1–2, cf. Vg.].

Let no man deceive himself here. For since the magistrate cannot be resisted without God being resisted at the same time, even though it seems that an unarmed magistrate can be despised with impunity, still God is armed to avenge mightily this contempt toward himself.

Moreover, under this obedience I include the restraint which private citizens ought to bid themselves keep in public, that they may not deliberately intrude in public affairs, or pointlessly invade the magistrate's office, or undertake anything at all politically. If anything in a public ordinance requires amendment, let them not raise a tumult, or put their hands to the task—all of them ought to keep their hands bound in this respect—but let them commit the matter to the judgment of the magistrate, whose hand alone here is free. I mean, let them not venture on anything without a command. For when the ruler gives his command, private citizens receive public authority. For as the counselors are commonly called the ears and eyes of the prince, so may one reasonably speak of those whom he has appointed by his command to do things, as the hands of the prince.

24. Obedience is also due the unjust magistrate.

But since we have so far been describing a magistrate who truly is what he is called, that is, a father of his country, and, as the poet expresses it, shepherd of his people, guardian of peace, protector of righteousness, and avenger of innocence—he who does not approve of such government must rightly be regarded as insane.

But it is the example of nearly all ages that some princes are careless about all those things to which they ought to have given heed, and, far from all care, lazily take their pleasure. Others, intent upon their own business, put up for sale laws, privileges, judgments, and letters of favor. Others drain the common people of their money, and afterward lavish it on insane largesse. Still others exercise sheer robbery, plundering houses, raping virgins and matrons, and slaughtering the innocent.

Consequently, many cannot be persuaded that they ought to recognize these as princes and to obey their authority as far as possible. For in such great disgrace, and among such crimes, so alien to the office not only of a magistrate but also of a man, they discern no appearance of the image of God which ought to have shone in the magistrate; while they see no trace of that minister of God, who had been appointed to praise the good, and to punish the evil [cf. I Peter 2:14, Vg.]. Thus, they also do not recognize as ruler him whose dignity and authority Scripture commends to us. Indeed, this inborn feeling has always been in the minds of men to hate and curse tyrants as much as to love and venerate lawful kings.

25. The wicked ruler a judgment of God.

But if we look to God's Word, it will lead us farther. We are not only subject to the authority of princes who perform their office toward us uprightly and faithfully as they ought, but also to the authority of all who, by whatever means, have got control of affairs, even though they perform not a whit of the princes' office. For despite the Lord's testimony that the magistrate's office is the highest gift of his beneficence to preserve the safety of men, and despite his appointment of bounds to the magistrates—he still declares at the same time that whoever they may be, they have their authority solely from him.

Indeed, he says that those who rule for the public benefit are true patterns and evidences of this beneficence of his; that they who rule unjustly and incompetently have been raised up by him to punish the wickedness of the people; that all equally have been endowed with that holy majesty with which he has invested lawful power.

I shall proceed no farther until I have added some sure testimonies of this thing. Yet, we need not labor to prove that a wicked king is the Lord's wrath upon the earth [Job 34:30, Vg.; Hos. 13:11; Isa. 3:4; 10:5; Deut. 28:29], for I believe no man will contradict me; and thus nothing more would be said of a king than of a robber who seizes your possessions, or an adulterer who pollutes your marriage bed, or of a murderer who seeks to kill you. For Scripture reckons all such calamities among God's curses.

But let us, rather, pause here to prove this, which does not so easily settle in men's minds. In a very wicked man utterly unworthy of all honor, provided he has the public power in his hands, that noble and divine power resides which the Lord has by his Word given to the ministers of his justice and judgment. Accordingly, he should be held in the same reverence and esteem by his subjects, in so far as public obedience is concerned, in which they would hold the best of kings if he were given to them.

26. Obedience to bad kings required in Scripture.

First, I should like my readers to note and carefully observe that providence of God, which the Scriptures with good reason so often recall to us, and its special operation in distributing kingdoms and appointing what kings he pleases. In Daniel, the Lord changes times and successions at times, removes kings and sets them up [Dan. 2:21, 37]. Likewise: "to the end that the living may know that the Most High rules the kingdom of men, and gives it to whom he will" [Dan. 4:17; cf. ch. 4:14, Vg.]. Although Scripture everywhere abounds with such passages, this prophecy particularly swarms with them. Now it is well enough known what kind of king Nebuchadnezzar was, who conquered Jerusalem—a strong invader and destroyer of others. Nevertheless, the Lord declares in Ezekiel that He has given him the land of Egypt for the service he had done him in devastating it [Ezek. 29:10–20]. And Daniel said to him: "You, O king, are a king of kings, to whom the God of heaven has given the kingdom, powerful, mighty, and glorious; to you, I say, he has given also all lands where the sons of men dwell, beasts of the forest and birds of the air: these he has given into your hand and made you rule over them" [Dan. 2:37–38, cf. Vg.]. Again, Daniel says to Nebuchadnezzar's son Belshazzar: "The Most High God gave Nebuchadnezzar, your father, kingship and magnificence, honor and glory; and because of the magnificence that he gave him, all peoples, tribes, and tongues were trembling and fearful before him" [Dan. 5:18–19, cf. Vg.]. When we hear that a king has been ordained by God, let us at once call to mind those heavenly edicts with regard to honoring and fearing a king; then we shall not hesitate to hold a most wicked tyrant in the place where the Lord had deigned to set him. Samuel, when he warned the people of Israel what sort of things they would suffer from their kings, said: "This shall be the right of the king that will reign over you: he will take your sons and put them to his chariot to make them his horsemen and to plow his fields and reap his harvest, and make his weapons. He will take your daughters to be perfumers and cooks and bakers. Finally, he will take your fields, your vineyards, and your best olive trees and will give them to his servants. He will take the tenth of your grain and of your vineyards, and will give it to his eunuchs and servants. He will take your menservants, maidservants, and asses and set them to his work. He will take the tenth of your flocks and you will be his servants" [I Sam. 8:11–17, with omissions; cf. Hebrew]. Surely, the kings would not do this by legal right, since the law trained them to all restraint [Deut. 17:16 ff.]. But it was called a right in relation to the people, for they had to obey it and were not allowed to resist. It is as if Samuel had said: The willfulness of kings will run to excess, but it will not be your part to restrain it; you will have only this left to you: to obey their commands and hearken to their word.

27. The case of Nebuchadnezzar in Jer., ch. 27.

But in Jeremiah, especially, there is a memorable passage, which (although rather long) it will not trouble me to quote because it very clearly defines this whole question. "I have made the earth and men, says the Lord, and the animals which are upon the face of the earth, with my great strength and outstretched arm; and I give it to him who is pleasing in my eyes. Now, therefore, I have given all these lands into the hand of Nebuchadnezzar . . . my servant. . . . All the nations and great kings shall serve him . . . , until the time of his own land comes. . . . And it shall be that any nation and kingdom that will not serve the king of Babylon, I shall visit that nation with sword, famine, and pestilence. . . . Therefore, serve the king of Babylon and live"

[Jer. 27:5–8, 17, cf. Vg.]. We see how much obedience the Lord willed to be paid to that abominable and cruel tyrant for no other reason than that he possessed the kingship. But it was by heavenly decree that he had been set upon the throne of the kingdom and assumed into kingly majesty, which it would be unlawful to violate. If we have continually present to our minds and before our eyes the fact that even the most worthless kings are appointed by the same decree by which the authority of all kings is established, those seditious thoughts will never enter our minds that a king should be treated according to his merits and that it is unfair that we should show ourselves subjects to him who, on his part, does not show himself a king to us.

28. *General testimonies of Scripture on the sanctity of the royal person.*

It is vain for anyone to object that that command was peculiar to the Israelites. For we must note with what reason the Lord confirms it: "I have given," he says, "the kingdom to Nebuchadnezzar" [Jer. 27:6, cf. Vg.]. "Therefore, serve him and live" [Jer. 27:17, cf. Vg.]. Let us not doubt that we ought to serve him to whom it is evident that the kingdom has been given. And when once the Lord advances any man to a kingly rank, he attests to us his determination that he would have him reign. For there are general testimonies of Scripture concerning this. Solomon, in the twenty-eighth chapter of The Proverbs, says: "Because of the iniquity of the land there are many princes" [Prov. 28:2 p.]. Likewise, the twelfth chapter of Job: "He takes away subjection from kings, and girds them again with a girdle" [Job 12:18 p.]. Once this has been admitted, nothing remains but that we should serve and live.

In Jeremiah the prophet, there is also another command of the Lord by which he enjoins his people to seek the peace of Babylon, where they have been sent as captives, and to pray to the Lord on its behalf, for in its peace will be their peace [Jer. 29:7]. Behold, the Israelites, divested of all their possessions, driven from their homes, led away into exile, and cast into pitiable bondage, are commanded to pray for the prosperity of their conqueror—not as we are commanded in other passages to pray for our persecutors [cf. Matt. 5:44], but in order that his kingdom may be preserved safe and peaceful, that under him they too may prosper. So David, already designated king by God's ordination and anointed with his holy oil, when he was persecuted by

Saul without deserving it, still regarded the head of his assailant as inviolable, because the Lord had sanctified it with the honor of the kingdom. "The Lord forbid," he said, "that I should do this thing before the Lord, to my lord, the Lord's anointed, to put forth my hand against him, since he is the Lord's anointed" [I Sam. 24:6, cf. Vg.]. Again: "My soul has spared you; and I have said, 'I shall not put forth my hand against my lord, for he is the Lord's anointed'" [I Sam. 24:11, cf. Vg.]. Again: "Who will put forth his hand against the anointed of the Lord and be innocent? . . . The Lord lives; unless the Lord strike him, or the day come for him to die, or he fall in battle, the Lord forbid that I should put forth my hand against the Lord's anointed" [I Sam. 26:9–11, cf. Vg.].

29. It is not the part of subjects but of God to vindicate the right.

We owe this attitude of reverence and therefore of piety toward all our rulers in the highest degree, whatever they may be like. I therefore the more often repeat this: that we should learn not to examine the men themselves, but take it as enough that they bear, by the Lord's will, a character upon which he has imprinted and engraved an inviolable majesty.

But (you will say) rulers owe responsibilities in turn to their subjects. This I have already admitted. But if you conclude from this that service ought to be rendered only to just governors, you are reasoning foolishly. For husbands are also bound to their wives, and parents to their children, by mutual responsibilities. Suppose parents and husbands depart from their duty. Suppose parents show themselves so hard and intractable to their children, whom they are forbidden to provoke to anger [Eph. 6:4], that by their rigor they tire them beyond measure. Suppose husbands most despitefully use their wives, whom they are commanded to love [Eph. 5:25] and to spare as weaker vessels [I Peter 3:7]. Shall either children be less obedient to their parents or wives to their husbands? They are still subject even to those who are wicked and undutiful.

Indeed, all ought to try not to "look at the bag hanging from their back," that is, not to inquire about another's duties, but every man should keep in mind that one duty which is his own. This ought particularly to apply to those who have been put under the power of others. Therefore, if we are cruelly tormented by a savage prince, if we are greedily despoiled by one who is avaricious or wanton, if we are neglected by a slothful one, if finally we are vexed for piety's sake by one who is impious and sacrilegious, let us first be mindful of our own misdeeds, which without doubt are chastised by such whips of the Lord [cf. Dan. 9:7]. By this, humility will restrain our impatience. Let us then also call this thought to mind, that it is not for us to remedy such evils; that only this remains, to implore the Lord's help, in whose hand are the hearts of kings, and the changing of kingdoms [Prov. 21:1 p.]. "He is God who will stand in the assembly of the gods, and will judge in the midst of the Gods" [Ps. 82:1 p.]. Before His face all kings shall fall and be crushed, and all the judges of the earth, that have not kissed his anointed [Ps. 2:10–11], and all those who have written unjust laws to oppress the poor in judgment and to do violence to the cause of the lowly, to prey upon widows and rob the fatherless [Isa. 10:1–2, cf. Vg.].

(Constitutional magistrates, however, ought to check the tyranny of kings; obedience to God comes first, 30–31)

30. When God intervenes, it is sometimes by unwitting agents.

Here are revealed his goodness, his power, and his providence. For sometimes he raises up open avengers from among his servants, and arms them with his command to punish the wicked government and deliver his people, oppressed in unjust ways, from miserable calamity. Sometimes he directs to this end the rage of men with other intentions and other endeavors. Thus he delivered the people of Israel from the tyranny of Pharaoh, through Moses [Ex. 3:7–10]; from the violence of Chusan, king of Syria, through Othniel [Judg. 3:9]; and from other servitudes through other kings or judges. Thus he tamed the pride of Tyre by the Egyptians, the insolence of the Egyptians by the Assyrians, the fierceness of the Assyrians by the Chaldeans; the arrogance of Babylon by the Medes and Persians, after Cyrus had already subjugated the Medes. The ungratefulness of the kings of Judah and Israel and their impious obstinacy toward his many benefits, he sometimes by the Assyrians, sometimes by the Babylonians, crushed and afflicted—although not all in the same way.

For the first kind of men, when they had been sent by God's lawful calling to carry out such acts, in taking up arms against kings, did not at all violate that majesty which is implanted in kings by God's ordination; but, armed from heaven, they subdued the lesser power with the greater just as it is lawful for kings to punish their subordinates. But the latter kind of men, although they were directed by God's hand whither he pleased, and executed his work unwittingly, yet planned in their minds to do nothing but an evil act.

31. Constitutional defenders of the people's freedom.

But however these deeds of men are judged in themselves, still the Lord accomplished his work through them alike when he broke the bloody scepters or arrogant kings and when he overturned intolerable governments. Let the princes hear and be afraid.

But we must, in the meantime, be very careful not to despise or violate that authority of magistrates, full of venerable majesty, which God has established by the weightiest decrees, even though it may reside with the most unworthy men, who defile it as much as they can with their own wickedness. For, if the correction of unbridled despotism is the Lord's to avenge, let us not at once think that it is entrusted to us, to whom no command has been given except to obey and suffer.

I am speaking all the while of private individuals. For if there are now any magistrates of the people, appointed to restrain the willfulness of kings (as in ancient times the ephors were set against the Spartan kings, or the tribunes of the people against the Roman consuls, or the demarchs against the senate of the Athenians; and perhaps, as things now are, such power as the three estates exercise in every realm when they hold their chief assemblies), I am so far from forbidding them to withstand, in accordance with their duty, the fierce licentiousness of kings, that, if they wink at kings who violently fall upon and assault the lowly common folk, I declare that their dissimulation involves nefarious perfidy, because they dishonestly betray the freedom of the people, of which they know that they have been appointed protectors by God's ordinance.

32. Obedience to man must not come before disobedience to God.

But in that obedience which we have shown to be due the authority of rulers, we are always to make this exception, indeed, to observe it as primary, that such obedience is never to lead us away from obedience to him, to whose will the desires of all kings ought to be subject, to whose decrees all their commands ought to yield, to whose majesty their scepters ought to be submitted. And how absurd would it be that in satisfying men you should incur the displeasure of him for whose sake you obey men themselves! The Lord, therefore, is the King of Kings, who, when he has opened his sacred mouth, must alone be heard, before all and above all men; next to him we are subject to those men who are in authority over us, but only in him. If they command anything against him, let it go unesteemed. And here let us not be concerned about all that dignity which the magistrates possess; for no harm is done to it when it is humbled before that singular and truly supreme power of God. On this consideration, Daniel denies that he has committed any offense against the king when he has not obeyed his impious edict [Dan. 6:22–23, Vg.]. For the king had exceeded his limits, and had not only been a wrongdoer against men, but, in lifting up his horns against God, had himself abrogated his power. Conversely, the Israelites are condemned because they were too obedient to the wicked proclamation of the king [Hos. 5:13]. For when Jeroboam molded the golden calves, they, to please him, forsook God's Temple and turned to new superstitions [I Kings 12:30]. With the same readiness, their descendants complied with the decrees of their kings. The prophet sharply reproaches them for embracing the king's edicts [Hos. 5:11]. Far, indeed, is the pretense of modesty from deserving praise, a false modesty with which the court flatterers cloak themselves and deceive the simple, while they deny that it is lawful for them to refuse anything imposed by their kings. As if God had made over his right to mortal men, giving them the rule over mankind! Or as if earthly power were diminished when it is subjected to its Author, in whose presence even the heavenly powers tremble as suppliants! I know with what great and present peril this constancy is menaced, because kings bear defiance with the greatest displeasure, whose "wrath is a messenger of death" [Prov. 16:14], says Solomon. But since this edict has been proclaimed by the heavenly herald, Peter —"We must obey God rather than men" [Acts 5:29]—let us comfort ourselves with the thought that we are rendering that obedience which the Lord requires when we suffer anything rather than turn aside from piety. And that our courage may not grow faint, Paul pricks us with another goad: That we have been redeemed by Christ at so great a price as our redemption cost him, so that we should not enslave ourselves to the wicked desires of men—much less be subject to their impiety [I Cor. 7:23].

GOD BE PRAISED

3

JAMES I
The Divine Right of Kings

The doctrine of the divine right of kings provided the classic expression of the view that political rulership must be exercised by individuals whose authority stems from divine sanction. It became a prominent ideological defense of absolute monarchy in the sixteenth and seventeenth centuries. It involved a major modification of the long-established doctrine that secular authority is based on divine origin. Throughout the Middle Ages the accepted view was that all authority—spiritual and temporal—comes from God, but nevertheless authority was not absolute and unlimited. Despite frequent jurisdictional disputes about the relation of secular and spiritual authorities, the two were seen as separate and distinct without the right of encroaching upon the other. Law was seen as rooted in customs and folkways, and thus belonging essentially to the people. The king, himself, it was commonly believed, was as much subject to the law as his subjects. Thus resistance to the king, when the fundamental law was believed to have been invaded, was considered to be a legal and moral right. This did not usually imply the right of individual resistance to secular authority, but it did mean that a variety of orders and corporations had rights against the king. By the fifteenth century it was generally accepted in England that the king should not make laws without consulting Parliament.

The period of the sixteenth-century religious wars produced a new type of resistance to royal power from religious minorities; their opposition was based on the argument that the authority of the ruler rests not only upon the will of God and not on mere custom, but on the fact that the people have agreed to set up rulers for certain purposes and therefore have the right to resist a tyrannical king. The theory of the divine right of kings appears as a defense of the established monarchies in England and

France against the political threat of religious minorities. The aim of James I (1566–1625), almost from the time he was proclaimed King of Scotland in 1567, was to escape from subservience to Scottish factions and to establish his claim to succeed Elizabeth I upon the throne of England. For these ends he was willing to use whatever means were necessary. After breaking the power of the Catholic faction in 1594, James I asserted himself against the Presbyterians and eventually was able to rule Scotland almost as absolutely as Elizabeth ruled England. It was at about this time that he expounded his exalted views of the nature of royal authority in the

True Law of Free Monarchies.

According to James I, kings are the "breathing images of God on earth"; they are not only God's lieutenants upon earth, and sit upon God's throne, but even by God himself they are called God. The divine origin of kingship, he contended, is vindicated in the Scriptures, where it is stated that God commanded Samuel to hear the people's voice in choosing and anointing them a king. But the king's authority derives from God, and the people do not have the right to disobey or defy the power of the monarch no matter how wicked or tyrannical he may be.

James I did not rest his argument solely upon a theological basis. The sovereign authority of the king also derives from natural law; it is analogous to the relation of a father to his children; of the head to the body, providing the care, guidance and direction without which the people would be a headless multitude, incapable of making laws. Finally, James was aware that the particular authority of the King of Scotland needed to be established on specific historical grounds, as well as upon general principles of government. The king's authority, he contended, was originally established by conquest over a few primitive barbarians. Kings were, therefore, in Scotland before any aristocratic estates, or ranks of man; land was distributed, states created and forms of government established. From this it follows that kings are the makers of laws. Once established, the king's authority passes to his successors by the principle of hereditary right.

As supreme sovereign authority, the prerogative of the king is absolute and unfettered: he cannot be considered subject to restraint by estates of the realm or by parliament. Subjects can claim no right of resistance to sovereign authority; even a wicked king must be endured as a penalty imposed by God for the sins of the people. Nor are judges entitled to question the prerogative of the Crown, which, in its basic essence, is a transcendent affair. "That which concerns the mystery of the king's power is not lawful to be disputed, for that is to wade into the weakness of princes and to take away the mystic reverence that belongs to them that sit in the throne of God." Ultimately, then, the theory of divine right constitutes a claim to legitimacy which requires no legal or rational justification.*

. . . There is not a thing so necessary to be known by the people of any land, next to the knowledge of their God, as the right knowledge of their allegiance, according to the form of government established among them, especially in a monarchy (which form of government, as resembling the Divinity, approaches nearest to perfect union, as all the learned and wise men from the beginning have agreed upon; Divinity being the perfection of all things). . . . Ignorance, and (which is worse) the seduced opinion of the multitude, blinded by those who think themselves able to teach and instruct the ignorant, procured the wrack and overthrow of sundry flourishing commonwealths; and reaped heavy calamities, threatening utter destruction upon others. . . .

I have chosen, then, only to set down in this short Treatise, the true grounds of the mutual duty, and allegiance between a free and absolute Monarchy, and his people. . . . First then, I will set down the true grounds, whereupon I am to build, out of the scriptures, since Monarchy is the true pattern of Divinity, as I have already said: next, from the fundamental Laws of our own Kingdom, which nearest must concern us; thirdly from the laws of Nature, by diverse similitudes drawn out of the same; and will conclude, later, by answering the most weighty and appearing incommodities that can be objected.

The Prince's duty to his subjects is so clearly set down in many places of the scripture, and so openly confessed by all the good princes, according to their oath in their Coronation, as not needing to be long therein, I shall, as shortly as I can, run through it.

Kings are called Gods[1] by the Prophetical King David because they

---

* The selection is from "The True Law of Free Monarchies: Or the Reciprocal and Mutual Duty Between a Free King and His Natural Subjects," in *The Political Works of James I*, introduction by C. H. McIlwain (Cambridge: Harvard University Press, 1918), pp. 53–57; 58; 59; 60–64; 66–69; 307–10. By permission. In order to render the excerpts from James I (written in Old English style) more readable, the editor has made some modifications: spelling has been modernized; certain Old English expressions have been translated into modern equivalents; and, in a few instances, minor changes have been made in sentence structure.

[1] Psal. 82 : 6.

sit upon God his Throne in the earth, and have the account of their administration to give unto him. Their office is *to minister justice and judgment to the people,*[2] as the same *David* said; *to advance the good, and punish evil,*[3] as he likewise said; *to establish good laws to his people, and procure obedience to the same,*[4] as diverse good Kings of *Judah*[5] did; *to procure the peace of the people,* as the same *David* said;[6] *to decide all controversies that can arise among them*[7] as *Solomon* did; *to be the Minister of God, for the weal of them that do well, and as the minister of God, to take vengeance upon those that do evil,*[8] as St. Paul said. And finally, *as a good Pastor, to go out and in before his people,*[9] as is said in the first of *Samuel; that through the Prince's prosperity the people's peace may be procured,*[10] as *Jeremie* said.

And therefore in the Coronation of our own Kings, as well as of every Christian Monarch, they give their Oath, first to maintain the Religion presently professed within their country, according to their laws, whereby it is established, and to punish all those that should press to alter, or disturb the profession thereof; And next to maintain all the allowable and good Laws made by their predecessors: to see them put in execution, and the breakers and violators thereof, to be punished, according to the tenor of the same: And lastly, to maintain the whole country, and every state therein, in all their ancient Privileges and Liberties, as well against all foreign enemies, as among themselves: And shortly to procure the weal and flourishing of his people, not only in maintaining and putting to execution the old allowable laws of the country, and by establishing of new (as necessity and evil manners will require) but by all other means possible to foresee and prevent all dangers that are likely to fall upon them, and to maintain concord, wealth, and civility among them, as a loving Father, and careful watchman, caring for them more than for himself, knowing himself to be ordained for them, and they not for him; and therefore accountable to that great God, who placed him as his

[2] Psal. 101.
[3] Psal. 101.
[4] 2 Kings 18.
[5] 2 Chron. 29; 2 Kings 22; and 23 : 2; Chron. 34 and 35.
[6] Psal. 72.
[7] 1 Kings 3.
[8] Rom. 13.
[9] 1 Sam. 8.
[10] Jer. 29.

lieutenant over them, upon the peril of his soul, to procure the weal of both souls and bodies, as far as in him lie, of all those that are committed to his charge. And this Oath in the Coronation is the clearest, civil, and fundamental Law, whereby the King's office is properly defined.

By the Law of Nature the King becomes a natural Father to all his Lieges at his Coronation: And as the Father, in fulfilling his fatherly duty, is bound to care for the nourishing, education, and virtuous government of his children; even so is the King bound to care for all his subjects. As all the toil and pain that the Father can take for his children; will be thought light and well bestowed by him, so that the effect thereof redound to their profit and weal; so ought the Prince to do towards his people. As the kindly Father ought to foresee all inconveniences and dangers that may arise towards his children, and though with the hazard of his own person press to prevent the same; so ought the King towards his people. As the Father's wrath and correction upon any of his children that offends ought to be by a Fatherly chastisement seasoned with pity, as long as there is any hope of amendment in them; so ought the King towards any of his Lieges that offend in that measure. And shortly, as the Father's chief joy ought to be in procuring his children's welfare, rejoicing at their weal, sorrowing and pitying at their evil, to hazard for their safety, travel for their rest, wake for their sleep; and in a word, to think that his earthly felicity and life stands and lies more in them, nor in himself; so ought a good Prince think of his people.

As to the other branch of his mutual and reciprocal band, is the duty and allegiance that the Lieges owe to their King: the ground whereof, I take out of the words of *Samuel*, dictated by God's Spirit, when God had given him commandment to hear the people's voice in choosing and anointing them a King. And because that place of Scripture being well understood, is so pertinent for our purpose, I have inserted herein the very words of the Text.

9 *Now therefore hearken to their voice: howbeit yet testify unto them, and show them the manner of the King, that shall reign over them.*

10 *So Samuel told all the words of the Lord unto the people that asked a King of him.*

11 *And he said, This shall be the manner of the King that shall reign over you: he will take your sons, and appoint them to his*

Chariots, and to be his horsemen, and some shall run before his Chariots.

12 *Also, he will make them his captains over thousands, and captains over fifties, and to eare his ground, and to reap his harvest, and to make instruments of war and the things that serve for his chariots:*

13 *He will also take your daughters, and make them Apothicaries, and Cooks, and Bakers.*

14 *And he will take your fields, and your vineyards, and your best Olive trees, and give them to his servants.*

15 *And he will take the tenth of your seed, and of your Vineyards, and give it to his Eunuchs, and to his servants.*

16 *And he will take your men servants, and your maid-servants, and the chief of your young men, and your asses, and put them to his work.*

17 *He will take the tenth of your sheep: and ye shall be his servants.*

18 *And ye shall cry out at that day, because of your King, whom ye have chosen you: and the Lord God will not hear you at that day.*

19 *But the people would not hear the voice of Samuel, but did say: Nay, but there shall be a King over us.*

20 *And we also will be all like other Nations, and our King shall Judge us, and go out before us, and fight our battles.*

That these words, and discourses of *Samuel* were dictated by God's Spirit, it needs no further probation, but that it is a place of Scripture: since the whole Scripture is dictated by that inspiration, as *Paul* said: which ground no good Christian will, or dare deny. Whereupon it must necessarily follow, that these speeches proceeded not from any ambition in *Samuel*, as one loath to quit the reins that he so long had ruled, and therefore desirous, by making odious the government of a King, to dissuade the people from their further importunate craving of one: For, as the text proves plainly, he then convened them to give them a resolute grant of their demand, as God by his own mouth commanded him saying,

Hearken to the voice of the people. . . .

And if you will consider the very words of the text in order, as they are set down, it shall plainly declare the obedience that the people owe to their King in all respects.

First, God commanded *Samuel* to do two things: the one, to grant the people their suit in giving them a King; the other, to forewarn them what some Kings will do to them so that they may not thereafter in their grudging and murmuring say, when they shall feel the snares here fore-spoken: We would never have had a king of God, in case when we craved him, had he let us know how we would have been used by him, as now we find but overlaid. And this is meant by these words:

Now therefore hearken unto their voice: howbeit yet testifie unto them, and show them the manner of the King that shall rule over them.

And next, Samuel, in execution of this commandment of God, he likewise did two things.

First, he declared unto them, what points of justice and equity their king will break in his behavior unto them: And next he put them out of hope, that weary as they will, they shall not have leave to shake off that yoke, which God through their importunity has laid upon them. . . .

Now then, since the erection of this Kingdom and Monarchy among the Jews, and the law thereof may, and ought to be, a pattern to all Christian and well-founded Monarchies, as being founded by God himself, who by his Oracle, and out of his own mouth gave the law thereof: what liberty can broiling spirits, and rebellious minds, claim justly to against any Christian Monarchy; since they can claim to no greater liberty on their part, nor the people of God might have done, and no greater tyranny was ever executed by any Prince or tyrant, whom they can object, nor was here fore-warned to the people of God, (and yet all rebellion countermanded unto them) if tyrannizing over men's persons, sons, daughters and servants; redacting noble houses, and men, and women of noble blood, to slavish and servile offices; and extortion, and spoils of their lands and goods to the prince's own private use and commodity, and of his courtiers, and servants, may be called a tyrannie?

And that this proposition grounded upon the Scripture, may the more clearly appear to be true by the practice often proved in the same book, we never read that ever the Prophets persuaded the people to rebel against the Prince, however wicked he was. . . .

To end, then, the ground of my proposition taken out of the Scripture, let two special and notable examples, one under the law, another under the Evangel, conclude this part of my allegiance. Under the law, *Jeremie* threatened the people of God with utter destruction for rebellion to *Nabuchadnezar* the king of Babel:[11] who although he was an idolatrous persecutor, a foreign King, a Tyrant, and usurper of their liberties, yet in respect they had once received and acknowledged him for their king, he not only commanded them to obey him, but even to pray for his prosperity, because in his prosperity stood their peace.[12]

And under the Evangel, that king, whom *Paul* bids the *Romans obey* and serve *for conscience' sake,* was *Nero* that bloody tyrant, an infamie to his age, and a monster to the world, being also an idolatrous persecutor, as the King of *Babel* was. If, then, Idolatry and defection from God, tyranny over their people, and persecution of the Saints, for their profession' sake, hindered not the Spirit of God to command his people under all highest pain to give them all due and hearty obedience for conscience' sake, giving to *Caesar* that which was *Caesar's,* and to God that which was God's, as Christ said; and that this practice throughout the book of God agrees with this law, which he made in the erection of that Monarchy (as is at length before deduced) what shameless presumption is it to any Christian people today to claim to that unlawfull liberty, which God refused to his own peculiar and chosen people?[13] Shortly, then, to take up in two or three sentences, grounded upon all these arguments, out of the law of God, the duty, and allegiance of the people to their lawful king, their obedience, I say, ought to be to him, as to God's Lieutenant in earth, obeying his commands in all things, except directly against God, as the commands of God's Minister, acknowledging him a Judge set by God over them, having power to Judge them, but to be Judged only by God, whom to only he must give count of his Judgement; fearing him as their Judge, loving him as their Father; praying for him as their protector; for his continuance, if he be good; for his amendment, if he be wicked; following and obeying his lawful commands, eschewing and flying his fury in his unlawful, without resistance, but by sobs and tears to God, according to that sentence used in the primitive church in the time of the persecution.

Preces, and Lachrymae sunt arma Ecclesiae.

Now, as for the describing the allegiance, that the lieges owe to their native King, out of the fundamental and civil Law, especially of

---

[11] Jer. 27.
[12] Jer. 29.
[13] Jer. 13.

this country, as I promised, the ground must first be set down of the first manner of establishing the Laws and form of government among us; that the ground being first right laid, we may thereafter build rightly thereupon. Although it be true (according to the affirmation of those that pride themselves to be the scourges of Tyrants) that in the first beginning of Kings rising among the Gentiles, in the time of the first age, diverse commonwealths and societies of men chose out one among themselves, who for his virtues and valour, being more eminent than the rest, was chosen by them, and set up in that place, to maintain the weakest in their right, to throw down oppressors, and to foster and continue the society among men; which could not otherwise, but by virtue of that unity, be well done: yet these examples are nothing pertinent to us; because our Kingdom and diverse other Monarchies are not in that case, but had their beginning in a far contrary fashion.

For as our Chronicles bear witness, this Ile, and especially our part of it, being scantly inhabited, but by very few, and they are barbarous and scant of civility, as number, there came our first King *Fergus,* with a great number with him, out of *Ireland,* which was long inhabited before us, and making himself master of the country, by his own friendship, and force, as well of the *Irelandmen* that came with him, as of the country-men that willingly fell to him, he made himself King and Lord, of the whole land, as of the whole inhabitants within the same. Thereafter he and his successors, a long while after their being Kings, made and established their laws from time to time, as the occasion required. So the truth is directly contrary in our state to the false affirmation of such seditious writers, as would persuade us, that the Laws and state of our country were established before the admitting of a King: where by the contrary you see it plainly proved, that a wise king coming in among barbarians, first established the estate and form of government, and thereafter made Laws by himself, and his successors.

The Kings were therefore in *Scotland* before any estates or ranks of men within the same, before any Parliaments were held, or laws made: and by them was the land distributed (which at the first was wholly theirs), states erected and discerned, and forms of government devised and established: And so it follows of necessity, that the Kings were the authors and makers of the Laws, and not the Laws of the kings. And to prove my assertion more clearly, it is evident by the rolls of our Chancellery (which contains our eldest and most

fundamental Laws) that the King is *Dominus omnium bonorum,* and
Dominus directus totius Dominij, the whole people being but his
vassals, and from him holding all their lands as their over-lord, who
according to good services done unto him, change their holdings from
tacke to few, from ward to blanch, erecting new Baronies, and uniting
old, without advice or authority of either Parliament or any other
subaltern Judicial seat: So as if wrong might be admitted in play
(albeit I grant wrong should be wrong in all persons) the King might
have a better colour for his pleasure, without further reason, to take
the land from his lieges, as overlord of the whole, and do with it as
pleases him, since all that they hold is of him; then, as foolish
writers say, the people might unmake the king, and put another in his
place: But either of them, as unlawful, and against the ordinance
of God, ought to be alike odious to be thought, much less put into
practice.

And according to these fundamental Laws already alleged, we daily
see that in the Parliament (which is nothing else but the head Court
of the king and his vassals) the laws are but demanded by his subjects, and only made by him at their supplication, and with their
advice: For albeit the King make daily statutes and ordinances,
enjoying such pain thereto as he thinks proper, without any advice of
Parliament or estates; yet it lies in the power of no Parliament to
make any kind of Law or Statute, without his Scepter be to it, for
giving it the force of a Law: And although diverse changes have been
in other countries of the blood Royal, and kingly house, the kingdom
being reft by conquest from one to another, as in our neighbour
country in *England* (which was never in ours), yet the same ground
of the King's right over all the land, and subjects thereof remains alike
in all other free Monarchies, as well as in this: For when the Bastard
of *Normandie* came into *England,* and made himself King, was it not
by force, and with a mighty army? Where he gave the Law, and took
none, changed the Laws, inverted the order of government, set down
the strangers, his followers, in many of the old possessor's places, as
at this day it well appears a great part of the Gentlemen in *England,*
have come of the Norman blood, and their old Laws, which to this
day they are ruled by, are written in his language, and not in theirs:
And yet his successors have with great happiness enjoyed the Crown
to this day; Whereof the like was also done by all those that con-
quested them before.

And for conclusion of this point, that the King is over-lord over the whole land, it is likewise daily proved by the Law of our hoardes, of want of Heiress, and of Bastardies: For if a hoard be found under the earth, because it is no more in the keeping or use of any person, it of the law pertains to the King. If a person, inheritor of any lands or goods, die without any sort of heiress, all his lands and goods return to the King. And if a bastard die unrehabilitated without heiress of his body (which rehabilitation lies only in the king's hands) all that he has likewise returns to the King. And as you see it manifest, that the King is over-lord of the whole land: so is he Master over every person that inhabit the same, having power over the life and death of every one of them: For although a Just Prince will not take the life of any of his subjects without a clear law; yet the same laws whereby he take them are made by himself, or his predecessors; and so the power flows always from him-self; as by daily experience we see, good and Just Princes will from time to time make new laws and statutes, adjoining the penalties to the breakers thereof, which before the law was made, had been no crime to the subject to have committed. Not that I deny the old definition of a King, and of a law; which makes the king to be a speaking law, and the Law a dumb King: for certainly a king that governs not by his law can neither be accountable to God for his administration, nor have a happy and established reign: For albeit it be true that I have at length proved, that the King is above the law, as both the author and giver of strength thereto; yet a good king will not only delight to rule his subjects by the law, but even will conform himself in his own actions thereunto, always keeping that ground, that the health of the common-wealth be his chief law: And where he sees the law doubtful or rigorous, he may interpret or miti-gate the same, lest otherwise *Summum ius* be *summa iniuria:* And therefore general laws, made publicly in Parliament, may upon known respects to the King by his authority be mitigated, and suspended upon causes only known to him.

As likewise, although I have said, a good king will frame all his actions to be according to the Law; yet is he not bound thereto but of his good will, and for good example-giving to his subjects: For as in the law of abstaining from eating of flesh in *Lenton,* the King will, for example's sake, make his own house to observe the Law; yet no man will think he needs to take a licence to eat flesh. And although by our Laws, the bearing and wearing of hag-buts and pistolets be forbidden, yet no man can find any fault in the King, for causing his train use them in any raid upon the Borderers, or other malefactors or rebellious

subjects. So, as I have already said, a good King, although he be
above the Law, will subject and frame his actions thereto, for
example's sake to his subjects, and of his own free-will, but not as
subject or bound thereto.

Since I have so clearly proven, then, out of the fundamental laws
and practice of this country, what right and power a King hath over
his land and subjects, it is easy to be understood, what allegiance and
obedience his lieges owe unto him; I mean always of such free
Monarchies as our king is, and not of elected Kings, and much less of
such sort of governors, as the dukes of *Venice* are, whose aristocratic
and limited government is nothing like free Monarchies; although the
malice of some writers has not been ashamed to deny any difference
between them. And if it be not lawful to any particular Lord's tenants
or vassals, upon whatsoever pretext, to control and displace their
Master, and over-lord . . . how much less may the subjects and vassals
of the great over-lord the King control or displace him? And since in
all inferior Judgements in the land, the people may not upon any respects displace their Magistrates, although but subaltern: for the people
of a borough, cannot displace their Provost before the time of their
election: nor in Ecclesiastical policy the flock can upon any pretense
displace the Pastor, nor Judge of him: yea, even the poor Schoolmaster cannot be displaced by his scholars: If these, I say (whereof
some are but inferior, subaltern, and temporal Magistrates, and none
of them equal in any sort to the dignity of a King), cannot be displaced for any occasion or pretext by those that are ruled by them:
how much less is it lawful upon any pretext to control or displace the
great Provost, and great Schoolmaster of the whole land: except by
inverting the order of all Law and reason, the commanded may be
made to command their commander, the Judged to judge their Judge,
and they that are governed, to govern their time about their Lord and
governour. . . .

And in case any doubts might arise in any part of this treatise, I
will (according to my promise) with the solution of four principal
and most weighty doubts, that the adversaries may object, conclude
this discourse. At first it is cast up by diverse sources, that employ
their pens upon Apologies for rebellions and treasons, that every man
is born to carry such a natural zeal and duty to his commonwealth, as
to his mother; that seeing it so rent and deadly wounded, as it will be
by wicked and tyrannous Kings, good Citizens will be forced, for the
natural zeal and duty they owe to their own native country, to put

their hand to work for freeing their commonwealth from such a pest.

Whereunto I give two answers: First, it is a sure Axiom in *Theology* that evil should not be done, that good may come of it: The wickedness, therefore, of the King can never make those that are ordained to be Judged by him, to become his Judges. And if it be not lawful to a private man to revenge his private injury upon his private adversary (since God has only given the sword to the Magistrate) how much less is it lawful to the people, or any part of them (who all are but private men, the authority being always with the Magistrate, as I have already proved) to take upon them the use of the sword, whom to it belongs not, against the public Magistrate, whom to only it belongs.

Next, in place of relieving the common-wealth out of distress (which is their only excuse and colour) they shall heap double distress and desolation upon it; and so their rebellion shall procure the contrary effects that they pretend it for: For a King cannot be imagined to be so unruly and tyrannous, but the commonwealth will be kept in better order, notwithstanding thereof, by him, then it can be by his overthrow. For first, all sudden mutations are perilous in commonwealths, hope being thereby given to all bare men to set up themselves, and fly with other men's feathers, the reins being loosed to all the insolencies that disordered people can commit by hope of impunity, because of the looseness of all things.

And next, it is certain that a King can never be so monstrously vicious, but that he will generally favor Justice, and maintain some order, except in the particulars, wherein his inordinate lusts and passions carry him away; where by the contrary, no King, being, nothing, is unlawful to none: And so the old opinion of the Philosophers proves true, That better it is to live in a Common-wealth, where nothing is lawful, than where all things are lawful to all men; the Common-wealth at that time resembling an untamed young horse that has cast his rider: For as the divine Poet *Dv Bartas* says, *Better it were to suffer some disorder in the estate, and some spots in the Common-wealth, than in pretending to reform, utterly to overthrow the Republic.*

The second objection they ground upon the curse that hangs over the commonwealth, where a wicked King reigns: and, say they, there cannot be a more acceptable deed in the sight of God, nor more dutiful to their common-weal, than to free the country of such a curse, and vindicate to them their liberty, which is natural to all creatures to crave.

Whereunto for answer, I grant indeed, that a wicked king is sent by God for a curse to his people, and a plague for their sins: but that it it is lawful to them to shake off that curse at their own hand, which God hath laid on them, that I deny, and may so do justly. Will any deny that the King of *Babel* was a curse to the people of God, as was plainly fore-spoken and threatened unto them in the prophecy of their captivity? And what was *Nero* to the Christian Church in his time? And yet *Jeremie* and *Paul* (as you have elsewhere heard) commanded them not only to obey them, but heartily to pray for their welfare.

It is certain then (as I have already by the Law of God sufficiently proved) that patience, earnest prayers to God, and amendment of their lives, are the only lawful means to move God to relieve them of that heavy curse. As for vindicating to themselves their own liberty, what lawful power have they to revoke to themselves against those privileges, which by their own consent before were so fully put out of their hands? For if a Prince cannot Justly bring back again to himself the privileges once bestowed by him or his predecessors upon any state or rank of his subjects; how much less may the subjects take from out of the Prince's hand that superiority, which he and his Predecessors have long brooked over them?

But the unhappy iniquitude of the time, which has often given over good success to their treasonable attempts, furnish them the ground of their third objection: For, say they, the fortunate success that God has so often given to such enterprises, proves plainly by the practice, that God favored the Justness of their quarrel.

To which I answer that it is true indeed, that all the success of battles, as well as other worldly things, lies only in God's hand: And therefore it is that in the Scripture he takes to himself the style of God or Hosts. But upon that general principle to conclude that he ever gives victory to the just quarrel would prove the *Philistines,* and diverse other neighbour enemies of the people of God, to have often had the just quarrel against the people of God, in respect of the many victories they obtained against them. And by that same argument, they had also Just quarrel against the Ark of God: For they won it in the field, and kept it long prisoner in their country. As likewise by all good writers, as well Theologians, as other, the Duels and singular combats are disallowed; which are only made upon pretense, that God will make known thereby the Justice of the quarrel: For we must consider that the innocent party is not innocent before God: And therefore God will often make those that have the wrong side revenge justly his quarrel; and when he has done so, cast his scourge in the fire; as he often did this to his own people, stirring up and strengthening their enemies, while they were humbled in his sight, and then delivered them in their hands. So God, as the great Judge, may Justly punish his Deputy, and for his rebellion against him stir up his rebels to meet him with the like: And when it is done, the part of the instrument is no better than the duel's part is in tempting and torturing such as God has committed to him as his hangman to do: Therefore, as I said in the beginning, it is often a very deceiving argument, to Judge of the cause by the event.

And the last objection is grounded upon the mutual pact and stipulation (as they call it) between the King and his people, at the time of his coronation: For there, say they, there is a mutual pact, and contract bound, and sworn between the king, and the people: Whereupon it follows, that if the one part of the contract or the covenant be broken upon the King's side, the people are no longer bound to keep their part of it, but are thereby freed of their oath: For (say they) a contract between two parties, of all Law frees the one party, if the other break the contract.

As to this contract allegedly made at the coronation of a King, although I deny any such contract to be made then, especially containing such a clause irritant as they allege; yet I confess, that a king at his coronation, or at the entry to his kingdom, willingly promises to his people, to discharge honourably and truly the office given him by God over them: But presuming that thereafter he breaks his promise to them never so inexcusable; the question is, who should be judge of the break. . . . I think no man that hath but the smallest entrance into the civil Law, will doubt that of all Law, either civil or municipal of any nation, a contract cannot be thought broken by the one party, and so the other likewise to be freed therefrom, except that first, a lawful trial and cognition be had by the ordinary Judge of the breakers thereof: Or else every man may be both party and Judge in his own cause; which is absurd once to be thought. Now in this contract (I say) between the king and his people, God is doubtless the only Judge, both because to him only the king must make account of his administration (as has often been said before) as likewise by the oath in the coronation, God is made Judge and revenger of the breakers: For in his presence, as only Judge of oaths, all oaths ought to be made. Then since God is the only Judge between the two contracting parties, the cognition and revenge must only appertain to him. It follows, therefore, of necessity, that God must first give sentence upon the King that breaks the contract, before the people can think themselves freed of their oath. What Justice then is it, that the party shall be both Judge and party, usurping upon himself the office of God, may by this argument easily appear: And shall it lie in the hands of headless multitude, when they please, to weary of subjection, to cast off the yoke of government that God has laid upon them, to judge and punish him, whom-by they should be Judged and punished, and in that case, wherein by their violence they show themselves to be most passionate parties, to use the office of an ungracious Judge or Arbiter? Nay, to speak truly of that case, as it stands between the king and his people, none of them ought to Judge of the other's break: For considering rightly the two parties at the time of their mutual promise, the King is the one party, and the whole people in one body are the other party. And therefore since it is certain, that a King, in case so it should fall out, that his people in one body had rebelled against him, he should not in that case, as thinking himself free of his promise and oath, become an utter enemy, and practice the wreak of his whole people and native country: although he ought Justly to punish the principal authours and bellowers of that universal rebellion: how much less, then, ought the people (that are always subject unto him, and naked of all authority on their part) seek to Judge and over-throw him? otherwise the people, as the one party contractors, shall no sooner challenge the King as breaker, but he as soon shall judge them as breakers: so as the victors making the tyners the traitors (as our proverb is) the party shall become both Judge and party in his own particular, as I have already said.

And it is here likewise to be noted, that the duty and allegiance, which the people swear to their prince, is not only bound to themselves, but likewise to their lawful heiress and posterity, the lineal succession of crowns being begun among the people of God, and happily continued in diverse christian commonwealths: So as no objection either of heresy, or whatsoever private statute or law may free the people from their oath-giving to their King, and his succession, established by the old fundamental laws of the kingdom: For, as he is their heritable over-lord, and so by birth, not by any right in the coronation, comes to his crown; it is alike unlawful (the crown, ever standing full) to displace him that succeeds thereto, as to eject the former: For at the very moment of the expiring of the king reigning, the nearest and lawful heir enters in his place: And so to refuse him, or intrude another, is not to hold out uncomming in, but to expel and put out their righteous King. And I trust at this time whole *France* acknowledges the superstitious rebellion of the liguers, who upon pretense of heresy, by force of arms held out so long, to the great desolation of their whole country, their native and righteous king from possessing of his own crown and natural kingdom. . . .

The State of MONARCHY is the most supreme thing upon earth: For Kings are not only God's Lieutenants upon earth, and sit upon God's throne, but even by God himself they are called Gods. There are three principal similitudes that illustrate the state of MONARCHY: One taken out of the word of God; and the two other out of the grounds of Policy and Philosophy. In the Scriptures Kings are called Gods, and so their power after a certain relation compared to the Divine power. Kings are also compared to Fathers of families: For a King is truly *Parens patriae,* the political father of his people. And lastly, Kings are compared to the head of this Microcosm of the body of man.

Kings are Justly called Gods, for that they exercise a manner or resemblance of Divine power upon earth: For if you will consider the Attributes to God, you shall see how they agree in the person of a King. God has power to create, or destroy, make, or unmake at his pleasure, to give life, or send death, to Judge all, and to be Judged nor accountable to none. To raise low things, and to make high things low at his pleasure, and to God are both soul and body due. And the like power have Kings: they make and unmake their subjects: they have power of raising, and casting down: of life, and of death: Judges over all their subjects, and in all causes, and yet accountable to none but God only. They have power to exalt low things, and abase high things, and make of their subjects like men at the Chess; A pawn to take a Bishop or a Knight, and to cry up, or down, any of their subjects, as they do their money. And to the King is due both the affection of the soul, and the services of the body of his subjects.

4

MACHIAVELLI
The Autonomy of Power

With Niccolò Machiavelli (1469-1527) one finds a major break with theories of legitimacy based upon the appeal to moral principle, higher law or divine sanction. Political power is an end in itself, divorced from questions of morality and religion, and the successful political ruler must be one who has the qualities and virtues necessary for the attainment of power: courage, intelligence and foresight; the capacity to seize opportunities presented by circumstance; skill in the techniques and strategies of warfare and diplomacy. Since power is the sole end of political action, all necessary means for achieving these goals are legitimate, including murder, violence, dishonesty and bad faith. This does not mean Machiavelli condoned immorality or violence for its own sake; he was simply indifferent to the question of moral principle. The only criterion for evaluating the prince is whether the means he uses are efficient and successful in attaining power. Because of his indifference to moral principle, and his advocacy of the doctrine that the end justifies the means, Machiavelli is commonly viewed as the quintessence of political evil and immorality.

There are, however, several interpretations which put Machiavelli's contribution in a more favorable light. One is that Machiavelli was a sincere admirer of the virtues of the Roman Republic, which is revealed in his less well-known work *The Discourses*. But because of what he saw as the moral corruption and degeneration of the Italian city-states, Machiavelli was convinced that the only effective government that was possible, at least in Italy in his time, was an absolute monarchy.

But perhaps the more widely influential appreciation of Machiavelli is that he was the first true "political scientist," basing his theory upon empirical description and analysis of what he saw to be the basic realities of human nature and the actual conditions of political behavior of the Italian city-states. As a contribution to the problem of defining the nature of political rule, Machiavelli provided a modern emphasis upon politics as the scientific study of the techniques and methods for the attainment of political power. Machiavelli's *Prince* is perhaps justly accused of being a textbook for totalitarian rule, but his general approach to the study of politics, it is often argued, contributes to our understanding of political rule in a democratic, as well as a totalitarian state. For Machiavelli confronts us with the dilemma of statesmanship as the effort to reconcile democratic principles with the inevitable realities of the struggle for power in both domestic and international affairs. He reminds us that the wise statesman, while respectful of the limits imposed by democratic processes, must be conversant with the techniques and stratagems for gaining access to political power.*

OF THOSE WHO HAVE ATTAINED THE POSITION OF PRINCE BY VILLAINY

But as there are still two ways of becoming prince which cannot be attributed entirely either to fortune or to ability, they must not be passed over, although one of them could be more fully discussed if we were treating of republics. These are when one becomes prince by some nefarious or villainous means, or when a private citizen becomes the prince of his country through the favour of his fellow-citizens. And in speaking of the former means, I will give two examples, one ancient, the other modern, without entering further into the merits of this method, as I judge them to be sufficient for any one obliged to imitate them.

Agathocles the Sicilian rose not only from private life but from the lowest and most abject position to be King of Syracuse. The son of a potter, he led a life of the utmost wickedness through all the stages of his fortune. Nevertheless, his wickedness was accompanied by such vigour of mind and body that, having joined the militia, he rose through its ranks to be praetor of Syracuse. Having been appointed to this position, and having decided to become prince, and to hold with violence and without the support of others that which had been constitutionally granted him; and having imparted his design to Hamilcar the Carthaginian, who was fighting with his armies in Sicily, he called together one morning the people and senate of Syracuse, as if he had to deliberate on matters of importance to the republic, and at a given signal had all the senators and the richest men of the people

* The selection is taken from Niccolò Machiavelli's *The Prince (Il Principe)*, trans. by Luigi Ricci (London : Oxford University Press). Used by permission.

killed by his soldiers. After their death he occupied and held rule over the city without any civil strife. And although he was twice beaten by the Carthaginians and ultimately besieged, he was able not only to defend the city, but leaving a portion of his forces for its defence, with the remainder he invaded Africa, and in a short time liberated Syracuse from the siege and brought the Carthaginians to great extremities, so that they were obliged to come to terms with him, and remain contented with the possession of Africa, leaving Sicily to Agathocles. Whoever considers, therefore, the actions and qualities of this man, will see few if any things which can be attributed to fortune; for, as above stated, it was not by the favour of any person, but through the grades of the militia, in which he had advanced with a thousand hardships and perils, that he arrived at the position of prince, which he afterwards maintained by so many courageous and perilous expedients. It cannot be called virtue to kill one's fellow-citizens, betray one's friends, be without faith, without pity, and without religion; by these methods one may indeed gain power, but not glory. For if the virtues of Agathocles in braving and overcoming perils, and his greatness of soul in supporting and surmounting obstacles be considered, one sees no reason for holding him inferior to any of the most renowned captains. Nevertheless his barbarous cruelty and inhumanity, together with his countless atrocities, do not permit of his being named among the most famous men. We cannot attribute to fortune or virtue that which he achieved without either.

In our own times, during the pontificate of Alexander VI, Oliverotto da Fermo had been left as a young fatherless boy under the care of his maternal uncle, Giovanni Fogliani, who brought him up, and sent him in early youth to soldier under Paolo Vitelli, in order that he might, trained in that hard school, obtain a good military position. On the death of Paolo he fought under his brother Vitellozzo, and in a very short time, being of great intelligence, and active in mind and body, he became one of the leaders of his troops. But deeming it servile to be under others, he resolved, with the help of some citizens of Fermo, who preferred servitude to the liberty of their country, and with the favour of the Vitelli, to occupy Fermo; he therefore wrote to Giovanni Fogliani, how, having been for many years away from home, he wished to come to see him and his city, and as far as possible to inspect his estates. And as he had only laboured to gain honour, in order that his fellow-citizens might see that he had not spent his time in vain, he wished to come honourably accompanied by one hundred horsemen, his friends and followers, and prayed him that he would be pleased to order that he should be received with honour by the citizens of Fermo, by which he would honour not only him, Oliverotto, but also himself, as he had been his pupil. Giovanni did not fail in any due courtesy towards his nephew; he caused him to be honourably received by the people of Fermo, and lodged him in his own houses. After waiting some days to arrange all that was necessary to his villainous projects, Oliverotto invited Giovanni Fogliani and all the principal men of Fermo to a grand banquet. After the dinner and the entertainments usual at such feasts, Oliverotto artfully introduced certain important matters of discussion, speaking of the greatness of Pope Alexander, and of his son Cesare, and of their enterprises. To which discourses Giovanni and others having replied, he all at once rose, saying that these matters should be spoken of in a more private place, and withdrew into a room where Giovanni and the other citizens followed him. They were no sooner seated than soldiers rushed out of hiding-places and killed Giovanni and all the others. After which massacre Oliverotto mounted his horse, rode through the town and besieged the chief magistrate in his palace, so that through fear they were obliged to obey him and form a government, of which he made himself prince. And all those being dead who, if discontented, could injure him, he fortified himself with new orders, civil and military, in such a way that within the year that he held the principality he was not only safe himself in the city of Fermo, but had become formidable to all his neighbours. And his overthrow would have been difficult, like that of Agathocles, if he had not allowed himself to be deceived by Cesare Borgia, when he captured the Orsini and Vitelli at Sinigaglia, as already related, where he also was taken, one year after the parricide he had committed, and strangled, together with Vitellozzo, who had been his teacher in ability and atrocity.

Some may wonder how it came about that Agathocles, and others like him, could, after infinite treachery and cruelty, live secure for many years in their country and defend themselves from external enemies without being conspired against by their subjects; although many others have, owing to their cruelty, been unable to maintain their position in times of peace, not to speak of the uncertain times of war. I believe this arises from the cruelties being exploited well or badly. Well committed may be called those (if it is permissible to use the word well of evil) which are perpetrated once for the need of securing one's self, and which afterwards are not persisted in, but are exchanged for measures as useful to the subjects as possible. Cruelties ill committed are those which, although at first few, increase rather than diminish with time. Those who follow the former method may remedy in some measure their condition, both with God and man; as did Agathocles. As to the others, it is impossible for them to maintain themselves.

Whence it is to be noted, that in taking a state the conqueror must arrange to commit all his cruelties at once, so as not to have to recur to them every day, and so as to be able, by not making fresh changes, to reassure people and win them over by benefiting them. Whoever acts otherwise, either through timidity or bad counsels, is always obliged to stand with knife in hand, and can never depend on his subjects, because they, owing to continually fresh injuries, are unable to depend upon him. For injuries should be done all together, so that being less tasted, they will give less offence. Benefits should be granted little by little, so that they may be better enjoyed. And above all, a prince must live with his subjects in such a way that no accident of good or evil fortune can deflect him from his course; for necessity arising in adverse times, you are not in time with severity, and the good that you do does not profit, as it is judged to be forced upon you, and you will derive no benefit whatever from it. . . .

THE DUTIES OF A PRINCE WITH REGARD TO THE MILITIA

A prince should therefore have no other aim or thought, nor take up any other thing for his study, but war and its organisation and discipline, for that is the only art that is necessary to one who commands, and it is of such virtue that it not only maintains those who are born princes, but often enables men of private fortune to attain to that rank. And one sees, on the other hand, that when princes think more of luxury than of arms, they lose their state. The chief cause of the loss of states, is the contempt of this art, and the way to acquire them is to be well versed in the same.

Francesco Sforza, through being well armed, became, from private status, Duke of Milan; his sons, through wishing to avoid the fatigue and hardship of war, from dukes became private persons. For among other evils caused by being disarmed, it renders you contemptible; which is one of those disgraceful things which a prince must guard against, as will be explained later. Because there is no comparison whatever between an armed and a disarmed man; it is not reasonable to suppose that one who is armed will obey willingly one who is unarmed; or that any unarmed man will remain safe among armed servants. For one being disdainful and the other suspicious, it is not possible for them to act well together. And therefore a prince who is ignorant of military matters, besides the other misfortunes already mentioned, cannot be esteemed by his soldiers, nor have confidence in them.

He ought, therefore, never to let his thoughts stray from the exercise of war; and in peace he ought to practise it more than in war, which he can do in two ways: by action and by study. As to action, he must, besides keeping his men well disciplined and exercised, engage continually in hunting, and thus accustom his body to hardships; and meanwhile learn the nature of the land, how steep the mountains are, how the valleys debouch, where the plains lie, and understand the nature of rivers and swamps. To all this he should devote great attention. This knowledge is useful in two ways. In the first place, one learns to know one's country, and can the better see how to defend it. Then by means of the knowledge and experience gained in one locality, one can easily understand any other that it may be necessary to observe; for the hills and valleys, plains and rivers of Tuscany, for instance, have a certain resemblance to those of other provinces, so that from a knowledge of the country in one province one can easily arrive at a knowledge of others. And that prince who is lacking in this skill is wanting in the first essentials of a leader; for it is this which teaches how to find the enemy, take up quarters, lead armies, plan battles and lay siege to towns with advantage.

Philopoemen, prince of the Achaei, among other praises bestowed on him by writers, is lauded because in times of peace he thought of nothing but the methods of warfare, and when he was in the country with his friends, he often stopped and asked them: If the enemy were on that hill and we found ourselves here with our army, which of us would have the advantage? How could we safely approach him maintaining our order? If we wished to retire, what ought we to do? If they retired, how should we follow them? And he put before them as they went along all the contingencies that might happen to an army, heard their opinion, gave his own, fortifying it by argument; so that thanks to these constant reflections there could never happen any incident when actually leading his armies for which he was not prepared.

But as to exercise for the mind, the prince ought to read history

and study the action of eminent men, see how they acted in warfare,
examine the causes of their victories and defeats in order to imitate
the former and avoid the latter, and above all, do as some men have
done in the past, who have imitated some one, who has been much
praised and glorified, and have always kept his deeds and actions before them, as they say Alexander the Great imitated Achilles, Caesar
Alexander, and Scipio Cyrus. And whoever reads the life of Cyrus
written by Xenophon, will perceive in the life of Scipio how gloriously
he imitated the former, and how, in chastity, affability, humanity, and
liberality Scipio conformed to those qualities of Cyrus as described
by Xenophon.

A wise prince should follow similar methods and never remain idle
in peaceful times, but industriously make good use of them, so that
when fortune changes she may find him prepared to resist her blows,
and to prevail in adversity.

OF THE THINGS FOR WHICH MEN, AND ESPECIALLY PRINCES, ARE PRAISED OR BLAMED

It now remains to be seen what are the methods and rules for a
prince as regards his subjects and friends. And as I know that many
have written of this, I fear that my writing about it may be deemed
presumptuous, differing as I do, especially in this matter, from the
opinions of others. But my intention being to write something of use
to those who understand, it appears to me more proper to go to the
real truth of the matter than to its imagination; and many have
imagined republics and principalities which have never been seen or
known to exist in reality; for how we live is so far removed from how
we ought to live, that he who abandons what is done for what ought
to be done, will rather learn to bring about his own ruin than his
preservation. A man who wishes to make a profession of goodness in
everything must necessarily come to grief among so many who are
not good. Therefore it is necessary for a prince, who wishes to maintain himself, to learn how not to be good, and to use this knowledge
and not use it, according to the necessity of the case.

Leaving on one side, then, those things which concern only an
imaginary prince, and speaking of those that are real, I state that all
men, and especially princes, who are placed at a greater height, are
reputed for certain qualities which bring them either praise or blame.
Thus one is considered liberal, another *misero* or miserly (using a

Tuscan term, seeing that *avaro* with us still means one who is rapaciously acquisitive and *misero* one who makes grudging use of his own); one a free giver, another rapacious; one cruel, another merciful; one a breaker of his word, another trustworthy; one effeminate and pusillanimous, another fierce and high-spirited; one humane, another haughty; one lascivious, another chaste; one frank, another astute; one hard, another easy; one serious, another frivolous; one religious, another an unbeliever, and so on. I know that every one will admit that it would be highly praiseworthy in a prince to possess all the above-named qualities that are reputed good, but as they cannot all be possessed or observed, human conditions not permitting of it, it is necessary that he should be prudent enough to avoid the scandal of those vices which would lose him the state, and guard himself if possible against those which will not lose it him, but if not able to, he can indulge them with less scruple. And yet he must not mind incurring the scandal of those vices, without which it would be difficult to save the state, for if one considers well, it will be found that some things which seem virtues would, if followed, lead to one's ruin, and some others which appear vices result in one's greater security and well being.

OF LIBERALITY AND NIGGARDLINESS

Beginning now with the first qualities above named, I say that it would be well to be considered liberal; nevertheless liberality such as the world understands it will injure you, because if used virtuously and in the proper way, it will not be known, and you will incur the disgrace of the contrary vice. But one who wished to obtain the reputation of liberality among men, must not omit every kind of sumptuous display, and to such an extent that a prince of this character will consume by such means all his resources, and will be at last compelled, if he wishes to maintain his name for liberality, to impose heavy taxes on his people, become extortionate, and do everything possible to obtain money. This will make his subjects begin to hate him, and he will be little esteemed being poor, so that having by this liberality injured many and benefited but few, he will feel the first little disturbance and be endangered by every peril. If he recognises this and wishes to change his system, he incurs at once the charge of niggardliness.

A prince, therefore, not being able to exercise this virtue of liberality without risk if it be known, must not, if he be prudent, object to be called miserly. In course of time he will be thought more liberal, when it is seen that by his parsimony his revenue is sufficient, that he can defend himself against those who make war on him, and undertake enterprises without burdening his people, so that he is really liberal to all those from whom he does not take, who are infinite in number, and niggardly to all to whom he does not give, who are few. In our times we have seen nothing great done except by those who have been esteemed niggardly; the others have all been ruined. Pope Julius II, although he had made use of a reputation for liberality in order to attain the papacy, did not seek to retain it afterwards, so that he might be able to wage war. The present King of France has carried on so many wars without imposing an extraordinary tax, because his extra expenses were covered by the parsimony he had so long practised. The present King of Spain, if he had been thought liberal, would not have engaged in and been successful in so many enterprises.

For these reasons a prince must care little for the reputation of being a miser, if he wishes to avoid robbing his subjects, if he wishes to be able to defend himself, to avoid becoming poor and contemptible, and not to be forced to become rapacious; this niggardliness is one of those vices which enable him to reign. If it is said that Caesar attained the empire through liberality, and that many others have reached the highest positions through being liberal or being thought so, I would reply that you are either a prince already or else on the way to become one. In the first case, this liberality is harmful; in the second, it is certainly necessary to be considered liberal. Caesar was one of those who wished to attain the mastery over Rome, but if after attaining it he had lived and had not moderated his expenses, he would have destroyed that empire. And should any one reply that there have been many princes, who have done great things with their armies, who have been thought extremely liberal, I would answer by saying that the prince may either spend his own wealth and that of his subjects or the wealth of others. In the first case he must be sparing, but for the rest he must not neglect to be very liberal. The liberality is very necessary to a prince who marches with his armies, and lives by plunder, sack and ransom, and is dealing with the wealth of others, for without it he would not be followed by his soldiers. And you may be very generous indeed with what is not the property of yourself or your subjects, as were Cyrus, Caesar, and Alexander; for spending the wealth of others will not diminish your reputation, but increase it, only spending your own resources will injure you. There is nothing which destroys itself so much as liberality, for by using it you lose the power of using it, and become either poor and despicable, or, to escape poverty, rapacious and hated. And of all things that a prince must guard against, the most important are being despicable or hated, and liberality will lead you to one or the other of these conditions. It is, therefore, wiser to have the name of a miser, which produces disgrace without hatred, than to incur of necessity the name of being rapacious, which produces both disgrace and hatred.

OF CRUELTY AND CLEMENCY, AND WHETHER IT IS BETTER TO BE LOVED OR FEARED

Proceeding to the other qualities before named, I say that every prince must desire to be considered merciful and not cruel. He must, however, take care not to misuse this mercifulness. Cesare Borgia was considered cruel, but his cruelty had brought order to the Romagna, united it, and reduced it to peace and fealty. If this is considered well, it will be seen that he was really much more merciful than the Florentine people, who, to avoid the name of cruelty, allowed Pistoia to be destroyed. A prince, therefore, must not mind incurring the charge of cruelty for the purpose of keeping his subjects united and faithful; for, with a very few examples, he will be more merciful than those who, from excess of tenderness, allow disorders to arise, from whence spring bloodshed and rapine; for these as a rule injure the whole community, while the executions carried out by the prince injure only individuals. And of all princes, it is impossible for a new prince to escape the reputation of cruelty, new states being always full of dangers. Wherefore Virgil through the mouth of Dido says:

> *Res dura, et regni novitas me talia cogunt*
> *Moliri, et late fines custode tueri.*

Nevertheless, he must be cautious in believing and acting, and must not be afraid of his own shadow, and must proceed in a temperate manner with prudence and humanity, so that too much confidence does not render him incautious, and too much diffidence does not render him intolerant.

From this arises the question whether it is better to be loved more than feared, or feared more than loved. The reply is, that one ought to be both feared and loved, but as it is difficult for the two to go together, it is much safer to be feared than loved, if one of the two

has to be wanting. For it may be said of men in general that they are
ungrateful, voluble, dissemblers, anxious to avoid danger, and
covetous of gain; as long as you benefit them, they are entirely yours;
they offer you their blood, their goods, their life, and their children,
as I have before said, when the necessity is remote; but when it approaches, they revolt. And the prince who has relied solely on their
words, with making other preparations, is ruined; for the friendship
which is gained by purchase and not through grandeur and nobility of
spirit is bought but not secured, and at a pinch is not to be expended
in your service. And men have less scruple in offending one who
makes himself loved than one who makes himself feared; for love is
held by a chain of obligation which, men being selfish, is broken
whenever it serves their purpose; but fear is maintained by a dread
of punishment which never fails.

Still, a prince should make himself feared in such a way that if he
does not gain love, he at any rate avoids hatred; for fear and the
absence of hatred may well go together, and will be always attained
by one who abstains from interfering with the property of his citizens
and subjects or with their women. And when he is obliged to take the
life of any one, let him do so when there is a proper justification and
manifest reason for it; but above all he must abstain from taking the
property of others, for men forget more easily the death of their father
than the loss of their patrimony. Then also pretexts for seizing property are never wanting, and one who begins to live by rapine will
always find some reason for taking the goods of others, whereas causes
for taking life are rarer and more fleeting.

But when the prince is with his army and has a large number of
soldiers under his control, then it is extremely necessary that he should
not mind being thought cruel; for without this reputation he could
not keep an army united or disposed to any duty. Among the note-
worthy actions of Hannibal is numbered this, that although he had
an enormous army, composed of men of all nations and fighting in
foreign countries, there never arose any dissension either among them
or against the prince, either in good fortune or in bad. This could not
be due to anything but his inhuman cruelty, which together with his
infinite other virtues, made him always venerated and terrible in the
sight of his soldiers, and without it his other virtues would not have
sufficed to produce that effect. Thoughtless writers admire on the one
hand his actions, and on the other blame the principal cause of them.

And that it is true that his other virtues would not have sufficed may be seen from the case of Scipio (famous not only in regard to his own times, but all times of which memory remains), whose armies rebelled against him in Spain, which arose from nothing but his excessive kindness, which allowed more licence to the soldiers than was consonant with military discipline. He was reproached with this in the senate by Fabius Maximus, who called him a corrupter of the Roman militia. Locri having been destroyed by one of Scipio's officers was not revenged by him, nor was the insolence of that officer punished, simply by reason of his easy nature; so much so, that some one wishing to excuse him in the senate, said that there were many men who knew rather how not to err, than how to correct the errors of others. This disposition would in time have tarnished the fame and glory of Scipio had he persevered in it under the empire, but living under the rule of the senate this harmful quality was not only concealed but became a glory to him.

I conclude, therefore, with regard to being feared and loved, that men love at their own free will, but fear at the will of the prince, and that a wise prince must rely on what is in his power and not on what is in the power of others, and he must only contrive to avoid incurring hatred, as has been explained.

IN WHAT WAY PRINCES MUST KEEP FAITH

How laudable it is for a prince to keep good faith and live with integrity, and not with astuteness, every one knows. Still the experience of our times shows those princes to have done great things who have had little regard for good faith, and have been able by astuteness to confuse men's brains, and who have ultimately overcome those who have made loyalty their foundation.

You must know, then, that there are two methods of fighting, the one by law, the other by force: the first method is that of men, the second of beasts; but as the first method is often insufficient, one must have recourse to the second. It is therefore necessary for a prince to know well how to use both the beast and the man. This was covertly taught to rulers by ancient writers, who relate how Achilles and many others of those ancient princes were given to Chiron the centaur to be brought up and educated under his discipline. The parable of this semi-animal, semi-human teacher is meant to indicate that a prince must know how to use both natures, and that the one without the other is not durable.

A prince being thus obliged to know well how to act as a beast must imitate the fox and the lion, for the lion cannot protect himself from traps, and the fox cannot defend himself from wolves. One must therefore be a fox to recognise traps, and a lion to frighten wolves. Those that wish to be only lions do not understand this. Therefore, a prudent ruler ought not to keep faith when by so doing it would be against his interest, and when the reasons which made him bind himself no longer exist. If men were all good, this precept would not be a good one; but as they are bad, and would not observe their faith with you, so you are not bound to keep faith with them. Nor have legitimate grounds ever failed a prince who wished to show colourable excuse for the non-fulfilment of his promise. Of this one could furnish an infinite number of modern examples, and show how many times peace has been broken, and how many promises rendered worthless, by the faithlessness of princes, and those that have been best able to imitate the fox have succeeded best. But it is necessary to be able to disguise this character well, and to be a great feigner and dissembler; and men are so simple and so ready to obey present necessities, that one who deceives will always find those who allow themselves to be deceived.

I will only mention one modern instance. Alexander VI did nothing else but deceive men, he thought of nothing else, and found the occasion for it; no man was ever more able to give assurances, or affirmed things with stronger oaths, and no man observed them less; however, he always succeeded in his deceptions, as he well knew this aspect of things.

It is not, therefore, necessary for a prince to have all the above-named qualities, but it is very necessary to seem to have them. I would even be bold to say that to possess them and always to observe them is dangerous, but to appear to possess them is useful. Thus it is well to seem merciful, faithful, humane, sincere, religious, and also to be so; but you must have the mind so disposed that when it is needful to be otherwise you may be able to change to the opposite qualities. And it must be understod that a prince, and especially a new prince, cannot observe all those things which are considered good in men, being often obliged, in order to maintain the state, to act against faith, against charity, against humanity, and against religion. And, therefore, he must have a mind disposed to adapt itself according to the wind, and as the variations of fortune dictate, and, as I said before, not deviate from what is good, if possible, but be able to do evil if constrained.

A prince must take great care that nothing goes out of his mouth which is not full of the above-named five qualities, and, to see and hear him, he should seem to be all mercy, faith, integrity, humanity, and religion. And nothing is more necessary than to seem to have this last quality, for men in general judge more by the eyes than by the hands, for every one can see, but very few have to feel. Everybody sees what you appear to be, few feel what you are, and those few will not dare to oppose themselves to the many, who have the majesty of the state to defend them; and in the actions of men, and especially of princes, from which there is no appeal, the end justifies the means. Let a prince therefore aim at conquering and maintaining the state, and the means will always be judged honourable and praised by every one, for the vulgar is always taken by appearances and the issue of the event; and the world consists only of the vulgar, and the few who are not vulgar are isolated when the many have a rallying point in the prince. A certain prince of the present time, whom it is well not to name, never does anything but preach peace and good faith, but he is really a great enemy to both, and either of them, had he observed them, would have lost him state or reputation on many occasions.

THAT WE MUST AVOID BEING DESPISED AND HATED

But as I have now spoken of the most important of the qualities in question, I will now deal briefly and generally with the rest. The prince must, as already stated, avoid those things which will make him hated or despised; and whenever he succeeds in this, he will have done his part, and will find no danger in other vices. He will chiefly become hated, as I said, by being rapacious, and usurping the property and women of his subjects, which he must abstain from doing, and whenever one does not attack the property or honour of the generality of men, they will live contented; and one will only have to combat the ambition of a few, who can be easily held in check in many ways. He is rendered despicable by being thought changeable, frivolous, effeminate, timid, and irresolute; which a prince must guard against as a rock of danger, and so contrive that his actions show grandeur, spirit, gravity, and fortitude; and as to the government of his subjects, let his sentence be irrevocable, and let him adhere to his decisions so that no one may think of deceiving or cozening him.

The prince who creates such an opinion of himself gets a great reputation, and it is very difficult to conspire against one who has a great reputation, and he will not easily be attacked, so long as it is known that he is capable and reverenced by his subjects. For a prince must have two kinds of fear: one internal as regards his subjects, one external as regards foreign powers. From the latter he can defend himself with good arms and good friends, and he will always have good friends if he has good arms; and internal matters will always remain quiet, if they are not perturbed by conspiracy and there is no disturbance from without; and even if external powers sought to attack him, if he has ruled and lived as I have described, he will always if he stands firm, be able to sustain every shock, as I have shown that Nabis the Spartan did. But with regard to the subjects, if not acted on from outside, it is still to be feared lest they conspire in secret, from which the prince may guard himself well by avoiding hatred and contempt, and keeping the people satisfied with him, which it is necessary to accomplish, as has been related at length. And one of the most potent remedies that a prince has against conspiracies, is that of not being hated by the mass of the people; for whoever conspires always believes that he will satisfy the people by the death of their prince; but if he thought to offend them by doing this, he would fear to engage in such an undertaking, for the difficulties that conspirators have to meet are infinite. Experience shows that there have been very many conspiracies, but few have turned out well, for whoever conspires cannot act alone, and cannot find companions except among those who are discontented; and as soon as you have disclosed your intention to a malcontent, you give him the means of satisfying himself, for by revealing it he can hope to secure everything he wants; to such an extent that seeing a certain gain by doing this, and seeing on the other hand only a doubtful one and full of danger, he must either be a rare friend to you or else a very bitter enemy to the prince if he keeps faith with you. And to express the matter in a few words, I say, that on the side of the conspirator there is nothing but fear, jealousy, suspicion, and dread of punishment which frightens him; and on the side of the prince there is the majesty of government, the laws, the protection of friends and of the state which guard him. When to these things is added the goodwill of the people, it is impossible that any one should have the temerity to conspire. For whereas generally a conspirator has to fear before the execution of his plot, in this case, having the people for an enemy, he must also fear after his crime is accomplished, and thus he is not able to hope for any refuge.

Numberless instances might be given of this, but I will content myself with one which took place within the memory of our fathers. Messer Annibale Bentivogli, Prince of Bologna, ancestor of the present Messer Annibale, was killed by the Canneschi, who conspired against him. He left no relations but Messer Giovanni, who was then an infant, but after the murder the people rose up and killed all the Canneschi. This arose from the popular goodwill that the house of Bentivogli enjoyed at that time, which was so great that, as there was nobody left after the death of Annibale who could govern the state, the Bolognese hearing that there was one of the Bentivogli family in Florence, who had till then been thought the son of a blacksmith, came to fetch him and gave him the government of the city, and it was governed by him until Messer Giovanni was old enough to assume the government.

I conclude, therefore, that a prince need trouble little about conspiracies when the people are well disposed, but when they are hostile and hold him in hatred, then he must fear everything and everybody. Well-ordered states and wise princes have studied diligently not to drive the nobles to desperation, and to satisfy the populace and keep it contented, for this is one of the most important matters that a prince has to deal with.

Among the kingdoms that are well ordered and governed in our time is France, and there we find numberless good institutions on which depend the liberty and security of the king; of these the chief is the parliament and its authority, because he who established that kingdom, knowing the ambition and insolence of the great nobles, deemed it necessary to have a bit in their mouths to check them. And knowing on the other hand the hatred of the mass of the people against the great, based on fear, and wishing to secure them, he did not wish to make this the special care of the king, to relieve him of the dissatisfaction that he might incur among the nobles by favouring the people, and among the people by favouring the nobles. He therefore established a third judge that, without direct charge of the king, kept in check the great and favoured the lesser people. Nor could any better or more prudent measure have been adopted, nor better precaution for the safety of the king and the kingdom. From which another notable rule can be drawn, that princes should let the carrying out of unpopular duties devolve on others, and bestow favours themselves. I conclude again by saying that a prince must esteem his nobles, but not make himself hated by the populace.

It may perhaps seem to some, that considering the life and death of

many Roman emperors that they are instances contrary to my
opinion, finding that some who always lived nobly and showed great
strength of character, nevertheless lost the empire, or were killed by
their subjects who conspired against them. Wishing to answer these
objections, I will discuss the qualities of some emperors, showing the
cause of their ruin not to be at variance with what I have stated, and
I will also meanwhile consider the things to be noted by whoever
reads the deeds of these times. I will content myself with taking all
those emperors who succeeded to the empire from Marcus the philosopher to Maximinus; these were Marcus, Commodus his son, Pertinax, Julianus, Severus, Antoninus, Caracalla his son, Macrinus,
Heliogabalus, Alexander, and Maximinus. And the first thing to note
is, that whereas other princes have only to contend against the ambition of the great and the insolence of the people, the Roman emperors
had a third difficulty, that of having to support the cruelty and avarice
of the soldiers, which was such that it was the cause of the ruin of
many, it being hardly possible to satisfy both the soldiers and the
people. For the people love tranquility, and therefore like pacific
princes, but the soldiers prefer a prince of military spirit, who is inso-
lent, cruel, and rapacious. They wish him to exercise these qualities
on the people so that they may get double pay and give vent to their
avarice and cruelty. Thus it came about that those emperors who, by
nature or art, had not such a reputation as could keep both parties in
check, were invariably ruined, and the greater number of them who
were raised to the empire being new men, knowing the difficulties of
these two opposite dispositions, confined themselves to satisfying the
soldiers, and thought little of injuring the people. This choice was
necessary, princes not being able to avoid being hated by someone.
They must first try not to be hated by the mass of the people; if they
cannot accomplish this they must use every means to escape the
hatred of the most powerful parties. And therefore these emperors,
who being new men had need of extraordinary favours, adhered to
the soldiers rather than to the people; whether this, however, was of
use to them or not, depended on whether the prince knew how to
maintain his reputation with them. From these causes it resulted that
Marcus, Pertinax, and Alexander, being all of modest life, lovers of
justice, enemies of cruelty, humane and benign, all came to a sad end
except Marcus. Marcus alone lived and died in honour, because he
succeeded to the empire by hereditary right and did not owe it either
to the soldiers or to the people; besides which, possessing many virtues

which made him revered, he kept both parties in their place as long as he lived and was never either hated or despised. But Pertinax was created emperor against the will of the soldiers, who being accustomed to live licentiously under Commodus, could not put up with the honest life to which Pertinax wished to limit them, so that having made himself hated, and to this contempt being added because he was old, he was ruined at the very beginning of his administration.

Whence it may be seen that hatred is gained as much by good works as by evil, and therefore, as I said before, a prince who wishes to maintain the state is often forced to do evil, for when that party, whether populace, soldiery, or nobles, whichever it be that you consider necessary to you for keeping your position, is corrupt, you must follow its humour and satisfy it, and in that case good works will be inimical to you. But let us come to Alexander, who was of such goodness, that among other things for which he is praised, it is said that in the fourteen years that he reigned no one was put to death by him without a fair trial. Nevertheless, being considered effeminate, and a man who allowed himself to be ruled by his mother, and having thus fallen into contempt, the army conspired against him and killed him.

Considering, on the other hand, the qualities of Commodus, Severus, Antoninus, Caracalla, and Maximinus, you will find them extremely cruel and rapacious; to satisfy the soldiers there was no injury which they would not inflict on the people, and all except Severus ended badly. Severus, however, had such abilities that by maintaining the soldiers friendly to him, he was able to reign happily, although he oppressed the people, for his virtues made him so admirable in the sight both of the soldiers and the people that the latter were, in some degree, astonished and stupefied, while the former were respectful and contented.

As the deeds of this ruler were great and notable for a new prince, I will briefly show how well he could use the qualities of the fox and the lion, whose natures, as I said before, it is necessary for a prince to imitate. Knowing the sloth of the Emperor Julianus, Severus, who was leader of the army in Slavonia, persuaded the troops that it would be well to go to Rome to avenge the death of Pertinax, who had been slain by the Praetorian guard, and under this pretext, without revealing his aspirations to the throne, marched with his army to Rome and was in Italy before his departure was known. On his arrival in Rome the senate elected him emperor through fear, and killed Julianus. There remained after this beginning two difficulties to be faced by

Severus before he could obtain the whole control of the empire: one is Asia, where Nigrinus, head of the Asiatic armies, had declared himself emperor; the other in the west from Albinus, who also aspired to the empire. As he judged it dangerous to show himself hostile to both, he decided to attack Nigrinus and deceive Albinus, to whom he wrote that having been elected emperor by the senate he wished to share that dignity with him; he sent him the title of Caesar and, by deliberation of the senate, he was declared his colleague; all of which was accepted as true by Albinus. But when Severus had defeated and killed Nigrinus, and pacified things in the East, he returned to Rome and charged Albinus in the senate with having, unmindful of the benefits received from him, traitorously sought to assassinate him, and stated that he was therefore obliged to go and punish his ingratitude. He then went to France to meet him, and there deprived him of both his position and his life.

Whoever examines in detail the actions of Severus, will find him to have been a very ferocious lion and an extremely astute fox, and will find him to have been feared and respected by all and not hated by the army; and will not be surprised that he, a new man, should have been able to hold so much power, since his great reputation defended him always from the hatred that his rapacity might have produced in the people. But Antoninus his son was also a man of great ability, and possessed qualities that rendered him admirable in the sight of the people and also made him popular with the soldiers, for he was a military man, capable of enduring the most extreme hardships, disdainful of delicate food, and every other luxury, which made him loved by all the armies. However, his ferocity and cruelty were so great and unheard of, through his having, after executing many private individuals, caused a large part of the population of Rome and all that of Alexandria to be killed, that he became hated by all the world and began to be feared by those about him to such an extent that he was finally killed by a centurion in the midst of his army. Whence it is to be noted that this kind of death, which proceeds from the deliberate action of a determined man, cannot be avoided by princes, since any one who does not fear death himself can inflict it, but a prince need not fear much on this account, as such men are extremely rare. He must only guard against committing any grave injury to any one he makes use of, or has about him for his service, like Antoninus had done, having caused the death with contumely of the brother of that centurion, and also threatened him every day, although he still retained him in his bodyguard, which was a foolish and dangerous thing to do, as the fact proved.

But let us cóme to Commodus, who might easily have kept the empire, having succeeded to it by heredity, being the son of Marcus, and it would have sufficed for him to follow in the steps of his father to have satisfied both the people and the soldiers. But being of a cruel and bestial disposition, in order to be able to exercise his rapacity on the people, he sought to favour the soldiers and render them licentious; on the other hand, by not maintaining his dignity, by often descending into the theatre to fight with gladiators and committing other contemptible actions, little worthy of the imperial dignity, he became despicable in the eyes of the soldiers, and being hated on the one hand and despised on the other, he was conspired against and killed.

There remains to be described the character of Maximinus. He was an extremely warlike man, and as the armies were annoyed with the effeminacy of Alexander, which we have already spoken of, he was elected emperor after the death of the latter. He did not enjoy it for long, as two things made him hated and despised: the one his base origin, as he had been a shepherd in Thrace, which was generally known and caused great disdain on all sides; the other, because he had at the commencement of his rule deferred going to Rome to take possession of the Imperial seat, and had obtained a reputation for great cruelty, having through his prefects in Rome and other parts of the empire committed many acts of cruelty. The whole world being thus moved by indignation for the baseness of his blood, and also by the hatred caused by fear of his ferocity, he was conspired against first by Africa and afterwards by the senate and all the people of Rome and Italy. His own army also joined them, for besieging Aquileia and finding it difficult to take, they became enraged at his cruelty, and seeing that he had so many enemies, they feared him less and put him to death.

I will not speak of Heliogabalus, of Macrinus, or Julianus, who being entirely contemptible were immediately suppressed, but I will come to the conclusion of this discourse by saying that the princes of our time have less difficulty than these in being obliged to satisfy in an extraordinary degree their soldiers in their states; for although they must have a certain consideration for them, yet any difficulty is soon settled, for none of these princes have armies that are inextricably bound up with the administration of the government and the rule of their provinces as were the armies of the Roman empire. If it was then necessary to satisfy the soldiers rather than the people, it was because the soldiers could do more than the people; now, it is more necessary for all princes, except the Turk and the Sultan, to satisfy the people than the soldiers, for the people can do more than the soldiers. I except the Turk, because he always keeps about him twelve thousand infantry and fifteen thousand cavalry, on which depend the security and strength of his kingdom; and it is necessary for him to postpone every other consideration to keep them friendly. It is the same with the kingdom of the Sultan, which being entirely in the hands of the soldiers, he is bound to keep their friendship regardless of the people. And it is to be noted that this state of the Sultan is different from that of all other princes, being similar to the Christian pontificate, which cannot be called either a hereditary kingdom or a new one, for the sons of the dead prince are not his heirs, but he who is elected to that position by those who have authority. And as this order is ancient it cannot be called a new kingdom, there being none of these difficulties which exist in new ones; as although the prince is new, the rules of that state are old and arranged to receive him as if he were their hereditary lord.

But returning to our matter, I say that whoever studies the preceding argument will see that either hatred or contempt were the causes of the ruin of the emperors named, and will also observe how it came about that, some of them acting in one way and some in another, in both ways there were some who had a fortunate and others an unfortunate ending. As Pertinax and Alexander were both new rulers, it was useless and injurious for them to try and imitate Marcus, who was a hereditary prince; and similarly with Caracalla, Commodus, and Maximinus it was pernicious for them to imitate Severus, as they had not sufficient ability to follow in his footsteps. Thus a new prince cannot imitate the actions of Marcus, in his dominions, nor is it necessary for him to imitate those of Severus; but he must take from Severus those things that are necessary to found his state, and from Marcus those that are useful and glorious for conserving a state that is already established and secure. . . .

HOW MUCH FORTUNE CAN DO IN HUMAN AFFAIRS AND HOW IT CAN BE OPPOSED

It is not unknown to me how many have been and are of opinion that worldly events are so governed by fortune and by God, that men cannot by their prudence change them, and that on the contrary there is no remedy whatever, and for this they may judge it to be useless to toil much about them, but let things be ruled by chance. This opinion has been more held in our day, from the great changes that have been seen, and are daily seen, beyond every human conjecture. When I think about them, at times I am partly inclined to share this opinion. Nevertheless, that our free will may not be altogether extinguished, I think it may be true that fortune is the ruler of half our actions, but that she allows the other half or thereabouts to be governed by us. I would compare her to an impetuous river that, when turbulent, inundates the plains, casts down trees and buildings, removes earth from this side and places it on the other; every one flees before it, and everything yields to its fury without being able to oppose it; and yet though it is of such a kind, still when it is quiet, men can make provision against it by dykes and banks, so that when it rises it will either go into a canal or its rush will not be so wild and dangerous. So it is with fortune, which shows her power where no measures have been taken to resist her, and directs her fury where she knows that no dykes or barriers have been made to hold her. And if you regard Italy, which has been the seat of these changes, and which has given the impulse to them, you will see her to be a country without dykes or banks of any kind. If she had been protected by proper measures, like Germany, Spain, and France, this inundation would not have caused the great changes that it has, or would not have happened at all.

This must suffice as regards opposition to fortune in general. But limiting myself more to particular cases, I would point out how one sees a certain prince to-day fortunate and to-morrow ruined, without seeing that he has changed in character or otherwise. I believe this arises in the first place from the causes that we have already discussed at length; that is to say, because the prince who bases himself entirely on fortune is ruined when fortune changes. I also believe that he is happy whose mode of procedure accords with the needs of the times, and similarly he is unfortunate whose mode of procedure is opposed to the times. For one sees that men in those things which lead them to the aim that each one has in view, namely, glory and riches, proceed in various ways; one with circumspection, another with impetuosity, one by violence, another by cunning, one with patience, another with the reverse; and each by these diverse ways may arrive at his aim. One sees also two cautious men, one of whom succeeds in his designs, and the other not, and in the same way two men succeed equally by different methods, one being cautious, the other impetuous, which arises only from the nature of the times, which does or does not conform to their method of procedure. From this it results, as I have said, that two men, acting differently, attain the same effect, and of two others acting in the same way, one attains his goal and not the other. On this depend also the changes in prosperity, for if it happens that time and circumstances are favourable to one who acts with caution and prudence he will be successful, but if time and circumstances change he will be ruined, because he does not change his mode of procedure. No man is found so prudent as to be able to adapt himself to this, either because he cannot deviate from that to which his nature disposes him, or else because having always prospered by walking in one path, he cannot persuade himself that it is well to leave it; and therefore the cautious man, when it is time to act suddenly, does not know how to do so and is consequently ruined; for if one could change one's nature with time and circumstances, fortune would never change.

Pope Julius II acted impetuously in everything he did and found the times and conditions so in conformity with that mode of procedure, that he always obtained a good result. Consider the first war that he made against Bologna while Messer Giovanni Bentivogli was still living. The Venetians were not pleased with it, neither was the King of Spain, France was conferring with him over the enterprise, notwithstanding which, owing to his fierce and impetuous disposition, he engaged personally in the expedition. This move caused both Spain and the Venetians to halt and hesitate, the latter through fear, the former through the desire to recover the entire kingdom of Naples. On the other hand, he engaged with him the King of France, because seeing him make this move and desiring his friendship in order to put down the Venetians, the king judged that he could not refuse him his troops without manifest injury. Thus Julius by his impetuous move achieved what no other pontiff with the utmost human prudence would have succeeded in doing, because, if he had waited till all arrangements had been made and everything settled before leaving Rome, as any other pontiff would have done, it would never have succeeded. For the king of France would have found a thousand excuses, and the others would have inspired him with a thousand fears. I will omit his other actions, which were all of this kind and which all succeeded well, and the shortness of his life did not suffer him to experience the contrary, for had times followed in which it was necessary to act with caution, his ruin would have resulted, for he would never have deviated from these methods to which his nature disposed him.

I conclude then that fortune varying and men remaining fixed in their ways, they are successful so long as these ways conform to cir-cumstances, but when they are opposed then they are unsuccessful. I certainly think that it is better to be impetuous than cautious, for fortune is a woman, and it is necessary, if you wish to master her, to conquer her by force; and it can be seen that she lets herself be over-come by the bold rather than by those who proceed coldly. And therefore, like a woman, she is always a friend to the young, because they are less cautious, fiercer, and master her with greater audacity.

5

LOCKE

The Rule of Numbers

Among the classics of Western political thought, the *Second Treatise of Civil Government* (1690) by John Locke (1632–1704), has become one of the most influential expressions of the democratic concept of popular sovereignty and majority rule. The English civil wars of the seventeenth century provided the setting for Locke's political philosophy: the struggle by Parliament to limit the power of the monarchy and to prevent the royal prerogative from destroying traditional English rights. Within Parliament, members of the land-owning gentry played a leading role in the protest against royal absolutism. When protest was insufficient, civil war broke out; the king was overthrown and a republican commonwealth was established under Oliver Cromwell in 1649. The difficulties of finding an acceptable form of parliamentary executive led to the restoration of Charles II to the throne in 1660. Although it was hoped that a practical equilibrium could be achieved, both Charles II and his successor, James II, sought to re-establish royal absolutism. This provoked the so-called Glorious Revolution of 1688, inaugurating the regime of William and Mary and establishing the principle of parliamentary supremacy.

Within this historical context, John Locke appears as a defender of the victorious Whigs in the revolution of 1688. Locke's theory of popular sovereignty is based on the social contract theory of government. According to this theory, man originally dwelled in a presocial state of nature governed by a law of nature decreeing that since all men are equal and independent, no one should harm another in the enjoyment of the rights of life, liberty and property. The state of nature, however, is beset by serious inconveniences because of the lack of a settled law, an impartial judge, or an effective executive power. Men thus agree to contract into a civil society in order to secure greater security for their natural rights and freedoms by an impartial law and adjudication. The legislative power becomes the supreme power of the commonwealth, but it is no more than a servant and trustee of the people, and its powers are subject to strict limits: it cannot be absolutely arbitrary over the lives and fortunes of the people; it cannot rule by arbitrary decrees but must dispense justice on the basis of standing laws and authorized judges; it cannot take from any man property without his consent; it cannot transfer power of making laws to any other hands. Ultimately the people retain the right of rebellion against an arbitrary or despotic government. Since men enter into society for the protection of property, when the legislative authority transgresses this fundamental rule it forfeits the power the people put into its hands, and the power devolves to the people, who have the right to resume their original state of liberty.

Locke's ideas have exercised a profound influence upon the American political heritage, the Declaration of Independence, the principles of the American Constitution, and the ideals of Jeffersonian democracy. As an approach to defining the nature of political rule, however, Locke's theory reveals a basic difficulty inherent in the fact that, while he recognizes the danger of tyranny by legislative or executive power, he fails to recognize that the people, themselves, may be tyrannical over individual or minority rights—a danger often stressed by conservative critics of popular democracy. The tension between majority rule and minority rights, as one of the perennial issues of American political evolution, is more fully explored in the concluding chapter.*

OF THE STATE OF NATURE

4. To understand political power aright, and derive it from its original, we must consider what estate all men are naturally in, and that is, a state of perfect freedom to order their actions, and dispose of their possessions and persons as they think fit, within the bounds of the law of Nature, without asking leave or depending upon the will of any other man.

A state also of equality, wherein all the power and jurisdiction is reciprocal, no one having more than another, there being nothing more evident than that creatures of the same species and rank, promiscuously born to all the same advantages of Nature, and the use of the same faculties, should also be equal one amongst another, without subordination or subjection, unless the lord and master of them all should, by any manifest declaration of his will, set one above another,

* The selection is taken from "The Second Treatise" in John Locke, *Of Civil Government, Two Treatises,* Everyman's Library edition, pp. 118–21, 164–66, 179–82, 183–90, 224–32. Reprinted by permission of E. P. Dutton and Co., Inc., New York, and J. M. Dent & Sons Ltd., London.

and confer on him, by an evident and clear appointment, an un-
doubted right to dominion and sovereignty.

5. This equality of men by Nature, the judicious Hooker looks
upon as so evident in itself, and beyond all question, that he makes it
the foundation of that obligation to mutual love amongst men on
which he builds the duties they owe one another, and from whence he
derives the great maxims of justice and charity. His words are:

"The like natural inducement hath brought men to know that it is
no less their duty to love others than themselves, for seeing those
things which are equal, must needs all have one measure; if I cannot
but wish to receive good, even as much at every man's hands, as any
man can wish unto his own soul, how should I look to have any part
of my desire herein satisfied, unless myself be careful to satisfy the
like desire, which is undoubtedly in other men weak, being of one and
the same nature: to have anything offered them repugnant to this
desire must needs, in all respects, grieve them as much as me: so that
if I do harm, I must look to suffer, there being no reason that others
should show greater measure of love to me than they have by me
showed unto them; my desire, therefore, to be loved of my equals in
Nature, as much as possible may be, imposeth upon me a natural
duty of bearing to themward fully the like affection. From which
relation of equality between ourselves and them that are as ourselves,
what several rules and canons natural reason hath drawn for direction
of life no man is ignorant." *(Eccl. Pol. i.)*

6. But though this be a state of liberty, yet it is not a state of
licence; though man in that state have an uncontrollable liberty to
dispose of his person or possessions, yet he has not liberty to destroy
himself, or so much as any creature in his possession, but where some
nobler use than its bare preservation calls for it. The state of Nature
has a law of Nature to govern it, which obliges every one, and reason,
which is that law, teaches all mankind who will but consult it, that
being all equal and independent, no one ought to harm another in his
life, health, liberty or possessions; for men being all the workmanship
of one omnipotent and infinitely wise Maker; all the servants of one
sovereign Master, sent into the world by His order and about His
business; they are His property, whose workmanship they are made
to last during His, not one another's pleasure. And, being furnished
with like faculties, sharing all in one community of Nature, there
cannot be supposed any such subordination among us that may
authorise us to destroy one another, as if we were made for one

another's uses, as the inferior ranks of creatures are for ours. Every one as he is bound to preserve himself, and not to quit his station wilfully, so by the like reason, when his own preservation comes not in competition, ought he as much as he can to preserve the rest of mankind, and not unless it be to do justice on an offender, take away or impair the life, or what tends to the preservation of the life, the liberty, health, limb, or goods of another.

7. And that all men may be restrained from invading others' rights, and from doing hurt to one another, and the law of Nature be observed, which willeth the peace and preservation of all mankind, the execution of the law of Nature is in that state put into every man's hands, whereby every one has a right to punish the transgressors of that law to such a degree as may hinder its violation. For the law of Nature would, as all other laws that concern men in this world, be in vain if there were nobody that in the state of Nature had a power to execute that law, and thereby preserve the innocent and restrain offenders; and if any one in the state of Nature may punish another for any evil he has done, every one may do so. For in that state of perfect equality, where naturally there is no superiority or jurisdiction of one over another, what any may do in prosecution of that law, every one must needs have a right to do.

8. And thus, in the state of Nature, one man comes by a power over another, but yet no absolute or arbitrary power to use a criminal, when he has got him in his hands, according to the passionate heats or boundless extravagancy of his own will, but only to retribute to him so far as calm reason and conscience dictate, what is proportionate to his transgression, which is so much as may serve for reparation and restraint. For these two are the only reasons why one man may lawfully do harm to another, which is that we call punishment. In transgressing the law of Nature, the offender declares himself to live by another rule than that of reason and common equity, which is that measure God has set to the actions of men for their mutual security, and so he becomes dangerous to mankind; the tie which is to secure them from injury and violence being slighted and broken by him, which being a trespass against the whole species, and the peace and safety of it, provided for by the law of Nature, every man upon this score, by the right he hath to preserve mankind in general, may restrain, or where it is necessary, destroy things noxious to them, and so may bring such evil on any one who hath transgressed that law, as may make his repent the doing of it, and thereby deter him, and, by

his example, others from doing the like mischief. And in this case, and upon this ground, every man hath a right to punish the offender, and be executioner of the law of Nature. . . .

OF THE BEGINNING OF POLITICAL SOCIETIES

95. Men being, as has been said, by Nature all free, equal, and independent, no one can be put out of this estate and subjected to the political power of another without his consent, which is done by agreeing with other men, to join and unite into a community for their comfortable, safe, and peaceable living, one amongst another, in a secure enjoyment of their properties, and a greater security against any that are not of it. This any number of men may do, because it injures not the freedom of the rest; they are left, as they were, in the liberty of the state of Nature. When any number of men have so consented to make one community or government, they are thereby presently incorporated, and make one body politic, wherein the majority have a right to act and conclude the rest.

96. For, when any number of men have, by the consent of every individual, made a community, they have thereby made that community one body, with a power to act as one body, which is only by the will and determination of the majority. For that which acts any community, being only the consent of the individuals of it, and it being one body, must move one way, it is necessary the body should move that way whither the greater force carries it, which is the consent of the majority, or else it is impossible it should act or continue one body, one community, which the consent of every individual that united into it agreed that it should; and so every one is bound by that consent to be concluded by the majority. And therefore we see that in assemblies empowered to act by positive laws where no number is set by that positive law which empowers them, the act of the majority passes for the act of the whole, and of course determines as having, by the law of Nature and reason, the power of the whole.

97. And thus every man, by consenting with others to make one body politic under one government, puts himself under an obligation to every one of that society to submit to the determination of the majority, and to be concluded by it; or else this original compact, whereby he with others incorporates into one society, would signify nothing, and be no compact if he be left free and under no other ties than he was in before in the state of Nature. For what appearance

would there be of any compact? What new engagement if he were no farther tied by any decrees of the society than he himself thought fit and did actually consent to? This would be still as great a liberty as he himself had before his compact, or any one else in the state of Nature, who may submit himself and consent to any acts of it if he thinks fit.

98. For if the consent of the majority shall not in reason be received as the act of the whole, and conclude every individual, nothing but the consent of every individual can make anything to be of the act of the whole, which, considering the infirmities of health and avocations of business, which in a number though much less than that of a commonwealth, will necessarily keep many away from the public assembly; and the variety of opinions and contrariety of interests which unavoidably happen in all collections of men, it is next impossible ever to be had. And, therefore, if coming into society be upon such terms, it will be only like Cato's coming into the theatre, *tantum ut exiret*. Such a constitution as this would make the mighty leviathan of a shorter duration than the feeblest creatures, and not let it outlast the day it was born in, which cannot be supposed till we can think that rational creatures should desire and constitute societies only to be dissolved. For where the majority cannot conclude the rest, there they cannot act as one body, and consequently will be immediately dissolved again.

99. Whosoever, therefore, out of a state of Nature unite into a community, must be understood to give up all the power necessary to the ends for which they unite into society to the majority of the community, unless they expressly agreed in any number greater than the majority. And this is done by barely agreeing to unite into one political society, which is all the compact that is, or needs be, between the individuals that enter into or make up a commonwealth. And thus, that which begins and actually constitutes any political society is nothing but the consent of any number of freemen capable of majority, to unite and incorporate into such a society. And this is that, and that only, which did or could give beginning to any lawful government in the world. . . .

OF THE ENDS OF POLITICAL SOCIETY AND GOVERNMENT

123. If man in the state of Nature be so free as has been said, if he be absolute lord of his own person and possessions, equal to the

greatest and subject to nobody, why will he part with his freedom, this empire, and subject himself to the dominion and control of any other power? To which it is obvious to answer, that though in the state of Nature he hath such a right, yet the enjoyment of it is very uncertain and constantly exposed to the invasion of others; for all being kings as much as he, every man his equal, and the greater part no strict observers of equity and justice, the enjoyment of the property he has in this state is very unsafe, very insecure. This makes him willing to quit this condition which, however free, is full of fears and continual dangers; and it is not without reason that he seeks out and is willing to join in society with others who are already united, or have a mind to unite for the mutual preservation of their lives, liberties and estates, which I call by the general name—property.

124. The great and chief end, therefore, of men uniting into commonwealths, and putting themselves under government, is the preservation of their property; to which in the state of Nature there are many things wanting.

Firstly, there wants an established, settled, known law, received and allowed by common consent to be the standard of right and wrong, and the common measure to decide all controversies between them. For though the law of Nature be plain and intelligible to all rational creatures, yet men, being biased by their interest, as well as ignorant for want of study of it, are not apt to allow of it as a law binding to them in the application of it to their particular cases.

125. Secondly, in the state of Nature there wants a known and indifferent judge, with authority to determine all differences according to the established law. For every one in that state being both judge and executioner of the law of Nature, men being partial to themselves, passion and revenge is very apt to carry them too far, and with too much heat in their own cases, as well as negligence and unconcernedness, make them too remiss in other men's.

126. Thirdly, in the state of Nature there often wants power to back and support the sentence when right, and to give it due execution. They who by any injustice offended will seldom fail where they are able by force to make good their injustice. Such resistance many times makes the punishment dangerous, and frequently destructive to those who attempt it.

127. Thus mankind, notwithstanding all the privileges of the state of Nature, being but in an ill condition while they remain in it are quickly driven into society. Hence it comes to pass, that we seldom

find any number of men live any time together in this state. The inconveniences that they are therein exposed to by the irregular and uncertain exercise of the power every man has of punishing the transgressions of others, make them take sanctuary under the established laws of government, and therein seek the preservation of their property. It is this makes them so willingly give up every one his single power of punishing to be exercised by such alone as shall be appointed to it amongst them, and by such rules as the community, or those authorised by them to that purpose, shall agree on. And in this we have the original right and rise of both the legislative and executive power as well as of the governments and societies themselves.

128. For in the state of Nature to omit the liberty he has of innocent delights, a man has two powers. The first is to do whatsoever he thinks fit for the preservation of himself and others within the permission of the law of Nature; by which law, common to them all, he and all the rest of mankind are one community, make up one society distinct from all other creatures, and were it not for the corruption and viciousness of degenerate men, there would be no need of any other, no necessity that men should separate from this great and natural community, and associate into lesser combinations. The other power a man has in the state of Nature is the power to punish the crimes committed against that law. Both these he gives up when he joins in a private, if I may so call it, or particular political society, and incorporates into any commonwealth separate from the rest of mankind.

129. The first power—viz., of doing whatsoever he thought fit for the preservation of himself and the rest of mankind, he gives up to be regulated by laws made by the society, so far forth as the preservation of himself and the rest of that society shall require; which laws of the society in many things confine the liberty he had by the law of Nature.

130. Secondly, the power of punishing he wholly gives up, and engages his natural force, which he might before employ in the execution of the law of Nature, by his own single authority, as he thought fit, to assist the executive power of the society as the law thereof shall require. For being now in a new state, wherein he is to enjoy many conveniencies from the labour, assistance, and society of others in the same community, as well as protection from its whole strength, he is to part also with as much of his natural liberty, in providing for himself, as the good, prosperity, and safety of the society shall require,

which is not only necessary but just, since the other members of the society do the like.

131. But though men when they enter into society give up the equality, liberty, and executive power they had in the state of Nature into the hands of society, to be so far disposed of by the legislative as the good of the society shall require, yet it being only with an intention in every one the better to preserve himself, his liberty and property (for no rational creature can be supposed to change his condition with an intention to be worse), the power of the society or legislative constituted by them can never be supposed to extend farther than the common good, but is obliged to secure every one's property by providing against those three defects above mentioned that made the state of Nature so unsafe and uneasy. And so, whoever has the legislative or supreme power of any commonwealth, is bound to govern by established standing laws, promulgated and known to the people, and not by extemporary decrees, by indifferent and upright judges, who are to decide controversies by those laws; and to employ the force of the community at home only in the execution of such laws, or abroad to prevent or redress foreign injuries and secure the community from inroads and invasion. And all this to be directed to no other end but the peace, safety, and public good of the people. . . .

OF THE EXTENT OF THE LEGISLATIVE POWER

134. The great end of men's entering into society being the enjoyment of their properties in peace and safety, and the great instrument and means of that being the laws established in that society, the first and fundamental positive law of all commonwealths is the establishing of the legislative power, as the first and fundamental natural law which is to govern even the legislative. Itself is the preservation of the society and (as far as will consist with the public good) of every person in it. This legislative is not only the supreme power of the commonwealth, but sacred and unalterable in the hands where the community have once placed it. Nor can any edict of anybody else, in what form soever conceived, or by what power soever backed, have the force and obligation of a law which has not its sanction from that legislative which the public has chosen and appointed; for without this the law could not have that which is absolutely necessary to its being a law, the consent of the society, over whom nobody can have a power to make laws but by their own consent and by authority

received from them; and therefore all the obedience, which by the most solemn ties any one can be obliged to pay, ultimately terminates in this supreme power, and is directed by those laws which it enacts. Nor can any oaths to any foreign power whatsoever, or any domestic subordinate power, discharge any member of the society from his obedience to the legislative, acting pursuant to their trust, nor oblige him to any obedience contrary to the laws so enacted or farther than they do allow, it being ridiculous to imagine one can be tied ultimately to obey any power in the society which is not the supreme.

135. Though the legislative, whether placed in one or more, whether it be always in being or only by intervals, though it be the supreme power in every commonwealth, yet, first, it is not, nor can possibly be, absolutely arbitrary over the lives and fortunes of the people. For it being but the joint power of every member of the society given up to that person or assembly which is legislator, it can be no more than those persons had in a state of Nature before they entered into society, and gave it up to the community. For nobody can transfer to another more power than he has in himself, and nobody has an absolute arbitrary power over himself, or over any other, to destroy his own life, or take away the life or property of another. A man, as has been proved, cannot subject himself to the arbitrary power of another; and having, in the state of Nature, no arbitrary power over the life, liberty, or possession of another, but only so much as the law of Nature gave him for the preservation of himself and the rest of mankind, this is all he doth, or can give up to the commonwealth, and by it to the legislative power, so that the legislative can have no more than this. Their power in the utmost bounds of it is limited to the public good of the society. It is a power that hath no other end but preservation, and therefore can never have a right to destroy, enslave, or designedly to impoverish the subjects; the obligations of the law of Nature cease not in society, but only in many cases are drawn closer, and have, by human laws, known penalties annexed to them to enforce their observation. Thus the law of Nature stands as an eternal rule to all men, legislators as well as others. The rules that they make for other men's actions, be conformable to the law of Nature—i.e., to the will of God, of which that is a declaration, and the fundamental law of Nature being the preservation of mankind, no human sanction can be good or valid against it.

136. Secondly, the legislative or supreme authority cannot assume to itself a power to rule by extemporary arbitrary decrees, but is

bound to dispense justice and decide the rights of the subject by promulgated standing laws, and known authorised judges. For the law of Nature being unwritten, and so nowhere to be found but in the minds of men, they who, through passion or interest, shall miscite or misapply it, cannot so easily be convinced of their mistake where there is no established judge; and so it serves not as it ought, to determine the rights and fence the properties of those that live under it, especially where every one is judge, interpreter, and executioner of it too, and that in his own case; and he that has right on his side, having ordinarily but his own single strength, hath not force enough to defend himself from injuries or punish delinquents. To avoid these inconveniences which disorder men's properties in the state of Nature, men unite into societies that they may have the united strength of the whole society to secure and defend their properties, and may have standing rules to bound it by which every one may know what is his. To this end it is that men give up all their natural power to the society they enter into, and the community put the legislative power into such hands as they think fit, with this trust, that they shall be governed by declared laws, or else their peace, quiet, and property will still be at the same uncertainty as it was in the state of Nature.

137. Absolute arbitrary power, or governing without settled standing laws, can neither of them consist with the ends of society and government, which men would not quit the freedom of the state of Nature for, and tie themselves up under, were it not to preserve their lives, liberties, and fortunes, and by stated rules of right and property to secure their peace and quiet. It cannot be supposed that they should intend, had they a power so to do, to give any one or more an absolute arbitrary power over their persons and estates, and put a force into the magistrate's hand to execute his unlimited will arbitrarily upon them; this were to put themselves into a worse condition than the state of Nature, wherein they had a liberty to defend their right against the injuries of others, and were upon equal terms of force to maintain it, whether invaded by a single man or many in combination. Whereas by supposing they have given up themselves to the absolute arbitrary power and will of a legislator, they have disarmed themselves, and armed him to make a prey of them when he pleases; he being in a much worse condition that is exposed to the arbitrary power of one man who has the command of a hundred thousand than he that is exposed to the arbitrary power of a hundred thousand single men, nobody being secure, that his will who has such a command is

better than that of other men, though his force be a hundred thousand times stronger. And, therefore, whatever form the commonwealth is under, the ruling power ought to govern by declared and received laws, and not by extemporary dictates and undetermined resolutions, for then mankind will be in a far worse condition than in the state of Nature if they shall have armed one or a few men with the joint power of a multitude, to force them to obey at pleasure the exorbitant and unlimited decrees of their sudden thoughts, or unrestrained, and till that moment, unknown wills, without having any measures set down which may guide and justify their actions. For all the power the government has, being only for the good of the society, as it ought not to be arbitrary and at pleasure, so it ought to be exercised by established and promulgated laws, that both the people may know their duty, and be safe and secure within the limits of the law, and the rulers, too, kept within their due bounds, and not be tempted by the power they have in their hands to employ it to purposes, and by such measures as they would not have known, and own not willingly.

138. Thirdly, the supreme power cannot take from any man any part of his property without his own consent. For the preservation of property being the end of government, and that for which men enter into society, it necessarily supposes and requires that the people should have property, without which they must be supposed to lose that by entering into society which was the end for which they entered into it; too gross an absurdity for any man to own. Men, therefore, in society having property, they have such a right to the goods, which by the law of the community are theirs, that nobody hath a right to take them, or any part of them, from them without their own consent; without this they have no property at all. For I have truly no property in that which another can by right take from me when he pleases against my consent. Hence it is a mistake to think that the supreme or legislative power of any commonwealth can do what it will, and dispose of the estates of the subject arbitrarily, or take any part of them at pleasure. This is not much to be feared in governments where the legislative consists wholly or in part in assemblies which are variable, whose members upon the dissolution of the assembly are subjects under the common laws of their country, equally with the rest. But in governments where the legislative is in one lasting assembly, always in being, or in one man as in absolute monarchies, there is danger still, that they will think themselves to have a distinct interest from the rest of the community, and so will be

apt to increase their own riches and power by taking what they think fit from the people. For a man's property is not at all secure, though there be good and equitable laws to set the bounds of it between him and his fellow-subjects, if he who commands those subjects have power to take from any private man what part he pleases of his property, and use and dispose of it as he thinks good.

139. But government, into whosesoever hands it is put, being as I have before showed, entrusted with this condition, and for this end, that men might have and secure their properties, the prince or senate, however it may have power to make laws for the regulating of property between the subjects one amongst another, yet can never have a power to take to themselves the whole, or any part of the subjects' property, without their own consent; for this would be in effect to leave them no property at all. And to let us see that even absolute power, where it is necessary, is not arbitrary by being absolute, but is still limited by that reason, and confined to those ends which required it in some cases to be absolute, we need look no farther than the common practice of martial discipline. For the preservation of the army, and in it of the whole commonwealth, requires an absolute obedience to the command of every superior officer, and it is justly death to disobey or dispute the most dangerous or unreasonable of them; but yet we see that neither the sergeant that could command a soldier to march up to the mouth of a cannon, or stand in a breach where he is almost sure to perish, can command that soldier to give him one penny of his money; nor the general that can condemn him to death for deserting his post, or not obeying the most desperate orders, cannot yet with all his absolute power of life and death dispose of one farthing of that soldier's estate, or seize one jot of his goods; whom yet he can command anything, and hang for the least disobedience. Because such a blind obedience is necessary to that end for which the commander has his power—viz., the preservation of the rest, but the disposing of his goods has nothing to do with it.

140. It is true governments cannot be supported without great charge, and it is fit every one who enjoys his share of the protection should pay out of his estate his proportion for the maintenance of it. But still it must be with his own consent—i.e., the consent of the majority, giving it either by themselves or their representatives chosen by them; for if any one shall claim a power to lay and levy taxes on the people by his own authority, and without such consent of the people, he thereby invades the fundamental law of property, and

subverts the end of government. For what property have I in that which another may by right take when he pleases to himself?

141. Fourthly. The legislative cannot transfer the power of making laws to any other hands, for it being but a delegated power from the people, they who have it cannot pass it over to others. The people alone can appoint the form of the commonwealth, which is by constituting the legislative, and appointing in whose hands that shall be. And when the people have said, "We will submit, and be governed by laws made by such men, and in such forms," nobody else can say other men shall make laws for them; nor can they be bound by any laws but such as are enacted by those whom they have chosen and authorised to make laws for them.

142. These are the bounds which the trust that is put in them by the society and the law of God and Nature have set to the legislative power of every commonwealth, in all forms of government. First: They are to govern by promulgated established laws, not to be varied in particular cases, but to have one rule for rich and poor, for the favourite at Court, and the countryman at plough. Secondly: These laws also ought to be designed for no other end ultimately but the good of the people. Thirdly: They must not raise taxes on the property of the people without the consent of the people given by themselves or their deputies. And this properly concerns only such governments where the legislative is always in being, or at least where the people have not reserved any part of the legislative to deputies, to be from time to time chosen by themselves. Fourthly: Legislative neither must nor can transfer the power of making laws to anybody else, or place it anywhere but where the people have. . . .

OF THE DISSOLUTION OF GOVERNMENT

211. He that will, with any clearness, speak of the dissolution of government, ought in the first place to distinguish between the dissolution of the society and the dissolution of the government. That which makes the community, and brings men out of the loose state of Nature into one politic society, is the agreement which every one has with the rest to incorporate and act as one body, and so be one distinct commonwealth. The usual, and almost only way whereby this union is dissolved, is the inroad of foreign force making a conquest upon them. For in that case (not being able to maintain and support themselves as one entire and independent body) the union belonging

to that body, which consisted therein, must necessarily cease, and so every one returns to the state he was in before, with a liberty to shift for himself and provide for his own safety, as he thinks fit, in some other society. Whenever the society is dissolved, it is certain the government of that society cannot remain. Thus conquerors' swords often cut up governments by the roots, and mangle societies to pieces, separating the subdued or scattered multitude from the protection of and dependence on that society which ought to have preserved them from violence. The world is too well instructed in, and too forward to allow of this way of dissolving of governments, to need any more to be said of it; and there wants not much argument to prove that where the society is dissolved, the government cannot remain; that being as impossible as for the frame of a house to subsist when the materials of it are scattered and displaced by a whirlwind, or jumbled into a confused heap by an earthquake.

212. Besides this overturning from without, governments are dissolved from within:

First: When the legislative is altered, civil society being a state of peace amongst those who are of it, from whom the state of war is excluded by the umpirage which they have provided in their legislative for the ending all differences that may arise amongst any of them; it is in their legislative that the members of a commonwealth are united and combined together into one coherent living body. This is the soul that gives form, life, and unity to the commonwealth; from hence the several members have their mutual influence, sympathy, and connection; and therefore when the legislative is broken, or dissolved, dissolution and death follows. For the essence and union of the society consisting in having one will, the legislative, when once established by the majority, has the declaring and, as it were, keeping of that will. The constitution of the legislative is the first and fundamental act of society, whereby provision is made for the continuation of their union under the direction of persons and bonds of laws, made by persons authorised thereunto, by the consent and appointment of the people, without which no one man, or number of men, amongst them can have authority of making laws that shall be binding to the rest. When any one, or more, shall take upon them to make laws whom the people have not appointed so to do, they make laws without authority, which the people are not therefore bound to obey; by which means they come again to be out of subjection, and may constitute to themselves a new legislative, as they think best, being in full liberty to resist the force of those who, without authority, would impose anything upon them. Every one is at the disposure of his own will, when those who had, by the delegation of the society, the declaring of the public will, are excluded from it, and others usurp the place who have no such authority or delegation.

213. This being usually brought about by such in the commonwealth, who misuse the power they have, it is hard to consider it aright, and know at whose door to lay it, without knowing the form of government in which it happens. Let us suppose then, the legislative placed in the concurrence of three distinct persons:—First, a single hereditary person having the constant, supreme, executive power, and with it the power of convoking and dissolving the other two within certain periods of time. Secondly, an assembly of hereditary nobility. Thirdly, an assembly of representatives chosen, *pro tempore,* by the people. Such a form of government supposed, it is evident:

214. First, that when such a single person or prince sets up his own arbitrary will in place of the laws which are the will of the society declared by the legislative, then the legislative is changed. For that being, in effect, the legislative whose rules and laws are put in execution, and required to be obeyed, when other laws are set up, and other rules pretended and enforced than what the legislative, constituted by the society, have enacted, it is plain that the legislative is changed. Whoever introduces new laws, not being thereunto authorised, by the fundamental appointment of the society, or subverts the old, disowns and overturns the power by which they were made, and so sets up a new legislative.

215. Secondly, when the prince hinders the legislative from assembling in its due time, or from acting freely, pursuant to those ends for which it was constituted, the legislative is altered. For it is not a certain number of men—no, nor their meeting, unless they have also freedom of debating and leisure of perfecting what is for the good of the society, wherein the legislative consists; when these are taken away, or altered, so as to deprive the society of the due exercise of their power, the legislative is truly altered. For it is not names that constitute governments, but the use and exercise of those powers that were intended to accompany them; so that he who takes away the freedom, or hinders the acting of the legislative in its due seasons, in effect takes away the legislative, and puts an end to the government.

216. Thirdly, when, by the arbitrary power of the prince, the electors

or ways of election are altered without the consent and contrary
to the common interest of the people, there also the legislative is
altered. For if others than those whom the society hath authorised
thereunto do choose, or in another way than what the society hath
prescribed, those chosen are not the legislative appointed by the
people.

217. Fourthly, the delivery also of the people into the subjection of
a foreign power, either by the prince or by the legislative, is certainly
a change of the legislative, and so a dissolution of the government.
For the end why people entered into society being to be preserved one
entire, free, independent society, to be governed by its own laws, this
is lost whenever they are given up into the power of another.

218. Why, in such a constitution as this, the dissolution of the
government in these cases is to be imputed to the prince is evident,
because he, having the force, treasure, and offices of the State to employ, and often persuading himself or being flattered by others, that,
as supreme magistrate, he is incapable of control; he alone is in a
condition to make great advances towards such changes under pretence of lawful authority, and has it in his hands to terrify or suppress
opposers as factious, seditious, and enemies to the government;
whereas no other part of the legislative, or people, is capable by themselves to attempt any alteration of the legislative without open and
visible rebellion, apt enough to be taken notice of, which, when it prevails, produces effects very little different from foreign conquest. Besides, the prince, in such a form of government, having the power of
dissolving the other parts of the legislative, and thereby rendering
them private persons, they can never, in opposition to him, or without
his concurrence, alter the legislative by a law, his consent being necessary to give any of their decrees that sanction. But yet so far as the
other parts of the legislative any way contribute to any attempt upon
the government, and do either promote, or not, what lies in them,
hinder such designs, they are guilty, and partake in this, which is certainly the greatest crime men can be guilty of one towards another.

219. There is one way more whereby such a government may be
dissolved, and that is: When he who has the supreme executive power
neglects and abandons that charge, so that the laws already made can
no longer be put in execution; this is demonstratively to reduce all to
anarchy, and so effectively to dissolve the government. For laws not
being made for themselves, but to be, by their execution, the bonds
of the society to keep every part of the body politic in its due place

and function. When that totally ceases, the government visibly ceases, and the people become a confused multitude without order or connection. Where there is no longer the administration of justice for the securing of men's rights, nor any remaining power within the community to direct the force, or provide for the necessities of the public, there certainly is no government left. Where the laws cannot be executed it is all one as if there were no laws, and a government without laws is, I suppose, a mystery in politics inconceivable to human capacity, and inconsistent with human society.

220. In these, and the like cases, when the government is dissolved, the people are at liberty to provide for themselves by erecting a new legislative differing from the other by the change of persons, or form, or both, as they shall find it most for their safety and good. For the society can never, by the fault of another, lose the native and original right it has to preserve itself, which can only be done by a settled legislative and a fair and impartial execution of the laws made by it. But the state of mankind is not so miserable that they are not capable of using this remedy till it be too late to look for any. To tell people they may provide for themselves by erecting a new legislative, when, by oppression, artifice, or being delivered over to a foreign power, their old one is gone, is only to tell them they may expect relief when it is too late, and the evil is past cure. This is, in effect, no more than to bid them first be slaves, and then to take care of their liberty, and, when their chains are on, tell them they may act like free men. This, if barely so, is rather mockery than relief, and men can never be secure from tyranny if there be no means to escape it till they are perfectly under it; and, therefore, it is that they have not only a right to get out of it, but to prevent it.

221. There is, therefore, secondly, another way whereby governments are dissolved, and that is, when the legislative, or the prince, either of them act contrary to their trust.

For the legislative acts against the trust reposed in them when they endeavour to invade the property of the subject, and to make themselves, or any part of the community, masters or arbitrary disposers of the lives, liberties, or fortunes of the people.

222. The reason why men enter into society is the preservation of their property; and the end while they choose and authorise a legislative is that there may be laws made, and rules set, as guards and fences to the properties of all the society, to limit the power and moderate the dominion of every part and member of the society. For

since it can never be supposed to be the will of the society that the
legislative should have a power to destroy that which every one
designs to secure by entering into society, and for which the people
submitted themselves to legislators of their own making: whenever
the legislators endeavour to take away and destroy the property of the
people, or to reduce them to slavery under arbitrary power, they put
themselves into a state of war with the people, who are thereupon
absolved from any farther obedience, and are left to the common
refuge which God hath provided for all men against force and violence. Whensoever, therefore, the legislative shall transgress this fundamental rule of society, and either by ambition, fear, folly, or corruption, endeavour to grasp themselves, or put into the hands of any
other, an absolute power over the lives, liberties, and estates of the
people, by this breach of trust they forfeit the power the people had
put into their hands for quite contrary ends, and it devolves to the
people, who have a right to resume their original liberty, and by the
establishment of a new legislative (such as they shall think fit), provide for their own safety and security, which is the end for which they
are in society. What I have said here concerning the legislative in
general holds true also concerning the supreme executor, who having
a double trust put in him, both to have a part in the legislative and
the supreme execution of the law, acts against both, when he goes
about to set up his own arbitrary will as the law of the society. He
acts also contrary to his trust when he employs the force, treasure,
and offices of the society to corrupt the representatives and gain them
to his purposes, when he openly pre-engages the electors, and pres-
cribes, to their choice, such whom he has, by solicitation, threats,
promises, or otherwise, won to his designs, and employs them to bring
in such who have promised beforehand what to vote and what to
enact. Thus to regulate candidates and electors, and new model the
ways of election, what is it but to cut up the government by the roots,
and poison the very fountain of public security? For the people having reserved to themselves the choice of their representatives as the
fence to their properties, could do it for no other end but that they
might always be freely chosen, and so chosen, freely act and advise
as the necessity of the commonwealth and the public good should,
upon examination and mature debate, be judged to require. This,
those who give their votes before they hear the debate, and have
weighed the reasons on all sides, are not capable of doing. To prepare
such an assembly as this, and endeavour to set up the declared

abettors of his own will, for the true representatives of the people, and the law-makers of the society, is certainly as great a breach of trust, and as perfect a declaration of a design to subvert the government, as is possible to be met with. To which, if one shall add rewards and punishments visibly employed to the same end, and all the arts of perverted law made use of to take off and destroy all that stand in the way of such a design, and will not comply and consent to betray the liberties of their country, it will be past doubt what is doing. What power they ought to have in the society who thus employ it contrary to the trust went along with it in its first institution, is easy to determine; and one cannot but see that he who has once attempted any such thing as this cannot any longer be trusted.

223. To this, perhaps, it will be said that the people being ignorant and always discontented, to lay the foundation of government in the unsteady opinion and uncertain humour of the people, is to expose it to certain ruin; and no government will be able long to subsist if the people may set up a new legislative whenever they take offence at the old one. To this I answer, quite the contrary. People are not so easily got out of their old forms as some are apt to suggest. They are hardly to be prevailed with to amend the acknowledged faults in the frame they have been accustomed to. And if there be any original defects, or adventitious ones introduced by time or corruption, it is not an easy thing to get them changed, even when all the world sees there is an opportunity for it. This slowness and aversion in the people to quit their old constitutions has in the many revolutions have been seen in this kingdom, in this and former ages, still kept us to, or after some interval of fruitless attempts, still brought us back again to our old legislative of king, lords and commons; and whatever provocations have made the crown be taken from some of our princes' heads, they never carried the people so far as to place it in another line.

224. But it will be said this hypothesis lays a ferment for frequent rebellion. To which I answer:

First: no more than any other hypothesis. For when the people are made miserable, and find themselves exposed to the ill usage of arbitrary power, cry up their governors as much as you will for sons of Jupiter, let them be sacred and divine, descended or authorised from Heaven; give them out for whom or what you please, the same will happen. The people generally ill treated, and contrary to right, will be ready upon any occasion to ease themselves of a burden that sits heavy upon them. They will wish and seek for the opportunity, which in the change, weakness, and accidents of human affairs, seldom delays long to offer itself. He must have lived but a little while in the world, who has not seen examples of this in his time; and he must have read very little who cannot produce examples of it in all sorts of governments in the world.

225. Secondly: I answer, such revolutions happen not upon every little mismanagement in public affairs. Great mistakes in the ruling part, many wrong and inconvenient laws, and all the slips of human frailty will be borne by the people without mutiny or murmur. But if a long train of abuses, prevarications, and artifices, all tending the same way, make the design visible to the people, and they cannot but feel what they lie under, and see whither they are going, it is not to be wondered that they should then rouse themselves, and endeavour to put the rule into such hands which may secure to them the ends for which government was at first erected, and without which, ancient names and specious forms are so far from being better, that they are much worse than the state of Nature or pure anarchy; the inconveniences being all as great and as near, but the remedy farther off and more difficult.

226. Thirdly: I answer, that this power in the people of providing for their safety anew by a new legislative when their legislators have acted contrary to their trust by invading their property, is the best fence against rebellion, and the probablest means to hinder it. For rebellion being an opposition, not to persons, but authority, which is founded only in the constitutions and laws of the government: those, whoever they be, who, by force, break through, and, by force, justify their violation of them, are truly and properly rebels. For when men, by entering into society and civil government, have excluded force, and introduced laws for the preservation of property, peace, and unity amongst themselves, those who set up force again in opposition to the laws, do *rebellare*—that is, bring back again the state of war, and are properly rebels, which they who are in power, by the pretence they have to authority, the temptation of force they have in their hands, and the flattery of those about them being likeliest to do, the properest way to prevent the evil is to show them the danger and injustice of it who are under the greatest temptation to run into it.

227. In both the forementioned cases, when either the legislative is changed, or the legislators act contrary to the end for which they were constituted, those who are guilty are guilty of rebellion. For if any one by force takes away the established legislative of any society, and

the laws by them made, pursuant to their trust, he thereby takes away the umpirage which every one had consented to for a peaceable decision of all their controversies, and a bar to the state of war amongst them. They who remove or change the legislative take away this decisive power, which nobody can have but by the appointment and consent of the people, and so destroying the authority which the people did, and nobody else can set up, and introducing a power which the people hath not authorised, actually introduce a state of war, which is that of force without authority; and thus by removing the legislative established by the society, in whose decisions the people acquiesced and united as to that of their own will, they untie the knot, and expose the people anew to the state of war. And if those, who by force take away the legislative, are rebels, the legislators themselves, as has been shown, can be no less esteemed so, when they who were set up for the protection and preservation of the people, their liberties and properties shall by force invade and endeavour to take them away; and so they putting themselves into a state of war with those who made them the protectors and guardians of their peace, are properly, and with the greatest aggravation, *rebellantes,* rebels.

6

ROUSSEAU
The Concept of the General Will

Jean-Jacques Rousseau's *Social Contract,* published in 1762, provides focus upon a central problem of political rule in democracy: the reconciliation of liberty with political authority. The basic problem, as Rousseau (1712–1778) put it, is to find a form of association which will defend and protect with the whole common force the person and goods of each associate and in which each, while uniting himself with all, may still obey himself alone and remain as free as before.

Just as Locke did, Rousseau utilized the contract theory as an explanation of the origin of political authority, but he differs from Locke in the view that, upon entrance into civil society from the state of nature, man surrenders all rights to the community.

The basic foundation of political authority is what Rousseau calls the General Will, the source of all law and the standard of what is just and unjust within a political community. The General Will is not equivalent to the "will of all," or the sum of particular wills both of which take into account expressions of private interest; it is an intrinsic standard of goodness inherent within the moral consensus of the political community. The General Will, as the expression of sovereign authority, cannot be represented by any organ of government; sovereignty is inalienable and indivisible. While Locke saw the people transfer sovereign power to the organs of government—legislative, executive and judicial—Rousseau foreclosed any transfer of sovereign power and insisted that it resides solely in the people. While Locke emphasized the importance of limits on political authority in behalf of individual rights, Rousseau maintained the absolute authority of the General Will, and by an ingenious piece of reasoning, he argued that individual freedom, properly conceived, can never be in conflict with the General Will. For the General Will is the embodiment of the common good or moral consensus of society which all individuals have helped to create. In obeying the General Will the individual citizen is thus exercising his true moral freedom in contrast to momentary impulses of selfish interest or appetite. Thus it is not meaningless to contend that when a dissenting individual is compelled to obey the General Will, he is being "forced to be free."

The major intent of the *Social Contract* is to formulate a theory of political rule derived from the model of a city-state democracy; Rousseau admired it as a type of integrated society in which common objectives could be realized without undue interference with individual desires. As an approach to defining the nature of political rule in modern democracy, however, Rousseau's theory is vulnerable to the basic criticism that it fails to recognize the essential role of political parties or representative bodies in the formulation of the General Will. At the same time, Rousseau appears to recognize that an unorganized mass cannot formulate the General Will on particular issues; since he rules out all other means of organizing public opinion, he falls back on the necessity of a wise legislator or lawgiver (not unlike Plato's philosopher-king) who establishes the original constitution and creates the general spirit of society which enables the people to achieve the true General Will. At this point, Rousseau's theory takes on implications that can be considered congenial to the spirit of authoritarian government. What Rousseau did not recognize is that within the complexities of the modern industrial state, the quest for a General Will requires the process of free discussion, negotiation and bargaining among conflicting interests within the framework of constitutional processes, political parties and representative organs.

Yet Rousseau's concept of the General Will makes an important contribution to democratic theory. The democratic concept of individual freedom cannot be viewed solely as a negative concept; it embodies a positive component in the recognition that individual self-expression and fulfillment can be given maximum realization only in a society in which there is a recogition of a common good which may require, in particular cases, restraints upon the actions of individuals. How to define the boundaries between particular claims of individuals and the claims of sovereign authority is, of course, one of the perennial problems of democratic theory, which Rousseau does not resolve. But Rousseau's theory is a classic statement of the kind of questions that must be probed in seeking to define the nature of political rule in modern democracy. Finally, it must be acknowledged that despite the difficulties of Rousseau's theory, the *Social Contract* has been an inspiration for the cause of popular democracy and revolutionary movements against political tyranny in the modern era.*

* The selection is from Jean-Jacques Rousseau, *The Social Contract and The Discourses,* trans. by G. D. H. Cole, Everyman's Library edition, pp. 3–16; 20–24; 30–35; 41; 77–80; 85–89. Reprinted by permission of E. P. Dutton & Co., Inc., New York, and J. M. Dent & Sons Ltd., London.

Man is born free; and everywhere he is in chains. One thinks himself the master of others, and still remains a greater slave than they. How did this change come about? I do not know. What can make it legitimate? That question I think I can answer.

If I took into account only force, and the effects derived from it, I should say: "As long as a people is compelled to obey, and obeys, it does well; as soon as it can shake off the yoke, and shakes it off, it does still better; for, regaining its liberty by the same right as took it away, either it is justified in resuming it, or there was no justification for those who took it away." But the social order is a sacred right which is the basis of all other rights. Nevertheless, this right does not come from nature, and must therefore be founded on conventions. Before coming to that, I have to prove what I have just asserted.

THE FIRST SOCIETIES

The most ancient of all societies, and the only one that is natural, is the family: and even so the children remain attached to the father only so long as they need him for their preservation. As soon as this need ceases, the natural bond is dissolved. The children, released from the obedience they owed to the father, and the father, released from the care he owed his children, return equally to independence. If they remain united, they continue so no longer naturally, but voluntarily; and the family itself is then maintained only by convention.

This common liberty results from the nature of man. His first law is to provide for his own preservation, his first cares are those which he owes to himself; and, as soon as he reaches years of discretion, he is the sole judge of the proper means of preserving himself, and consequently becomes his own master.

The family then may be called the first model of political societies: the ruler corresponds to the father, and the people to the children; and all, being born free and equal, alienate their liberty only for their own advantage. The whole difference is that, in the family, the love of the father for his children repays him for the care he takes of them, while, in the State, the pleasure of commanding takes the place of the love which the chief cannot have for the peoples under him.

Grotius denies that all human power is established in favour of the governed, and quotes slavery as an example. His usual method of reasoning is constantly to establish right by fact. It would be possible to employ a more logical method, but none could be more favourable to tyrants.

It is then, according to Grotius, doubtful whether the human race belongs to a hundred men, or that hundred men to the human race: and, throughout his book, he seems to incline to the former alternative, which is also the view of Hobbes. On this showing, the human species is divided into many herds of cattle, each with its ruler, who keeps guard over them for the purpose of devouring them.

As a shepherd is of a nature superior to that of his flock, the shepherds of men, i.e. their rulers, are of a nature superior to that of the peoples under them. Thus, Philo tells us, the Emperor Caligula reasoned, concluding equally well either that kings were gods, or that men were beasts.

The reasoning of Caligula agrees with that of Hobbes and Grotius. Aristotle, before any of them, had said that men are by no means equal naturally, but that some are born for slavery, and others for dominion.

Aristotle was right; but he took the effect for the cause. Nothing can be more certain than that every man born in slavery is born for slavery. Slaves lose everything in their chains, even the desire of escaping from them: they love their servitude, as the comrades of Ulysses loved their brutish condition. If then there are slaves by nature, it is because there have been slaves against nature. Force made the first slaves, and their cowardice perpetuated the condition.

I have said nothing of King Adam, or Emperor Noah, father of the three great monarchs who shared out the universe, like the children of Saturn, whom some scholars have recognized in them. I trust to getting due thanks for my moderation; for, being a direct descendant of one of the princes, perhaps of the eldest branch, how do I know that a verification of titles might not leave me the legitimate king of the human race? In any case, there can be no doubt that Adam was sovereign of the world, as Robinson Crusoe was of his island, as long as he was its only inhabitant; and this empire had the advantage that the monarch, safe on his throne, had no rebellions, wars, or conspirators to fear.

THE RIGHT OF THE STRONGEST

The strongest is never strong enough to be always the master, unless he transforms strength into right, and obedience into duty. Hence

the right of the strongest, which, though to all seeming meant ironi-
cally, is really laid down as a fundamental principle. But are we never
to have an explanation of this phrase? Force is a physical power, and
I fail to see what moral effect it can have. To yield to force is an act
of necessity, not of will—at the most, an act of prudence. In what
sense can it be a duty?

Suppose for a moment that this so-called "right" exists. I maintain
that the sole result is a mass of inexplicable nonsense. For, if force
creates right, the effect changes with the cause: every force that is
greater than the first succeeds to its right. As soon as it is possible to
disobey with impunity, disobedience is legitimate; and, the strongest
being always in the right, the only thing that matters is to act so as to
become the strongest. But what kind of right is that which perishes
when force fails? If we must obey perforce, there is no need to obey
because we ought; and if we are not forced to obey, we are under no
obligation to do so. Clearly, the word "right" adds nothing to force:
in this connection, it means absolutely nothing.

Obey the powers that be. If this means yield to force, it is a good
precept, but superfluous: I can answer for its never being violated. All
power comes from God, I admit; but so does all sickness: does that
mean that we are forbidden to call in the doctor? A brigand surprises
me at the edge of a wood: must I not merely surrender my purse on
compulsion; but, even if I could withhold it, am I in conscience
bound to give it up? For certainly the pistol he holds is also a
power.

Let us then admit that force does not create right, and that we are
obliged to obey only legitimate powers. In that case, my original
question recurs.

SLAVERY

Since no man has a natural authority over his fellow, and force
creates no right, we must conclude that conventions form the basis of
all legitimate authority among men.

If an individual, says Grotius, can alienate his liberty and make
himself the slave of a master, why could not a whole people do the
same and make itself subject to a king? There are in this passage
plenty of ambiguous words which would need explaining: but let us
confine ourselves to the word *alienate*. To alienate is to give or to sell.
Now, a man who becomes the slave of another does not give himself;

he sells himself, at the least for his subsistence: but for what does a people sell itself? A king is so far from furnishing his subjects with their subsistence that he gets his own only from them; and, according to Rabelais, kings do not live on nothing. Do subjects then give their persons on condition that the king takes their goods also? I fail to see what they have left to preserve.

It will be said that the despot assures his subjects civil tranquillity. Granted; but what do they gain, if the wars his ambition brings down upon them, his insatiable avidity, and the vexatious conduct of his ministers press harder on them than their own dissentions would have done? What do they gain, if the very tranquillity they enjoy is one of their miseries? Tranquillity is found also in dungeons; but is that enough to make them desirable places to live in? The Greeks imprisoned in the cave of the Cyclops lived there very tranquilly, while they were awaiting their turn to be devoured.

To say that a man gives himself gratuitously, is to say what is absurd and inconceivable; such an act is null and illegitimate, from the mere fact that he who does it is out of his mind. To say the same of a whole people is to suppose a people of madmen; and madness creates no right.

Even if each man could alienate himself, he could not alienate his children: they are born men and free; their liberty belongs to them, and no one but they has the right to dispose of it. Before they come to years of discretion, the father can, in their name, lay down conditions for their preservation and well-being, but he cannot give them irrevocably and without conditions: such a gift is contrary to the ends of nature, and exceeds the rights of paternity. It would therefore be necessary, in order to legitimize an arbitrary government, that in every generation the people should be in a position to accept or reject it; but, were this so, the government would be no longer arbitrary.

To renounce liberty is to renounce being a man, to surrender the rights of humanity and even its duties. For him who renounces everything no indemnity is possible. Such a renunciation is incompatible with man's nature; to remove all liberty from his will is to remove all morality from his acts. Finally, it is an empty and contradictory convention that sets up, on the one side, absolute authority, and, on the other, unlimited obedience. Is it not clear that we can be under no obligation to a person from whom we have the right to exact everything? Does not this condition alone, in the absence of equivalence or exchange, in itself involve the nullity of the act? For what right can my slave have against me, when all that he has belongs to me, and, his right being mine, this right of mine against myself is a phrase devoid of meaning?

Grotius and the rest find in war another origin for the so-called right of slavery. The victor having, as they hold, the right of killing the vanquished, the latter can buy back his life at the price of his liberty; and this convention is the more legitimate because it is to the advantage of both parties.

But it is clear that this supposed right to kill the conquered is by no means deducible from the state of war. Men, from the mere fact that, while they are living in their primitive independence, they have no mutual relations stable enough to constitute either the state of peace or the state of war, cannot be naturally enemies. War is constituted by a relation between things, and not between persons; and, as the state of war cannot arise out of simple personal relations, but only out of real relations, private war, or war of man with man, can exist neither in the state of Nature, where there is no constant property, nor in the social state, where everything is under the authority of the laws.

Individual combats, duels, and encounters, are acts which cannot constitute a state; while the private wars, authorized by the Establishments of Louis IX, King of France, and suspended by the Peace of God, are abuses of feudalism, in itself an absurd system if ever there was one, and contrary to the principles of natural right and to all good polity.

War then is a relation, not between man and man, but between State and State, and individuals are enemies only accidentally, not as men, nor even as citizens, but as soldiers; not as members of their country, but as its defenders. Finally, each State can have for enemies only other States, and not men; for between things disparate in Nature there can be no real relation.

Furthermore, this principle is in conformity with the established rules of all times and the constant practice of all civilized peoples. Declarations of war are intimations less to powers than to their subjects. The foreigner, whether king, individual, or people, who robs, kills, or detains the subjects, without declaring war on the prince, is not an enemy, but a brigand. Even in real war, a just prince, while laying hands, in the enemy's country, on all that belongs to the public, respects the lives and goods of individuals: he respects rights on which his own are founded. The object of the war being the destruction of the hostile State, the other side has a right to kill its defenders, while they are bearing arms; but as soon as they lay them down and surrender, they cease to be enemies or instruments of the enemy, and become once more merely men, whose life no one has any right to take. Sometimes it is possible to kill the State without killing a single one of its members; and war gives no right which is not necessary to the gaining of its object. These principles are not those of Grotius: they are not based on the authority of poets, but derived from the nature of reality and based on reason.

The right of conquest has no foundation other than the right of the strongest. If war does not give the conqueror the right to massacre the conquered peoples, the right to enslave them cannot be based upon a right which does not exist. No one has a right to kill an enemy except when he cannot make him a slave, and the right to enslave him cannot therefore be derived from the right to kill him. It is accordingly an unfair exchange to make him buy at the price of his liberty his life, over which the victor holds no right. Is it not clear that there is a vicious circle in founding the right of life and death on the right of slavery, and the right of slavery on the right of life and death?

Even if we assume this terrible right to kill everybody, I maintain that a slave made in war, or a conquered people, is under no obligation to a master, except to obey him as far as he is compelled to do so. By taking an equivalent for his life, the victor has not done him a favour; instead of killing him without profit, he has killed him usefully. So far then is he from acquiring over him any authority in addition to that of force, that the state of war continues to subsist between them: their mutual relation is the effect of it, and the usage of the right of war does not imply a treaty of peace. A convention has indeed been made; but this convention, so far from destroying the state of war, presupposes its continuance.

So, from whatever aspect we regard the question, the right of slavery is null and void, not only as being illegitimate, but also because it is absurd and meaningless. The words *slave* and *right* contradict each other, and are mutually exclusive. It will always be equally foolish for a man to say to a man or to a people: "I make with you a convention wholly at your expense and wholly to my advantage; I shall keep it as long as I like, and you will keep it as long as I like."

THAT WE MUST ALWAYS GO BACK TO A FIRST
CONVENTION

Even if I granted all that I have been refuting, the friends of despotism would be no better off. There will always be a great difference between subduing a multitude and ruling a society. Even if scattered individuals were successively enslaved by one man, however numerous they might be, I still see no more than a master and his slaves, and certainly not a people and its ruler; I see what may be termed an aggregation, but not an association; there is as yet neither public good nor body politic. The man in question, even if he has enslaved half the world, is still only an individual; his interest, apart from that of others, is still a purely private interest. If this same man comes to die, his empire, after him, remains scattered and without unity, as an oak falls and dissolves into a heap of ashes when the fire has consumed it.

A people, says Grotius, can give itself to a king. Then, according to Grotius, a people is a people before it gives itself. The gift is itself a civil act, and implies public deliberation. It would be better, before examining the act by which a people gives itself to a king, to examine that by which it has become a people; for this act, being necessarily prior to the other, is the true foundation of society.

Indeed, if there were no prior convention, where, unless the election were unanimous, would be the obligation on the minority to submit to the choice of the majority? How have a hundred men who wish for a master the right to vote on behalf of ten who do not? The law of majority voting is itself something established by convention, and presupposes unanimity, on one occasion at least.

THE SOCIAL COMPACT

I suppose men to have reached the point at which the obstacles in the way of their preservation in the state of Nature show their power of resistance to be greater than the resources at the disposal of each individual for his maintenance in that state. That primitive condition can then subsist no longer; and the human race would perish unless it changed its manner of existence.

But, as men cannot engender new forces, but only unite and direct existing ones, they have no other means of preserving themselves than the formation, by aggregation, of a sum of forces great enough to overcome the resistance. These they have to bring into play by means of a single motive power, and cause to act in concert.

This sum of forces can arise only where several persons come together: but, as the force and liberty of each man are the chief instruments of his self-preservation, how can he pledge them without harming his own interests, and neglecting the care he owes to himself? This difficulty, in its bearing on my present subject, may be stated in the following terms:

The problem is to find a form of association which will defend and protect with the whole common force the person and goods of each associate, and in which each, while uniting himself with all, may still obey himself alone, and remain as free as before. This is the fundamental problem of which the *Social Contract* provides the solution.

The clauses of this contract are so determined by the nature of the act that the slightest modification would make them vain and ineffective; so that, although they have perhaps never been formally set forth, they are everywhere the same and everywhere tacitly admitted and recognized, until, on the violation of the social compact, each regains his original rights and resumes his natural liberty, while losing the conventional liberty in favour of which he renounced it.

These clauses, properly understood, may be reduced to one—the total alienation of each associate, together with all his rights, to the whole community; for, in the first place, as each gives himself absolutely, the conditions are the same for all; and, this being so, no one has any interest in making them burdensome to others.

Moreover, the alienation being without reserve, the union is as perfect as it can be, and no associate has anything more to demand: for, if the individuals retained certain rights, as there would be no common superior to decide between them and the public, each, being on one point his own judge, would ask to be so on all; the state of Nature would thus continue, and the association would necessarily become inoperative or tyrannical.

Finally, each man, in giving himself to all, gives himself to nobody; and as there is no associate over which he does not acquire the same right as he yields others over himself, he gains an equivalent for everything he loses, and an increase of force for the preservation of what he has.

If then we discard from the social compact what is not of its essence, we shall find that it reduces itself to the following terms:

"Each of us puts his person and all his power in common under the supreme direction of the general will, and, in our corporate capacity, we receive each member as an indivisible part of the whole."

At once, in place of the individual personality of each contracting party, this act of association creates a moral and collective body, composed of as many members as the assembly contains voters, and receiving from this act its unity, its common identity, its life, and its will. This public person, so formed by the union of all other persons, formerly took the name of *city,* and now takes that of *Republic* or *body politic;* it is called by its members *State* when passive, *Sovereign* when active, and *Power* when compared with others like itself. Those who are associated in it take collectively the name of *people,* and severally are called citizens, as sharing in the sovereign power, and *subjects,* as being under the laws of the State. But these terms are often confused and taken one for another: it is enough to know how to distinguish them when they are being used with precision.

THE SOVEREIGN

This formula shows us that the act of association comprises a mutual undertaking between the public and the individuals, and that each individual, in making a contract, as we may say, with himself, is bound in a double capacity; as a member of the Sovereign he is bound to the individuals, and as a member of the State to the Sovereign. But the maxim of civil right, that no one is bound by undertakings made to himself, does not apply in this case; for there is a great difference between incurring an obligation to yourself and incurring one to a whole of which you form a part.

Attention must further be called to the fact that public deliberation, while competent to bind all the subjects to the Sovereign, because of the two different capacities in which each of them may be regarded, cannot, for the opposite reason, bind the Sovereign to itself; and that it is consequently against the nature of the body politic for the Sovereign to impose on itself a law which it cannot infringe. Being able to regard itself in only one capacity, it is in the position of an individual who makes a contract with himself; and this makes it clear that there neither is nor can be any kind of fundamental law binding on the body of the people—not even the social contract itself. This does not mean that the body politic cannot enter into undertakings with others, provided the contract is not infringed by them; for in relation to what is external to it, it becomes a simple being, an individual.

But the body politic or the Sovereign, drawing its being wholly from the sanctity of the contract, can never bind itself, even to an outsider, to do anything derogatory to the original act, for instance, to alienate any part of itself, or to submit to another Sovereign. Violation of the act by which it exists would be self-annihilation; and that which is itself nothing can create nothing.

As soon as this multitude is so united in one body, it is impossible to offend against one of the members without attacking the body, and still more to offend against the body without the members resenting it. Duty and interest therefore equally oblige the two contracting parties to give each other help; and the same men should seek to combine, in their double capacity, all the advantages dependent upon that capacity.

Again, the Sovereign, being formed wholly of the individuals who compose it, neither has nor can have any interest contrary to theirs; and consequently the sovereign power need give no guarantee to its subjects, because it is impossible for the body to wish to hurt all its members. We shall also see later on that it cannot hurt any in particular. The Sovereign, merely by virtue of what it is, is always what it should be.

This, however, is not the case with the relation of the subjects to the Sovereign, which, despite the common interest, would have no security that they would fulfil their undertakings, unless it found means to assure itself of their fidelity.

In fact, each individual, as a man, may have a particular will contrary or dissimilar to the general will which he has as a citizen. His particular interest may speak to him quite differently from the common interest: his absolute and naturally independent existence may make him look upon what he owes to the common cause as a gratuitous contribution, the loss of which will do less harm to others than the payment of it is burdensome to himself; and, regarding the moral person which constitutes the State as a *persona ficta,* because not a man, he may wish to enjoy the rights of citizenship without being ready to fulfil the duties of a subject. The continuance of such an injustice could not but prove the undoing of the body politic.

In order then that the social compact may not be an empty formula, it tacitly includes the undertaking, which alone can give force to the rest, that whoever refuses to obey the general will shall be compelled to do so by the whole body. This means nothing less than that he will be forced to be free; for this is the condition which, by giving each citizen to his country, secures him against all personal dependence. In this lies the key to the working of the political machine; this alone legitimizes civil undertakings which, without it, would be absurd, tyrannical, and liable to the most frightful abuses.

THE CIVIL STATE

The passage from the state of nature to the civil state produces a very remarkable change in man, by substituting justice for instinct in his conduct, and giving his actions the morality they had formerly lacked. Then only, when the voice of duty takes the place of physical impulses and right of appetite, does man, who so far had considered only himself, find that he is forced to act on different principles, and to consult his reason before listening to his inclinations. Although, in this state, he deprives himself of some advantages which he got from Nature, he gains in return others so great, his faculties are so stimulated and developed, his ideas so extended, his feelings so ennobled, and his whole soul so uplifted, that, did not the abuses of this new condition often degrade him below that which he left, he would be bound to bless continually the happy moment which took him from it for ever, and, instead of a stupid and unimaginative animal, made him an intelligent being and a man.

Let us draw up the whole account in terms easily commensurable. What man loses by the social contract is his natural liberty and an unlimited right to everything he tries to get and succeeds in getting; what he gains is civil liberty and the proprietorship of all he possesses. If we are to avoid mistake in weighing one against the other, we must clearly distinguish natural liberty, which is bounded only by the strength of the individual, from civil liberty, which is limited by general will; and possession, which is merely the effect of force or the right of the first occupier, from property, which can be founded only on a positive title.

We might, over and above all this, add, to what man acquires in the civil state, moral liberty, which alone makes him truly master of himself; for the mere impulse of appetite is slavery, while obedience to a law which we prescribe to ourselves is liberty. But I have already said too much on this head, and the philosophical meaning of the word liberty does not now concern us. . . .

THAT THE SOVEREIGNTY IS INALIENABLE

The first and most important deduction from the principles we have so far laid down is that the general will alone can direct the State according to the object for which it was instituted, i.e. the common good: for if the clashing of particular interests made the establishment of societies necessary, the agreement of these very interests made it possible. The common element in these different interests is what forms the social tie; and, were there no point of agreement between them all, no society could exist. It is solely on the basis of this common interest that every society should be governed.

I hold then that Sovereignty, being nothing less than the exercise of the general will, can never be alienated, and that the Sovereign, who is no less than a collective being, cannot be represented except by himself: the power indeed may be transmitted, but not the will.

In reality, if it is not impossible for a particular will to agree on some point with the general will, it is at least impossible for the agreement to be lasting and constant; for the particular will tends, by its very nature, to partiality, while the general will tends to equality. It is even more impossible to have any guarantee of this agreement; for even if it should always exist, it would be the effect not of art, but of chance. The Sovereign may indeed say: "I now will actually what this man wills, or at least what he says he wills"; but it cannot say: "What he wills to-morrow, I too shall will" because it is absurd for the will to bind itself for the future, nor is it incumbent on any will to consent to anything that is not for the good of the being who wills. If then the people promises simply to obey, by that very act it dissolves itself and loses what makes it a people; the moment a master exists, there is no longer a Sovereign, and from that moment the body politic has ceased to exist.

This does not mean that the commands of the rulers cannot pass for general wills, so long as the Sovereign, being free to oppose them, offers no opposition. In such a case, universal silence is taken to imply the consent of the people. This will be explained later on.

THAT SOVEREIGNTY IS INDIVISIBLE

Sovereignty, for the same reason as makes it inalienable, is indivisible; for will either is, or is not, general; it is the will either of the body of the people, or only of a part of it. In the first case, the will, when declared, is an act of Sovereignty and constitutes law: in the second, it is merely a particular will, or act of magistracy—at the most a decree.

But our political theorists, unable to divide Sovereignty in principle, divide it according to its object: into force and will; into legislative power and executive power; into rights of taxation, justice, and war; into internal administration and power of foreign treaty. Sometimes they confuse all these sections, and sometimes they distinguish them; they turn the Sovereign into a fantastic being composed of several connected pieces: it is as if they were making man of several bodies, one with eyes, one with arms, another with feet, and each with nothing besides. We are told that the jugglers of Japan dismember a child before the eyes of the spectators; then they throw all the members into the air one after another, and the child falls down alive and whole. The conjuring tricks of our political theorists are very like that; they first dismember the body politic by an illusion worthy of a fair, and then join it together again we know not how.

This error is due to a lack of exact notions concerning the Sovereign authority, and to taking for part of it what are only emanations from it. Thus, for example, the acts of declaring war and making peace have been regarded as acts of Sovereignty; but this is not the case, as these acts do not constitute law, but merely the application of a law, a particular act which decides how the law applies, as we shall see clearly when the idea attached to the word "law" has been defined.

If we examined the other divisions in the same manner, we should find that, whenever Sovereignty seems to be divided, there is an illusion: the rights which are taken as being part of Sovereignty are really all subordinate, and always imply supreme wills of which they only sanction the execution.

It would be impossible to estimate the obscurity this lack of exactness has thrown over the decisions of writers who have dealt with political right, when they have used the principles laid down by them to pass judgment on the respective rights of kings and peoples. Every one can see, in Chapters III and IV of the first book of Grotius, how the learned man and his translator, Barbeyrac, entangle and tie themselves up in their own sophistries, for fear of saying too little or too much of what they think, and so offending the interests they have to conciliate. Grotius, a refugee in France, ill content with his own country, and desirous of paying his court to Louis XIII, to whom his book is dedicated, spares no pains to rob the peoples of all their rights and invest kings with them by every conceivable artifice. This would also have been much to the taste of Barbeyrac, who dedicated his translation to George I of England. But unfortunately the expulsion of James II, which he called his "abdication," compelled him to use all reserve, to shuffle and to tergiversate, in order to avoid making William out a usurper. If these two writers had adopted the true principles, all difficulties would have been removed, and they would have been always consistent; but it would have been a sad truth for them to tell, and would have paid court for them to no one save the people. Moreover, truth is no road to fortune, and the people dispenses neither ambassadorships, nor professorships, nor pensions.

WHETHER THE GENERAL WILL IS FALLIBLE

It follows from what has gone before that the general will is always right and tends to the public advantage; but it does not follow that the deliberations of the people are always equally correct. Our will is always for our own good, but we do not always see what that is; the people is never corrupted, but it is often deceived, and on such occasions only does it seem to will what is bad.

There is often a great deal of difference between the will of all and the general will; the latter considers only the common interest, while the former takes private interest into account, and is no more than a sum of particular wills: but take away from these same wills the pluses and minuses that cancel one another, and the general will remains as the sum of the differences.

If, when the people, being furnished with adequate information, held its deliberations, the citizens had no communication one with another, the grand total of the small differences would always give the general will, and the decision would always be good. But when factions arise, and partial associations are formed at the expense of the great association, the will of each of these associations becomes general in relation to its members, while it remains particular in relation to the State: it may then be said that there are no longer as many votes as there are men, but only as many as there are associations. The differences become less numerous and give a less general result. Lastly, when one of these associations is so great as to prevail over all the rest, the result is no longer a sum of small differences, but a single difference; in this case there is no longer a general will, and the opinion which prevails is purely particular.

It is therefore essential, if the general will is to be able to express itself, that there should be no partial society within the State, and that each citizen should think only his own thoughts: which was indeed the sublime and unique system established by the great Lycurgus. But if there are partial societies it is best to have as many as possible and to prevent them from being unequal, as was done by Solon, Numa, and Servius. These precautions are the only ones that can guarantee that the general will shall be always enlightened and that the people shall in no way deceive itself. . . .

LAW

. . . I therefore give the name "Republic" to every State that is governed by Laws, no matter what the form of its administration may be: for only in such a case does the public interest govern, and the *res publica* rank as a *reality*. Every legitimate government is republican; what government is I will explain later on.

Laws are, properly speaking, only the conditions of civil association. The people, being subject to the Laws, ought to be their author: the conditions of the society ought to be regulated solely by those who come together to form it. But how are they to regulate them? Is it to be by common agreement, by a sudden inspiration? Has the body politic and organ to declare its will? Who can give it the foresight to formulate and announce its acts in advance? Or how is it to announce them in the hour of need? How can a blind multitude, which often does not know what it wills, because it rarely knows what is good for it, carry out for itself so great and difficult an enterprise as a system of legislation? Of itself the people wills always the good, but of itself it by no means always sees it. The general will is always in the right, but the judgment which guides it is not always enlightened. It must be got to see objects as they are, and sometimes as they ought to appear to it; it must be shown the good road it is in search of, secured from the seductive influences of individual wills, taught to see times and spaces as a series, and made to weigh the attractions of present and sensible advantages against the danger of distant and hidden evils. The individuals see the good they reject; the public wills the good it does not see. All stand equally in need of guidance. The former must be compelled to bring their wills into conformity with their reason; the latter must be taught to know what it wills. If that is done, public enlightenment leads to the union of understanding and will in the social body: the parts are made to work exactly together, and the whole is raised to its highest power. This makes a legislator necessary.

THE LEGISLATOR

In order to discover the rules of society best suited to nations, a superior intelligence beholding all the passions of men without experiencing any of them would be needed. This intelligence would have to be wholly unrelated to our nature, while knowing it through and through; its happiness would have to be independent of us, and yet ready to occupy itself with ours; and lastly, it would have, in the march of time, to look forward to a distant glory, and, working in one century, be able to enjoy in the next. It would take gods to give men laws.

What Caligula argued from the facts, Plato, in the dialogue called the *Politicus,* argued in defining the civil or kingly man, on the basis of right. But if great princes are rare, how much more so are great legislators! The former have only to follow the pattern which the latter have to lay down. The legislator is the engineer who invents the machine, the prince merely the mechanic who sets it up and makes it go. "At the birth of societies," says Montesquieu, "the rulers of Republics establish institutions, and afterwards the institutions mould the rulers."

He who dares to undertake the making of a people's institutions ought to feel himself capable, so to speak, of changing human nature, of transforming each individual, who is by himself a complete and solitary whole, into part of a greater whole from which he in a manner receives his life and being; of altering man's constitution for the purpose of strengthening it; and of substituting a partial and moral existence for the physical and independent existence nature has conferred on us all. He must, in a word, take away from man his own resources and give him instead new ones alien to him, and incapable of being made use of without the help of other men. The more completely these natural resources are annihilated, the greater and the more lasting are those which he acquires, and the more stable and perfect the new institutions; so that if each citizen is nothing and can do nothing without the rest, and the resources acquired by the whole are equal or superior to the aggregate of the resources of all the individuals, it may be said that legislation is at the highest possible point of perfection.

The legislator occupies in every respect an extraordinary position in the State. If he should do so by reason of his genius, he does so no less by reason of his office, which is neither magistracy, nor Sovereignty. This office, which sets up the Republic, nowhere enters into its constitution; it is an individual and superior function, which has nothing in common with human empire; for if he who holds command over men ought not to have command over the laws, he who has command over the laws ought not any more to have it over men; or else his laws would be the ministers of his passions and would often merely serve to perpetuate his injustices: his private aims would inevitably mar the sanctity of his work.

When Lycurgus gave laws to his country, he began by resigning the throne. It was the custom of most Greek towns to entrust the establishment of their laws to foreigners. The Republics of modern Italy in many cases followed this example; Geneva did the same and profited by it. Rome, when it was most prosperous, suffered a revival of all the crimes of tyranny, and was brought to the verge of destruction, because it put the legislative authority and the sovereign power into the same hands.

Nevertheless, the decemvirs themselves never claimed the right to pass any law merely on their own authority. "Nothing we propose to you," they said to the people, "can pass into law without your consent. Romans, be yourselves the authors of the laws which are to make you happy."

He, therefore, who draws up the laws has, or should have, no right of legislation, and the people cannot, even if it wishes, deprive itself of this incommunicable right, because, according to the fundamental compact, only the general will can bind the individuals, and there can be no assurance that a particular will is in conformity with the general will, until it has been put to the free vote of the people. This I have said already; but it is worth while to repeat it.

Thus in the task of legislation we find together two things which appear to be incompatible: an enterprise too difficult for human powers, and, for its execution, an authority that is no authority.

There is a further difficulty that deserves attention. Wise men, if they try to speak their language to the common herd instead of its own, cannot possibly make themselves understood. There are a thousand kinds of ideas which it is impossible to translate into popular language. Conceptions that are too general and objects that are too remote are equally out of its range: each individual, having no taste for any other plan of government than that which suits his particular interest, finds it difficult to realize the advantages he might hope to draw from the continual privations good laws impose. For a young people to be able to relish sound principles of political theory and follow the fundamental rules of statecraft, the effect would have to become the cause; the social spirit, which should be created by these institutions, would have to preside over their very foundation; and men would have to be before law what they should become by means of law. The legislator therefore, being unable to appeal to either force or reason, must have recourse to an authority of a different order, capable of constraining without violence and persuading without convincing.

This is what has, in all ages, compelled the fathers of nations to have recourse to divine intervention and credit the gods with their own wisdom, in order that the peoples, submitting to the laws of the State as to those of nature, and recognizing the same power in the formation of the city as in that of man, might obey freely, and bear with docility the yoke of the public happiness.

This sublime reason, far above the range of the common herd, is that whose decisions the legislator puts into the mouth of the immortals, in order to constrain by divine authority those whom human prudence could not move. But it is not anybody who can make the gods speak, or get himself believed when he proclaims himself their interpreter. The great soul of the legislator is the only miracle that can prove his mission. Any man may grave tablets of stone, or buy an oracle, or feign secret intercourse with some divinity, or train a bird to whisper in his ear, or find other vulgar ways of imposing on the people. He whose knowledge goes no further may perhaps gather round him a band of fools; but he will never found an empire, and his extravagances will quickly perish with him. Idle tricks form a passing tie; only wisdom can make it lasting. The Judaic law, which still subsists, and that of the child of Ishmael, which, for ten centuries, has ruled half the world, still proclaim the great men who laid them down; and, while the pride of philosophy or the blind spirit of faction sees in them no more than lucky impostures, the true political theorist admires, in the institutions they set up, the great and powerful genius which presides over things made to endure.

We should not, with Warburton, conclude from this that politics and religion have among us a common object, but that, in the first periods of nations, the one is used as a instrument for the other....

THE PEOPLE

... What people, then, is a fit subject for legislation? One which, already bound by some unity of origin, interest, or convention has never yet felt the real yoke of law; one that has neither customs nor superstitions deeply ingrained; one which stands in no fear of being overwhelmed by sudden invasion; one which, without entering into its neighbour's quarrels, can resist each of them single-handed, or get the help of one to repel another; one in which every member may be known by every other, and there is no need to lay on any man burdens too heavy for a man to bear; one which can do without other peoples, and without which all others can do, one which is neither rich nor poor, but self-sufficient; and, lastly, one which unites the consistency of an ancient people with the docility of a new one. Legislation is made difficult less by what it is necessary to build up than by what has to be destroyed; and what makes success so rare is the impossibility of finding natural simplicity together with social requirements. All these conditions are indeed rarely found united, and therefore few States have good constitutions.

There is still in Europe one country capable of being given laws—Corsica. The valour and persistence with which that brave people has regained and defended its liberty well deserves that some wise man should teach it how to preserve what it has won. I have a feeling that some day that little island will astonish Europe. ...

DEPUTIES OR REPRESENTATIVES

As soon as public service ceases to be the chief business of the citizens, and they would rather serve with their money than with their persons, the State is not far from its fall. When it is necessary to march out to war, they pay troops and stay at home: when it is necessary to meet in council, they name deputies and stay at home. By reason of idleness and money, they end by having soldiers to enslave their country and representatives to sell it.

It is through the hustle of commerce and the arts, through the greedy self-interest of profit, and through softness and love of amenities that personal services are replaced by money payments. Men surrender a part of their profits in order to have time to increase them at leisure. Make gifts of money, and you will not be long without chains. The word "finance" is a slavish word, unknown in the city-state. In a country that is truly free, the citizens do everything with their own arms and nothing by means of money; so far from paying to be exempted from their duties, they would even pay for the privilege of fulfilling them themselves. I am far from taking the common view: I hold enforced labour to be less opposed to liberty than taxes.

The better the constitution of a State is, the more do public affairs encroach on private in the minds of the citizens. Private affairs are even of much less importance, because the aggregate of the common happiness furnishes a greater proportion of that of each individual, so that there is less for him to seek in particular cares. In a well-ordered city every man flies to the assemblies: under a bad government no one cares to stir a step to get to them, because no one is interested in what happens there, because it is foreseen that the general will will not prevail, and lastly because domestic cares are all-absorbing. Good laws lead to the making of better ones; bad ones bring about worse. As soon as any man says of the affairs of the State *What does it matter to me?* the State may be given up for lost.

The lukewarmness of patriotism, the activity of private interest, the vastness of States, conquest, and the abuse of government suggested the method of having deputies or representatives of the people in the national assemblies. These are what, in some countries, men have presumed to call the Third Estate. Thus the individual interest of two orders is put first and second; the public interest occupies only the third place.

Sovereignty, for the same reason as makes it inalienable, cannot be represented; it lies essentially in the general will, and will does not admit of representation: it is either the same, or other; there is no intermediate possibility. The deputies of the people, therefore, are not and cannot be its representatives; they are merely its stewards, and can carry through no definitive acts. Every law the people has not ratified in person is null and void—is, in fact, not a law. The people of England regards itself as free; but it is grossly mistaken; it is free only during the election of members of parliament. As soon as they are elected, slavery overtakes it, and it is nothing. The use it makes of the short moments of liberty it enjoys shows indeed that it deserves to lose them.

The idea of representation is modern; it comes to us from feudal government, from that iniquitous and absurd system which degrades humanity and dishonours the name of man. In ancient republics and even in monarchies, the people never had representatives; the word itself was unknown. It is very singular that in Rome, where the tribunes were so sacrosanct, it was never even imagined that they could usurp the functions of the people, and that in the midst of so great a multitude they never attempted to pass on their own authority a single *plebiscitum*. We can, however, form an idea of the difficulties caused sometimes by the people being so numerous, from what happened in the time of the Gracchi, when some of the citizens had to cast their votes from the roofs of buildings.

Where right and liberty are everything, disadvantages count for nothing. Among this wise people everything was given its just value, its lictors were allowed to do what its tribunes would never have dared to attempt; for it had no fear that its lictors would try to represent it.

To explain, however, in what way the tribunes did sometimes represent it, it is enough to conceive how the government represents the Sovereign. Law being purely the declaration of the general will, it is clear that, in the exercise of the legislative power, the people cannot be represented; but in that of the executive power, which is only the force that is applied to give the law effect, it both can and should be represented. We thus see that if we looked closely into the matter we should find that very few nations have any laws. However that may be, it is certain that the tribunes, possessing no executive power, could never represent the Roman people by right of the powers entrusted to them, but only by usurping those of the senate.

In Greece, all that the people had to do, it did for itself; it was constantly assembled in the public square. The Greeks lived in a mild climate; they had no natural greed; slaves did their work for them; their great concern was with liberty. Lacking the same advantages, how can you preserve the same rights? Your severer climates add to your needs; for half the year your public squares are uninhabitable; the flatness of your languages unfits them for being heard in the open air; you sacrifice more for profit than for liberty, and fear slavery less than poverty.

What then? Is liberty maintained only by the help of slavery? It may be so. Extremes meet. Everything that is not in the course of nature has its disadvantages, civil society most of all. There are some unhappy circumstances in which we can only keep our liberty at others' expense, and where the citizen can be perfectly free only when the slave is most a slave. Such was the case with Sparta. As for you, modern peoples, you have no slaves, but you are slaves yourselves;

you pay for their liberty with your own. It is in vain that you boast of this preference; I find in it more cowardice than humanity.

I do not mean by all this that it is necessary to have slaves, or that the right of slavery is legitimate: I am merely giving the reasons why modern peoples, believing themselves to be free, have representatives, while ancient peoples had none. In any case, the moment a people allows itself to be represented, it is no longer free: it no longer exists.

All things considered, I do not see that it is possible henceforth for the Sovereign to preserve among us the exercise of its rights, unless the city is very small. But if it is very small, it will be conquered? No. I will show later on how the external strength of a great people may be combined with the convenient polity and good order of a small State. . . .

THAT THE GENERAL WILL IS INDESTRUCTIBLE

As long as several men in assembly regard themselves as a single body, they have only a single will which is concerned with their common preservation and general well-being. In this case, all the springs of the State are vigorous and simple and its rules clear and luminous; there are no embroilments or conflicts of interests; the common good is everywhere clearly apparent, and only good sense is needed to perceive it. Peace, unity, and equality are the enemies of political subtleties. Men who are upright and simple are difficult to deceive because of their simplicity, lures and ingenious pretexts fail to impose upon them, and they are not even subtle enough to be dupes. When, among the happiest people in the world, bands of peasants are seen regulating affairs of State under an oak, and always acting wisely, can we help scorning the ingenious methods of other nations, which make themselves illustrious and wretched with so much art and mystery?

A State so governed needs very few laws; and, as it becomes necessary to issue new ones, the necessity is universally seen. The first man to propose them merely says what all have already felt, and there is no question of factions or intrigues or eloquence in order to secure the passage into law of what every one has already decided to do, as soon as he is sure that the rest will act with him.

Theorists are led into error because, seeing only States that have been from the beginning wrongly constituted, they are struck by the impossibility of applying such a policy to them. They make great game of all the absurdities a clever rascal or an insinuating speaker might get the people of Paris or London to believe. They do not know that Cromwell would have been put to "the bells" by the people of Berne, and the Duc de Beaufort on the treadmill by the Genevese.

But when the social bond begins to be relaxed and the State to grow weak, when particular interests begin to make themselves felt and the smaller societies to exercise an influence over the larger, the common interest changes and finds opponents: opinion is no longer unanimous; the general will ceases to be the will of all; contradictory views and debates arise; and the best advice is not taken without question.

Finally, when the State, on the eve of ruin, maintains only a vain, illusory, and formal existence, when in every heart the social bond is broken, and the meanest interest brazenly lays hold of the sacred name of "public good," the general will becomes mute: all men, guided by secret motives, no more give their views as citizens than if the State had never been; and iniquitous decrees directed solely to private interest get passed under the name of laws.

Does it follow from this that the general will is exterminated or corrupted? Not at all: it is always constant, unalterable, and pure; but it is subordinated to other wills which encroach upon its sphere. Each man, in detaching his interest from the common interest, sees clearly that he cannot entirely separate them; but his share in the public mishaps seems to him negligible beside the exclusive good he aims at making his own. Apart from this particular good, he wills the general good in his own interest, as strongly as any one else. Even in selling his vote for money, he does not extinguish in himself the general will, but only eludes it. The fault he commits is that of changing the state of the question, and answering something different from what he is asked. Instead of saying, by his vote, "It is to the advantage of the State," he says, "It is of advantage to this or that man or party that this or that view should prevail." Thus the law of public order in assemblies is not so much to maintain in them the general will as to secure that the question be always put to it, and the answer always given by it.

I could here set down many reflections on the simple right of voting in every act of Sovereignty—a right which no one can take from the citizens—and also on the right of stating views, making proposals, dividing and discussing, which the government is always most careful to leave solely to its members; but this important subject would need a treatise to itself, and it is impossible to say everything in a single work.

VOTING

It may be seen, from the last chapter, that the way in which general business is managed may give a clear enough indication of the actual state of morals and the health of the body politic. The more concert reigns in the assemblies, that is, the nearer opinion approaches unanimity, the greater is the dominance of the general will. On the other hand, long debates, dissensions, and tumult proclaim the ascendancy of particular interests and the decline of the State.

This seems less clear when two or more orders enter into the constitution, as patricians and plebeians did at Rome; for quarrels between these two orders often disturbed the comitia, even in the best days of the Republic. But the exception is rather apparent than real; for then, through the defect that is inherent in the body politic, there were, so to speak, two States in one, and what is not true of the two together is true of either separately. Indeed, even in the most stormy times, the *plebiscita* of the people, when the senate did not interfere with them, always went through quietly and by large majorities. The citizens having but one interest, the people had but a single will.

At the other extremity of the circle, unanimity recurs; this is the case when the citizens, having fallen into servitude, have lost both liberty and will. Fear and flattery then change votes into acclamation; deliberation ceases, and only worship or malediction is left. Such was the vile manner in which the senate expressed its views under the emperors. It did so sometimes with absurd precautions. Tacitus observes that, under Otho, the senators, while they heaped curses on Vitellius, contrived at the same time to make a deafening noise, in order that, should he ever become their master, he might not know what each of them had said.

On these various considerations depend the rules by which the methods of counting votes and comparing opinions should be regulated, according as the general will is more or less easy to discover, and the State more or less in its decline.

There is but one law which, from its nature, needs unanimous consent. This is the social compact; for civil association is the most voluntary of all acts. Every man being born free and his own master, no one, under any pretext whatsoever, can make any man subject without his consent. To decide that the son of a slave is born a slave is to decide that he is not born a man.

If then there are opponents when the social compact is made, their opposition does not invalidate the contract, but merely prevents them from being included in it. They are foreigners among citizens. When the State is instituted, residence constitutes consent; to dwell within its territory is to submit to the Sovereign.

Apart from this primitive contract, the vote of the majority always binds all the rest. This follows from the contract itself. But it is asked how a man can be both free and forced to conform to wills that are not his own. How are the opponents at once free and subject to laws they have not agreed to?

I retort that the question is wrongly put. The citizen gives his consent to all the laws, including those which are passed in spite of his opposition, and even those which punish him when he dares to break any of them. The constant will of all the members of the State is the general will; by virtue of it they are citizens and free. When in the popular assembly a law is proposed, what the people is asked is not exactly whether it approves or rejects the proposal, but whether it is in conformity with the general will, which is their will. Each man, in giving his vote, states his opinion on that point; and the general will is found by counting votes. When therefore the opinion that is contrary to my own prevails, this proves neither more nor less than that I was mistaken, and that what I thought to be the general will was not so. If my particular opinion had carried the day I should have achieved the opposite of what was my will; and it is in that case that I should not have been free.

This presupposes, indeed, that all the qualities of the general will still reside in the majority: when they cease to do so, whatever side a man may take, liberty is no longer possible.

In my earlier demonstration of how particular wills are substituted for the general will in public deliberation, I have adequately pointed out the practicable methods of avoiding this abuse; and I shall have more to say of them later on. I have also given the principles for determining the proportional number of votes for declaring that will. A difference of one vote destroys equality; a single opponent destroys unanimity; but between equality and unanimity, there are several grades of unequal division, at each of which this proportion may be fixed in accordance with the condition and the needs of the body politic.

There are two general rules that may serve to regulate this relation. First, the more grave and important the questions discussed, the nearer should the opinion that is to prevail approach unanimity.

Secondly, the more the matter in hand calls for speed, the smaller the prescribed difference in the numbers of votes may be allowed to become: where an instant decision has to be reached, a majority of one vote should be enough. The first of these two rules seems more in harmony with the laws, and the second with practical affairs. In any case, it is the combination of them that gives the best proportions for determining the majority necessary.

7

BURKE
The Authority of Tradition

The democratic principle of legitimacy stemming from the influence of Locke and Rousseau has been subject to vigorous challenge by the conservative political philosophy of Edmund Burke (1729–1797). The central premise of Burke's political philosophy is that political rule must be founded upon the authority of tradition rather than the rule of numbers or electoral decision. The British constitution, as Burke viewed it, is not a matter of momentary choice but the deliberate election of ages and generations, made of peculiar circumstances, dispositions and habits which declare themselves over a long period of time. It thus possesses an authority which derives from prescription: it is a constitution whose sole authority is that it has existed time out of mind. This prescription, Burke believed, creates a presumption in favor of any settled scheme, against any untried project or temporary arrangements by popular elections. Burke did not deny the necessity of reform, but this must be slow and gradual rather than violent and revolutionary. Burke distinguished between genuine reform and mere innovation, which is bound to be crude, harsh, undigested and imprudent. Wise statesmanship must combine a disposition to preserve with the ability to improve, avoiding extremes of tearing down blindly or resisting change at all cost.

The question of who should rule proceeds logically from Burke's emphasis upon the prescriptive character of tradition and convention—aristocracy and wealth, he believed, are repositories of vested wisdom and experience. It was for this reason that Burke opposed the extension of universal suffrage and favored the idea of "virtual representation": the view that it is the duty of a statesman not to act as a delegate of his constituents but to consider the general good on the basis of his own enlightened conscience and judgment. One of the most significant contributions of Burke's theory is his view of the qualities necessary for the task of wise statesmanship. Political judgment he contends, requires a prudential, or practical, wisdom, different in character from the generalized, abstract reasoning of the academician, capable of taking into account exceptions and modifications; the variable, transient aspects of circumstances. The wise statesman is thus able to recognize the difference between genuine reform and mere innovation; an ability which requires a vigorous mind, powers of combination and comparison; an understanding fruitful in expedience; the ability to reconcile, balance and compensate conflicting principles in the affairs of men.

Burke's political philosophy embodies a constructive criticism of liberal ideology and a keen insight into the problem of political rule and statesmanship. But his analysis is vulnerable to criticism on several points. Burke rightly emphasizes that wise statesmanship must be founded upon a prudent regard for the importance of tradition and the capacity to distinguish between genuine reform and revolutionary disruption. But he fails to tell us how moderate evolutionary reform can be fostered in the face of a political tyranny which does not allow for democratic, constitutional processes. Under these circumstances, if revolutionary action must be condemned, then Burke's philosohy becomes a convenient ideology for defense of an unjust status quo. The second difficulty is the lack of any convincing evidence that political wisdom and wise statesmanship are most likely to be found among members of an aristocracy or the owners of property; he does not provide any convincing evidence that the members of these classes are more dedicated to the general good or less disposed than others to promote the selfish interests of their class. Burke fails to recognize the democratic assumption that legitimate political rule is possible only in a system where no particular class or interest is allowed to assume dominant power and where political leadership must be accountable to the citizen body through the exercise of universal suffrage.

THE BRITISH CONSTITUTION*

... If you are desirous of knowing the spirit of our constitution, and the policy which predominated in that great period which has secured it to this hour, pray look for both in our histories, in our records, in our acts of parliament, and journals of parliament, and not in the sermons of the Old Jewry, and the after-dinner toasts of the Revolution Society. In the former you will find other ideas and another language. Such a claim is as ill-suited to our temper and wishes as it is unsupported by any appearance of authority. The very idea of the fabrication of a new government is enough to fill us with

* From "The Revolution in France" (1970), *The Works of Edmund Burke,* Vol. 2 (London: Henry Bohn), pp. 304–8.

disgust and horror. We wished at the period of the Revolution, and do now wish, to derive all we possess as *an inheritance from our fore-fathers.* Upon that body and stock of inheritance we have taken care not to inoculate any scion alien to the nature of the original plant. All the reformations we have hitherto made have proceeded upon the principle of reverence to antiquity; and I hope, nay I am persuaded, that all those which possibly may be made hereafter, will be carefully formed upon analogical precedent, authority, and example.

Our oldest reformation is that of Magna Charta. You will see that Sir Edward Coke, that great oracle of our law, and indeed all the great men who follow him, to Blackstone, are industrious to prove the pedigree of our liberties. They endeavour to prove, that the ancient charter, the Magna Charta of King John, was connected with another positive charter from Henry I., and that both the one and the other were nothing more than a reaffirmance of the still more ancient standing law of the kingdom. In the matter of fact, for the greater part, these authors appear to be in the right; perhaps not always; but if the lawyers mistake in some particulars, it proves my position still the more strongly; because it demonstrates the powerful prepossession towards antiquity, with which the minds of all our lawyers and legis-lators, and of all the people whom they wish to influence, have been always filled; and the stationary policy of this kingdom in considering their most sacred rights and franchises as an *inheritance.*

In the famous law of the 3rd of Charles I., called the *Petition of Right,* the parliament says to the king, "Your subjects have *inherited* this freedom," claiming their franchises not on abstract principles "as the rights of men," but as the rights of Englishmen, and as a patri-mony derived from their forefathers. Selden, and the other profoundly learned men, who drew this Petition of Right, were as well acquainted, at least, with all the general theories concerning the "rights of men," as any of the discoursers in our pulpits, or on your tribune; full as well as Dr. Price, or as the Abbe Sieyes. But, for reasons worthy of that practical wisdom which superseded their theoretic science, they preferred this positive, recorded, *hereditary* title to all which can be dear to the man and the citizen, to that vague speculative right, which exposed their sure inheritance to be scrambled for and torn to pieces by every wild, litigious spirit.

The same policy pervades all the laws which have since been made for the preservation of our liberties. In the 1st of William and Mary, in the famous statute, called the Declaration of Right, the two Houses

utter not a syllable of "a right to frame a government for themselves."
You will see, that their whole care was to secure the religion, laws,
and liberties, that had been long possessed, and had been lately endangered. "Taking into their most serious consideration the *best*
means for making such an establishment, that their religion, laws, and
liberties might not be in danger of being again subverted," they
auspicate all their proceedings, by stating as some of those *best* means,
"in the *first place*" to do "as their *ancestors in like cases have usually*
done for vindicating their *ancient* rights and liberties, to *declare*"—
and then they pray the king and queen, "that it may be *declared* and
enacted, that *all and singular* the rights and liberties *asserted and
declared,* are the true *ancient* and indubitable rights and liberties of
the people of this kingdom."

You will observe, that from Magna Charta to the Declaration of
Right, it has been the uniform policy of our constitution to claim and
assert our liberties, as an *entailed inheritance* derived to us from our
forefathers, and to be transmitted to our posterity; as an estate
specially belonging to the people of this kingdom, without any reference whatever to any other more general or prior right. By this means
our constitution preserves a unity in so great a diversity of its parts.
We have an inheritable crown; an inheritable peerage; and a House
of Commons and a people inheriting privileges, franchises, and liberties, from a long line of ancestors.

This policy appears to me to be the result of profound reflection;
or rather the happy effect of following nature, which is wisdom without reflection, and above it. A spirit of innovation is generally the
result of a selfish temper, and confined views. People will not look
forward to posterity, who never look backward to their ancestors.
Besides, the people of England well know, that the idea of inheritance
furnishes a sure principle of conservation, and a sure principle of
transmission; without at all excluding a principle of improvement. It
leaves acquisition free; but it secures what it acquires. Whatever
advantages are obtained by a state proceeding on these maxims, are
locked fast as in a sort of family settlement; grasped as in a kind of
mortmain for ever. By a constitutional policy, working after the pattern of nature, we receive, we hold, we transmit our government and
our privileges, in the same manner in which we enjoy and transmit
our property and our lives. The institutions of policy, the goods of
fortune, the gifts of providence, are handed down to us, and from us,
in the same course and order. Our political system is placed in a just

correspondence and symmetry with the order of the world, and with
the mode of existence decreed to a permanent body composed of
transistory parts; wherein, by the disposition of a stupendous wisdom,
moulding together the great mysterious incorporation of the human
race, the whole, at one time, is never old, or middle-aged, or young,
but, in a condition of unchangeable constancy, moves on through the
varied tenor of perpetual decay, fall, renovation, and progression.
Thus, by preserving the method of nature in the conduct of the state,
in what we improve, we are never wholly new; in what we retain we
are never wholly obsolete. By adhering in this manner and on those
principles to our forefathers, we are guided not by the superstition of
antiquarians, but by the spirit of philosophic analogy. In this choice
of inheritance we have given to our frame of polity the image of a
relation in blood; binding up the constitution of our country with our
dearest domestic ties; adopting our fundamental laws into the bosom
of our family affections; keeping inseparable, and cherishing with the
warmth of all their combined and mutually reflected charities, our
state, our hearths, our sepulchres, and our altars.

Through the same plan of a conformity to nature in our artificial
institutions, and by calling in the aid of her unerring and powerful
instincts, to fortify the fallible and feeble contrivances of our reason,
we have derived several other, and those no small benefits, from considering our liberties in the light of an inheritance. Always acting as if
in the presence of canonized forefathers, the spirit of freedom, leading
in itself to misrule and excess, is tempered with an awful gravity. This
idea of a liberal descent inspires us with a sense of habitual native
dignity, which prevents that upstart insolence almost inevitably
adhering to and disgracing those who are the first acquirers of any
distinction. By this means our liberty becomes a noble freedom. It
carries an imposing and majestic aspect. It has a pedigree and illus-
trating ancestors. It has its bearings and its ensigns armorial. It has
its gallery of portraits; its monumental inscriptions; its records, evidences, and titles. We procure reverence to our civil institutions on
the principle upon which nature teaches us to revere individual men;
on account of their age, and on account of those from whom they are
descended. All your sophisters cannot produce anything better
adapted to preserve a rational and manly freedom than the course

that we have pursued, who have chosen our nature rather than our speculations, our breasts rather than our inventions, for the great conservatories and magazines of our rights and privileges. . . .

THE AUTHORITY OF PRESCRIPTION*

. . . Our constitution is a prescriptive constitution; it is a constitution whose sole authority is that it has existed time out of mind. It is settled in these *two* portions against one, legislatively; and in the whole of the judicature, the whole of the federal capacity, of the executive, the prudential, and the financial administration, in one alone. Nor was your House of Lords and the prerogatives of the Crown settled on any adjudication in favour of natural rights, for they could never be so partitioned. Your king, your lords, your judges, your juries, grand and little, are all prescriptive; and what proves it is the disputes not yet concluded, and never near becoming so, when any of them first originated. Prescription is the most solid of all titles, not only to property, but, which is to secure that property, to government. They harmonize with each other, and give mutual aid to one another. It is accompanied with another ground of authority in the constitution of the human mind,—presumption. It is a presumption in favour of any settled scheme of government against any untried project, that a nation has long existed and flourished under it. It is a better presumption even of the *choice* of a nation, far better than any sudden and temporary arrangement by actual election. Because a nation is not an idea only of local extent, and individual momentary aggregation; but it is an idea of continuity, which extends in time as well as in numbers and in space. And this is a choice not of one day, or one set of people, not a tumultuary and giddy choice; it is a deliberate election of ages and of generations; it is a constitution made by what is ten thousand times better than choice, it is made by the peculiar circumstances, occasions, tempers, dispositions, and moral, civil, and social habitudes of the people, which disclose themselves only in a long space of time. It is a vestment, which accommodates itself to the body. Nor is prescription of government formed upon blind unmeaning prejudices —for man is a most unwise and a most wise being. The individual is foolish, when they act without deliberation; but the species is wise, and, when time is given to it, as a species it always acts right. . . .

* From "On the Reform of Representation in the House of Commons" (1782), *Works*, Vol. 6, pp. 146–47.

THE FOUNDATIONS OF CIVIL SOCIETY*

Far am I from denying in theory, full as far is my heart from with-
holding in practice, (if I were of power to give or to withhold,) the
real rights of men. In denying their false claims of right, I do not
mean to injure those which are real, and are such as their pretended
rights would totally destroy. If civil society be made for the advantage
of man, all the advantages for which it is made become his right. It is
an institution of beneficence; and law itself is only beneficence acting
by a rule. Men have a right to live by that rule; they have a right to
do justice, as between their fellows, whether their fellows are in public
function or in ordinary occupation. They have a right to the fruits of
their industry and to the means of making their industry fruitful. They
have a right to the acquisitions of their parents; to the nourishment
and improvement of their offspring; to instruction in life, and to consolation in death. Whatever each man can separately do, without
trespassing upon others, he has a right to do for himself; and he has
a right to a fair portion of all which society, with all its combinations
of skill and force, can do in his favour. In this partnership all men
have equal rights; but not to equal things. He that has but five shil-
lings in the partnership, has as good a right to it, as he that has five
hundred pounds has to his larger proportion. But he has not a right
to an equal dividend in the product of the joint stock; and as to the
share of power, authority, and direction which each individual ought
to have in the management of the state, that I must deny to be amongst
the direct original rights of man in civil society; for I have in my contemplation the civil social man, and no other. It is a thing to be settled
by convention.

If civil society be the offspring of convention, that convention must
be its law. That convention must limit and modify all the descriptions
of constitution which are formed under it. Every sort of legislative,
judicial, or executory power are its creatures. They can have no being
in any other state of things; and how can any man claim under the
conventions of civil society, rights which do not so much as suppose
its existence? rights which are absolutely repugnant to it? One of the
first motives to civil society, and which becomes one of its fundamental rules, is, *that no man should be judge in his own cause.* By
this each person has at once divested himself of the first fundamental
right of uncovenanted man, that is, to judge for himself, and to assert

* From "The Revolution in France," *Works,* Vol. 2, pp. 331–35; 368–69.

his own cause. He abdicates all right to be his own governor. He inclusively, in a great measure, abandons the right of self-defence, the first law of nature. Men cannot enjoy the rights of an uncivil and of a civil state together. That he may obtain justice, he gives up his right of determining what it is in points the most essential to him. That he may secure some liberty, he makes a surrender in trust of the whole of it.

Government is not made in virtue of natural rights, which may and do exist in total independence of it; and exist in much greater clearness, and in a much greater degree of abstract perfection: but their abstract perfection is their practical defect. By having a right to everything they want everything. Government is a contrivance of human wisdom to provide for human *wants*. Men have a right that these wants should be provided for by this wisdom. Among these wants is to be reckoned the want, out of civil society, of a sufficient restraint upon their passions. Society requires not only that the passions of individuals should be subjected, but that even in the mass and body, as well as in the individuals, the inclinations of men should frequently be thwarted, their will controlled, and their passions brought into subjection. This can only be done *by a power out of themselves;* and not, in the exercise of its function, subject to that will and to those passions which it is its office to bridle and subdue. In this sense the restraints on men, as well as their liberties, are to be reckoned among their rights. But as the liberties and the restrictions vary with times and circumstances, and admit of infinite modifications, they cannot be settled upon any abstract rule; and nothing is so foolish as to discuss them upon that principle.

The moment you abate anything from the full rights of men, each to govern himself, and suffer any artificial, positive limitation upon those rights, from that moment the whole organization of government becomes a consideration of convenience. This it is which makes the constitution of a state, and the due distribution of its powers, a matter of the most delicate and complicated skill. It requires a deep knowledge of human nature and human necessities, and of the things which facilitate or obstruct the various ends, which are to be pursued by the mechanism of civil institutions. The state is to have recruits to its strength, and remedies to its distempers. What is the use of discussing a man's abstract right to food or medicine? The question is upon the method of procuring and administering them. In that deliberation I shall always advise to call in the aid of the farmer and the physician, rather than the professor of metaphysics.

The science of constructing a commonwealth, or renovating it, or reforming it, is, like every other experimental science, not to be taught *a priori*. Nor is it a short experience that can instruct us in that practical science; because the real effects of moral causes are not always immediate; but that which in the first instance is prejudicial may be excellent in its remoter operation; and its excellence may arise even from the ill effects it produces in the beginning. The reverse also happens: and very plausible schemes, with very pleasing commencements, have often shameful and lamentable conclusions. In states there are often some obscure and almost latent causes, things which appear at first view of little moment, on which a very great part of its prosperity or adversity may most essentially depend. The science of government being therefore so practical in itself, and intended for such practical purposes, a matter which requires experience, and even more experience than any person can gain in his whole life, however sagacious and observing he may be, it is with infinite caution that any man ought to venture upon pulling down an edifice, which has answered in any tolerable degree for ages the common purposes of society, or on building it up again, without having models and patterns of approved utility before his eyes.

These metaphysic rights entering into common life, like rays of light which pierce into a dense medium, are, by the laws of nature, refracted from their straight line. Indeed in the gross and complicated mass of human passions and concerns, the primitive rights of men undergo such a variety of refractions and reflections, that it becomes absurd to talk of them as if they continued in the simplicity of their original direction. The nature of man is intricate; the objects of society are of the greatest possible complexity: and therefore no simple disposition or direction of power can be suitable either to man's nature, or to the quality of his affairs. When I hear the simplicity of contrivance aimed at and boasted of in any new political constitutions, I am at no loss to decide that the artificers are grossly ignorant of their trade, or totally negligent of their duty. The simple governments are fundamentally defective, to say no worse of them. If you were to contemplate society in but one point of view, all these simple modes of polity are infinitely captivating. In effect each would answer its single end much more perfectly than the more complex is able to attain all its complex purposes. But it is better that the whole should be imperfectly and anomalously answered, than that, while some parts are provided for with great exactness, others might be totally neglected, or perhaps materially injured, by the over-care of a favourite member.

The pretended rights of these theorists are all extremes: and in proportion as they are metaphysically true, they are morally and politically false. The rights of men are in a sort of *middle,* incapable of definition, but not impossible to be discerned. The rights of men in governments are their advantages; and these are often in balances between differences of good; in compromises sometimes between good and evil, and sometimes between evil and evil. Political reason is a computing principle; adding, subtracting, multiplying, and dividing, morally and not metaphysically, or mathematically, true moral denominations.

By these theorists the right of the people is almost always sophistically confounded with their power. The body of the community, whenever it can come to act, can meet with no effectual resistance; but till power and right are the same, the whole body of them has no right inconsistent with virtue, and the first of all virtues, prudence. Men have no right to what is not reasonable, and to what is not for their benefit; for though a pleasant writer said, *Liceat perire poetis,* when one of them, in cold blood, is said to have leaped into the flames of a volcanic revolution, *Ardentem frigidus Aetnam insiluit,* I consider such a frolic rather as an unjustifiable poetic licence, than as one of the franchises of Parnassus; and whether he were poet, or divine, or politician, that chose to exercise this kind of right, I think that more wise, because more charitable, thoughts would urge me rather to save the man, than to preserve his brazen slippers as the monuments of his folly. . . .

Society is indeed a contract. Subordinate contracts for objects of mere occasional interest may be dissolved at pleasure—but the state ought not to be considered as nothing better than a partnership agreement in a trade of pepper and coffee, calico or tobacco, or some other such low concern, to be taken up for a little temporary interest, and to be dissolved by the fancy of the parties. It is to be looked on with other reverence; because it is not a partnership in things subservient only to the gross animal existence of a temporary and perishable nature. It is a partnership in all science; a partnership in all art; a partnership in every virtue, and in all perfection. As the ends of such a partnership cannot be obtained in many generations, it becomes a partnership not only between those who are living, but between those who are living, those who are dead, and those who are to be born.

Each contract of each particular state is but a clause in the great primaeval contract of eternal society, linking the lower with the higher natures, connecting the visible and invisible world, according to a fixed compact sanctioned by the inviolable oath which holds all physical and all moral natures, each in their appointed place. This law is not subject to the will of those, who by an obligation above them, and infinitely superior, are bound to submit their will to that law. The municipal corporations of that universal kingdom are not morally at liberty at their pleasure, and on their speculations of a contingent improvement, wholly to separate and tear asunder the bands of their subordinate community, and to dissolve it into an unsocial, uncivil, unconnected chaos of elementary principles. It is the first and supreme necessity only, a necessity that is not chosen, but chooses, a necessity paramount to deliberation, that admits no discussion, and demands no evidence, which alone can justify a resort to anarchy. This necessity is no exception to the rule; because this necessity itself is a part too of that moral and physical disposition of things, to which man must be obedient by consent or force: but if that which is only submission to necessity should be made the object of choice, the law is broken, nature is disobeyed, and the rebellious are outlawed, cast forth, and exiled, from this world of reason, and order, and peace, and virtue, and fruitful penitence, into the antagonist world of madness, discord, vice, confusion, and unavailing sorrow.

THE REPRESENTATION OF PROPERTY*

Nothing is a due and adequate representation of a state, that does not represent its ability as well as its property. But as ability is a vigorous and active principle, and as property is sluggish, inert, and timid, it never can be safe from the invasions of ability, unless it be, out of all proportion, predominant in the representation. It must be represented too in great masses of accumulation, or it is not rightly protected. The characteristic essence of property, formed out of the combined principles of its acquisition and conservation, is to be *unequal*. The great masses therefore which excite envy, and tempt rapacity, must be put out of the possibility of danger. Then they form a natural rampart about the lesser properties in all their gradations. The same quantity of property, which is by the natural course of

* From "The Revolution in France," *Works*, Vol. 2, pp. 324–26.

things divided among many, has not the same operation. Its defensive power is weakened as it is diffused. In this diffusion each man's portion is less than what, in the eagerness of his desires, he may flatter himself to obtain by dissipating the accumulations of others. The plunder of the few would indeed give but a share inconceivably small in the distribution to the many. But the many are not capable of making this calculation; and those who lead them to rapine never intend this distribution.

The power of perpetuating our property in our families is one of the most valuable and interesting circumstances belonging to it, and that which tends the most to the perpetuation of society itself. It makes our weakness subservient to our virtue; it grafts benevolence even upon avarice. The possessors of family wealth, and of the distinction which attends hereditary possession, (as most concerned in it,) are the natural securities for this transmission. With us the House of Peers is formed upon this principle. It is wholly composed of hereditary property and hereditary distinction; and made therefore the third of the legislature; and, in the last event, the sole judge of all property in all its subdivisions. The House of Commons too, though not necessarily, yet in fact, is always so composed, in the far greater part. Let those large proprietors be what they will, and they have their chance of being amongst the best, they are, at the very worst, the ballast in the vessel of the commonwealth. For though hereditary wealth, and the rank which goes with it, are too much idolized by creeping sycophants, and the blind, abject admirers of power, they are too rashly slighted in shallow speculations of the petulant, assuming, short-sighted coxcombs of philosophy. Some decent, regulated pre-eminence, some preference (not exclusive appropriation) given to birth, is neither unnatural, nor unjust, nor impolitic.

It is said, that twenty-four millions ought to prevail over two hundred thousand. True; if the constitution of a kingdom be a problem of arithmetic. This sort of discourse does well enough with the lamp-post for its second: to men who *may* reason calmly, it is ridiculous. The will of the many, and their interest, must very often differ; and great will be the difference when they make an evil choice. A government of five hundred country attornies and obscure curates is not good for twenty-four millions of men, though it were chosen by eight and forty millions; nor is it the better for being guided by a dozen of persons of quality, who have betrayed their trust in order to obtain that power. At present, you seem in everything to have strayed out of the high road of nature. The property of France does not govern it. Of course property is destroyed, and rational liberty has no existence. All you have got for the present is a paper circulation, and a stock-jobbing constitution: and, as to the future, do you seriously think that the territory of France, upon the republican system of eighty-three independent municipalities, (to say nothing of the parts that compose them,) can ever be governed as one body, or can ever be set in motion by the impulse of one mind? When the National Assembly has completed its work, it will have accomplished its ruin. These commonwealths will not long bear a state of subjection to the republic of Paris. They will not bear that this one body should monopolize the captivity of the king, and the dominion over the assembly calling itself national. Each will keep its own portion of the spoil of the church to itself; and it will not suffer either that spoil, or the more just fruits of their industry, or the natural produce of their soil, to be sent to swell the insolence, or pamper the luxury, of the mechanics of Paris. In this they will see none of the equality, under the pretence of which they have been tempted to throw off their allegiance to their sovereign, as well as the ancient constitution of their country. There can be no capital city in such a constitution as they have lately made. They have forgot, that when they framed democratic governments, they had virtually dismembered their country. The person, whom they persevere in calling king, has not power left to him by the hundredth part sufficient to hold together this collection of republics. The republic of Paris will endeavour indeed to complete the debauchery of the army, and illegally to perpetuate the assembly, without resort to its constituents, as the means of continuing its despotism. It will make efforts, by becoming the heart of a boundless paper circulation, to draw everything to itself; but in vain. All this policy in the end will appear as feeble as it is now violent.

THE OBLIGATION OF THE REPRESENTATIVE*

Certainly, gentlemen, it ought to be the happiness and glory of a representative to live in the strictest union, the closest correspondence, and the most unreserved communication with his constituents. Their wishes ought to have great weight with him; their opinion, high respect; their business, unremitted attention. It is his duty to sacrifice his repose, his pleasures, his satisfactions, to theirs; and above all,

* From "To the Electors at Bristol" (1774), *Works*, Vol. 1, pp. 446–48.

ever, and in all cases, to prefer their interest to his own. But his un-
biased opinion, his mature judgment, his enlightened conscience, he
ought not to sacrifice to you, to any man, or to any set of men living.
These he does not derive from your pleasure; no, nor from the law
and the constitution. They are a trust from Providence, for the abuse
of which he is deeply answerable. Your representative owes you, not
his industry only, but his judgment; and he betrays, instead of serving
you, if he sacrifices it to your opinion.

My worthy colleague says, his will ought to be subservient to
yours. If that be all, the thing is innocent. If government were a matter of will upon any side, yours, without question, ought to be
superior. But government and legislation are matters of reason and
judgment, and not of inclination; and what sort of reason is that, in
which the determination precedes the discussion; in which one set of
men deliberate, and another decide; and where those who form the
conclusion are perhaps three hundred miles distant from those who
hear the arguments?

To deliver an opinion, is the right of all men; that of constituents
is a weighty and respectable opinion, which a representative ought
always to rejoice to hear; and which he ought always most seriously
to consider. But *authoritative* instructions; *mandates* issued, which
the member is bound blindly and implicitly to obey, to vote, and to
argue for, though contrary to the clearest conviction of his judgment
and conscience—these are things utterly unknown to the laws of this
land, and which arise from a fundamental mistake of the whole order
and tenor of our constitution.

Parliament is not a *congress* of ambassadors from different and
hostile interests; which interests each must maintain, as an agent and
advocate, against other agents and advocates; but parliament is a
deliberative assembly of *one* nation, with *one* interest, that of the
whole; where, not local purposes, not local prejudices, ought to guide,
but the general good, resulting from the general reason of the whole.
You choose a member indeed; but when you have chosen him, he is
not member of Bristol, but he is a member of *parliament*. If the local
constituent should have an interest, or should form an hasty opinion,
evidently opposite to the real good of the rest of the community, the
member for that place ought to be as far, as any other, from any
endeavour to give it effect. I beg pardon for saying so much on this
subject. I have been unwillingly drawn into it; but I shall ever use a
respectful frankness of communication with you. Your faithful friend,

your devoted servant, I shall be to the end of my life: a flatterer you
do not wish for. On this point of instructions, however, I think it
scarcely possible we ever can have any sort of difference. Perhaps I
may give you too much, rather than too little, trouble.

THE IDEAL OF PRUDENTIAL WISDOM*

The subversion of a government, to deserve any praise, must be
considered but as a step preparatory to the formation of something
better, either in the scheme of the government itself, or in the persons
who administer it, or in both. These events cannot in reason be
separated. For instance, when we praise our Revolution of 1688,
though the nation in that act was on the defensive, and was justified
in incurring all the evils of a defensive war, we do not rest there. We
always combine with the subversion of the old government, the happy
settlement which followed. When we estimate that revolution, we
mean to comprehend in our calculation both the value of the thing
parted with, and the value of the thing received in exchange.

The burthen of proof lies heavily on those who tear to pieces the
whole frame and contexture of their country, that they could find no
other way of settling a government fit to obtain its rational ends,
except that which they have pursued by means unfavourable to all
the present happiness of millions of people, and to the utter ruin of
several hundreds of thousands. In their political arrangements, men
have no right to put the well-being of the present generation wholly
out of the question. Perhaps the only moral trust with any certainty
in our hands, is the care of our own time. With regard to futurity, we
are to treat it like a ward. We are not so to attempt an improvement
of his fortune, as to put the capital of his estate to any hazard.

It is not worth our while to discuss, like sophisters, whether, in no
case, some evil, for the sake of some benefit, is to be tolerated. Nothing universal can be rationally affirmed on any moral or any political
subject. Pure metaphysical abstraction does not belong to these matters. The lines of morality are not like ideal lines of mathematics.
They are broad and deep as well as long. They admit of exceptions;
they demand modifications. These exceptions and modifications are
not made by the process of logic, but by the rules of prudence. Prudence is not only the first in rank of the virtues political and moral,

* From "An Appeal from the New to Old Whigs" (1791), *Works*, Vol 3, pp.
15–16.

but she is the director, the regulator, the standard of them all. Metaphysics cannot live without definition; but prudence is cautious how she defines. Our courts cannot be more fearful in suffering fictitious cases to be brought before them for eliciting their determination on a point of law, than prudent moralists are in putting extreme and hazardous cases of conscience upon emergences not existing. Without attempting therefore to define, what never can be defined, the case of a revolution in government, this I think may be safely affirmed, that a sore and pressing evil is to be removed, and that a good, great in its amount and unequivocal in its nature, must be probable almost to certainty, before the inestimable price of our own morals, and the well-being of a number of our fellow-citizens, is paid for a revolution. If ever we ought to be economists even to parsimony, it is in the voluntary production of evil. Every revolution contains in it something of evil.

REFORM AND REVOLUTION*

... The errors and defects of old establishments are visible and palpable. It calls for little ability to point them out; and where absolute power is given, it requires but a word wholly to abolish the vice and the establishment together. The same lazy but restless disposition, which loves sloth and hates quiet, directs the politicians, when they come to work for supplying the place of what they have destroyed. To make everything the reverse of what they have seen is quite as easy as to destroy. No difficulties occur in what has never been tried. Criticism is almost baffled in discovering the defects of what has not existed; and eager enthusiasm and cheating hope have all the wide field of imagination, in which they may expatiate with little or no opposition.

At once to preserve and to reform is quite another thing. When the useful parts of an old establishment are kept, and what is superadded is to be fitted to what is retained, a vigorous mind, steady, persevering attention, various powers of comparison and combination, and the resources of an understanding fruitful in expedients, are to be exercised; they are to be exercised in a continued conflict with the combined force of opposite vices, with the obstinacy that rejects all improvement, and the levity that is fatigued and disgusted with everything of which it is in possession. But you may object—"A

* From "The Revolution in France," *Works,* Vol. 2, pp. 438–40.

process of this kind is slow. It is not fit for an assembly, which glories in performing in a few months the work of ages. Such a mode of reforming, possibly, might take up many years." Without question it might; and it ought. It is one of the excellencies of a method in which time is amongst the assistants, that its operation is slow, and in some cases almost imperceptible. If circumspection and caution are a part of wisdom, when we work only upon inanimate matter, surely they become a part of duty too, when the subject of our demolition and construction is not brick and timber, but sentient beings, by the sudden alteration of whose state, condition, and habits, multitudes may be rendered miserable. But it seems as if it were the prevalent opinion in Paris, that an unfeeling heart, and an undoubting confidence, are the sole qualifications for a perfect legislator. Far different are my ideas of that high office. The true lawgiver ought to have a heart full of sensibility. He ought to love and respect his kind, and to fear himself. It may be allowed to his temperament to catch his ultimate object with an intuitive glance; but his movements towards it ought to be deliberate. Political arrangement, as it is a work for social ends, is to be only wrought by social means. There mind must conspire with mind. Time is required to produce that union of minds which alone can produce all the good we aim at. Our patience will achieve more than our force. If I might venture to appeal to what is so much out of fashion in Paris, I mean to experience, I should tell you, that in my course I have known, and, according to my measure, have co-operated with great men; and I have never yet seen any plan which has not been mended by the observations of those who were much inferior in understanding to the person who took the lead in the business. By a slow but well-sustained progress, the effect of each step is watched; the good or ill success of the first gives light to us in the second; and so, from light to light, we are conducted with safety through the whole series. We see that the parts or the system do not clash. The evils latent in the most promising contrivances are provided for as they arise. One advantage is as little as possible sacrificed to another. We compensate, we reconcile, we balance. We are enabled to unite into a consistent whole the various anomalies and contending principles that are found in the minds and affairs of men. From hence arises, not an excellence in simplicity, but one far superior, an excellence in composition. Where the great interests of mankind are concerned through a long succession of generations, that succession ought to be admitted into some share in the councils which are so deeply to affect them. If justice requires this, the work itself requires the aid of more minds than one age can furnish. It is from this view of things that the best legislators have been often satisfied with the establishment of some sure, solid, and ruling principle in government; a power like that which some of the philosophers have called a plastic nature; and having fixed the principle, they have left it afterwards to its own operation.

8

CARLYLE
The Hero as Ruler

Thomas Carlyle (1795–1881) was one of the most vigorous polemicists of the Victorian age and, like Edmund Burke, a leading figure in the conservative reaction against the ideological tenets of liberalism. He viewed popular democracy as the leadership of ignoble, unvaliant and fatuous men. Democracy, by its very nature, is a self-canceling business, producing in the long run a net result of zero. In Carlyle's view, it is the everlasting privilege of the foolish to be governed by the wise: to be guided in the right path by those who know better than they. "Find in any country the Ablest Man that exist there; raise *him* to the supreme place and loyally reverence him; you have a perfect government for that country; no ballot box, parliamentary eloquence, voting or constitution-building can improve it a whit."

Carlyle's hero theory, as the belief that political rule should be exercised by the man of exceptional wisdom and ability, resembles, in some respects, Plato's concept of the philosopher-king. For Carlyle, however, the world cannot be understood through philosophical meditation upon a realm of transcendental forms; it is inherent in the process of historical growth and evolution; a truth that never is, but is always in the process of *becoming*. The heroic leader is the indispensable agent of historical evolution and progress; his distinctive quality is the capacity for bold, audacious action based upon an intuitive, rather than a philosophical, grasp of historical reality: history is the biography of great individuals. In his firm acceptance of power and wrongdoing as inevitable features of the historical process and his view that the hero must be immersed in the equivocations and compromises of actual life, Carlyle is close to the spirit and tradition of Machiavelli.

As a contribution to the problem of political rule, Carlyle provides a needed emphasis upon the role and importance of superior individuals in politics, and he rightly deplores tendencies in mass democracy which encourage mediocrity, ignorance and incompetence. The objection to Carlyle's polemic, however, is that he presents an image of popular democracy in its worst possible manifestations without recognizing the historical evidence that Western parliamentary governments have produced superior as well as mediocre leadership. But perhaps the more basic objection to Carlyle's theory is the unwarranted assumption that so-called heroic leaders possess the virtues which should entitle them to command reverence and respect of the people they rule. Modern history is testimony to the fact that political rulers, such as Hitler and Mussolini, were men of undoubtedly superior abilities and talents, but few would be disposed to attribute to them qualities of nobility or enlightened statesmanship. Herein lies the basic justification of constitutional democracy: the commitment to the principle of limited government and the accountability of leadership to the electoral body as an essential means to protect the citizenship against the danger of political tyranny and the abuse of power by self-styled "heroic individuals."

THE HERO AS DIVINITY*

We have undertaken to discourse here for a little on Great Men, their manner of appearance in our world's business, how they have shaped themselves in the world's history, what ideas men formed of them, what work they did;—on Heroes, namely, and on their reception and performance; what I call Hero-worship and the Heroic in human affairs. Too evidently this is a large topic; deserving quite other treatment than we can expect to give it at present. A large topic; indeed, an illimitable one; wide as Universal History itself. For, as I take it, Universal History, the history of what man has accomplished in this world, is at bottom the History of the Great Men who have worked here. They were the leaders of men, these great ones; the modellers, patterns, and in a wide sense creators, of whatsoever the general mass of men contrived to do or to attain; all things that we see standing accomplished in the world are properly the outer material result, the practical realisation and embodiment, of Thoughts that dwelt in the Great Men sent into the world: the soul of the whole world's history, it may justly be considered, were the history of these. Too clearly it is a topic we shall do no justice to in this place!

One comfort is, that Great Men, taken up in any way, are profitable company. We cannot look, however imperfectly, upon a great man,

* From Thomas Carlyle, *On Heroes, Hero-Worship and the Heroic in History* (New York : Robert M. McBride and Co.), pp. 3–4; 16–19; 243–47.

without gaining something by him. He is the living light-fountain, which it is good and pleasant to be near. The light which enlightens, which has enlightened the darkness of the world; and this not as a kindled lamp only, but rather as a natural luminary shining by the gift of Heaven; a flowing light-fountain, as I say, of native original insight, of manhood and heroic nobleness;—in whose radiance all souls feel that it is well with them. On any terms whatsoever, you will not grudge to wander in such neighbourhood for a while. These Six classes of Heroes, chosen out of widely-distant countries and epochs, and in mere external figure differing altogether, ought, if we look faithfully at them, to illustrate several things for us. Could we see *them* well, we should get some glimpses into the very marrow of the world's history. How happy, could I but, in any measure, in such times as these, make manifest to you the meanings of Heroism; the divine relation (for I may well call it such) which in all times unites a Great Man to other men; and thus, as it were, not exhaust my subject, but so much as break ground on it! At all events, I must make the attempt. . . .

I am well aware that in these days Hero-worship, the thing I call Hero-worship, professes to have gone-out, and finally ceased. This, for reasons which it will be worth while some time to inquire into, is an age that as it were denies the existence of great men; denies the desirableness of great men. Show our critics a great man, a Luther for example, they begin to what they call 'account' for him; not to worship him, but take the dimensions of him,—and bring him out to be a little kind of man! He was the 'creature of the Time,' they say; the Time called him forth, the Time did everything, he nothing—but what we the little critic could have done too! This seems to me but melancholy work. The Time call forth? Alas, we have known Times *call* loudly enough for their great man; but not find him when they called! He was not there; Providence had not sent him; the Time, *calling* its loudest, had to go down to confusion and wreck because he would not come when called. For if we will think of it, no Time need have gone to ruin, could it have *found* a man great enough, a man wise and good enough: wisdom to discern truly what the Time wanted, valour to lead it on the right road thither; these are the salvation of any Time. But I liken common languid Times, with their unbelief, distress, perplexity, with their languid doubting characters and embarrassed circumstances, impotently crumbling-down into ever worse distress towards final ruin,—all this I liken to dry dead fuel, waiting for the lightning out of Heaven that shall kindle it. The great man, with his free force direct out of God's own hand, is the lightning. His word is the wise healing word which all can believe in. All blazes round him now, when he has once struck on it, into fire like his own. The dry mouldering sticks are thought to have called him forth. They did want him greatly; but as to calling him forth—!—Those are critics of small vision, I think, who cry: "See, is it not the sticks that made the fire?" No sadder proof can be given by a man of his own littleness than disbelief in great men. There is no sadder symptom of a generation than such general blindness to the spiritual lightning, with faith only in the heap of barren dead fuel. It is the last consummation of unbelief. In all epochs of the world's history, we shall find the Great Man to have been the indispensable saviour of his epoch; —the lightning, without which the fuel never would have burnt. The History of the World, I said already, was the Biography of Great Men.

Such small critics do what they can to promote unbelief and universal spiritual paralysis: but happily they cannot always completely succeed. In all times it is possible for a man to arise great enough to feel that they and their doctrines are chimeras and cobwebs. And what is notable, in no time whatever can they entirely eradicate out of living men's hearts a certain altogether peculiar reverence for Great Men; genuine admiration, loyalty, adoration, however dim and perverted it may be. Hero-worship endures forever while man endures. Boswell venerates his Johnson, right truly even in the Eighteenth century. The unbelieving French believe in their Voltaire; and burst-out round him into very curious Hero-worship, in that last act of his life, when they 'stifle him under roses.' It has always seemed to me extremely curious this of Voltaire. Truly, if Christianity be the highest instance of Hero-worship, then we may find here in Voltairism one of the lowest! He whose life was that of a kind of Antichrist, does again on this side exhibit a curious contrast. No people ever were so little prone to admire at all as those French of Voltaire. *Persiflage* was the character of their whole mind; adoration had nowhere a place in it. Yet see! The old man of Ferney comes-up to Paris; an old, tottering, infirm man of eighty-four years. They feel that he too is a kind of Hero; that he has spent his life in opposing error and injustice, delivering Calases, unmasking hypocrites in high places;—in short that *he* too, though in a strange way, has fought like a valiant man.

They feel withal that, if *persiflage* be the great thing, there never was such a *persifleur*. He is the realised ideal of every one of them; the thing they are all wanting to be; of all Frenchmen the most French. *He* is properly their god,—such god as they are fit for. Accordingly all persons, from the Queen Antoinette to the Douanier at the Porte St. Denis, do they not worship him? People of quality disguise themselves as tavern-waiters. The Maitre de Poste, with a broad oath, orders his Postilion: *"Va bon train;* thou art driving M. de Voltaire." At Paris his carriage is 'the nucleus of a comet, whose train fills whole streets.' The ladies pluck a hair or two from his fur, to keep it as a sacred relic. There was nothing highest, beautifullest, noblest in all France, that did not feel this man to be higher, beautifuller, nobler.

Yes, from Norse Odin to English Samuel Johnson, from the divine Founder of Christianity to the withered Pontiff of Encyclopedism, in all times and places, the Hero has been worshiped. It will ever be so. We all love great men; love, venerate and bow-down submissive before great men: nay can we honestly bow-down to anything else? Ah, does not every true man feel that he is himself made higher by doing reverence to what is really above him? No nobler or more blessed feeling dwells in man's heart. And to me it is very cheering to consider that no sceptical logic, or general triviality, insincerity and aridity of any Time and its influences can destroy this noble inborn loyalty and worship that is in man. In times of unbelief, which soon have to become times of revolution, much down-rushing, sorrowful decay and ruin is visible to everybody. For myself in these days, I seem to see in this indestructibility of Hero-worship the everlasting adamant lower than which the confused wreck of revolutionary things cannot fall. The confused wreck of things crumbling and even crashing and tumbling all round us in these revolutionary ages, will get down so far; *no* farther. It is an eternal corner-stone, from which they can begin to build themselves up again. That man, in some sense or other, worships Heroes; that we all of us reverence and must ever reverence Great Men: this is, to me, the living rock amid all rushings-down whatsoever;—the one fixed point in modern revolutionary history, otherwise as if bottomless and shoreless.

THE HERO AS KING

We come now to the last form of Heroism; that which we call Kingship. The Commander over Men; he to whose will our wills are to be

subordinated, and loyally surrender themselves, and find their welfare
in doing so, may be reckoned the most important of Great Men. He
is practically the summary for us of *all* the various figures of Heroism;
Priest, Teacher, whatsoever of earthly or of spiritual dignity we can
fancy to reside in a man, embodies itself here, to *command* over us,
to furnish us with constant practical teaching, to tell us for the day
and hour what we are to *do*. He is called *Rex*, Regulator, *Roi:* our
own name is still better; King, *Könning*, which means *Canning*,
Ableman.

Numerous considerations, pointing towards deep, questionable, and
indeed unfathomable regions, present themselves here: on the most of
which we must resolutely for the present forbear to speak at all. As
Burke said that perhaps fair *Trial by Jury* was the soul of Government, and that all legislation, administration, parliamentary debating,
and the rest of it, went on, in 'order to bring twelve impartial men
into a jury-box;'—so, by much stronger reason, may I say here, that
the finding of your *Ableman,* and getting him invested with the *symbols of ability,* with dignity, worship *(worth-*ship), royalty, kinghood,
or whatever we call it, so that *he* may actually have room to guide
according to his faculty of doing it,—is the business, well or ill accomplished, of all social procedure whatsoever in this world! Hustings-
speeches, Parliamentary motions, Reform Bills, French Revolutions,
all mean at heart this; or else nothing. Find in any country the Ablest
Man that exists there; raise *him* to the supreme place, and loyally
reverence him: you have a perfect government for that country; no
ballot-box, parliamentary eloquence, voting, constitution-building, or
other machinery whatsoever can improve it a whit. It is in the perfect
state; an ideal country. The Ablest Man; he means also the truest-
hearted, justest, the Noblest Man: what he *tells us to do* must be precisely the wisest, fittest, that we could anywhere or anyhow learn;—
the thing which it will in all ways behove us, with right loyal thank-
fulness, and nothing doubting, to do! Our *doing* and life were then,
so far as government could regulate it, well regulated; that were the
ideal of constitutions.

Alas, we know very well that Ideals can never be completely embodied in practice. Ideals must ever lie a very great way off; and we
will right thankfully content ourselves with any not intolerable
approximation thereto! Let no man, as Schiller says, too querulously
'measure by a scale of perfection the meagre product of reality' in
this poor world of ours. We will esteem him no wise man; we will

esteem him a sickly, discontented, foolish man. And yet, on the other
hand, it is ever to be forgotten that Ideals do exist; that if they be not
approximated to at all, the whole matter goes to wreck! Infallibly.
No bricklayer builds a wall *perfectly* perpendicular, mathematically
this is not possible; a certain degree of perpendicularity suffices him;
and he, like a good bricklayer, who must have done with his job,
leaves it so. And yet if he sway *too much* from the perpendicular;
above all, if he throw plummet and level quite away from him, and
pile brick on brick heedless, just as it comes to hand—! Such bricklayer, I think, is in a bad way. *He* has forgotten himself: but the Law
of Gravitation does not forget to act on him; he and his wall rush-
down into confused welter of ruin!—

This is the history of all rebellions, French Revolutions, social
explosions in ancient or modern times. You have put the too *Un*able
Man at the head of affairs! The too ignoble, unvaliant, fatuous man.
You have forgotten that there is any rule, or natural necessity whatever, of putting the Able Man there. Brick must lie on brick as it may
and can. Unable Simulacrum of Ability, *quack,* in a word, must adjust
himself with quack, in all manner of administration of human things;
—which accordingly lie unadministered, fermenting into unmeasured
masses of failure, of indigent misery: in the outward, and in the inward or spiritual, miserable millions stretch-out the hand for their due
supply, and it is not there. The 'law of gravitation' acts; Nature's
laws do none of them forget to act. The miserable millions burst-forth
into Sansculottism, or some other sort of madness: bricks and bricklayer lie as a fatal chaos!—

Much sorry stuff, written some hundred years ago or more, about
the 'Divine right of Kings,' moulders unread now in the Public Libraries of this country. Far be it from us to disturb the calm process by
which it is disappearing harmlessly from the earth, in those repositories! At the same time, not to let the immense rubbish go without
leaving us, as it ought, some soul of it behind,—I will say that it did
mean something; something true, which it is important for us and all
men to keep in mind. To assert that in whatever man you chose to
lay hold of (by this or the other plan of clutching at him); and clapt
a round piece of metal on the head of, and called King,—there
straightway came to reside a divine virtue, so that *he* became a kind
of god, and a Divinity inspired him with faculty and right to rule over
you to all lengths: this,—what can we do with this but leave it to rot
silently in the Public Libraries? But I will say withal, and that is what

these Divine-right men meant, That in Kings, and in all human Authorities, and relations that men god-created can from among each other, there is verily either a Divine Right or else a Diabolic Wrong; one or the other of these two! For it is false altogether, what the last Sceptical Century taught us, that this world is a steam engine. There is a God in this world; and a God's sanction, or else the violation of such, does look-out from all ruling and obedience, from all moral acts of men. There is no act more moral between men than that of rule and obedience. Woe to him that claims obedience when it is not due; woe to him that refuses it when it is! God's law is in that, I say, however the Parchment-laws may run: there is a Divine Right or else a Diabolic Wrong at the heart of every claim that one man makes upon another.

It can do none of us harm to reflect on this: in all the relations of life it will concern us; in Loyalty and Royalty, the highest of these. I esteem the modern error, That all goes by self-interest and the checking and balancing of greedy knaveries, and that, in short, there is nothing divine whatever in the association of men, a still more despicable error, natural as it is to an unbelieving century, than that of a 'divine right' in people *called* Kings. I say, Find me the true Könning, King, or Ableman, and he *has* a divine right over me. That we knew in some tolerable measure how to find him, and that all men were ready to acknowledge his divine right when found: this is precisely the healing which a sick world is everywhere, in these ages seeking after! The true King, as guide of the practical, has ever something of the Pontiff in him,—guide of the spiritual, from which all practice has its rise. This too is a true saying, that the *King* is head of the *Church.*—But we will leave the Polemic stuff of a dead century to lie quiet on its bookshelves.

THE PRESENT TIME*

For universal *Democracy,* whatever we may think of it, has declared itself as an inevitable fact of the days in which we live; and he who has any chance to instruct, or lead, in his days, must begin by admitting that: new street-barricades, and new anarchies, still more scandalous if still less sanguinary, must return and again return, till governing persons everywhere know and admit that. Democracy, it

* From Thomas Carlyle, *Latter-Day Pamphlets* (London: Chapman and Hall), pp. 7–21; 25–26.

may be said everywhere, is here:—for sixty years now, ever since the grand or *First* French Revolution, that fact has been terribly announced to all the world; in message after message, some of them very terrible indeed; and now at last all the world ought really to believe it. That the world does believe it; that even Kings now as good as believe it, and know, or with just terror surmise, that they are but temporary phantasm Playactors, and that Democracy is the grand, alarming, imminent and indisputable Reality: this, among the scandalous phases we witnessed in the last two years, is a phasis full of hope: a sign that we are advancing closer and closer to the very problem itself, which it will behove us to solve or die;—that all fighting and campaigning and coalitioning in regard to the *existence* of the Problem, is hopeless and superfluous henceforth. The gods have appointed it *so*; no Pitt, nor body of Pitts or mortal creatures can appoint it otherwise. Democracy, sure enough, is here: one knows not how long it will keep hidden underground even in Russia;—and here in England, though we object to it resolutely in the form of street-barricades and insurrectionary pikes, and decidedly will not open doors to it on those terms, the tramp of its million feet is on all streets and thoroughfares, the sound of its bewildered thousandfold voice is in all writings and speakings, in all thinkings and modes and activities of men: the soul that does not now, with hope or terror, discern *it,* is not the one we address on this occasion.

What *is* Democracy; this huge inevitable Product of the Destinies, which is everywhere the portion of our Europe in these latter days? There lies the question for us. Whence comes it, this universal big black Democracy; whither tends it; what is the meaning of it? A meaning it must have, or it would not be here. If we can find the right meaning of it, we may, wisely submitting or wisely resisting and controlling, still hope to live in the midst of it; if we cannot find the right meaning, if we find only the wrong or no meaning in it, to live will not be possible!—The whole social wisdom of the Present Time is summoned, in the name of the Giver of Wisdom, to make clear to itself, and lay deeply to heart with an eye to strenuous valiant practice and effort, what the meaning of this universal revolt of the European Populations, which calls itself Democracy, and decides to continue permanent, may be.

Certainly it is a drama full of action, event fast following event; in which curiosity finds endless scope, and there are interests at stake, enough to rivet the attention of all men, simple and wise. Whereat the idle multitude lift-up their voices, gratulating, celebrating sky-high; in rhyme and prose announcement, more than plentiful, that *now* the New Era, and long-expected Year One of Perfect Human Felicity has come. Glorious and immortal people, sublime French citizens, heroic barricades; triumph of civil and religious liberty—O Heaven! one of the inevitablest private miseries, to an earnest man in such circumstances, is this multitudinous efflux of oratory and psalmody, from the universal foolish human throat; drowning for the moment all reflection whatsoever, except the sorrowful one that you are fallen in an evil, heavy-laden, long-eared age, and must resignedly bear your part in the same. The front wall of your wretched old crazed dwelling, long denounced by you to no purpose, having at last fairly folded itself over, and fallen prostrate into the street, the floors, as may happen, will still hang-on by the mere beam-ends, and coherency of old carpentry, though in a sloping direction, and depend there till certain poor rusty nails and wormeaten dovetailing give way:—but is it cheering in such circumstances, that the whole household burst-forth into celebrating the new joys of light and ventilation, liberty and picturesqueness of position, and thank God that now they have got a house to their mind? My dear household, cease singing and psalmodying; lay aside your fiddles, take out your work-implements, if you have any; for I can say with confidence the laws of gravitation are still active, and rusty nails, wormeaten dovetailings, and secret coherency of old carpentry, are not the best basis for a household!—In the lanes of Irish cities, I have heard say, the wretched people are sometimes found living, and perilously boiling their potatoes, on such swing-floors and inclined planes hanging-on by the joist-ends; but I did not hear that they sang very much in celebration of such lodging. No, they slid gently about, sat near the back wall, and perilously boiled their potatoes, in silence for most part!—

High shouts of exultation, in every dialect, by every vehicle of speech and writing, rise from far and near over this last avatar of Democracy in 1848; and yet, to wise minds, the first aspect it presents seems rather to be one of boundless misery and sorrow. What can be more miserable than this universal hunting-out of the high dignitaries, solemn functionaries, and potent, grave and reverend signiors of the world; this stormful rising-up of the inarticulate dumb masses everywhere, against those who pretended to be speaking for them and guiding them? These guides, then, were mere blind men only pretending to see? These rulers were not ruling at all; they had merely got-on the

attributes and clothes of rulers, and were surreptitiously drawing the
wages, while the work remained undone? The Kings were Sham-
Kings, playacting as at Drury Lane;—and what were the people
withal that took them for real?

It is probably the hugest disclosure of *falsity* in human things that
was ever at one time made. These reverend Dignitaries that sat amid
their far-shining symbols and long-sounding, long-admitted profes-
sions, were mere Impostors, then? Not a true thing they were doing,
but a false thing. The story they told men was a cunningly-devised
fable; the gospels they preached to them were *not* an account of man's
real position in this world, but an incoherent fabrication, of dead
ghosts and unborn shadows, of traditions, cants, indolences, coward-
icies,—a falsity of falsities, which at last *ceases* to stick together.
Wilfully and against their will, these high units of mankind were
cheats, then; and the low millions who believed in them were dupes,
—a kind of *inverse* cheats, too, or they would not have believed in
them so long. A universal *Bankruptcy of Imposture;* that may be the
brief definition of it. Imposture everywhere declared once more to be
contrary to Nature; nobody will change its word into an act any
farther:—fallen insolvent; unable to keep its head up by these false
pretences, or make its pot boil any more for the present! A more
scandalous phenomenon, wide as Europe, never afflicted the face of
the sun. Bankruptcy everywhere; foul ignomiy, and the abomination
or desolation, in all high places: odious to look upon, as the carnage
of a battle-field on the morrow morning;—a massacre not of the inno-
cents; but a universal tumbling of Impostors and of Impostures into
the street!—

Such a spectacle, can we call it joyful? There is a joy in it, to the
wise man too; yes, but a joy full of awe, and as it were sadder than
any sorrow,—like the vision of immortality, unattainable except
through death and the grave! And yet who would not, in his heart of
hearts, feel piously thankful that Imposture has fallen bankrupt? By all
means let it fall bankrupt; in the name of God let it do so, with whatever misery to itself and to all of us. Imposture, be it known then,—
known it must and shall be,—is hateful, unendurable to God and
man. Let it understand this everywhere; and swiftly make ready for
departure, wherever it yet lingers; and let it learn never to return, if
possible! The eternal voices, very audibly again, are speaking to proclaim this message, from side to side of the world. Not a very cheering
message, but a very indispensable one.

Alas, it is sad enough that Anarchy is here; that we are not permitted to regret its being here,—for who that had, for this divine Universe, an eye which was human at all, could wish that Shams of any kind, especially that Sham-Kings should continue? No: at all costs, it is to be prayed by all men that Shams may *cease*. Good Heavens, to what depths have we got, when this to many a man seems strange! Yet strange to many a man it does seem; and to many a solid Englishman, wholesomely digesting his pudding among what are called the cultivated classes, it seems strange exceedingly; a mad ignorant notion, quite heterodox, and big with mere ruin. He has been used to decent forms long since fallen empty of meaning, to plausible modes, solemnities grown ceremonial,—what you in your iconoclast humour call shams,—all his life long; never heard that there was any harm in them, that there was any getting-on without them. Did not cotton spin itself, beef grow, and groceries and spiceries come in from the East and the West, quite comfortably by the side of shame? Kings reigned, what they were pleased to call reigning; lawyers pleaded, bishops preached, and honourable members perorated; and to crown the whole, as if it were all real and no sham there, did not scrip continue saleable, and the banker pay in bullion, or paper with a metallic basis? "The greatest sham, I have always thought, is he that would destroy shams."

Even so. To such depth have *I*, the poor knowing person of this epoch, got;—almost below the level of lowest humanity, and down towards the state of apehood and oxhood! For never till in quite recent generations was such a scandalous blasphemy quietly set forth among the sons of Adam; never before did the creature called man believe generally in his heart that lies were the rule in this Earth; that in deliberate long-established lying could there be help or salvation for him, could there be at length other than hindrance and destruction for him. O Heavyside, my solid friend, this is the sorrow of sorrows: what on earth can become of us till this accursed enchantment, the general summary and consecration of delusions, be cast forth from the heart and life of one and all! Cast forth it will be; it must, or we are tending at all moments,—whitherward I do not like to name. Alas, and the casting of it out, to what heights and what depths will it lead us, in the sad universe mostly of lies and shams and hollow phantasms (grown very ghastly now), in which, as in a safe home, we have lived this century or two! To heights and depths of social and individual *divorce* from delusions—of 'reform' in right sacred earnest, of indispensable amendment, and stern sorrowful abrogation and order to depart—such as cannot well be spoken at present; as dare scarcely be thought at present; which nevertheless are very inevitable, and perhaps rather imminent several of them! Truly we have a heavy task of work before us; and there is a pressing call that we should seriously begin upon it, before it tumble into an inextricable mass, in which there will be no working, but only suffering and hopelessly perishing!—

Or perhaps Democracy, which we announce as now come, will itself manage it? Democracy, once modelled into suffrages, furnished with ballot-boxes and suchlike, will itself accomplish the salutary universal change from Delusive to Real, and make a new blessed world of us by and by?—To the great mass of men, I am aware, the matter presents itself quite on this hopeful side. Democracy they consider to *be* a kind of 'Government.' The old model, formed long since, and brought to perfection in England now two hundred years ago, has proclaimed itself to all Nations as the new healing for every woe; "Set-up a Parliament," the Nations everywhere say, when the old King is detected to be a Sham-King, and hunted out or not; "set-up a Parliament; let us have suffrages, universal 'suffrages;' and all either at once or by due degrees will be 'right,' and a real Millennium come!" Such is their way of construing the matter.

Such, alas, is by no means my way of construing the matter; if it were, I should have had the happiness of remaining silent, and been without call to speak here. It is because the contrary of all this is deeply manifest to me, and appears to be forgotten by multitudes of my contemporaries, that I have had to undertake addressing a word to them. The contrary of all this;—and the farther I look into the roots of all this, the more hateful, ruinous and dismal does the state of mind all this could have originated in appear to me. To examine this recipe of a Parliament, how fit it is for governing Nations, nay how fit it may now be, in these new times, for governing England itself where we are used to it so long: this, too, is an alarming inquiry, to which all thinking men, and good citizens of their country, who have an ear for the small still voices and eternal intimations, across the temporary clamours and loud blaring proclamations, are now solemnly invited. Invited by the rigorous fact itself; which will one day, and that perhaps soon, demand practical decision or redecision of it from us,—with enormous penalty if we decide it wrong! I think we shall all have to consider this question, one day; better perhaps now than later, when the leisure may be less. If a Parliament, with suffrages and universal or any conceivable kind of suffrages, *is* the method, then certainly let us set about discovering the kind of suffrages, and rest no moment till we have got them. But it is possible a Parliament may not be the method! Possible the inveterate notions of the English People may have settled it as the method, and the Everlasting Laws of Nature may have settled it as not the method! Not the whole method; nor the method at all, if taken as the whole? If a Parliament with never such suffrages is *not* the method settled by this latter authority, then it will urgently behove us to become aware of that fact, and to quit such method;—we may depend upon it, however unanimous *we* be, every step taken in that direction will, by the Eternal Law of things, be a step *from* improvement, not towards it.

Not towards it, I say, if so! Unanimity of voting—that will do nothing for us if *so*. Your ship cannot double Cape Horn by its excellent plans of voting. The ship may vote this and that, above decks and below, in the most harmonious exquisitely constitutional manner: the ship, to get round Cape Horn, will find a set of conditions already voted for, and fixed with adamantine rigour by the ancient Elemental Powers, who are entirely careless how you vote. If you can, by voting or without voting, ascertain these conditions, and valiantly conform to them, you will get round the Cape: if you cannot,—the ruffian Winds will blow you ever back again; the inexorable Icebergs, dumb privy-councillors from Chaos, will nudge you with most chaotic 'admonition;' you will be flung half-frozen on the Patagonian cliffs, or admonished into shivers by your iceberg councillors, and sent sheer down to Davy Jones, and will never get round Cape Horn at all! Unanimity on board ship;—yes indeed, the ship's crew may be very unanimous, which doubtless, for the time being, will be very comfortable to the ship's crew, and to their Phantasm Captain if they have one: but if the tack they unanimously steer upon is guiding them into the belly of the Abyss, it will not profit them much!—Ships accordingly do not use the ballot-box at all; and they reject the Phantasm species of Captains: one wishes much some other Entities,—since all entities lie under the same rigorous set of laws,—could be brought to show as much wisdom, and sense at least of self-preservation, the *first* command of Nature. Phantasm Captains with unanimous votings: this is considered to be all the law and all the prophets, at present.

If a man could shake-out of his mind the universal noise of political doctors in this generation and in the last generation or two, and

consider the matter face to face, with his own sincere intelligence
looking at it, I venture to say he would find this a very extraordinary
method of navigating, whether in the Straits of Magellan or the un-
discovered Sea of Time. To prosper in this world, to gain felicity,
victory and improvement, either for a man or a nation, there is but
one thing requisite, That the man or nation can discern what the true
regulations of the Universe are in regard to him and his pursuit, and
can faithfully and steadfastly follow these. These will lead him to
victory; whoever it may be that sets him in the way of these,—were it
Russian Autocrat, Chartist Parliament, Grand Lama, Force of Public
Opinion, Archbishop of Canterbury, M'Croudy the Seraphic Doctor
with his Last-evangel of Political Economy,—sets him in the sure way
to please the Author of this Universe, and is his friend of friends. And
again, whoever does the contrary is, for a like reason, his enemy of
enemies. This may be taken as fixed.

And now by what method ascertain the monition of the gods in
regard to our affairs? How decipher, with best fidelity, the eternal
regulation of the Universe; and read, from amid such confused embroilments of human clamour and folly, what the real Divine Message
to us is? A divine message, or eternal regulation of the Universe,
there verily is, in regard to every conceivable procedure and affair of
man: faithfully following this, said procedure or affair will prosper,
and have the whole Universe to second it, and carry it, across the
fluctuating contradictions, towards a victorious goal; not following
this, mistaking this, disregarding this, destruction and wreck are certain for every affair. How find it? All the world answers me, "Count
heads; ask Universal Suffrage, by the ballot-boxes, and that will tell."
Universal Suffrage, ballot-boxes, count of heads? Well,—I perceive
we have got into strange spiritual latitudes indeed. Within the last
half century or so, either the Universe or else the heads of
men must have altered very much. Half a century ago, and down
from Father Adam's time till then, the Universe, wherever I could
hear tell of it, was wont to be of somewhat obstruse nature; by no
means carrying its secret written on its face, legible to every passerby;
on the contrary, obstinately hiding its secret from all foolish, slavish,
wicked, insincere persons, and partially disclosing it to the wise and
noble-minded alone, whose number was not the majority in my time!

Or perhaps the chief end of man being now, in these improved
epochs, to make money and spend it, his interests in the Universe
have become amazingly simplified of late; capable of being voted-on

with effect by almost anybody? 'To buy in the cheapest market, and sell in the dearest': truly if that is the summary of his social duties, and the final divine-message he has to follow, we may trust him extensively to vote upon that. But if it is *not*, and never was, or can be? If the Universe will not carry on its divine bosom any common-wealth of mortals that have no higher aim,—being still 'a Temple and Hall of Doom,' not a mere Weaving-shop and Cattle-pen? If the un-fathomable Universe has decided to *reject* Human Beavers pretending to be Men; and will abolish, pretty rapidly perhaps, in hideous mud-deluges, their 'markets' and them, unless they think of it?—In that case it were better to think of it: and the Democracies and Universal Suffrages, I can observe, will require to modify themselves a good deal!

Historically speaking, I believe there was no Nation that could subsist upon Democracy. Of ancient Republics, and *Demoi* and *Populi,* we have heard much; but it is now pretty well admitted to be nothing to our purpose;—a universal-suffrage republic, or a general-suffrage one, or any but a most-limited-suffrage one, never came to light, or dreamed of doing so, in ancient times. When the mass of the population were slaves, and the voters intrinsically a kind of *kings,* or men born to rule others; when the voters were *real* 'aristocrats' and manageable dependents of such,—then doubtless voting, and con-fused jumbling of talk and intrigue, might, without immediate des-truction, or the need of a Cavaignac to intervene with cannon and sweep the streets clear of it, go on; and beautiful developments of manhood might be possible beside it, for a season. Beside it; or even, if you will, by means of it, and in virtue of it, though that is by no means so certain as is often supposed. Alas, no: the reflective consti-tutional mind has misgivings as to the origin of old Greek and Roman nobleness; and indeed knows not how this or any other human noble-ness could well be 'originated,' or brought to pass, by voting or with-out voting, in this world, except by the grace of God very mainly;—and remembers, with a sigh, that of the Seven Sages themselves no fewer than three were bits of Despotic Kings, . . . 'Tyrants' so-called (such being greatly wanted there); and that the other four were very far from Red Republicans, if of any political faith whatever! We may quit the Ancient Classical concern, and leave it to College-clubs and speculative debating-societies, in these late days.

Of the various French Republics that have been tried, or that are still on trial,—of these also it is not needful to say any word. But there is one modern instance of Democracy nearly perfect, the Republic of the United States, which has actually subsisted for three-score years or more, with immense success as is affirmed; to which many still appeal, as to a sign of hope for all nations, and a 'Model Republic.' Is not America an instance in point? Why should not all Nations subsist and flourish on Democracy, as America does?

Of America it would ill beseem any Englishman, and me perhaps as little as another, to speak unkindly, to speak *unpatriotically,* if any of us even felt so. Sure enough, America is a great, and in many respects a blessed and hopeful phenomenon. Sure enough, these hardy millions of Anglo-saxon men prove themselves worthy of their genealogy; and, with the axe and plough and hammer, if not yet with any much finer kind of implements, are triumphantly clearing-out wide spaces, seedfields for the sustenance and refuge of mankind, arenas for the future history of the world; doing, in their day and generation, a creditable and cheering feat under the sun. But as to a Model Republic, or a model anything, the wise among themselves know too well that there is nothing to be said. Nay the title hitherto to be a Commonwealth or Nation at all, . . . is, strictly considered, still a thing they are but striving for, and indeed have not yet done much towards attaining. Their Constitution, such as it may be, was made here, not there; went over with them from the Old-Puritan English workshop ready-made. Deduct what they carried with them from England ready-made—their common English Language, and that same Constitution, or rather elixir of constitutions, their inveterate and now, as it were, inborn reverence for the Constable's Staff; two quite immense attainments, which England had to spend much blood, and valiant sweat of brow and brain, for centuries long, in achieving; —and what new elements of polity or nationhood, what noble new phasis of human arrangement, or social device worthy of Prometheus or of Epimetheus, yet comes to light in America? Cotton-crops and Indian-corn and dollars come to light; and half a word of untilled land, where populations that respect the constable can live, for the present *without* Government: this comes to light; and the profound sorrow of all nobler hearts, here uttering itself as silent patient unspeakable ennui, there coming out as vague elegiac wailings, that there is still next to nothing more. 'Anarchy *plus* a street constable': that also is anarchic to me, and other than quite lovely!

I foresee, too, that long before the waste lands are full, the very street-constable, on these poor terms, will have become impossible: without the waste lands, as here in our Europe, I do not see how he could continue possible many weeks. Cease to brag to me of America, and its model institutions and constitutions. To men in their sleep there is nothing granted in this world: nothing, or as good as nothing, to men that sit idly *caucusing* and ballot-boxing on the graves of their heroic ancestors, saying, "It is well, it is well!" Corn and bacon are granted: not a very sublime boon, on such conditions; a boon moreover which, on such conditions, cannot last! No: America too will have to strain its energies, in quite other fashion than this; to crack its sinews, and all-but break its heart, as the rest of us have had to do, in thousand-fold wrestle with the Pythons and mud-demons, before it can become a habitation for the gods. America's battle is yet to fight; and we, sorrowful though nothing doubting, will wish her strength for it. New Spiritual Pythons, plenty of them; enormous Megatherions, as ugly as were ever born of mud, loom huge and hideous out of the twilight Future on America; and she will have her own agony, and her own victory, but on other terms than she is yet quite aware of. Hitherto she but ploughs and hammers, in a very successful manner; hitherto, in spite of her 'roast-goose with apple-sauce,' she is not much. 'Roast-goose with apple-sauce for the poorest working-man': well, surely that is something,—thanks to your respect for the street-constable, and to your continents of fertile waste land;—but that, even if it could continue is by no means enough; that is not even an instalment towards what will be required of you. My friend, brag not yet of our American cousins! Their quantity of cotton, dollars, industry and resources, I believe to be almost unspeakable; but I can by no means worship the life of these. What great human soul, what great thought, what great noble thing that one could worship, or loyally admire, has yet been produced there? None: the American cousins have yet done none of these things. "What they have done?" growls Smelfungus, tired of the subject: "They have doubled their population every twenty years. They have begotten, with a rapidity beyond recorded example, Eighteen Millions of the greatest *bores* ever seen in this world before,—that hitherto is their feat in History!"—And so we leave them, for the present; and cannot predict the success of Democracy, on this side of the Atlantic, from their example.

Alas, on this side of the Atlantic and on that, Democracy, we apprehend, is forever impossible! So much, with certainty of loud astonished contradiction from all manner of men at present, but with sure appeal to the Law of Nature and the ever-abiding Fact, may be suggested and asserted once more. The Universe itself is a Monarchy and Hierarchy; large liberty of 'voting' there, all manner of choice, utmost free-will, but with conditions inexorable and immeasurable annexed to every exercise of the same. A most free commonwealth of voters;' but with Eternal Justice to preside over it, Eternal Justice enforced by Almighty Power! This is the model of 'constitutions'; this: nor in any Nation where there has not yet (in some supportable and withal some constantly-increasing degree) been confided to the *Noblest,* with his select series of *Nobler,* the divine everlasting duty of directing and controlling the Ignoble, has the 'Kingdom of God,' which we all pray for, 'come,' nor can 'His will' even *tend* to be 'done on Earth as it is in Heaven' till then. My Christian friends, and indeed my Sham-Christian and Anti-Christian, and all manner of men, are invited to reflect on this. They will find it to be the truth of the case. The Noble in the high place, the Ignoble in the low; that is, in all times and in all countries, the Almighty Maker's Law.

To raise the Sham-Noblest, and solemnly consecrate *him* by whatever method, new-devised, or slavishly adhered to from old wont, this, little as we may regard it, is, in all times and countries, a practical blasphemy, and Nature will in no wise forget it. Alas, there lies the origin, the fatal necessity, of modern Democracy everywhere. It is the Noblest, not the Sham-Noblest; it is God-Almighty's Noble, not the Court-Tailor's Noble, nor the Able-Editor's Noble, that must in some approximate degree, be raised to the supreme place; he and not a counterfeit,—under penalties! Penalties deep as death, and at length terrible as hell-on-earth, my constitutional friend!—Will the ballot-box raise the Noblest to the chief place; does any sane man deliberately believe such a thing? That nevertheless is the indispensable result, attain it how we may: if that is attained, all is attained; if not that, nothing. He that cannot believe the ballot-box to be attaining it, will be comparatively indifferent to the ballot-box. Excellent for keeping the ship's crew at peace under their Phantasm Captain; but unserviceable, under such, for getting round Cape Horn. Alas, that there should be human beings requiring to have these things argued of, at this late time of day!

I say, it is the everlasting privilege of the foolish to be governed by the wise; to be guided in the right path by those who know it better than they. This is the first 'right of man;' compared with which all other rights are as nothing,—mere superfluities, corollaries which will follow of their own accord out of this; if they be not contradictions to this, and less than nothing! To the wise it is not a privilege; far other indeed. Doubtless, as bringing preservation to their country, it implies preservation to themselves withal; but intrinsically it is the harshest duty a wise man, if he be indeed wise, has laid to his hand. A duty which he would fain enough shirk; which accordingly, in these sad times of doubt and cowardly sloth, he has long everywhere been endeavouring to reduce to its minimum, and has in fact in most cases nearly escaped altogether. It is an ungoverned world; a world which we flatter ourselves will henceforth need no governing. On the dust of our heroic ancestors we too sit ballot-boxing, saying to one another, It is well, it is well! By inheritance of their noble struggles, we have been permitted to sit slothful so long. By noble toil, not by shallow laughter and vain talk, they made this English Existence from a savage forest into an arable inhabitable field for us; and we, idly dreaming it would grow spontaneous crops forever,—find it now in a too questionable state; peremptorily requiring real labour and agriculture again. Real 'agriculture' is not pleasant, much pleasanter to reap and winnow (with ballot-box or otherwise) than to plough!

Who would govern that can get along without governing? He that is fittest for it, is of all men the unwillingest unless constrained. By multifarious devices we have been endeavouring to dispense with governing; and by very superficial speculations, of *laissez-faire,* supply-and-demand, etc., etc., to persuade ourselves that it is best so. The Real Captain, unless it be some Captain of mechanical Industry hired by Mammon, where is he in these days? Most likely, in silence, in sad isolation somewhere, in remote obscurity; trying if, in an evil ungoverned time, he cannot at least govern himself. The Real Captain undiscoverable; the Phantasm Captain everywhere very conspicuous: —it is thought Phantasm Captains, aided by ballot-boxes, are the true method, after all. They are much the pleasantest for the time being! And so no *Dux* or Duke of any sort, in any province of our affairs, now *leads:* the Duke's Bailiff *leads,* what little leading is required for getting-in the rents; and the Duke merely rides in the state-coach. It is everywhere so: and now at last we see a world all rushing towards strange consummations, because it is and has long been so! . . .

Reader, did you ever hear of 'Constituted Anarchy'? Anarchy; the choking, sweltering, deadly and killing rule of No-rule; the consecration of cupidity, and braying folly, and dim stupidity and baseness, in most of the affairs of men? Slop-shirts attainable three-halfpence cheaper, by the ruin of living bodies and immortal souls? Solemn

Bishops and high Dignitaries, *our* divine 'Pillars of Fire by night,'
debating meanwhile, with their largest wigs and gravest look, upon
something they call 'prevenient grace'? Alas, our noble men of
genius, Heaven's *real* messengers to us, they also rendered nearly
futile by the wasteful time;—preappointed they everywhere, and
assiduously trained by all their pedagogues and monitors, to 'rise in
Parliament,' to compose orations, write books, or in short speak
words, for the approval of reviewers; instead of doing real kingly
work to be approved of by the gods! Our 'Government,' a highly 'responsible' one; responsible to no God that I can hear of, but to the
twenty-seven million *gods* of the shilling gallery. A Government
tumbling and drifting on the whirlpools and mud-deluges, floating
atop in a conspicuous manner, no-whither,—like the carcass of a
drowned ass. Authentic *Chaos* come up into this sunny Cosmos again;
and all men singing *Gloria in excelsis* to it. In spirituals and tem-
porals, in field and workshop, from Manchester to Dorsetshire, from
Lambeth Palace to the Lanes of Whitechapel, wherever men meet and
toil and traffic together,—Anarchy, Anarchy; and only the street-
constable (though with ever-increasing difficulty) still maintaining
himself in the middle of it; that so, for one thing, this blessed
exchange of slop-shirts for the souls of women may transact itself in
a peaceable manner!—I, for my part, do profess myself in eternal
opposition to this, and discern well that universal Ruin has us in the
wind, unless we can get out of this. My friend Crabbe, in a late number of his *Intermittent Radiator,* pertinently enough exclaims:

'When shall we have done with all this of British Liberty, Voluntary Principle, Dangers of Centralisation, and the like? It is really
getting too bad. For British Liberty, it seems, the people cannot be
taught to read. British Liberty, shuddering to interfere with the rights
of capital, takes six or eight millions of money annually to feed the
idle labourer whom it dare not employ. For British Liberty we live
over poisonous cess-pools, gully-drains, and detestable abominations;
and omnipotent London cannot sweep the dirt out of itself. British
Liberty produces—what? Floods of Hansard Debates every year, and
apparently little else at present. If these are the results of British
Liberty, I, for one, move we should lay it on the shelf a little, and
look-out for something other and farther. We have achieved British
Liberty hundreds of years ago; and are fast growing, on the strength
of it, one of the most absurd populations the Sun, among his great
Museum of Absurdities, looks down upon at present.'

9

PARETO
The Dominance of Elites

The approach to political rule expounded by Vilfredo Pareto (1848–1923) derives from what he conceived to be a scientific view of society freed from moral evaluations or metaphysical assumptions. Pareto grew up in an age dominated by the belief in democracy, progress and the perfectability of man. By the end of the century, however, these optimistic doctrines were all under open attack, and parliamentary institutions of liberal democratic states seemed to be disintegrating. From this time on, one finds increasing antirationalist approaches to the study of social behavior, and Pareto was one of the leading writers who contributed to this reaction. According to Pareto, man is motivated mainly by nonlogical factors: what he called *residues,* or instincts. Among these are several which are of particular significance to his analysis of political types. One class *(residues of combination)* is the tendency characteristic of human beings to combine or manipulate things and thoughts. A second class *(group persistences)* are drives which lead to the worship, defense and protection of established combinations. According to Pareto, there are two principal types of individuals. One group is that of the "foxes," strong in the residues of the first class: an adventurous, speculative type who lives by his wits and relies on fraud, deceit and cleverness. The other is the quality of "lions," predominant in residues of the second class; a conservative type, patriotic and loyal to tradition, tied to family, state and church. This type values character more than intelligence, talks much of "duty," and relies more on force than on intelligence. Pareto believed that society is divided into two strata: elites (or rulers) and nonelites (those who are ruled). The elite itself is divided into a governing and non-governing elite, and within the governing elite there is a still similar group or committee which exercises effective control. This is true whether a government is called a democracy, aristocracy, monarchy or dictatorship. Whether or not universal suffrage is practiced, it is always an oligarchy that rules; the art of government, Pareto was convinced, depends on the exercise of deceit and violence.

The elitist doctrine of Pareto has been interpreted on two different levels. One level of interpretation would perceive in Pareto a species of modern Machiavellianism: a justification for political rule by social elites who possess the qualities of the fox and the lion. From the view that such elites are inevitable tendencies in social behavior, it is an easy transition to the view that therefore such elites must possess qualities or abilities that give them the *right* to rule.

Another level of interpretation, however, is that Pareto (just as Machiavelli) must be regarded as an example of the modern trend toward scientific analysis of social phenomena where the focus of concern is not on the question of moral legitimacy or who *ought* to rule but rather what groups or classes do *in fact* exercise power in government. But even if one accepts this interpretation of Pareto, it obviously presents a serious challenge to the democratic claim of legitimacy, since it embodies the contention that popular rule is based on false and illusory foundations.

In the effort to cope with the challenge presented by elitist analysis, the defense of democratic theory involves two different types of response. One is to argue that the concept of elitism is not scientifically sound: crucial questions (such as the nature of power held by elites; the relation of elites to actual governing power; the character of limits upon power, etc.) are not satisfactorily answered. But the more important point is that even if one concedes the general proposition that governing power is invariably exercised by elites or minorities, it does not follow that democratic assumptions have been destroyed. For the essence of democracy, it may be contended, is not the determination of actual decisions by the electorate, but a system in which those who govern must acquire power by a competitive struggle for the people's vote and in which power exercised by elite groups can be subjected to constitutional checks and restraints.*

Social elites and their circulation. Suppose we begin by giving a theoretical definition of the thing we are dealing with, making it as exact as possible, and then go on to see what practical considerations we can replace it with to get a first approximation. Let us for the moment completely disregard considerations as to the good or bad, useful or harmful, praiseworthy or reprehensible character of the various traits in individuals, and confine ourselves to degrees—to

---

* The selections are from Vilfredo Pareto, *The Mind and Society: A Treatise of General Sociology* (New York: Dover Publications, 1935), pp. 1421–32; 1510–27; 1566–92. By permission of the Pareto Fund, New York.

whether, in other words, the trait in a given case be slight, average, intense, or more exactly, to the index that may be assigned to each individual with reference to the degree, or intensity, in him of the trait in question.

Let us assume that in every branch of human activity each individual is given an index which stands as a sign of his capacity, very much the way grades are given in the various subjects in examinations in school. The highest type of lawyer, for instance, will be given 10. The man who does not get a client will be given 1—reserving zero for the man who is an out-and-out idiot. To the man who has made his millions—honestly or dishonestly as the case may be—we will give 10. To the man who has earned his thousands we will give 6; to such as just manage to keep out of the poor-house, 1, keeping zero for those who get in. To the woman "in politics," such as the Aspasia of Pericles, the Maintenon of Louis XIV, the Pompadour of Louis XV, who has managed to infatuate a man of power and play a part in the man's career, we shall give some higher number, such as 8 or 9; to the strumpet who merely satisfies the senses of such a man and exerts no influence on public affairs, we shall give zero. To a clever rascal who knows how to fool people and still keep clear of the penitentiary, we shall give 8, 9, or 10, according to the number of geese he has plucked and the amount of money he has been able to get out of them. To the sneak-thief who snatches a piece of silver from a restaurant table and runs away into the arms of a policeman, we shall give 1. To a poet like Carducci we shall give 8 or 9 according to our tastes; to a scribbler who puts people to rout with his sonnets we shall give zero. For chess-players we can get very precise indices, noting what matches, and how many, they have won. And so on for all the branches of human activity.

We are speaking, remember, of an actual, not a potential, state. If at an English examination a pupil says: "I could know English very well if I chose to; I do not know any because I have never seen fit to learn," the examiner replies: "I am not interested in your alibi. The grade for what you know is zero." If, similarly, someone says: "So-and-so does not steal, not because he couldn't, but because he is a gentleman," we reply: "Very well, we admire him for his self-control, but his grade as a thief is zero."

There are people who worship Napoleon Bonaparte as a god. There are people who hate him as the lowest of criminals. Which are right? We do not choose to solve that question in connexion with a quite different matter. Whether Napoleon was a good man or a bad man, he was certainly not an idiot, nor a man of little account, as millions of others are. He had exceptional qualities, and that is enough for us to give him a high ranking, though without prejudice of any sort to questions that might be raised as to the ethics of his qualities or their social utility.

In short, we are here as usual resorting to scientific analysis, which distinguishes one problem from another and studies each one separately. As usual, again, we are replacing imperceptible variations in absolutely exact numbers with the sharp variations corresponding to groupings by class, just as in examinations those who are passed are sharply and arbitrarily distinguished from those who are "failed," and just as in the matter of physical age we distinguish children from young people, the young from the aged.

So let us make a class of the people who have the highest indices in their branch of activity, and to that class give the name of *elite*.

For the particular investigation with which we are engaged, a study of the social equilibrium, it will help if we further divide that class into two classes: a *governing elite,* comprising individuals who directly or indirectly play some considerable part in government, and a *non-governing elite,* comprising the rest.

A chess champion is certainly a member of the *elite,* but it is no less certain that his merits as a chess-player do not open the doors to political influence for him; and hence unless he has other qualities to win him that distinction, he is not a member of the governing *elite.* Mistresses of absolute monarchs have oftentimes been members of the *elite,* either because of their beauty or because of their intellectual endowments; but only a few of them, who have had, in addition, the particular talents required by politics, have played any part in government.

So we get two strata in a population: (1) A lower stratum, the *non-elite,* with whose possible influence on government we are not just here concerned; then (2) a higher stratum, *the elite,* which is divided into two: (a) a governing *elite;* (b) a non-governing *elite.*

In the concrete, there are no examinations whereby each person is assigned to his proper place in these various classes. That deficiency is made up for by other means, by various sorts of labels that serve the purpose after a fashion. Such labels are the rule even where there are examinations. The label "lawyer" is affixed to a man who is supposed to know something about the law and often does, though sometimes again he is an ignoramus. So, the government *elite* contains individuals who wear labels appropriate to political offices of a certain altitude—ministers, Senators, Deputies, chief justices, generals, colonels, and so on—making the apposite exceptions for those who have found their way into that exalted company without possessing qualities corresponding to the labels they wear.

Such exceptions are much more numerous than the exceptions among lawyers, physicians, engineers, millionaires (who have made their own money), artists of distinction, and so on; for the reason, among others, that in these latter departments of human activity the labels are won directly by each individual, whereas in the *elite* some of the labels—the label of wealth, for instance—are hereditary. In former times there were hereditary labels in the governing *elite* also— in our day hardly more than the label of king remains in that status; but if direct inheritance has disappeared, inheritance is still powerful indirectly; and an individual who has inherited a sizable patrimony can easily be named Senator in certain countries, or can get himself elected to the parliament by buying votes or, on occasion, by wheed- ling voters with assurances that he is a democrat of democrats, a Socialist, an Anarchist. Wealth, family, or social connexions also help in many other cases to win the label of the *elite* in general, or of the governing *elite* in particular, for persons who otherwise hold no claim upon it.

In societies where the social unit is the family the label worn by the head of the family also benefits all other members. In Rome, the man who became Emperor generally raised his freedmen to the higher class, and oftentimes, in fact, to the governing *elite*. For that matter, now more, now fewer, of the freedmen taking part in the Roman government possessed qualities good or bad that justified their wear- ing the labels which they had won through imperial bounty. In our societies, the social unit is the individual; but the place that the indi- vidual occupies in society also benefits his wife, his children, his con- nexions, his friends.

If all these deviations from type were of little importance, they might be disregarded, as they are virtually disregarded in cases where a diploma is required for the practice of a profession. Everyone knows that there are persons who do not deserve their diplomas, but experience shows that on the whole such exceptions may be over- looked.

One might, further, from certain points of view, at least, disregard deviations if they remained more or less constant quantitatively—if there were only a negligible variation in proportions between the total of a class and the people who wear its label without possessing the qualities corresponding.

As a matter of fact, the real cases that we have to consider in our societies differ from those two. The deviations are not so few that they can be disregarded. Then again, their number is variable, and the variations give rise to situations having an important bearing on the social equilibrium. We are therefore required to make a special study of them.

Furthermore, the manner in which the various groups in a population intermix has to be considered. In moving from one group to another an individual generally brings with him certain inclinations, sentiments, attitudes, that he has acquired in the group from which he comes, and that circumstance cannot be ignored.

To this mixing, in the particular case in which only two groups, the *elite,* and the *non-elite,* are envisaged, the term "circulation of elites" has been applied—in French, *circulation des elites* [or in more general terms "class-circulation"].

In conclusion we must pay special attention (1), in the case of one single group, to the proportions between the total of the group and the number of individuals who are nominally members of it but do not possess the qualities requisite for effective membership; and then (2), in the case of various groups, to the ways in which transitions from one group to the other occur, and to the intensity of that movement—that is to say, to the velocity of the circulation.

Velocity in circulation has to be considered not only absolutely but also in relation to the supply of and the demand for certain social elements. A country that is always at peace does not require many soldiers in its governing class, and the production of generals may be overexuberant as compared with the demand. But when a country is in a state of continuous warfare many soldiers are necessary, and though production remains at the same level it may not meet the demand. That, we might note in passing, has been one of the causes for the collapse of many aristocracies.

Another example. In a country where there is little industry and little commerce, the supply of individuals possessing in high degree the qualities requisite for those types of activity exceeds the demand. Then industry and commerce develop and the supply, though remaining the same, no longer meets the demand.

We must not confuse the state of law with the state of fact. The latter alone, or almost alone, has a bearing on the social equilibrium. There are many examples of castes that are legally closed, but into which, in point of fact, new-comers make their way, and often in large numbers. On the other hand, what difference does it make if a caste is legally open, but conditions *de facto* prevent new accessions to it? If a person who acquires wealth thereby becomes a member of the governing class, but no one gets rich, it is as if the class were closed; and if only a few get rich, it is as if the law erected serious barriers against access to the caste. Something of that sort was observable towards the end of the Roman Empire. People who acquired wealth entered the order of the curials. But only a few individuals made any money. Theoretically we might examine any number of groups. Practically we have to confine ourselves to the more important. We shall proceed by successive approximations, starting with the simple and going on to the complex.

Higher class and lower class in general. The least we can do is to divide society into two strata: a higher stratum, which usually contains the rulers, and a lower stratum, which usually contains the ruled. That fact is so obvious that it has always forced itself even upon the most casual observation, and so for the circulation of individuals between the two strata. Even Plato had an inkling of class-circulation and tried to regulate it artificially. The "new man," the upstart, the *parvenu,* has always been a subject of interest, and literature has analyzed him unendingly. Here, then, we are merely giving a more exact form to things that have long been perceived more or less vaguely. Above, we noted a varying distribution of residues in the various social groupings, and chiefly in the higher and the lower class. Such heterogeneousness is a fact perceived by the most superficial glance.

Changes in Class I and Class II residues occurring within the two social strata have an important influence in determining the social equilibrium. They have been commonly observed by laymen under a special form, as changes in "religious" sentiments, so called, in the higher stratum of society. It has often been noted that there were times when religious sentiments seemed to lose ground, others when they seemed to gain in strength, and that such undulations corresponded to social movements of very considerable scope. The uniformity might be more exactly described by saying that in the higher stratum of society Class II residues gradually lose in strength, until now and again they are reinforced by tides upwelling from the lower stratum.

Religious sentiments were very feeble in the higher classes in Rome towards the end of the Republic; but they gained notably in strength thereafter, through the rise to the higher classes of men from the lower, of foreigners that is, freedmen, and others, whom the Roman Empire raised in station. They gained still further in intensity in the days of the decadent Roman Empire, when the government passed into the hands of a military plebs and a bureaucracy originating in the lower classes. That was a time when the predominance of Class II residues made itself manifest in a decadence in literature and in the arts and sciences, and in invasions by Oriental religions and especially Christianity.

The Protestant Reformation in the sixteenth century, the Puritan Revolution in Cromwell's day in England, the French Revolution of 1789, are examples of great religious tides originating in the lower classes and rising to engulf the sceptical higher classes. An instance in our day would be the United States of America, where this upward thrust of members of lower classes strong in Class II residues is very intense; and in that country one witnesses the rise of no end of strange and wholly unscientific religions—such as Christian Science—that are utterly at war with any sort of scientific thinking, and a mass of hypocritical laws for the enforcement of morality that are replicas of laws of the European Middle Ages.

The upper stratum of society, the *elite,* nominally contains certain groups of people, not always very sharply defined, that are called aristocracies. There are cases in which the majority of individuals belonging to such aristocracies actually possess the qualities requisite for remaining there; and then again there are cases where considerable numbers of the individuals making up the class do not possess those requisites. Such people may occupy more or less important places in the governing *elite* or they may be barred from it.

In the beginning, military, religious, and commercial aristocracies and plutocracies—with a few exceptions not worth considering—must have constituted parts of the governing *elite* and sometimes have made up the whole of it. The victorious warrior, the prosperous merchant, the opulent plutocrat, were men of such parts, each in his own field, as to be superior to the average individual. Under those circumstances the label corresponded to an actual capacity. But as time goes by, considerable, sometimes very considerable, differences arise between the capacity and the label; while on the other hand, certain aristocracies originally figuring prominently in the rising *elite* end by constituting an insignificant element in it. That has happened especially to military aristocracies.

Aristocracies do not last. Whatever the causes, it is an incontestable fact that after a certain length of time they pass away. History is a graveyard of aristocracies. The Athenian "People" was an aristocracy as compared with the remainder of a population of resident aliens and slaves. It vanished without leaving any descent. The various aristocracies of Rome vanished in their time. So did the aristocracies of the Barbarians. Where, in France, are the descendants of the Frankish conquerors? The genealogies of the English nobility have been very exactly kept; and they show that very few families still remain to claim descent from the comrades of William the Conqueror. The rest have vanished. In Germany the aristocracy of the present day is very largely made up of descendants of vassals of the lords of old. The populations of European countries have increased enormously during the past few centuries. It is as certain as certain can be that the aristocracies have not increased in proportion.

They decay not in numbers only. They decay also in quality, in the sense that they lose their vigour, that there is a decline in the proportions of the residues which enabled them to win their power and hold it. The governing class is restored not only in numbers, but—and that is the more important thing—in quality, by families rising from the lower classes and bringing with them the vigour and the proportions of residues necessary for keeping themselves in power. It is also restored by the loss of its more degenerate members.

If one of those movements comes to an end, or worse still, if they both come to an end, the governing class crashes to ruin and often sweeps the whole of a nation along with it. Potent cause of disturbance in the equilibrium is the accumulation of superior elements in the lower classes and, conversely, of inferior elements in the higher classes. If human aristocracies were like thoroughbreds among animals, which reproduce themselves over long periods of time with approximately the same traits, the history of the human race would be something altogether different from the history we know.

In virtue of class-circulation, the governing *elite* is always in a state of slow and continuous transformation. It flows on like a river, never being today what it was yesterday. From time to time sudden and violent disturbances occur. There is a flood—the river overflows its banks. Afterwards, the new governing *elite* again resumes its slow transformation. The flood has subsided, the river is again flowing normally in its wonted bed.

Revolutions come about through accumulations in the higher strata of society—either because of a slowing-down in class-circulation, or from other causes—of decadent elements no longer possessing the residues suitable for keeping them in power, and shrinking from the use of force; while meantime in the lower strata of society elements of superior quality are coming to the fore, possessing residues suitable for exercising the functions of government and willing enough to use force.

In general, in revolutions the members of the lower strata are captained by leaders from the higher strata, because the latter possess the intellectual qualities required for outlining a tactic, while lacking the combative residues supplied by the individuals from the lower strata.

Violent movements take place by fits and starts, and effects therefore do not follow immediately on their causes. After a governing class, or a nation, has maintained itself for long periods of time on force and acquired great wealth, it may subsist for some time still without using force, buying off its adversaries and paying not only in gold, but also in terms of the dignity and respect that it had formerly enjoyed and which constitute, as it were, a capital. In the first stages of decline, power is maintained by bargainings and concessions, and people are so deceived into thinking that that policy can be carried on indefinitely. So the decadent Roman Empire bought peace of the Barbarians with money and honours. So Louis XVI, in France, squandering in a very short time an ancestral inheritance of love, respect, and almost religious reverence for the monarchy, managed, by making repeated concessions, to be the King of the Revolution. So the English aristocracy managed to prolong its term of power in the second half of the nineteenth century down to the dawn of its decadence which was heralded by the "Parliament Bill" in the first years of the twentieth. . . .

The use of force in society. Societies in general subsist because alive and vigorous in the majority of their constituent members are sentiments corresponding to residues of sociality (Class IV). But there are also individuals in human societies in whom some at least of those sentiments are weak or indeed actually missing. That fact has two interesting consequences, which stand in apparent contradiction, one of them threatening the dissolution of a society, the other making for its progress in civilization. What at bottom is there is continuous movement, but it is a movement that may progress in almost any direction.

It is evident that if the requirement of uniformity (residues IV–B) were so strongly active in all individuals in a given society as to prevent even one of them from breaking away in any particular from the uniformities prevalent in it, such a society would have no internal causes for dissolution; but neither would it have any causes for change, whether in the direction of an increase, or of a decrease, in the utility of the individuals or of the society. On the other hand if the requirement of uniformity were to fail, society would not hold together, and each individual would go his own way, as lions and tigers, birds of prey, and other animals do. Societies that endure and change are therefore situated in some intermediate condition between those two extremes.

A homogeneous society might be imagined in which the requirement of uniformity would be the same in all individuals, and would correspond to the intermediate state just mentioned. But observation shows that that is not the case with human societies. Human societies are essentially heterogeneous, and the intermediate state is attained because the requirement of uniformity is very strong in some individuals, moderately strong in others, very feeble in still others, and almost entirely absent in a few. The average is found not in each individual, but in the group comprising them all. One may add as a datum of fact that the number of individuals in whom the requirement of uniformity is stronger than the average requisite of the intermediate state in which the society is situated is much greater than the number of individuals in whom the requirement is weaker than that average, and very very much greater than the number in whom it is entirely missing.

For the reader who has followed us thus far it is needless to add that, in view of the effects of this greater or lesser potency of the sentiments of uniformity, one may foresee out of hand that two theologies will put in an appearance, one of which will glorify the immobility of one or another uniformity, real or imaginary, the other of which will glorify movement, progress, in one direction or another. That is what has actually happened in history. There have been popular Olympuses where the gods fixed and determined once and for all how human society was to be; and then, too, Olympuses of utopian reformers, who derived from their exalted minds conceptions of forms from which human society was never never more to deviate. On the other hand, from the days of ancient Athens down to our own, the lord gods of Movement in a Certain Direction have listened to the prayers of their faithful and now sit triumphant in our latter-day Olympus, where Progress Optimus Maximus reigns in sovereign majesty. So that intermediate situation of society has usually been attained as the resultant of many forces, prominent among them the two categories mentioned, which envisage different imaginary goals and correspond to different classes of residues.

To ask whether or not force ought to be used in a society, whether the use of force is or is not beneficial, is to ask a question that has no meaning; for force is used by those who wish to preserve certain uniformities and by those who wish to overstep them; and the violence of the ones stands in contrast and in conflict with the violence of the others. In truth, if a partisan of a governing class disavows the use of force, he means that he disavows the use of force by insurgents trying to escape from the norms of the given uniformity. On the other hand, if he says he approves of the use of force, what he really means is that he approves of the use of force by the public authority to constrain insurgents to conformity. Conversely, if a partisan of the subject class says he detests the use of force in society, what he really detests is the use of force by constituted authorities in forcing dissidents to conform; and if, instead, he lauds the use of force, he is thinking of the use of force by those who would break away from certain social uniformities.

Nor is there any particular meaning in the question as to whether the use of violence to enforce existing uniformities is beneficial to society, or whether it is beneficial to use force in order to overstep them; for the various uniformities have to be distinguished to see which of them are beneficial and which deleterious to society. Nor, indeed, is that enough; for it is further necessary to determine whether the utility of the uniformity is great enough to offset the harm that will be done by using violence to enforce it, or whether detriment from the uniformity is great enough to overbalance the damage that will be caused by the use of force in subverting it; in which detriment and damage we must not forget to reckon the very serious drawback involved in the anarchy that results from any frequent use of violence to abolish existing uniformities, just as among the benefits and utilities of maintaining frankly injurious uniformities must be counted the strength and stability they lend to the social order. So, to solve the problem as to the use of force, it is not enough to solve the other problem as to the utility, in general, of certain types of social organization; it is essential also and chiefly to compute all the advantages and all the drawbacks, direct and indirect. Such a course leads to the solution of a scientific problem; but it may not be and oftentimes is not the course that leads to an increase in social utility. It is better, therefore, if it be followed only by people who are called upon to solve a scientific problem or, to some limited extent, by certain individuals belonging to the ruling class; whereas social utility is oftentimes best served if the members of the subject class, whose function it is not to lead but to act, accept one of the two theologies according to the case—either the theology that enjoins preservation of existing uniformities, or the theology that counsels change.

What we have just said serves to explain, along with the theoretical difficulties, how it comes about that the solutions that are usually found for the general problem have so little and sometimes no bearing on realities. Solutions of particular problems come closer to the mark because, situated as they are in specific places and times, they present fewer theoretical difficulties; and because practical empiricism implicitly takes account of any circumstances that theory, until it has been carried to a state of high perfection, cannot explicitly appraise.

Considering violations of material conformities among modern civilized peoples, we see that, in general, the use of violence in repressing them is the more readily condoned in proportion as the violation can be regarded as an individual anomaly designed to attain some individual advantage, and the less readily condoned in proportion as the violation appears as a collective act aiming at some collective advantage, and especially if its apparent design be to replace general norms prevailing with certain other general norms.

That states all that there is in common between the large numbers of facts in which a distinction is drawn between so-called private and so-called political crimes. A distinction, and often a very sharp distinction, is drawn between the individual who kills or steals for his own benefit and the individual who commits murder or theft with the intent of benefiting a party. In general, civilized countries grant extradition for the former, but refuse it for the latter. In the same way one notes a continually increasing leniency towards crimes committed during labour strikes or in the course of other economic, social, or political struggles. There is a more and more conspicuous tendency to meet such aggressions with merely passive resistance, the police power being required not to use arms, or else permitted to do so only in cases of extreme necessity. Such cases never arise in practice. So long as the policeman is alive, the necessity is held not to be extreme, and it is bootless, after all, to recognize the extremity after he is in his grave and no longer in a position to profit by the considerate permission to use his revolver. Punishment by judicial process is also becoming less and less vigorous. Criminals are either not convicted or, being convicted, are released in virtue of some probation law, failing of which, they can still rely on commutations, individual pardons, or general amnesties, so that, sum total, they have little or nothing to fear from the courts. In a word, in a vague, cloudy, confused sort of way, the notion is coming to the fore that an existing government may make some slight use of force against its enemies, but no great amount of force, and that it is under all circumstances to be condemned if it carries the use of force so far as to cause the death of considerable numbers, of a small number, a single one, of its enemies; nor can it rid itself of them, either, by putting them in prison or otherwise.

What now are the correlations that subsist between this method of applying force and other social facts? We note, as usual, a sequence of actions and reactions, in which the use of force appears now as cause, now as effect. As regards the governing class, one gets, in the main, five groups of facts to consider: 1. A mere handful of citizens, so long as they are willing to use violence, can force their will upon public officials who are not inclined to meet violence with equal violence. If the reluctance of the officials to resort to force is primarily motivated by humanitarian sentiments, that result ensues very readily; but if they refrain from violence because they deem it wiser to use some other means, the effect is often the following: 2. To prevent or resist violence, the governing class resorts to "diplomacy," fraud, corruption—governmental authority passes, in a word, from the lions to the foxes. The governing class bows its head under the threat of violence, but it surrenders only in appearances, trying to turn the flank of the obstacle it cannot demolish in frontal attack. In the long run that sort of procedure comes to exercise a far-reaching influence on the selection of the governing class, which is now recruited only from the foxes, while the lions are blackballed. The individual who best knows the arts of sapping the strength of the foes of "graft" and of winning back by fraud and deceit what seemed to have been surrendered under pressure of force, is now leader of leaders. The man who has bursts of rebellion, and does not know how to crook his spine at the proper times and places, is the worst of leaders, and his presence is tolerated among them only if other distinguished endowments offset and defect. 3. So it comes about that the residues of the combination-instinct (Class I) are intensified in the governing class, and the residues of group-persistence (Class II) debilitated; for the combination-residues supply, precisely, the artistry and resourcefulness required for evolving ingenious expedients as substitutes for open resistance, while the residues of group-persistence stimulate open resistance, since a strong sentiment of group-persistence cures the spine of all tendencies to curvature. 4. Policies of the governing class are not planned too far ahead in time. Predominance of the combination instincts and enfeeblement of the sentiments of group-persistence result in making the governing class more satisfied with the present and less thoughtful of the future. The individual comes to prevail, and by far, over family, community, nation. Material interests and interests of the present or a near future come to prevail over the ideal interests of community or nation and interests of the distant future. The impulse is to enjoy the present without too much thought for the morrow. 5. Some of these phenomena become observable in international relations as well. Wars become essentially economic. Efforts are made to avoid conflicts with the powerful and the sword is rattled only before the weak. Wars are regarded more than anything else as speculations. A country is often unwittingly edged towards war by nursings of economic conflicts which, it is expected, will never get out of control and turn into armed conflicts. Not seldom, however, a war will be forced upon a country by peoples who are not so far advanced in the evolution that leads to the predominance of Class I residues.

As regards the subject class, we get the following relations, which correspond in part to the preceding: 1. When the subject class contains a number of individuals disposed to use force and with capable leaders to guide them, the governing class is, in many cases, overthrown and another takes its place. That is easily the case where governing classes are inspired by humanitarian sentiments primarily, and very very easily if they do not find ways to assimilate the exceptional indivduals who come to the front in the subject classes. A humanitarian aristocracy that is closed or stiffly exclusive represents the maximum of insecurity. 2. It is far more difficult to overthrow a governing class that is adept in the shrewd use of chicanery, fraud, corruption; and in the highest degree difficult to overthrow such a class when it successfully assimilates most of the individuals in the subject class who show those same talents, are adept in those same arts, and might therefore become the leaders of such plebeians as are disposed to use violence. Thus left without leadership, without talent, disorganized, the subject class is almost always powerless to set up any lasting regime. 3. So the combination-residues (Class I) become to some extent enfeebled in the subject class. But that phenomenon is in no way comparable to the corresponding reinforcement of those same residues in the governing class; for the governing class, being composed, as it is, of a much smaller number of individuals, changes considerably in character from the addition to it or withdrawal from it of relatively small numbers of individuals; whereas shifts of identical numbers produce but slight effects in the enormously greater total of the subject class. For that matter the subject class is still left with many individuals possessed of combination-instincts that are applied not to politics or activities connected with politics but to arts and trades independent of politics. That circumstance lends stability to societies, for the governing class is required to absorb only a small number of new individuals in order to keep the subject class deprived of leadership. However, in the long run the differences in temperament between the governing class and the subject class become gradually accentuated, the combination-instincts tending to predominate in the ruling class, and instincts of group-persistence in the subject class. When that difference becomes sufficiently great, revolution occurs. 4. Revolution often transfers power to a new governing class, which exhibits a reinforcement in its instincts of group-persistence and so adds to its designs of present enjoyment aspirations towards ideal enjoyments presumably attainable at some future time—scepticism in part gives way to faith. 5. These considerations must to some extent be applied to international relations. If the combination-instincts are reinforced in a given country beyond a certain limit, as compared with the instincts of group-persistence, that country may be easily vanquished in war by another country in which that change in relative proportions has not occurred. The potency of an ideal as a pilot to victory is observable in both civil and international strife. People who lose the habit of applying force, who acquire the habit of considering policy from a commercial standpoint and of judging it only in terms of profit and loss, can readily be induced to purchase peace; and it may well be that such a transaction taken by itself is a good one, for war might have cost more money than the price of peace. Yet experience shows that in the long run, and taken in con-nexion with the things that inevitably go with it, such practice leads a country to ruin. The combination-instincts rarely come to prevail in the whole of a population. More commonly that situation arises in the upper strata of society, there being few if any traces of it in the lower and more populous classes. So when a war breaks out one gazes in amazement on the energies that are suddenly manifested by the masses at large, something that could in no way have been foreseen by studying the upper classes only. Sometimes, as happened in the case of Carthage, the burst of energy may not be sufficient to save a country, because a way may have been inadequately prepared for and be incompetently led by the ruling classes, and soundly prepared for and wisely led by the ruling classes of the enemy country. Then again, as happened in the wars of the French Revolution, the energy in the masses may be great enough to save a country because, though the war may have been badly prepared for by its ruling classes, pre-parations and leadership have been even worse in the ruling classes of the enemy country, a circumstance that gives the constituent mem-bers of the lower strata of society time to drive their ruling class from power and replace it with another of greater energy and possessing the instincts of group-persistence in greater abundance. Still again, as happened in Germany after the disaster at Jena, the energy of the masses may spread to the higher classes and spur them to an activity that proves most effective as combining able leadership with enthusi-astic faith.

These, then, are the main, the outstanding phenomena, but other phenomena of secondary or incidental importance also figure. Not-able among such is the fact that if a ruling class is unable or unwilling or incompetent to use force to eradicate violations of uniformities in private life, anarchic action on the part of the subject class tends to make up for the deficiency. It is well known to history that the private vendetta languishes or recurs in proportion as public authority con-tinues or ceases to replace it. It has been seen to recur in the form of lynchings in the United States, and even in Europe. Whenever the influence of public authority declines, little states grow up within the state, little societies within society. So, whenever judicial process fails, private or group justice replaces it, and *vice versa*. In international relations, the tinselling of humanitarian and ethical declamation is just a dressing for an underlying force. The Chinese considered them-selves the superiors in civilization of the Japanese, and perhaps they were, but they lacked a military aptitude that the Japanese, in virtue of a surviving remnant of feudal "barbarism," possessed in abundance. So the poor Chinese were attacked by hordes of Europeans— whose exploits in China, as Sorel well says, remind one of the feats of the Spanish *conquistadores* in the Americas. They suffered murder, rapine, and pillage at European hands, and then paid an indemnity into the bargain; whereas the Japanese came off victorious over the Russians and now exact respect from everybody. A few centuries back, the subtle diplomacy of the Christian lords of Constantinople did not save them from ruin under the impact of the fanaticism and might of the Turks; and now, in this year 1913, on the very same spot, the victors show that they have deteriorated in their fanaticism and in their power and, in their turn reposing illusory hopes in the diplomatic arts, are defeated and overthrown by the vigour of their sometime subjects. Grievous the hallucination under which those statesmen labour who imagine that they can replace the use of force with unarmed law. Among the many examples that one might point to are Sulla's constitution in ancient Rome and the conservative constitution of the Third Republic in France. Sulla's constitution fell because the armed force that might have compelled respect for it was not maintained. The constitution of Augustus endured because his successors were in a position to rely on the might of the legions. When the Commune had been defeated and overthrown, Thiers decided that his government ought to find its support rather in the law than in armed force. As a result his laws were scattered like leaves before the hurricane of democratic plutocracy. We need say nothing of Louis XVI of France, who thought he could halt the Revolution with his royal veto, for his was the illusion of a spineless weakling who was soon to lose what little head he had.

All such facts as a rule present themselves in the guise of derivations. In one direction we get theories that condemn the use of violence by the subject class in whatever case, in the other direction theories that censure its use by public authority.

Ruling-class theories, when the requirement of logic is not too keenly felt, appeal simply to sentiments of veneration for holders of power, or for abstractions such as "the state," and to sentiments of disapprobation for individuals who try to disturb or subvert existing orders. Then when it is deemed advisable to satisfy the need of logic, the effort is to create a confusion between the violation of an established uniformity for the individual's exclusive profit and a violation designed to further some collective interest or some new uniformity. The aim in such a derivation is to carry over to the social or political act the reprobation that is generally visited upon common crime. Frequent in our day are reasonings in some way connected with the theology of Progress. Not a few of our modern governments have revolutionary origins. How condemn the revolutions that might be tried against them without repudiating the forefathers? That is attended to by invoking a new divine right: Insurrection was legitimate enough against governments of the past, where authority was based on force; it is not legitimate against modern governments, where the authority is based on "reason." Or else: Insurrection was legitimate against kings and oligarchies; it is never legitimate against "the People." Or again: Rebellion is justifiable where there is no universal suffrage, but not where that panacea is the law of the land. Or again: Revolt is useless and therefore reprehensible in all countries where "the People" are able to express their "will." Then finally— just to give some little satisfaction to their Graces, the Metaphysicists: Insurrection cannot be tolerated where a "state of law" exists. I hope I shall be excused if I do not define that very sweet entity here. For all of most painstaking researches on my part, it remains an entity altogether unknown to me, and I should much rather be asked to give the zoological pedigree of the Chimaera.

Again as usual, no one of these derivations has any exact meaning. All governments use force, and all assert that they are founded on reason. In the fact, whether universal suffrage prevails or not, it is always an oligarchy that governs, finding ways to give to the "will of the people" that expression which the few desire, from the "royal law" that bestowed the *imperium* on the Roman Emperors down to the votes of a legislative majority elected in one way or another, from the plebiscite that gave the empire to Napoleon III down to the universal suffrage that is shrewdly bought, steered, and manipulated by our "speculators." Who is this new god called Universal Suffrage? He is no more exactly definable, no less shrouded in mystery, no less beyond the pale of reality, than the hosts of other divinities; nor are there fewer and less patent contradictions in his theology than in theirs. Worshippers of Universal Suffrage are not led by their god. It is they who lead him—and by the nose, determining the forms in which he must manifest himself. Oftentimes, proclaiming the sanctity of "majority rule," they resist "majority rule" by obstructionist tactics, even though they form but small minorities, and burning incense

to the goddess Reason, they in no wise disdain, in certain cases,
alliances with Chicanery, Fraud, and Corruption. . . .

Government and its forms. Among the complex phenomena that
are observable in a society, of very great importance is the system of
government. That is closely bound up with the character of the governing class, and both stand in a relationship of interdependence with
all other social phenomena.

Oftentimes, as usual, too much importance has been attached to
forms at the expense, somewhat, of substance; and the thing chiefly
considered has been the form that the political regime assumed. However, in France, especially during the reign of Napoleon III, and more
particularly among economists, a tendency developed to ascribe little
or no importance to forms of government, and not only that, to substance as well. That was going to another extreme, and exclusively
"political" theories of society were met with exclusively "economic"
theories, among them the theory of economic determinism—the usual
mistake disregarding mutual correlation in social phenomena.

Those who attach supreme significance to forms of government find
it very important to answer the question, "What is the best form of
government?" But that question has little or no meaning unless the
society to which the government is to be applied is specified and
unless some explanation is given of the term "best," which alludes in
a very indefinite way to the various individual and social utilities.
Although that has now and then been sensed, consideration of governmental forms has given rise to countless derivations leading up to
this or that political myth, both derivations and myths being worth
exactly zero from the logico-experimental standpoint, but both of
them—or, rather the sentiments that they manifest—having, it may
be, effects of great consequence in the way of influencing human
conduct. It cannot be doubted that the sentiments manifested by the
monarchial, republican, oligarchic, democratic, and still other faiths,
have played and continue to play no mean part in social phenomena,
as is the case with the sentiments underlying other religions. The
"divine rights" of the prince, of the aristocracy, of the people, the
proletariat, the majority—or any other divine right that might be
imagined—have not the slightest experimental validity. We must
therefore consider them extrinsically only, as facts, as manifestations
of sentiments, operating, like other traits in the human beings that go
to make up a given society, to determine its mode of being, its form.
To say that no one of these "rights" has any experimental foundation

does not, of course, in any way impugn the utility to society with which it may be credited. Such an inference would be justified if the statement were a derivation, since in such reasonings it is generally taken for granted that anything that is not rational is harmful. But the question of utility is left untouched when the statement is rigorously logico-experimental, since then it contains no such implicit premise.

Here, as in dealing with other subjects of the kind, we stumble at the very first step on difficulties of terminology. That is natural enough: the objective investigations that we are trying to make require an objective terminology, whereas the subjective discussions that are commonly conducted can get along with the subjective terminology of ordinary parlance. Everyone recognizes that in our day "democracy" is tending to become the political system of all civilized peoples. But what is the exact meaning of the term "democracy"? It is even more vague than that vaguest of terms, "religion." We must therefore leave it to one side and turn to the facts that it covers.

One observes at the outset a pronounced tendency on the part of modern civilized peoples to use a form of government where legislative power rests largely with an assembly elected by a part at least of the citizens. One further notes a tendency to augment that power and increase the number of citizens electing the assembly.

In Switzerland, by way of exception, the legislative powers of the elective assembly are limited by the popular referendum, and in the United States they are to some extent checked by the federal courts. An attempt to limit them by plebiscite was made in France at the instance of Napoleon III. It met with no success, though one could not definitely assert that that was due to any inherent defect in the scheme itself, since the government that was created by it was destroyed by the armed forces of a foreign enemy. The tendency to increase numbers of voters is general, and along that road, for the time being, there is no going back. The franchise is continually being extended. After giving it to adult men, the idea is now to grant it to women. It is not beyond the range of possibility that it may be extended as regards age.

Underlying such forms, which are more or less the same with all civilized peoples, there are great differences in substance, like names being given to unlike things. The power of the legislative assembly varies all the way from a maximum to a minimum. In France both the Chamber of Deputies and the Senate are elective. For the purposes of our investigation, therefore, they may be regarded as a single

assembly, which is, one may say, absolutely sovereign and has no
limits to its power. In Italy, the power of the Chamber has a theoretical check in the Senate, an actual check in the monarchy. In England,
once upon a time, the power of the House of Commons found in the
House of Lords an actual check that is now very much attenuated,
and in the monarchy another that has likewise become largely nominal. In the United States the President is elected independently of the
Congress and effectively limits its power. In Germany the States'
Council and, to a still greater extent, the Emperor, supported by the
military caste, constituted very considerable checks on the power of the
Reichstag. So gradually we come to Russia, where the Duma has very
little power, and to Japan, where the elective assembly has almost none
at all. We may overlook Turkey and the republics of Central America,
where the legislative assemblies are more or less fanciful entities.

We need not linger on the fiction of "popular representation"—
poppycock grinds no flour. Let us go on and see what substance
underlies the various forms of power in the governing classes. Ignor-
ing exceptions, which are few in number and of short duration, one
finds everywhere a governing class of relatively few individuals that
keeps itself in power partly by force and partly by the consent of the
subject class, which is much more populous. The differences lie principally, as regards substance, in the relative proportions of force and
consent; and as regards forms, in the manners in which the force is
used and the consent obtained.

As we have elsewhere observed, if the consent were unanimous
there would be no need to use force; but that extreme is unknown to
fact. Another extreme has a few concrete illustrations—the case where
a despot keeps himself in power by armed force against a hostile
population (such cases all belong to the past); and then the case where
a foreign power holds a reluctant people in subjection—of that there
are still quite a few examples in the present. The reason why the
equilibrium is much more unstable in the first case than in the other
has to be sought in the prevalence of differing residues. The residues
working in the satellites of the despot are not essentially different
from those working in the despot's subjects, so that there is no faith
available to inspire, and at the same time to restrain, the use of force;
and as was the case with the praetorians, the janissaries, and the
Mamelukes, satellites are readily tempted to make capricious use of
their power, or else to abandon defence of the despot against the
people. The ruling nation, on the other hand, generally differs in

usages and customs and sometimes in language and religion, from the subject nation. There is a difference in residues, therefore, and so plenty of faith to inspire use of force. But there may be plenty of faith in the subject nation to inspire resistance to oppression; and that is how, in the long run, the equilibrium may chance to be upset.

It is in fear of that very outcome that conquering peoples try to assimilate their subject peoples, and when that can be done, it is by all odds the best way for them to assure their dominion. They often fail because they try to change residues by violence instead of taking advantages of existing residues. Rome had the faculty for this latter in pre-eminent degree, and so was able to assimilate the many peoples about her in Latium, Italy, and the Mediterranean basin.

We have had incidental occasion already to remark that the policies of governments are the more effective, the more adept they are at utilizing existing residues, the less effective, the less skilful, and in general total failures when they set out to change residues by force; and to tell the truth, almost all explanations as to the success or failure of certain policies of this or that government come down in the end to that principle.

Many people are prevented by derivations from recognizing the principle. If *A,* for instance, is the derivation that expresses certain sentiments of the subject class, another derivation, *B,* is readily found which at bottom expresses the sentiments of the dominant class but which the latter regards as a valid and convincing refutation of *A.* In that confidence it concludes that it will be an easy matter to force *B* upon the subject class, since that will be a mere question of opening their eyes to a truth so obvious. So the conflict between sentiments becomes a conflict between derivations or, in other terms, a mere battle of words. Others see the realities a little more clearly but use sophistries. They dwell at length on the advantages of a people's having unity of faith in certain matters, but neglect entirely to consider whether that can be accomplished without incurring very serious disadvantages that would offset or more than offset the advantages. Still others implicitly assume that for a person to take advantage of the sentiments of others without sharing them, he must necessarily have a purpose that is dishonest and detrimental to society, and so they condemn such conduct outright as worthy only of a wicked hypocrite.

To utilize the sentiments prevalent in a society for attaining a given purpose is in itself neither beneficial nor detrimental to society. The utility, or the detriment, depends upon the result achieved. If the result is beneficial, one gets a utility; if harmful, a detriment. Nor can it be said that when a governing class works for a result that will be advantageous to itself regardless of whether it will be beneficial, or the reverse, to its subject class, the latter is necessarily harmed. Countless the cases where a governing class working for its own exclusive advantage has further promoted the welfare of a subject class. In a word, utilization of the residues prevailing in a society is just a means, and its value the value of the results achieved.

Along with residues, considered as instruments of governing, come interests, and at times these are the only available agents for modifying residues. It is important, however, not to forget that naked interests alone, taken apart from sentiments, may indeed be a powerful instrument for influencing individuals showing a predominance of Class I residues and so for influencing numerous elements in a governing class; but that taken in that way by themselves, apart from sentiments, they have very little influence upon individuals showing a predominance of Class II residues, and consequently upon the subject class as a whole. One may say, in general and speaking very roughly, that the governing class has a clearer view of its own interests because its vision is less obscured by sentiments, whereas the subject class is less aware of its interests because its vision is more clouded by sentiments; and that, as a result, the governing class is in a position to mislead the subject class into serving the interests of the governing class; but that those interests are not necessarily opposite to the interests of the subject class, often in fact coincide with them, so that in the end the deception may prove beneficial to the subject class.

Consent and force appear in all the course of history as instruments of governing. They come forward in the legendary days of the *Iliad* and *Odyssey* to make the power of the Greek kings secure. They are discernible in the legends of the Roman kings. Later on, in historical times, in Rome they are busy under both Republic and Empire; and it is by no means to be taken for granted that the government of Augustus enjoyed any less support in the subject class than the various governments the last years of the Republic managed to secure. And so coming on through the Barbarian kings and the mediaeval republics down to the divine-right potentates of two or three centuries ago, and finally to our modern democratic regimes, we find all along the same mixture of force and consent.

Just as derivations are much more variable than the residues that underlie them, so the forms in which force and consent express themselves are much more variable than the sentiments and interests in which they originate; and the differences in the relative proportions of force and consent are in large part due to varying relative proportions of sentiments and interests. The parallel between derivations and forms of government goes farther still. They both have less influence upon the social equilibrium than do the sentiments and interests that underlie them. That fact has also been perceived by many scholars, but they have tended to go a little too far in asserting that forms of government are altogether matters of indifference.

A governing class is present everywhere, even where there is a despot, but the forms under which it appears are widely variable. In absolute governments a sovereign occupies the stage alone. In so-called democratic governments it is the parliament. But behind the scenes in both cases there are always people who play a very important role in actual government. To be sure they must now and again bend the knee to the whims of ignorant and domineering sovereigns or parliaments, but they are soon back at their tenacious, patient, never-ending work, which is of much the greater consequence. In the Roman *Digesta* one may read truly splendid constitutions bearing the names of very wretched Emperors, just as in our day we have very fair legal codes that have been enacted by fairly brainless parliaments. The cause in both cases is the same: The sovereign leaves everything to his legal advisers, in some cases not even divining what they are having him do—and parliaments today even less than many a shrewd leader or king. And least of all King Demos! And such blindness on his part has at times helped to effect betterments in conditions of living in the face of his prejudices, not to mention much-needed steps in behalf of national defence. King Demos, good soul, thinks he is following his own devices. In reality he is following the lead of his rulers. But that very very often turns out to the advantage of his rulers only, for they, from the days of Aristotle down to our own, have made lavish use of the arts of bamboozling King Demos. Our plutocrats, like those of the late Roman Republic, are at all times busy making money, either on their own account or to sate the hungry maws of their partisans and accomplices; and for anything else they care little or nothing. Among the derivations which they use to show that their rule is to the advantage of a country, interesting is the assertion that the public is better qualified to pass on general questions than on special ones. The fact, in reality, is the precise opposite. One has to talk only for a very brief time with an uneducated person to see that he grasps special questions, which are usually concrete, much more clearly than general questions, which as a rule are abstract. But abstract questions have the advantage for people in power that whatever the answers that are given them by the public, they will be able to draw any inference they choose from them. The people sends to parliament men who are pledged to abolish interest on capital and "surplus value" in industry, and check the "greed" of the "speculators" (general questions); and those representatives now directly, now indirectly by helping others, increase the public debt beyond all bounds and consequently the interest paid to capital, maintain and in fact increase the "surplus value" enjoyed by manufacturers (many of whom fatten on political demagoguery), and put the government of the nation into the hands of speculators such as Volpi, who concluded the Peace of Lausanne, or of cabinet ministers such as Caillaux and Lloyd George.

The governing class is not a homogeneous body. It too has a government—a smaller, choicer class (or else a leader, or a committee) that effectively and practically exercises control. Sometimes that fact is visible to the eye, as in the case of the Ephors of Sparta, the Council of Ten in Venice, the favourite ministers of absolute sovereigns, or the "bosses" in parliaments. At other times it is more or less hidden from view, as in the "caucus" in England, the political convention in the United States, the cliques of "speculator" chieftains who function in France and Italy, and so on. The tendency to personify abstractions or merely to think of them as objective realities inclines many people to picture the governing class as a person, or at least as a concrete unit, and imagine that it knows what it wants and executes by logical procedures designs which it had conceived in advance. In just such terms do anti-Semites think of the Jews, and many Socialists of the *"bourgeoisie"* (though others, coming closer to realities, think of the middle class as a "system" functioning to some extent quite aside from any design on the part of its members). Ruling classes, like other social groups, perform both logical and non-logical actions, and the chief element in what happens is in fact the order, or system, not the conscious will of individuals, who indeed may in certain cases be carried by the system to points where they would never have gone of deliberate choice. In speaking of "speculators," we must not think of them as actors in a melodrama who administer and rule the world, executing wicked designs by stratagem dark. Such a conception of them would be no more real than a fairy-story. Speculators are just people who keep their mind on their business, and being well supplied with Class I residues, take advantage of them to make money, following lines of least resistance, as after all everybody else does. They hold no meetings where they congregate to plot common designs, nor have they any other devices for reaching a common accord. That accord comes about automatically; for if in a given set of circumstances there is one line of procedure where the advantage is greatest and the resistance least, the majority of those who are looking for it will find it, and though each of them will be following it on his own account, it will seem, without being so, that they are all acting in common accord. But at other times they will be carried along by the sheer force of the system to which they belong, involuntarily, and indeed against their wills, following the course that is required of the system. Fifty years ago "speculators" had no conception whatever of the state of affairs that prevails today and to which their activities have brought them. The road they have followed has been the resultant of an infinitude of minor acts, each determined by the present advantage. As is the case with all social phenomena, it has been the resultant of certain forces operating in conjunction with certain ties and in the face of certain obstacles. When we say that at the present time our speculators are laying the foundations for a war by continually increasing public expenditures, we in no sense mean that they are doing that deliberately—quite to the contrary! They are continually increasing public expenditures and fanning economic conflicts not in order to bring on a war, but in order to make a direct profit in each little case. But that cause, though an important one, is not the main cause. There is another of greater importance—their appeal to sentiments of patriotism in the masses at large, as a device for governing. Furthermore, the speculators in the various countries are in competition with each other and are using armaments to exact concessions from rivals. Other similar causes are operating, and they all are leading to increases in armaments without that's being in any sense the consequences of preconceived design. Not only that. Those men who are rich in Class I residues sense intuitively, without needing to reason or theorize, that if a great and terrible war should occur, one of its possible consequences might be that they would have to give way to men who are rich in Class II residues. To such a war they are opposed in virtue of the same instinct that prompts the stag to run from the lion, though they are glad to take on little colonial wars, which they can superintend without any danger to themselves. It is on such interests and sentiments, not on any deliberate, premeditated resolve, that their activities depend, and these accordingly may eventually carry them to some objective that they may be aiming at, but also quite as readily to points where they would never have dreamed of going. Some day the war they have made way for but not wanted may break out; and then it will be a consequence of the past activities of the speculators, but not of any intent they have had either at that time or ever. So the speculators of ancient Rome brought on the fall of the Republic and the dictatorships of Caesar and Augustus, but without knowing that they were headed in those directions and without the slightest desire to reach those goals.

In dealing with speculators, as with other elements in the social order, the ethical aspect and the aspect of social utility have to be kept sharply distinguished. The speculators are not to be condemned from the standpoint of social utility because they do things that are censured by one or other of the current ethical systems; nor are they to be absolved from any given ethical standpoint because they have proved socially beneficial. The utility depends upon the circumstances in which the activities of the speculators are carried on, and specifically upon the relative proportions of speculators to persons strong in Class II residues, either in the population at large or in the governing classes. To determine and appraise such utility is a quantitative, not a qualitative, problem. In our day, for instance, the enormous development of economic production, the spread of civilization to new countries, the remarkable rise in standards of living among all civilized peoples, are in large part the work of speculators. But they have been able to do that work because they came from populations in which Class II residues were numerous and strong: and it is doubtful, indeed it is hardly probable, that benefits such as these could be realized if there were any great decline in the Class II residues in our masses at large or even merely in our governing classes.

To have a concrete instance of the applications of the instruments of governing just described, one might consider the case of Italy during the Depretis regime. How could that politician ever have been master of the Italian Chamber and the country for so many years? He was not the leader of a victorious army. He had none of the eloquence that stirs the emotions of men. He had none of the prestige born of high achievement. He was not forced upon the country by a king. What, then, the source of his strength? Only one answer is possible:

He was a past master at utilizing the sentiments and interests then prevailing in the country, and more especially the interests, and so becoming really the leader of the syndicate of speculators that was then ruling the country and to a large extent holding the substance of the power of which he enjoyed only the semblance. He made many speculators rich men by protective tariffs, railway deals, government contracts in which the state was robbed right and left, banking irregularities that were later exposed. Never was bandit chieftain more lavish towards his confederates in pillage and plunder. Crispi was an interlude. His was an administration that set out to modify residues and cared little for the interests of speculators. He aspired to creating sentiments of nationalism in a people that had no sense of country, and his work, like the work of all men who have tried what he tried, came to nothing. Instead of using the Socialists, he fought them and so had their more intelligent and active leaders against him. And hostile or indifferent were the speculators, to whom he tossed few if any bones to pick. In a word, the conditions of the economic period in which he ruled were all in his disfavour. He fell incidentally as the result of a defeat in Abyssinia, but he could not have lasted long in power in any event. Remarkable the contrast between him and his successor, Giolitti, who was truly a master in the art of using interests and sentiments. He, no less than Depretis, made himself the leader of the speculator class and the protector of "big business"; and since money was required for helping the latter, and the banks had their money tied up in government loans, he provided the government with funds by founding the insurance monopoly, so making the money in the banks available for "big business." Sentiments he had a gift for using in a truly marvellous way, never overlooking a single one. Crispi had striven to create nationalist sentiments in the country, and he had striven in vain. Giolitti found them ready-made, and exploited them lavishly and ever with success. He never dreamed of fighting Socialism. He billed and cooed with its leaders till he got them—as he himself said—to "pack Marx away in the attic." Others he tamed to such an extent that they came to deserve their nickname as "the King's Socialists." He lavished money on the Socialist cooperatives, and that he was in a position to do, because economic conditions were in his favor; just as they had been unfavorable to Crispi; and those same conditions allowed him to carry the Libyan adventure to a successful conclusion and defer to the Greek calends the liquidation of the huge public debt that was incurred in connexion with his policies. Friendly with the Socialists, at least with such among them as were not too savage and staunch, he was not unfriendly to the Clericals, and if he did not tame them, he at least made them more tractable, and could depend on them extensively at election time. Taking advantage of an enthusiastic public consensus in sentiments of nationalism, he broke up the close-knit body of Republicans and reduced that party to a small nucleus of zealots blindly keeping faith with their principles. He extended the franchise to strike terror into the hearts of the *bourgeoisie* and make himself its protector, meanwhile doing his utmost to look like the patron of the popular parties. In a word, there was not a sentiment nor an interest in Italy of which he failed to make clever use for his purposes, so piling success on success and going through with the Libyan enterprise, which was something far more costly and dangerous than the Abyssinian venture that had proved so fatal to Crispi. It is said that he did not want the war with Turkey and fought it only as a sop to certain sentiments, using it as an instrument of governing. Like all men preponderantly endowed with Class I residues, he could use sentiments, but he did not understand them. He could never see how they could still be strong in the masses at large when they showed themselves so pliant in the popular leaders whom he flattered and cajoled. He therefore had no accurate perception of their social significance. That was no great hindrance to him in his deft manoeuvres from moment to moment; but it prevented him from having any broad view of the future that he was meantime preparing. But that, after all, did not worry him greatly—his eye was wholly on the present. In fighting the Libyan War, he was striking a grievous blow at the Ottoman Empire and so bringing on the Balkan War, and as a result profoundly altering the balance in Europe. Yet he made no efforts to strengthen the military and naval forces of his country with a view to oncoming wars. He refused to increase army and navy appropriations in the degree required because he did not care to exasperate the tax-payers, and especially because he needed the votes of the Socialists. On the other hand, he made loud boast of the fact that in spite of his war he had maintained or increased expenditures on public works and in subventions of various kinds to voters. He concealed the amounts the war had cost by disguising them in his budget reports, postponing payment of them to the future. He increased the public debt clandestinely by issuing long-term treasury bonds, so filling the coffers of commercial and savings-banks but with grave risks of danger to come. By such devices he made ready to have

his war and yet conceal its costs. The policy was momentarily convenient, for by those devices he was able to satisfy both the elements
who wanted the war and the elements who were unwilling to shoulder
its inevitable consequences. But it postponed and aggravated the difficulties that it failed to solve.

In this particular case one sees, as under a magnifying lens, the
kind of thing that speculators generally tend to do. The great predominance of Class I and the virtual absence of Class II residues in
Giolitti and his followers first was a great help and then ended by
being a great handicap to their power, which was all but shattered by
fifty or more Socialist Deputies who were sent to the parliament by
the elections of 1913 and who were strong in Class II residues. Before
that campaign the Socialist party had had to choose between "trans-
formism" and "intransigence" (non-compromise) in other words,
between following a course more particularly featured by Class I residues and a course prevailingly featured by Class II residues. As
usually happens with both nations and parties, the Socialist leaders
were inclined to follow the first course; but a great tidal wave came
surging up from the masses and bore new leaders to the fore, and
then swept them, with a few survivors from among the old, along the
second course, where sentiments predominated. That was fortunate for
the Socialist party, for it was in that way placed in a favourable position for giving battle to a government that had no convictions and no
faith. And in that we have a particular instance of a development
that is general and with which we shall have to deal at some length.
In other words, we discover that the greatest strength of a party lies
not in the exclusive predominance of Class I residues or of Class II
residues, but in a combination of residues from the two classes in certain relative proportions.

The interlude provided by the administration of Luzzatti confirms
these inferences. Luzzatti had been of great help to elements that
profited by protective tariffs, but they had no further need of him
when he became Prime Minister—at that time protection was in no
danger, and once water has gone over the dam it comes no more to
the mill. Furthermore, Luzzatti was far from being as good a representative of the speculators as Giolitti had been, nor did he have
Giolitti's faculty for using sentiments without sharing them. For that
reason Giolitti remained the actual "boss" during Luzzatti's turn in
power and took power away from him with the greatest ease when he
judged the moment opportune. Likewise Sonnino, who is far superior

to many another statesman in Italy so far as education and political thinking are concerned, has never been able to last long in power, because he lacks either the ability or the inclination to act as a faithful agent of the band of speculators. In France, Rouvier was frequently "boss" of the parliament simply because of his merits as leader of a similar band, and his last ministry came to an end not because of difficulties at home but because of difficulties abroad. Caillaux's strength lies altogether in the speculators who are gathered about him. But it would be wiser for us not to stop at these names or any other list of the kind and imagine that we are dealing with situations peculiar to certain individuals, certain political systems, certain countries. They are closely bound up with a social system in which speculators make up the governing *elite*. In England the election campaigns against the House of Lords were backed financially by speculators led by so-called Liberal ministers. In Germany the great manufacturing and financial interests reach the very foot of the throne, though that choice spot is still to some extent disputed by the military caste. In the United States Wilson and Bryan went into power as professed and probably sincere opponents of trusts and financiers, but actually they worked in their favour in maintaining anarchy in Mexico with a view to securing a President there who would be subservient to American finance. And those pacifists carried their self-composure to the extent of inviting Mexico to attend the Peace Congress at The Hague at the very moment when the American navy was attacking Ver Cruz, killing men, women and children! The recent past is very much like the present. In France Louis Napoleon Bonaparte was able to become Napoleon III only because he had become the leader of the speculators, while in Italy administrations of the past have fallen through unawareness of the importance of speculators or through disregarding or neglecting them. It would perhaps be going too far, though not very much too far, to say that if the governments of the King of Naples and his other neighbours had made a concession of the "Railways of the South" to private interests, and promoted other similar enterprises, they would not have been overthrown. For years and years French and Italian liberals have tired our ear-drums with their praises of the English parliamentary system, which they have held up as a model before the whole world. Some of them may possibly have been ignorant of the extraordinary corruption which features that system and has been so excellently described by Ostrogorski. But others must certainly have known of it, and if they have held their peace, it has been in deference to the principle that wolf does not eat wolf.

For purposes of maintaining its power the governing class uses individuals from the subject class, who may be grouped in two divisions corresponding to the two principal instruments for holding power secure. The one group used force, and is made up of soldiers, police of one sort or another, and the *bravi* of a day gone by; the other uses skill, and ranges in character and in time all the way from the clientage of the old Roman politicians to the clienteles of our contemporary politicians. Those two groups are always with us, but never in the same actual proportions, nor, much less, in the same visible proportions. One extreme is marked by the Rome of the praetorians, where the chief *de facto* instrument of governing, and even more so the visible instrument, was armed force. The other extreme is represented by the United States of America, where the chief actual instrument of governing, and to a somewhat lesser extent the apparent instrument, is the political "machine." These cliques work in various ways. The principal way is the least conspicuous. The administration in power "looks after" the interests of the speculators, and often without any explicit understanding with them. A protectionist government, for instance, gets the confidence and the support of the manufacturers it protects without having to come to explicit terms with all of them, though it may have some agreement with outstanding individuals. The situation is the same with public works, though agreement with the big contractors is becoming the rule. Other ways are better known—they are less important from the social standpoint, but are commonly regarded as more important from the ethical standpoint. Among them is the bribery of voters, elected officials, government ministers, newspaperowners, and other such persons, which has its counterpart under systems of absolutism in the bribery of courtiers, favourites, male and female, officials, generals, and so on—an old form of corruption that has not altogether disappeared. Such means have been employed in all periods of history, from the days of ancient Athens and republican Rome down to our own; but they are really the consequences of government by a class that forces its way into power by cunning and rules by cunning. And that is why the numberless attempts which have been made to "purify" politics have been failures and still remain such. Witch-grass may be cut as often as one chooses, but it sprouts only the more rankly if the roots are left untouched. Our democracies in France, Italy, England, and the United

States are tending more and more to become demagogic plutocracies and may be following that road on the way to one of those radical transformations that have been witnessed in the past.

Barring some few exceptions, chief among them the conferring of honours and decorations by governments, money has to be spent to secure the support both of armed force and of political "machines." It is not enough, therefore, to be willing to use such instruments—one has to be able to. That capacity is correlated with the production of wealth, and the production of wealth, in its turn, is not independent of the manner in which armed force and the political following are utilized. The problem therefore is a complex one and has to be considered synthetically. Analytically, one may say that armed force in many cases costs less than the "machine," but in certain other cases the "machine" may prove to be more favourable to the production of wealth; and that has to be taken into account in striking the balance.

Evolution towards "democracy" seems to stand in strict correlation with the increased use of that instrument of governing which involves resort to artifice and to the "machine," as against the instrument of force. In ancient times that was clearly observable towards the end of the Republic in Rome, where there was a conflict between precisely those two instrumentalities, force winning the final victory in the Empire. It is even more apparent in our own day, when the regimes in many "democratic" countries might be defined as a sort of feudalism that is primarily economic and in which the principal instrument of governing is the manipulation of political followings, whereas the military feudalism of the Middle Ages used force primarily as embodied in vassalage. A political system in which "the people" expresses its "will"—given but not granted that it has one—without cliques, intrigues, "combines," "gangs," exists only as a pious wish of theorists. It is not to be observed in reality, either in the past or in the present, either in our Western countries or in any others.

Such phenomena, long the subject of remark, are usually described as aberrations, or "degenerations," of "democracy"; but when and where one may be introduced to the perfect, or even the merely decent, state from which said aberration or "degeneration" has occurred, no one ever manages to tell. The best that can be said is that when democracy was an opposition party it did not show as many blemishes as it does at present; but that is a trait common to almost all opposition parties, which lack not so much the will as the chance to go wrong.

It is further to be noted that the defects in various systems of government may differ from each other, but, taking things as a whole, it cannot be held that one type of regime is very different in that respect from any other. The criticisms that are levelled at modern democracy are not greatly different from those that were levelled at ancient democracies, the Athenian, for instance; and if there are cases of corruption in democracies old and new, it would not be difficult to find cases just as bad in absolute and constitutional monarchies, in oligarchical governments, and in any other sort of regime.

10

FASCISM

Race, State Worship and the Rule of Force

Fascist doctrine of political rulership should be seen in relation to several of its main ideological components. The keystone of Italian Fascism was the concept of the all-powerful and omnipotent state which is not only the giver of laws and the founder of institutions but the source of the spiritual and moral values of all individuals and groups who compose it. Fascism thus stands in radical opposition to liberal, individualist views of the state and the principle of majority rule. According to Benito Mussolini (1883–1945), government can never be based on popular majorities: Fascism affirms the irremedial and beneficent inequality of man which cannot be leveled by universal suffrage. Italian Fascism proclaimed the indispensable role of the heroic leader who stands at the vortex of the state, born of the needs of the time; he is seen to be a man of courage with a sincerity of purpose, a strong belief in the role he is destined to play, and knowledge of the truth through his supreme gift of intuition.

The Nazi theory of leadership stems from the concept of the German *Volk,* a common consciousness of solidarity and organic unity in which the myth of Aryan racial supremacy was a dominant component. According to Nazi theory, all progress is a struggle for survival in which particular racial groups contend for supremacy. The so-called Aryan race, it was alleged, produced all that has moral and cultural value in modern European civilization. Struggle also takes place within the race, giving rise to a natural elite at whose head is the leader: the man of genius, heroic qualities and intuitive vision in whose name everything is done and whose actions can never be questioned. The *Führer* is considered to be the bearer of the people's will, independent of all groups, associations, interests and civil laws but bound by laws inherent in the nature of the people.

Although the leader is thus considered to be representative of the collective will of the people, Fascism repudiates the democratic concept of parliamentary government and majority rule. The broad mass of the people is considered incapable of intelligent or enlightened judgment; government by majority rule, according to Adolf Hitler (1889–1945), sins against the basic aristocratic principle of nature. The power of the leader, however, is seen to be dependent on the fanatical devotion of the masses, which must be secured through effective use of the methods and techniques of propaganda.

Common to German and Italian Fascism is a repudiation of the pacifist aspects of liberalism and socialism and affirmation of force and power as the determining factors of politics. The dominance of the strong over the weak is seen as an inevitable fact of the struggle for existence and the basis for all great accomplishments and achievements. This approach to politics is closely related to the deeply irrational character of Fascist ideology: its emphasis upon action rather than concern for theory; its commitment to the belief that the path to greatness and achievement is not a matter of thought and reason but heroic will to power; its glorification of feeling, sentiment and racial intuition.

In its affirmation of the all-powerful, heroic leader, Fascism shows strong continuity with previous traditions of authoritarian political rule. What is unique in Fascism, however, is its thoroughgoing totalitarianism: the emphasis upon absolute state power, not only in the political sphere, but state control and supervision of economic activity, education, the arts and the mass media in the interests of promoting Fascist objectives and principles. The legitimate province of the state is the total society: no area of individual or group interests can be considered outside the sphere of state control and regulation.

The outcome of World War II destroyed Fascism as a major political movement, but its ideas and principles did not die with Hitler and Mussolini; certain of its basic features are embodied in the governments of Spain and Portugal; its ideas continue to find strong exponents in most Western nations. Conditions of severe economic and social crisis could easily bring about a more widespread revival of Fascism as a serious challenge to democracy.

The selections from Fascist sources presented in this volume are designed to present ideas expressed by two of the chief leaders of Fascism in the modern era: Adolf Hitler and Benito Mussolini. Hitler became chancellor of Germany in 1933, inaugurating a program of totalitarianism, external expansion, terrorization and war scarcely equaled in all history. Hitler was an impassioned orator, and many of the basic concepts of German Nazism are revealed in his speeches to the German nation. Mussolini was the founder of the Fascist Party in Italy and dictator from 1922 until his death in 1945. The selection from Mussolini first appeared in a contribution to the *Enciclopedia Italiana* in 1932, and it is generally considered to be one of the most famous statements of the philosophy of Fascism.

a. MUSSOLINI

*The Doctrine of Fascism**

Like every sound political conceptions, Fascism is both practice and thought; action in which a doctrine is immanent, and a doctrine which, arising out of a given system of historical forces, remains embedded in them and works there from within. Hence it has a form correlative to the contingencies of place and time, but it has also a content of thought which raises it to a formula of truth in the higher level of the history of thought. In the world one does not act spiritually as a human will dominating other wills without a conception of the transient and particular reality under which it is necessary to act, and of the permanent and universal reality in which the first has its being and its life. In order to know men it is necessary to know man; and in order to know man it is necessary to know reality and its laws. There is no concept of the State which is not fundamentally a concept of life, philosophy or intuition, a system of ideas which develops logically or is gathered up into a vision or into a faith, but which is always, at least virtually, an organic conception of the world.

Thus Fascism could not be understood in many of its practical manifestations as a party organization, as a system of education, as a discipline, if it were not always looked at in the light of its whole way of conceiving life, a spiritual way. The world seen through Fascism is not this material world which appears on the surface, in which man is an individual separated from all others and standing by himself, and in which he is governed by a natural law that makes him instinctively live a life of selfish and momentary pleasure. The man of Fascism is an individual who is nation and fatherland, which is a moral law, binding together individuals and the generations into a tradition and a mission, suppressing the instinct for a life enclosed within the brief round of pleasure in order to restore within duty a higher life free from the limits of time and space; a life in which the individual, through the denial of himself, through the sacrifice of his own private interests, through death itself, realizes that completely spiritual existence in which his value as a man lies.

* From *The Social and Political Doctrines of Contemporary Europe*, Michael Oakeshott, ed. (Cambridge University Press, 1939), pp. 164–68; 170–79. Used by permission.

Therefore it is a spiritualized conception, itself the result of the general reaction of modern times against the flabby materialistic positivism of the nineteenth century. Anti-positivistic, but positive: not sceptical, nor agnostic, nor pessimistic, nor passively optimistic, as are, in general, the doctrines (all negative) that put the centre of life outside man, who with his free will can and must create his own world. Fascism desires an active man, one engaged in activity with all his energies: it desires a man virilely conscious of the difficulties that exist in action and ready to face them. It conceives of life as a struggle, considering that it behoves man to conquer for himself that life truly worthy of him, creating first of all in himself the instrument (physical, moral, intellectual) in order to construct it. Thus for the single individual, thus for the nation, thus for humanity. Hence the high value of culture in all its forms (art, religion, science), and the enormous importance of education. Hence also the essential value of work, with which man conquers nature and creates the human world (economic, political, moral, intellectual).

This positive conception of life is clearly an ethical conception. It covers the whole of reality, not merely the human activity which controls it. No action can be divorced from moral judgement; there is nothing in the world which can be deprived of the value which belongs to everything in its relation to moral ends. Life, therefore, as conceived by the Fascist, is serious, austere, religious: the whole of it is poised in a world supported by the moral and responsible forces of the spirit. The Fascist disdains the "comfortable" life.

Fascism is a religious concept in which man is seen in his immanent relationship with a superior law and with an objective Will that transcends the particular individual and raises him to conscious membership of a spiritual society. Whoever has seen in the religious politics of the Fascist regime nothing but mere opportunism has not understood that Fascism besides being a system of government is also, and above all, a system of thought.

Fascism is an historical conception, in which man is what he is only in so far as he works with the spiritual process in which he finds himself, in the family or social group, in the nation and in the history in which all nations collaborate. From this follows the great value of tradition, in memories, in language, in customs, in the standards of social life. Outside history man is nothing. Consequently Fascism is opposed to all the individualistic abstractions of a materialistic nature like those of the eighteenth century; and it is opposed to all Jacobin utopias and innovations. It does not consider that "happiness" is possible upon earth, as it appeared to be in the desire of the economic literature of the eighteenth century, and hence it rejects all teleological theories according to which mankind would reach a definitive stabilized condition at a certain period in history. This implies putting oneself outside history and life, which is a continual change and coming to be. Politically, Fascism wishes to be a realistic doctrine; practically, it aspires to solve only the problems which arise historically of themselves and that of themselves find or suggest their own solution. To act among men, as to act in the natural world, it is necessary to enter into the process of reality and to master the already operating forces.

Against individualism, the Fascist conception is for the State; and it is for the individual in so far as he coincides with the State, which is the conscience and universal will of man in his historical existence. It is opposed to classical Liberalism, which arose from the necessity of reacting against absolutism, and which brought its historical purpose to an end when the State was transformed into the conscience and will of the people. Liberalism denied the State in the interests of the particular individual; Fascism reaffirms the State as the true reality of the individual. And if liberty is to be the attribute of the real man, and not of that abstract puppet envisaged by individualistic Liberalism, Fascism is for liberty. And for the only liberty which can be a real thing, the liberty of the State and of the individual within the State. Therefore, for the Fascist, everything is in the State, and nothing human or spiritual exists, much less has value, outside the State. In this sense Fascism is totalitarian, and the Fascist State, the synthesis and unity of all values, interprets, develops and gives strength to the whole life of the people.

Outside the State there can be neither individuals nor groups (political parties, associations, syndicates, classes). Therefore Fascism is opposed to Socialism, which confines the movement of history within the class struggle and ignores the unity of classes established in one economic and moral reality in the State; and analogously it is opposed to class syndicalism. Fascism recognizes the real exigencies for which the socialist and syndicalist movement arose, but while recognizing them wishes to bring them under the control of the State and give them a purpose within the corporative system of interests reconciled within the unity of the State.

Individuals form classes according to the similarity of their interests, they form syndicates according to differentiated economic activities within these interests; but they form first, and above all, the State, which is not to be thought of numerically as the sum-total of individuals forming the majority of a nation. And consequently Fascism is opposed to Democracy, which equates the nation to the majority, lowering it to the level of that majority; nevertheless it is the purest form of democracy if the nation is conceived, as it should be, qualitatively and not quantitatively, as the most powerful idea (most powerful because most moral, most coherent, most true) which acts within the nation as the conscience and the will of a few, even of One, which ideal tends to become active within the conscience and the will of all—that is to say, of all those who rightly constitute a nation by reason of nature, history or race, and have set out upon the same line of development and spiritual formation as one conscience and one sole will. Not a race, nor a geographically determined region, but as a community historically perpetuating itself, a multitude unified by a single idea, which is the will to existence and to power: consciousness of itself, personality.

This higher personality is truly the nation in so far as it is the State. It is not the nation that generates the State, as according to the old naturalistic concept which served as the basis of the political theories of the national States of the nineteenth century. Rather the nation is created by the State, which gives to the people, conscious of its own moral unity, a will and therefore an effective existence. The right of a nation to independence derives not from a literary and ideal consciousness of its own being, still less from a more or less unconscious and inert acceptance of a *de facto* situation, but from an active consciousness, from a political will in action and ready to demonstrate its own rights: that is to say, from a state already coming into being. The State, in fact, as the universal ethical will, is the creator of right.

The nation as the State is an ethical reality which exists and lives in so far as it develops. To arrest its development is to kill it. Therefore the State is not only the authority which governs and gives the form of laws and the value of spiritual life to the wills of individuals, but it is also a power that makes its will felt abroad, making it known and respected, in other words, demonstrating the fact of its universality in all the necessary directions of its development. It is consequently organization and expansion, at least virtually. Thus it can be likened to the human will which knows no limits to its development and realizes itself in testing its own limitlessness.

The Fascist State, the highest and most powerful form of personality, is a force, but a spiritual force, which takes over all the
forms of the moral and intellectual life of man. It cannot therefore
confine itself simply to the functions of order and supervision as
Liberalism desired. It is not simply a mechanism which limits the
sphere of the supposed liberties of the individual. It is the form, the
inner standard and the discipline of the whole person; it saturates the
will as well as the intelligence. Its principle, the central inspiration of
the human personality living in the civil community, pierces into the
depths and makes its home in the heart of the man of action as well
as of the thinker, of the artist as well as of the scientist: it is the soul
of the soul. . . .

Above all, Fascism, in so far as it considers and observes the future
and the development of humanity quite apart from the political considerations of the moment, believes neither in the possibility nor in
the utility of perpetual peace. It thus repudiates the doctrine of Pacifism—born of renunciation of the struggle and an act of cowardice in
the face of sacrifice. War alone brings up to their highest tension all
human energies and puts the stamp of nobility upon the peoples who
have the courage to meet it. All other trials are substitutes, which
never really put a man in front of himself in the alternative of life and
death. A doctrine, therefore, which begins with a prejudice in favour
of peace is foreign to Fascism; as are foreign to the spirit of Fascism,
even though acceptable by reason of the utility which they might
have in given political situations, all internationalistic and socialistic
systems which, as history proves, can be blown to the winds when
emotional, idealistic and practical movements storm the hearts of
peoples. Fascism carries over this anti-pacifist spirit even into the lives
of individuals. The proud motto of the *Squadrista, "Me ne frego,"*
written on the bandages of a wound is an act of philosophy which is
not only stoical, it is the epitome of a doctrine that is not only political: it is education for combat, the acceptance of the risks which it
brings; it is a new way of life for Italy. Thus the Fascist accepts and
loves life, he knows nothing of suicide and despises it; he looks on
life as duty, ascent, conquest: life which must be noble and full: lived
for oneself, but above all for those others near and far away, present
and future.

The "demographic" policy of the regime follows from these
premises. Even the Fascist does in fact love his neighbour, but this
"neighbour" is not for him a vague and ill-defined concept; love for

one's neighbour does not exclude necessary educational severities, and still less differentiations and distances. Fascism rejects universal concord, and, since it lives in the community of civilized peoples, it keeps them vigilantly and suspiciously before its eyes, it follows their states of mind and the changes in their interests and it does not let itself be deceived by temporary and fallacious appearances.

Such a conception of life makes Fascism the precise negation of that doctrine which formed the basis of the so-called Scientific or Marxian Socialism: the doctrine of historical Materialism, according to which the history of human civilizations can be explained only as the struggle of interest between the different social groups and as arising out of change in the means and instruments of production. That economic improvements—discoveries of raw materials, new methods of work, scientific inventions—should have an importance of their own, no one denies, but that they should suffice to explain human history to the exclusion of all other factors is absurd: Fascism believes, now and always, in holiness and in heroism, that is in acts in which no economic motive—remote or immediate—plays a part. With this negation of historical materialism, according to which men would be only by-products of history, who appear and disappear on the surface of the waves while in the depths the real directive forces are at work, there is also denied the immutable and irreparable "class struggle" which is the natural product of this economic conception of history, and above all it is denied that the class struggle can be the primary agent of social changes. Socialism, being thus wounded in these two primary tenets of its doctrine, nothing of it is left save the sentimental aspiration—old as humanity—towards a social order in which the sufferings and the pains of the humblest folk could be alleviated. But here Fascism rejects the concept of an economic "happiness" which would be realized socialistically and almost automatically at a given moment of economic evolution by assuring to all a maximum prosperity. Fascism denies the possibility of the materialistic conception of "happiness" and leaves it to the economists of the first half of the eighteenth century; it denies, that is, the equation of prosperity with happiness, which would transform men into animals with one sole preoccupation: that of being well-fed and fat, degraded in consequence to a merely physical existence.

After Socialism, Fascism attacks the whole complex of democratic ideologies and rejects them both in their theoretical premises and in their applications or practical manifestations. Fascism denies that the majority, through the mere fact of being a majority, can rule human societies; it denies that this majority can govern by means of a periodical consultation; it affirms the irremediable, fruitful and beneficient inequality of men, who cannot be levelled by such a mechanical and extrinsic fact as universal suffrage. By democratic regimes we mean those in which from time to time the people is given the illusion of being sovereign, while true effective sovereignty lies in other, perhaps irresponsible and secret, forces. Democracy is a regime without a king, but with very many kings, perhaps more exclusive, tyrannical and violent than one king even though a tyrant. This explains why Fascism, although before 1922 for reasons of expediency it made a gesture of republicanism, renounced it before the March on Rome, convinced that the question of the political forms of a State is not pre-eminent to-day, and that studying past and present monarchies, past and present Republics, it becomes clear that monarchy and republic are not to be judged *sub specie aeternitatis,* but represent forms in which the political evolution, the history, the tradition, the psychology of a given country are manifested. Now Fascism overcomes the antithesis between monarchy and republic which retarded the movements of democracy, burdening the former with every defect and defending the latter as the regime of perfection. Now it has been seen that there are inherently reactionary and absolutistic republics, and monarchies that welcome the most daring political and social innovations.

"Reason, Science," said Renan (who was inspired before Fascism existed) in one of his philosophical Meditations, "are products of humanity, but to expect reason directly from the people and through the people is a chimera. It is not necessary for the existence of reason that everybody should know it. In any case, if such an initiation should be made, it would not be made by means of base democracy, which apparently must lead to the extinction of every difficult culture, and every higher discipline. The principle that society exists only for the prosperity and the liberty of the individuals who compose it does not seem to conform with the plans of nature, plans in which the species alone is taken into consideration and the individual seems to be sacrificed. It is strongly to be feared lest the last word of democracy thus understood (I hasten to say that it can also be understood in other ways) would be a social state in which a degenerate mass would have no other care than to enjoy the ignoble pleasures of vulgar men."

Thus far Renan. Fascism rejects in democracy the absurd

conventional lie of political equalitarianism clothed in the dress of collective irresponsibility and the myth of happiness and indefinite progress. But if democracy can be understood in other ways, that is, if democracy means not to relegate the people to the periphery of the State, then Fascism could be defined as an "organized, centralized, authoritarian democracy."

In face of Liberal doctrines, Fascism takes up an attitude of absolute opposition both in the field of politics and in that of economics. It is not necessary to exaggerate—merely for the purpose of present controversies—the importance of Liberalism in the past century, and to make of that which was one of the numerous doctrines sketched in that century a religion of humanity for all times, present and future. Liberalism flourished for no more than some fifteen years. It was born in 1830, as a reaction against the Holy Alliance that wished to drag Europe back to what it had been before 1789, and it had its year of splendour in 1848 when even Pius IX was a Liberal. Immediately afterwards the decay set in. If 1848 was a year of light and poetry, 1849 was a year of darkness and of tragedy. The Republic of Rome was destroyed by another Republic, that of France. In the same year Marx launched the gospel of the religion of Socialism with the famous *Communist Manifesto*. In 1851 Napoleon III carried out his unliberal *coup d'etat* and ruled over France until 1870, when he was dethroned by a popular revolt, but as a consequence of a military defeat which ranks among the most resounding that history can relate. The victor was Bismarck, who never knew the home of the religion of liberty or who were its prophets. It is symptomatic that a people of high culture like the Germans should have been completely ignorant of the religion of liberty during the whole of the nineteenth century. It was, there, no more than a parenthesis, represented by what has been called the "ridiculous Parliament of Frankfort" which lasted only a season. Germany has achieved her national unity outside the doctrines of Liberalism, against Liberalism, a doctrine which seems foreign to the German soul, a soul essentially monarchial, whilst Liberalism is the historical and logical beginning of anarchism. The stages of German unity are the three wars of 1864, 1866 and 1870, conducted by "Liberals" like Moltke and Bismarck. As for Italian unity, Liberalism has had in it a part absolutely inferior to the share of Mazzini and of Garibaldi, who were not Liberals. Without the intervention of the unliberal Napoleon we should not have gained Lombardy, and without the help of the unliberal Bismarck at Sadowa and Sedan, very probably we should not have gained Venice in 1866; and in 1870 we should not have entered Rome. From 1870–1915 there occurs the period in which the very priests of the new creed had to confess the twilight of their religion: defeated as it was by decadence in literature, by activism in practice. Activism: that is to say, Nationalism, Futurism, Fascism. The "Liberal" century, after having accumulated an infinity of Gordian knots, tried to untie them by the hetacomb of the World War. Never before has any religion imposed such a cruel sacrifice. Were the gods of Liberalism thirsty for blood? Now Liberalism is about to close the doors of its deserted temples because the peoples feel that its agnosticism in economics, its indifferentism in politics and in morals, would lead, as they have led, the States to certain ruin. In this way one can understand why all the political experiences of the contemporary world are anti-Liberal, and it is supremely ridiculous to wish on that account to class them outside of history; as if history were a hunting ground reserved to Liberalism and its professors, as if Liberalism were the definitive and no longer surpassable message of civilization.

But the Fascist repudiations of Socialism, Democracy, Liberalism must not make one think that Fascism wishes to make the world return to what it was before 1789, the year which has been indicated as the year of the beginning of the liberal-democratic age. One does not go backwards. The Fascist doctrine has not chosen De Maistre as its prophet. Monarchial absolutism is a thing of the past and so also is every theocracy. So also feudal privileges and division into impenetrable and isolated castes have had their day. The theory of Fascist authority has nothing to do with the police State. A party that governs a nation in a totalitarian way is a new fact in history. References and comparisons are not possible. Fascism takes over from the ruins of Liberal Socialistic democratic doctrines those elements which still have a living value. It preserves those that can be called the established facts of history, it rejects all the rest, that is to say the idea of a doctrine which holds good for all times and all peoples. If it is admitted that the nineteenth century has been the century of Socialism, Liberalism and Democracy, it does not follow that the twentieth must also be the century of Liberalism, Socialism and Democracy. Political doctrines pass; peoples remain. It is to be expected that this century may be that of authority, a century of the "Right," a Fascist century. If the nineteenth was the century of the individual (Liberalism means individualism) it may be expected that this one may be the century of "collectivism" and therefore the century of the State. That a new doctrine should use the still vital elements of other doctrines is perfectly logical. No doctrine is born quite new, shining, never before seen. No doctrine can boast of an absolute "originality." It is bound, even if only historically, to other doctrines that have been, and to develop into other doctrines that will be. Thus the scientific socialism of Marx is bound to the Utopian Socialism of the Fouriers, the Owens and the Saint-Simons; thus the Liberalism of the nineteenth century is connected with the whole "Enlightenment" of the eighteenth century. Thus the doctrines of democracy are bound to the *Encyclopedie*. Every doctrine tends to direct the activity of men towards a determined objective; but the activity of man reacts upon the doctrine, transforms it, adapts it to new necessities or transcends it. The doctrine itself, therefore, must be, not words, but an act of life. Hence, the pragmatic veins in Fascism, its will to power, its will to be, its attitude in the face of the fact of "violence" and of its own courage.

The keystone of Fascist doctrine is the conception of the State, of its essence, of its tasks, of its ends. For Fascism the State is an absolute before which individuals and groups are relative. Individuals and groups are "thinkable" in so far as they are within the State. The Liberal State does not direct the interplay and the material and spiritual development of the groups, but limits itself to registering the results; the Fascist State has a consciousness of its own, a will of its own, on this account it is called an "ethical" State. In 1929, at the first quinquennial assembly of the regime, I said: For Fascism, the State is not the night-watchman who is concerned only with the personal security of the citizens; nor is it an organization for purely material ends, such as that of guaranteeing a certain degree of prosperity and a relatively peaceful social order, to achieve which a council of administration would be sufficient, nor is it a creation of mere politics with no contract with the material and complex reality of the lives of the individuals and the life of peoples. The State, as conceived by Fascism and as it acts, is a spiritual and moral fact because it makes concrete the political, juridical, economic organization of the nation and such an organization is, in its origin and in its development, a manifestation of the spirit. The State is the guarantor of internal and external security, but it is also the guardian and the transmitter of the spirit of the people as it has been elaborated through the centuries in language, custom, faith. The State is not only present, it is also past, and above all future. It is the State which, transcending the brief limit of individual lives, represents the immanent conscience of the nation. The forms in which states express themselves change, but the necessity of the State remains. It is the State which educates citizens for civic virtue, makes them conscious of their mission, calls them in unity; harmonizes their interests in justice; hands on the achievements of thought in the sciences, the arts, in law, in human solidarity; it carries men from the elementary life of the tribe to the highest human expression of power which is Empire; it entrusts to the ages the names of those who died for its integrity or in obedience to its laws; it puts forward as an example and recommends to the generations that are to come the leaders who increased its territory and the men of genius who gave it glory. When the sense of the State declines and the disintegrating and centrifugal tendencies of individuals and groups prevail, national societies move to their decline.

From 1929 up to the present day these doctrinal positions have been strengthened by the whole economico-political evolution of the world. It is the State alone that grows in size, in power. It is the State alone that can solve the dramatic contradictions of capitalism. What is called the crisis cannot be overcome except by the State, within the State. Where are the shades of Jules Simons who, at the dawn of liberalism, proclaimed that "the State must strive to render itself unnecessary and to prepare for its demise"; of the MacCullochs who, in the second half of the last century, affirmed that the State must abstain from too much governing? And faced with the continual, necessary and inevitable interventions of the State in economic affairs what would the Englishman Bentham now say, according to whom industry should have asked of the State only to be left in peace? Or the German Humboldt, according to whom the "idle" State must be considered the best? It is true that the second generation of liberal economists was less extremist than the first, and already Smith himself opened, even though cautiously, the door to State intervention in economics. But when one says liberalism, one says the individual; when one says Fascism, one says the State. But the Fascist State is unique; it is an original creation. It is not reactionary, but revolutionary in that it anticipates the solutions of certain universal problems. These problems are no longer seen in the same light: in the sphere of politics they are removed from party rivalries, from the supreme power of parliament, from the irresponsibility of assemblies; in the sphere of economics they are removed from the sphere of the syndicates' activities—activities that were ever widening their scope and increasing their power, both on the workers' side and on the employers'—removed from their struggles and their designs; in the moral sphere they are divorced from ideas of the need for order, discipline and obedience, and lifted into the plane of the moral commandments of the fatherland. Fascism desires the State to be strong, organic and at the same time founded on a wide popular basis. The Fascist State has also claimed for itself the field of economics and, through the corporative, social and educational institutions which it has created, the meaning of the State reaches out to and includes the farthest off-shoots; and within the State, framed in their respective organizations, there revolve all the political, economic and spiritual forces of the nation. A State founded on millions of individuals who recognize it, feel it, are ready to serve it, is not the tyrannical State of the medieval lord. It has nothing in common with the absolutist States that existed either before or after 1789. In the Fascist State the individual is not suppressed, but rather multiplied, just as in a regiment a soldier is not weakened but multiplied by the number of his comrades. The Fascist State organizes the nation, but it leaves sufficient scope to individuals; it has limited useless or harmful liberties and has preserved those that are essential. It cannot be the individual who decides in this matter, but only the State.

The Fascist State does not remain indifferent to the fact of religion in general and to that particular positive religion which is Italian Catholicism. The State has no theology, but it has an ethic. In the Fascist State religion is looked upon as one of the deepest manifestations of the spirit; it is, therefore, not only respected, but defended and protected. The Fascist State does not create a "God" of its own, as Robespierre once, at the height of the Convention's foolishness, wished to do; nor does it vainly seek, like Bolshevism, to expel religion from the minds of men; Fascism respects the God of the ascetics, of the saints, of the heroes, and also God as seen and prayed to by the simple and primitive heart of the people.

The Fascist State is a will to power and to government. In it the tradition of Rome is an idea that has force. In the doctrine of Fascism Empire is not only a territorial, military or mercantile expression, but spiritual or moral. One can think of an empire, that is to say a nation that directly or indirectly leads other nations, without needing to conquer a single square kilometre of territory. For Fascism the tendency to Empire, that is to say, to the expansion of nations, is a manifestation of vitality; its opposite, staying at home, is a sign of decadence: peoples who rise or re-rise are imperialist, peoples who die are renunciatory. Fascism is the doctrine that is most fitted to represent the aims, the states of mind, of a people, like the Italian people, rising again after many centuries of abandonment or slavery to foreigners. But Empire calls for discipline, co-ordination of forces, duty and sacrifice; this explains many aspects of the practical working of the regime and the direction of many of the forces of the State and the necessary severity shown to those who would wish to oppose this spontaneous and destined impulse of the Italy of the twentieth century, to oppose it in the name of the superseded ideologies of the nineteenth, repudiated wherever great experiments of political and social transformation have been courageously attempted: especially where, as now, peoples thirst for authority, for leadership, for order. If every age has its own doctrine, it is apparent from a thousand signs that the doctrine of the present age is Fascism. That it is a doctrine of life is shown by the fact that it has resuscitated a faith. That this faith has conquered minds is proved by the fact that Fascism has had its dead and its martyrs.

Fascism henceforward has in the world the universality of all those doctrines which, by fulfilling themselves, have significance in the history of the human spirit. . . .

The National Fascist Party is a civil militia for the service of the nation. Its objective: to realize the greatness of the Italian people. From its beginnings, which are indistinguishable from the renaissance of the Italian conscience and the will to victory, until now, the party has always thought of itself as in a state of war, at first in order to combat those who were stifling the will of the nation, to-day and from henceforth to defend and increase the power of the Italian people. Fascism is not merely an Italian organization connected with a programme partly realized and partly still to be realized; it is above all a faith which has had its confessors, and under the impulse of which the new Italians work as soldiers, pledged to achieve victory in the struggle between the nation and its enemies. The Party is an essential part of this new organization and its function is fundamental and indispensable to the vitality of the regime. In the hour of vigil, its organization was fixed according to the necessities of battle, and the people recognized the Duce by the marks of his will, his strength and his achievements. In the heat of the struggle, action took precedence of law. Every state was marked by a conquest, and the assemblies were only gatherings of officers and men dominated by the memory of the dead. Without dogmatic formulas or rigid projects, Fascism knows that victory lies in the possibility of its own continuous renewal. Fascism lives to-day in terms of the future, and regards the new generations as forces destined to achieve the ends appointed by our will. Without order and hierarchy, there can be neither discipline nor effort nor education of the people, which must receive light and guidance from that high place where is to be found the complete vision of rewards, tasks, functions and merits, and where the only guidance is in the general interest.

b. HITLER

Race and the Leadership Principle*

In order to understand the diseases from which a people suffers, it is first necessary to understand how a people is built up. Almost all the peoples of the world are composed to day of different racial primary elements *(Grundstoffen)*. These original elements are each characterized by different capacities. Only in the primitive functions of life can men be considered as precisely like each other. Beyond these primitive functions they immediately begin to be differentiated in their characters, their dispositions, and capacities. The differences between the individual races, both in part externally and, of course, also in their inner natures, can be quite enormous and in fact are so. The gulf between the lowest creature which can still be styled man and our highest races is greater than that between the lowest type of man and the highest ape.

If on this earth there were not some races which to-day determine its cultural appearance, it would hardly be possible to speak of any such thing as human civilization *(Kultur)*. For this neither climate nor education can be regarded as responsible, but only man himself who was endowed by providence with this capacity.

But if this cultural capacity is fundamentally inherent in certain races, its full effect is realized only under certain favourable

* From *The Speeches of Adolph Hitler,* April 1922–August 1939, an English translation of representative passages arranged under subjects, Norman H. Baynes, ed., Vol. 1 (London : Oxford University Press, 1942), pp. 464–80. Published by Oxford University Press for the Royal Institute of International Affairs. Used by permission.

circumstances. Man as an individual, whatever powers he may have in himself, will be incapable of higher achievements unless he can place the powers of many in the service of a single idea, a single conception, a single will and can unite them for a single action.

A glance at Nature shows us that creatures belonging to a pure race, not merely corporeally but in character and capacities, are more or less of equal value. This equality is the greatest hindrance in the way of formation of any community in work *(Arbeitsgemeinschaft);* for since every higher civilization receives its stamp through achievements which are possible only through uniting the forces of human labour, it is thus essential that a number of individuals must sacrifice a part of their individual freedom and must subject themselves to a single will. However much reason may counsel such a course, in reality it would be difficult amongst those who are complete equals to demonstrate the reasons why in the last resort one must be in a position to assert his will as against that of others.

The two conceptions—Command and Obedience—however, exercise quite another and more compelling force when folk of *different* value come into conflict or association with each other, and then through the action of the stronger section are bound together in pursuit of a common purpose.

The most primitive form of association for a common purpose can already be traced at the moment when man forces his supremacy upon the animals, tears them from the freedom of their former life, and builds them into his own life-process without troubling himself whether his animal-helper consents thereto or not.

But long ago man has proceeded in the same way with his fellow-man. The higher race—at first "higher" in the sense of possessing a greater gift for organization—subjects to itself a lower race and thus constitutes a relationship which now embraces races of unequal value. Thus there results the subjection of a number of people under the will often of only a few persons, a subjection based simply on the right of the stronger, a right which, as we see it in Nature, can be regarded as the sole conceivable right because founded on reason. The wild mustang does not take upon itself the yoke imposed by man either voluntarily or joyfully; neither does one people welcome the violence of another.

But, despite this, in the course of a long development this compulsion has very often been converted into a blessing for all parties. Thus were formed those communities which created the essential features of human organization through the welding together of different races. And this organization always demands the subjection of the will and the activity of many under the will and the energy of a single individual. As men come to discover the astonishing results of this concentration of their capacity and labour force they begin to recognize not merely the expediency but also the necessity of such action. And thus it is that a great and significant Aryan civilization did not arise where Aryans alone were living in racial purity, but always where they formed a vital association with races otherwise constituted, an association founded not on mixture of blood but on the basic of an organic community of purpose. And what was at first undoubtedly felt by the conquered as bitter compulsion later became in spite of this even for them a blessing. Unconsciously in the master-people there grew up ever more clearly and vitally a recognition of the ethical demand that their supremacy must be no arbitrary rule but must be controlled by a noble reasonableness. The capacity to subdue others was not given to them by Providence in order to make the subjects feel that the lordship of their conqueror was a meaningless tyranny, a mere oppression: that capacity was given that through the union of the conqueror's genius with the strength of the conquered they might create for both alike an existence which because it was useful was not degrading to man.

However this process of the formation of a people and a State was begun, its beginning signified the close of humanity's communistic age. For Communism is not a higher state of development; rather it is the most primitive form of life—the starting-point.

Men of completely similar characteristics, men who are precisely like each other and endowed with the same capacities, will be of necessity also alike in their achievement. This condition is realized in the case of peoples who are throughout of one and the same race. Where these conditions are realized, the individual result of the activity of each will correspond only with the general average of all.... In this case it can be a question only of quite primitive values, and the condition for any clear definition of the idea of property is lacking because of the absence of any differentiation in achievement which is essential for the rise of such a concept. Equal achievement carries with it the equal division of the results of that achievement. In such a state Communism is therefore a natural and morally comprehensible ordering of society. But when men of very different values have met together, the result of their achievements will also be different, that is to say that the race which stands higher in the scale of quality will contribute more to the sum total of common work than the race which is lower in the qualitative scale. And in particular men's capacities will lie on different levels. The primitive capacity of the one race will from the first produce values other than those more highly developed or otherwise constituted values produced by the other partner in the common life. As a consequence the administration of the labour-product will necessarily lead to a division which proceeds from a consideration of the character of the achievement, in other words: that which has been created will be administered as property on the same basis as that of its origin. The conception of private property is thus inseparably connected with the conviction that the capacities of men are different alike in character and in value and thus, further, that men themselves are different in character and value.

But one cannot in one sphere of life accept this difference in value —which I will now call difference in talent—as giving rise to a moral claim on the result produced by this superiority and then go on to deny that difference in another sphere. That would be to act illogically. . . . One cannot in fact proceed to maintain that all alike have the same capacity for politics, that is for the most important sphere in the entire conduct of life.

While it is denied that everyone in a nation is capable of administering a court or a factory or of appointing its administration, yet that they are all capable of administering the State or of appointing its administrators is solemnly certified in the name of democracy.

But here is a direct contradiction: either because of equal capacity men are equally capable of administering a State, and then the maintenance of the concept of property is not only unjust but simply stupid, or men are in truth not in a position to take into their common administration as common property that sum total of material and cultural treasure which the nation as a whole has created, and then in that case they are far less in a position to govern the State in common. . . . The State does not owe its existence to all but only to a definite section—the section which formerly created the State and which still supports and maintains it. This view is not unjust or hard: it is simply a statement of the truth. . . . The German people arose in no other way than did almost all of the truly creative civilized peoples *(Kulturvölker)* in the world of which we have any knowledge. A race, though small in numbers yet with capacities for organization and possessing a creative gift in the sphere of culture, in the course of many centuries spread itself over other peoples, absorbing some, adapting itself to others. All the different elements of which our people is composed naturally brought with them into this alliance their special capacities; but the alliance itself was created solely by a single core which fashioned both people and State. This core-people caused its language to prevail not, of course, without borrowings from its subjects, and in the end it subdued all for such a length of time to a common destiny that the life of the people which controlled the State became indissolubly united with the life of the other parts which were gradually fused into and on to it. Thus in course of time out of the conquerors and the conquered there was long since created a single community. And that community is our German people of to-day, and as it is to-day we love it and cling to it. In the course of its thousand years of history all its very varied characteristics, each of them so different from the other, have become familiar and dear. So great is this community of which we all form a part that we rejoice at every contribution which adds to our wealth. We do not ask to what section of our people we owe our several talents and capacities; each section must guard and foster its special gift. For one cannot only infer from the fact of race that certain capacities will be present, one can also start from the capacities and infer the race. That means, for instance, that it is not necessary first to discover musically gifted persons through the fact of their race in order to entrust to them the encouragement of music, but Music discloses the race by discovering the capacity.

Life sets to every single man the question of his descent on the day when he chooses his calling. All individuals in a people learn of the different functions of life but each function awakes a special echo only in one part of the people, in that part which through its origin was originally qualified to be the special representative *(Träger)* of this function and was thereby called to this task. How little the choice of a calling has to do with any weighing of economic profit or loss is most clearly shown by the fact that that choice is allowed to take place at an age when every condition for forming such a judgement is lacking, and more than that: we say in so many words that "the boy ought to be born for something." And that can mean only that we leave him to decide unconsciously and yet consciously. Unconsciously, since he is scarcely capable of estimating the material consequences of his choice; consciously, since in place of any such estimation he

obeys an inner voice which counsels him more truly than any superficial human understanding could ever do. For what a wonderful
thing it is when an eleven-year-old boy in his peasant village begins
to draw or carve and cannot tear himself away from a passion which
offers him oh! so little practical advantage, and then in the end, as a
great master, presents to the nation works which are immortal. That
which never moves thousands in their lives casts its spell over
hundreds because it corresponds with their inborn talent. The sole
interest of a people must be that this voice of inherited talent should
always be given a hearing. For this voice gives to the people, not men
under the violence of compulsion since they were never inwardly
born for such an activity, but men filled with a passion and therefore
devoted to their task.

And just as in all spheres of life we cannot feel any jealousy when
those who are specially born thereto, i.e. endowed from the outset,
exercise decisive influence, so it is in the sphere of the political safe-
guarding of that which in the course of the millennia has become for
us a people. Just as the unmusical person will not feel himself injured
or insulted because not he, but one who is musically gifted, composes
music or conducts an orchestra, so in every other sphere the appointment of qualified persons cannot be regarded as a slight by those who
have no capacities in that field. And in fact this does not occur; only
a conscious perversion could breed such madness.

Starting from the fact that any created thing can be maintained
only by the same force which created it, it follows that the body of a
people *(Volkskörper)* can be maintained only by those forces which
called it into being and which through their capacity for organization
welded it together and solidified it. Thus all who love their people
and wish for its maintenance must therefore see to it that that part of
the people can bring its political capacities into play which formerly
was responsible for the political formation and development of this
community.

For he who delivers up the political leadership of the nation to any
other force than that which formerly during the course of long periods
of time created the nation sooner or later does but open up the way
for anyone to seize that leadership.

We cling to our people just as it is: we love it in all its inner many-
sidedness and in all the external wealth which has resulted therefrom:
we would not that this community should cease to exist in this world
simply because the wrong part of the people was entrusted with its

political leadership. And that is precisely what has happened. Since the *bourgeoisie,* as a new class, claimed and received the political leadership of the nation, the reasonable organic evolution was interrupted in the most important sphere of all. The German *bourgeoisie* as a social body was the product of a selection which was based essentially less upon political than upon economic functions. The Liberalistic age through the introduction of money and property as the standard of valuation in the *bourgeoisie* produced a social class *(Schicht)* which corresponded with its own essential character. That many members of this social class did produce outstanding achievements in many spheres not concerned with material interests is not really connected with any valuation based upon the *bourgeois* idea, but rather with those fundamental racial values which survived in them. But in themselves these have no relation to the concept of the *bourgeoisie;* for membership of this social class all that was necessary was talent in the economic sphere which was evidenced by good fortune and a talent in the mental or cultural sphere which similarly could be turned into some form of economic success. In no case for determining membership of this class were such characteristics as valour or heroism the decisive test. On the contrary: since economic life has for the most part more un-heroic than heroic features, the German *bourgeoisie* had very little heroic about it: it was rather economic. And the *bourgeoisie* parties were a true reflection of this cast of soul—associations of hucksters, void of any capacity for a real leadership of the people.

And the people felt that. For that is the remarkable thing. Since from different racial cores a people came into being, each part learned gradually to tolerate the other—so long as it remained within its own sphere. Thus the people tolerates music only when it is good music, that is, when it is practised by that part of the people which is born for music. It tolerates those engineers only who understand the law of their craft and, thank God! it tolerates only those politicians whose calling is written on their brows.

Our whole life runs its course between leadership and following. The higher the development of a people the more complicated is its life. In no sphere is man any longer master of himself, his whole life is determined by considerations of others. Everywhere he is led and continuously he must obey. The time for his sleep, the time for his toil is dictated for him by the will of another, and when he begins his morning work that work runs in a channel which others determine and supervise. . . . Each takes his share in this violation of freedom, and yet all this is borne willingly and patiently. In every sphere of our cultural life leadership is readily recognized as soon as it is obvious that it is an inborn capacity. The lad observes this not merely through achievement, but he perceives it without any hesitation from a man's behaviour. The boy at school feels instinctively the calling of his teacher: one master he obeys, against others he declares open rebellion. The people tests through resistance in all spheres of life the capacity of leaders and above all in the political field. . . . Just as any company feels itself deserted, unfortunate, and unhappy in spirit when its tried leader falls, so unconsciously every people collapses when its leadership fails. Men justly feel themselves betrayed if they have through the centuries grown great in a community which can no longer be sustained because the part of the community responsible for sustaining it suddenly ceases to do so.

But with the claim of the German *bourgeoisie* to lead the nation a class of society presented itself to the people as leaders which was never born to the task. And the people recognized the fact and with instinctive certainty rejected its claim. So it became conceivable that an alien race could have the audacity with its primitive watchword to tear open an ancient wound in the midst of our people and through the proletariat could seek to undertake the organization of those who in the absence of leaders truly born to the task had become leaderless.

And this serves also to explain how it was that a *bourgeoisie* which was not in the least destined for political leadership sought to transfer to the political sphere the methods and usages of economic life. For with the anonymous share in a limited liability company corresponds the anonymous voting-paper, and with the majority of shareholders corresponds the parliamentary coalition!

And it was clear that with either of these it was impossible to find any logical, ethical, or moral foundation for the conception of private property. And the farther the age lapsed into these internal contradictions, the easier it was for an alien race, consistently pursuing its purpose, to foster the people's mistrust in its political leadership—a mistrust that had already instinctively arisen—and to shatter completely all confidence in that leadership. But since the *bourgeoisie* had founded itself upon the completely non-political concept of individual property, the opposition amongst the people quite naturally based itself on that section which was and still is quite incapable of creating an organization and therefore suddenly rediscovered in Communism the expression of the most primitive form of existence—a form of expression which had in the dim past been its own. It is thus no chance that hand in hand with this there went a retrogression in all spheres of culture—systematically propagated and carried into effect by Communism and its leaders.

For the same reason it is also quite natural that this *bourgeoisie*, being a completely inorganic political leadership and possessing no native talent or capacity for its task, must break down in face of the attack on Marxism while there could be no thought of bringing about a change in the situation through the *bourgeoisie* or by means of its political organizations. . . . And thus the question which arose after the collapse of the year 1918 was only this: first, whether there yet remained in our people a sufficiently large core of that part of the race which formerly had begun and effected the creation of our people and which therefore can alone be capable of leading and sustaining the people in the future, and secondly whether one could discover this part and entrust it with the leadership.

And it was further clear that, since the new formation of our society had developed out of economic functions, the capacity for political leadership could in no way be presumed to be necessarily identifiable with the social position of the individual German, that is to say, that men drawn from lower economic or social classes might be well fitted to lead the people just as on the other hand members of the highest social classes, especially those who represented economic or financial interests, would have to be rejected. The inborn talent necessary for our purpose—that alone must be decisive; our task was to discover these men out of all the different towns, callings, and classes.

This was in truth a Socialistic action, for in so far as I seek, for every function in life, to find from my people the man who was born for this task in order to hand over to him in this sphere full responsibility without considering to what economic or social class he belongs, I am acting in the interest of *all*. But if the word "Socialism" is to have any meaning at all, then that meaning can only be that with iron justice, that is with profound insight, on each man should be placed that share in the maintenance of the people as a whole which corresponds with his inborn talent and his value. This principle is the expression of a lofty justice because it is in itself logical and reasonable; it can be applied to all the functions of life and therefore to the entire sphere of the political leadership of a people.

The decisive problem which alone remained was thus: What was the method by which one was to find these men who as successors of the former creators of the body of our people and therefore as their heirs could to-day maintain their work? Here there was but one possibility: one could not from the race infer the capacity, but one had to infer from the capacity the racial fitness for the task. But one could establish the fact of capacity from the way in which individual men responded to the new idea which we had to proclaim. This is the infallible method by which to seek the men whom one wishes to find, for each man listens only to the note to which his inmost being is attuned. If you preach private gain all the egoists will join you . . . but if you demand sacrifice and courage, bravery, loyalty, faith, and heroism then that part of the people which calls these virtues its own will join your ranks. And always it was this factor which made history, and the content of that which we embrace under the word "history" is the formation of peoples and of States and their maintenance.

And thus it was that in the year 1919 I set forth a programme, I defined a tendency which was consciously a blow in the face of the pacifist-democratic world. If there were still in our people men of the kind we needed, then victory was certain. For this fanaticism in decision and in action was bound to draw to itself men of kindred nature. Wherever those who possessed these characteristics might be, they were bound one day to hear the voice which was that of their blood, and willy-nilly they would follow the Movement which was the expression of their own inmost being. That might take five, ten, or twenty years, but gradually there grew up within the State of Democracy the State of Authority, within the Reich of lamentable absurdity a core of fanatical devotion and ruthless determination. There was only one possible danger which might oppose this development—that the opponent might understand the principle, might clearly grasp these ideas and then avoid all opposition, or on the other hand that he might with the last extreme of brutality annihilate the new association at the very beginning and nip it in the bud.

But neither one nor the other happened. The time was no longer capable of making a decision and carrying through such an annihilation, nor had it the nerve, or rather it had not sufficient understanding, for a completely passive attitude which should avoid any conflict. Instead it began to tyrannize over the young Movement according to a *bourgeois* standard and thus supported the process of natural selection in the happiest way. After that it was only a question of the time when the leadership of the nation would fall into the hands of this hardened human material. And so I was able to wait for fourteen years, ever more and more assured that our hour must come. For in these years just as a magnet draws to itself the steel splinters so did our Movement gather together from all classes and callings and walks of life the forces in the German people which can form and also maintain States.

Once more it was proved that one may well be able to control a great business and yet be incapable of leading even a group of eight men. And on the other hand it was shown that from peasants' rooms and workmen's huts came the born leaders, for that was the wonderful thing in this period when we were propagating our idea—that its waves spread over the whole country and drew man after man, woman after woman under its spell. While *bourgeois* politicians were asking questions about our programme they never dreamed that hundreds of thousands were devoting themselves to this Movement simply because their inner receiver was adjusted to the wave-length of this idea. . . . And therein lies the Movement's mighty mission of reconciliation between the classes. A new valuation of men begins—not according to the standards of Liberalistic thought but according to the measures which Nature has determined. And the more the opponent believed that he could check the development through terrorism applied only in such doses as his character allowed him to use, the more he encouraged it. Nietzsche's word that a blow which does not fell a strong man only strengthens him found its verification a thousandfold. Every blow increased our defiance, every persecution increased our resolution, and that which did fall away proved in its falling away to be the greatest good fortune for the Movement.

And gradually the nation felt the rise of a new political leadership and more and more it yielded itself to that leadership, because it instinctively perceived in it something of that force to which formerly it owed its birth. The very people that in the Liberal epoch lay in continual strife with its leaders now stands more and more as one man behind its new leaders. The miracle in which our opponents refused to believe has become accomplished fact. . . . Out of forty-five million adult men three million fighters have organized themselves: they represent the political leadership of the nation. . . . Into their hands the people in full confidence has placed its destiny. But thereby the organization has undertaken a solemn obligation: it must see to it that this core whose mission it is to safeguard the stability of the political leadership in Germany must be preserved for all time.

The task of the Movement is to secure that through a skilful method in the choice of recruits only those are received into membership who will never change the inmost character of these forces which sustain our nation. It must realize that it is not the number of members of the core which counts but only its inner worth and thus its inner homogeneity. The Movement must make it clear that the selection of members in the future must proceed according to the same rigorous principles which a stern fate has imposed upon us in the past.

That which was formerly in part secured by the compulsion exercised by our opponents must now in the future be replaced by our own rigour. We must never hesitate to remove from this community anything which in its essential character does not belong to it. We must therefore in the course of time make more severe the conditions for membership, not lower or weaken them.

And this core of the Movement must never forget that it has to seek its reinforcements from the whole body of the people. It has an unceasing work to lead the whole nation to adopt its principles, i.e. it must secure their living allegiance. Only through this unbroken work with the people, for the people and about the people will a really close tie be formed, only so will it gain the capacity to recognize that part of the people which will provide it with its selected material. For those charged with the selection of members capable of political leadership must keep most careful watch to see that no real genius is living in the people without being observed and received into the ranks.

If the class of the political leaders of a nation overlooks or disregards those in the people who have inborn talents, then that class itself must bear the responsibility if that inborn talent at length creates its own field of activity, even if it were only like Spartacus to organize the slaves. In the long run it is not through any enforced respect for an incapable leadership which has become unworthy of its position that the born genius can be forced to refuse obedience to the imperious command of its own ego. The people has the right to demand that in the sphere of politics as in all other spheres of public life its ablest sons should not be neglected.

c. HITLER

*The Strong over the Weak**

Wars supposedly are not necessary among civilized peoples. The supposition is that disputes among nations are no longer necessary, for they are represented to be merely the expression of the oppression of one class by the particular bourgeois group dominating at the time. In the case of actual differences of opinions between nations, a court of arbitration is supposed to decide. The question, however, whether the judges of this court would have the power to bring the respective parties before the bar remains unanswered. Would a state be able to bring an accused into court if it did not have the police behind it? It is the same in the life of nations, and in the final analysis it is always a sort of divine ordeal that decides. The power which nations can bring to bear is a decisive factor. It is evident that the stronger has the right before God and the world to enforce his will. History shows that the right as such does not mean a thing, unless it is backed up by great power. If one does not have the power to enforce this right, that right alone will profit him absolutely nothing. The stronger have always been victorious. The whole of nature is a continuous struggle between strength and weakness, an eternal victory of the strong over the weak. All nature would be full of decay if it were otherwise. And the states which do not wish to recognize this law will decay. If you need an example of this kind of decay, look at the present German Reich. (Munich, April 13, 1923; *Voelkischer Beobachter*, April 15–16, 1923.)

SELF-PRESERVATION

Fundamentally, all genuine politics is an inspiration, a search for the preservation of a people. Food, drink and love—all are based on the drive for self-preservation. We do not know what role fate has intended for our people. Our chief desire is that it will be preserved in the future. We feel a moral obligation to preserve the race, to foster it, and to exalt it.

* This and the following selections on the same theme are taken from *Hitler's Words,* Gordon Prange, ed. (American Council on Public Affairs, 1944), pp. 3–13; 42–43. By permission.

So it is that the most fundamental question of politics is: How shall we provide daily bread for our people? "Lord give us this day our daily bread." . . . We understand this prayer only in the respect that we work for our daily bread and then beseech the Lord to bless our work.

In the life of nations, too, the struggle for daily bread is the first problem of politics. This problem is determined by the people itself, the size of its population, and the soil which it occupies. It is no accident, therefore, that a people, namely the Jews, whose existence has never rested on this basis, live as a parasite and has no soil and no homeland. All politics that reject this principle as the basis of a people's existence miscarries and is futile. (Nuremberg, July 4, 1926; *Voelkischer Beobachter,* July 7, 1926.)

ONLY FORCE RULES

The fundamental motif through all the centuries has been the principle that force and power are the determining factors. All development is struggle. Only force rules. Force is the first law. A struggle has already taken place between original man and his primeval world. Only through struggle have states and the world become great. If one should ask whether this struggle is gruesome, then the only answer could be: For the weak, yes, for humanity as a whole, no.

World history proves that in the struggle between nations, that race has always won out whose drive for self-preservation was the more pronounced, the stronger. . . . Unfortunately, the contemporary world stresses internationalism instead of the innate values of race, democracy and the majority instead of the worth of the great leader. Instead of everlasting struggle the world preaches cowardly pacifism and everlasting peace. These three things, considered in the light of their ultimate consequences, are the causes of the downfall of all humanity. The practical result of conciliation among nations is the renunciation of a people's own strength and their voluntary enslavement. (Essen, Nov. 22, 1926; *Voelkischer Beobachter,* Nov. 26, 1926.)

POLITICS IS STRUGGLE

What is politics? One of the great men of our nation once said: Politics is struggle. And Clemenceau, one of our most bitter enemies, said: Politics is war. Both men are right. Politics is the struggle of a people for its existence on this earth. It is a struggle for the present and a struggle for the future. The prayer reads: Lord, give us this day our daily bread. Even this Christian prayer shows that the struggle for daily bread actuates mankind—every one of us, day in and day out. (Vilsbiburg, March 6, 1927; *Voelkischer Beobachter,* March 8, 1927.)

THE NONSENSE OF HUMANITARIANISM

The inventions of mankind are the result of the eternal struggle. Never would aviation have progressed so remarkably had it not been for the War, had not countless thousands sacrificed their lives in this cruel struggle against nature. The struggle against the great beasts is ended, but it is being inexorably carried on against the tiny creatures— against bacteria and bacilli. There is no Marxian reconciliation on this score; it is either you or I, life or death, either extermination or servitude.

From (various) examples we arrive at the fundamental conclusion that there is no humanitarianism but only an external struggle, a struggle which is the prerequisite for the development of humanity.

The borderline between man and the animal is established by man himself. The position which man enjoys today is his own accomplishment. We see before us the Aryan race which is manifestly the bearer of all culture. The true representative of all humanity. All inventions in the field of transportation must be credited to the members of a particular race. Our entire industrial science is without exception the work of the Nordics. All great composers from Beethoven to Richard Wagner are Aryans, even though they were born in Italy or France. Do not say that art is international. The tango, the shimmy, and the jazzband are international but they are not art. Man owes everything that is of any importance to the principle of struggle and to one race which has carried itself forward successfully. Take away the Nordic Germans and nothing remains but the dance of apes.... Because we recognize the fact that our people can endure only through struggle, we National Socialists are fighters. (Munich, April 2, 1927; *Voelkischer Beobachter,* April 5, 1927.)

THE INEVITABILITY OF IMPERIALISM

Who is an imperialist? An imperialist is every father who begets a child and desires that his child live. An imperialist is every mother who bears a child and tries to keep her child from starving. For the realization of these goals, mankind must travel the roads of struggle, either economic struggle or struggle with weapons for life and food. Every people that is healthy shows that it has the drive to preserve itself. Only that people is healthy, therefore, which is imperial, which has the will to live. (Munich, June 3, 1927; *Voelkischer Beobachter,* June 5, 1927.)

STRUGGLE—THE SOURCE OF STRENGTH

Politics is nothing else than the struggle of a people for its existence in this world; it is the external battle of a people, for better or for worse, for its existence on this planet. How does this struggle take place? Great men of world history have described it. Frederick the Great said that politics is the art of serving one's people with all the means at one's disposal; according to Bismarck, politics is the art of the possible. . . . Clemenceau declared that the politics of peace was nothing else than the continuation of war with other means. Clausewitz asserted that war was nothing else than the continuation of politics with other weapons. In reality, then, politics is the struggle of a people with all weapons to the limit of its power for its existence on this earth.

With what question is struggle primarily related? It is the drive for self-preservation which leads to struggle—that is, the question of love and hunger. These are the two fundamental primitive forces around which everything on this earth centers. The total space on which life is carried on is circumscribed. This leads to a struggle of one against the other for this limited area. In addition, this area is more restricted for certain groups than for others so that their existence is dependent upon the preservation of the particular region which they inhabit.

Thus, the struggle for daily bread becomes in reality a struggle for the soil which produces this daily bread; that is, for space itself. It is an iron principle: the weak fail in order that the strong may live. . . . From all the innumerable creatures a complete species rises and becomes the master of the rest. Such a one is man—the most brutal, the most resolute creature on earth. He knows nothing but the extermination of his enemies in the world. . . . This struggle, this battle, has not been carried on by all men in the same way. Certain species stand out, and at the top of the list is the Aryan. The Aryan has forged the weapons with which mankind has made itself master of the animal world. There is scarcely anything in existence which when traced back to its origin cannot claim an Aryan as its creator. ... Never have votes and majorities added one iota to the culture of mankind. Every accomplishment is solely the result of the work and energy of great men, and as such, a flaming protest against the inertia of the masses.

How does this process then take place? It is an eternal struggle. Every achievement is nothing else than the result of a struggle of give-and-take. Every new invention is a triumph over an old one. Every record is a struggle against that which exists. Every championship performance is a conquest of that which prevailed previously.

Hence the following principles result: The value of man is determined in the first place by his inner racial virtues; second, by the ability of the race to bring forth men who in turn become leaders in the struggle for advancement; third, this entire process takes place in the form of eternal struggle. As a consequence struggle is the father of all things in this world. (Munich, Nov. 21, 1927; *Voelkischer Beobachter,* Nov. 23, 1927.)

NATURAL SELECTION AMONG NATIONS

What is the most powerful force that dominates human life? First, it is the drive for momentary self-preservation, the satisfaction of hunger; second, the drive to propagate the race, the gratification of love. These two drives dominate the individual. They compel him to work. From this fact one thing in particular is apparent, namely, that when all living creatures in this world are motivated by the same drive —that is, the preservation of life at any price—then they are forced into a competitive struggle.

Man must make use of his powers. He must struggle and fight. There is no achievement without breaking down resistance. Every new deed of mankind signifies the conquest of a previous one. We see that in mankind individual giants continuously tower over the rest. There are always certain nations which proceed in advance of all the others, nations which in the eternal struggle with nature are able to discover her secrets and to make them available for the rest of humanity. These nations are thereby able to open the gates of culture for other peoples. By means of this eternal struggle, the individual nations are sifted out. ...

Why is the position of the German people so desperate? Because we need power for every enterprise. Force determines the way of life. Right exists only when it is created and protected by power and force.

It bespeaks the greatness of a people if it can find the strength to raise itself upward. But when a people dances negro dances and listens only to jazz music, then we need not be surprised if it should perish, and seek out parliamentary monstrosities. He who does not honor his past is not worthy of a better future. A people must be taught to struggle. Struggle must be brought to the realization of a people. (Neustadt an der Aisch, Jan. 15, 1928; *Voelkischer Beobachter,* Jan. 20, 1928.)

THE FIGHT FOR LIFE

The idea of struggle is as old as life itself, for life is only preserved because other living things perish through struggle. The two most powerful drives of man, those of hunger and love, presuppose for their satisfaction an unending struggle. In this struggle, the stronger, the more able win, while the less able, the weak, lose. Struggle is the father of all things. Only through struggle has man raised himself above the animal world. Even today it is not by the principles of humanity that man lives or is able to preserve himself above the animal world, but solely by means of the most brutal struggle. As it is with the individual so it is in the destiny of nations. Only by struggle are the strong able to raise themselves above the weak. And every people that loses out in this eternally shifting struggle has, according to the laws of nature, received its just desert. A *Weltanschauung* that denies the idea of struggle is contrary to nature and will lead a people that is guided by it to destruction. The road that must be traveled by a people which wishes to develop itself still higher is not the road of comfort and ease, but the road of relentless struggle. For if you do not fight for life, then life will never be won. (Kulmbach, Feb. 5, 1928; *Voelkischer Beobachter,* Feb. 9, 1928.)

ORIGINALITY PLUS BRUTALITY

The will to live leads beyond the limitations of the present to the struggle for the prerequisites of life. Struggle is the impulse of self-preservation in nature. Man has become great through struggle.

The first fundamental of any rational *Weltanschauung* is the fact that on earth and in the universe force alone is decisive. Whatever goal man has reached is due to his originality plus his brutality. Whatever man possesses today in the field of culture is the culture of the Aryan race. The Aryan has stamped his character on the whole world. The basis for all development is the creative urge of the individual, not the vote of majorities. The genius of the individual is decisive, not the spirit of the masses. All life is bound up in three theses: Struggle is the father of all things, virtue lies in blood, leadership is primary and decisive.

Because the German people has forgotten this, it has collapsed. And if the German people does not again acquire power, that is, power in the sense of values and will, then no other choice is left the German people but to perish. There will never be a solution of the German problem until we return to the three fundamental principles which control the existence of every nation: The concept of struggle, the purity of blood, and the ingenuity of the individual. (Chemnitz, April 2, 1928; *Voelkischer Beobachter,* April 7, 1928.)

PEACE BY THE SWORD

Politics is history in the making. History is the story of a people's struggle for survival. There is no distinction between war and peace. Struggle is ever present. A latent peace is only possible when one is either a free lord or a slave. The final decision lies with the sword.

In the power of the sword lies the vital strength of a nation. There is, therefore, no difference between domestic policy and foreign policy. The one is the support of the other and in turn presupposes the existence of the other. Politics cannot be carried out without the recognition of certain fundamental principles: the principle of struggle, the purity of blood, and the ideal of the leader. (Munich, May 2, 1928; *Voelkischer Beobachter,* May 4, 1928.)

POWER AGAINST POWER

The battlefield is the final test of the foreign policy of a people. Even in the Soviet State the ultimate consideration is the possibility of preserving the nation on the field of arms. If a nation is unable to do this, then its foreign policy is destined to destruction from the very beginning. The state which is unable to preserve itself in war can possess diplomatic leadership a thousand times over and still not be able to meet the final demands of battle. Whoever is unable to meet the power of his enemy with power of his own must sacrifice any active espousal of his own interests; he will be forced from one dictate to another instead of from one treaty to another. We must do away with the misleading idea that Germany has concluded treaties in the past few years. Instead, she has signed dictates as a consequence of a perfectly senseless foreign policy.

The goal of foreign policy is the preservation of a people's means of subsistence; it is nothing else than the preservation of the life of a nation. The path to this goal will, in the final analysis, always be war. The means will be the might of the nation as it is set up in its military organization, plus clever political leadership, which chooses the course of policy wisely and then employs the means ingeniously. Any foreign policy, therefore, is linked up with the power constituted in the nation, and a resourceful organization of this power, namely the military.

It is impossible in the long run to carry out our foreign policy without building up the army. If this is not done, the results will always be negative. It is the function of domestic policy to build up the army as a means by which foreign policy can attain its ultimate goals. Domestic policy must follow lines which make possible the creation of powerful armed forces. Only when foreign policy and domestic policy work hand in hand can the problem of the subsistence of a people be solved.

Bismarck had the backing of instruments of power. He had a civil administration of great efficiency, a mighty army supported by a noble tradition and the constitution of a monarchial state. Nevertheless, this same Bismarck realized that the pursuit of his foreign policy would only be possible if it were supported by the above-mentioned factors of power. These in turn were reinforced by his diplomacy, and through the Prussian Army there was created the instrument which would realize the goals of the foreign policy of the state.

What was the most insane thing which the November traitors did? One cannot say that it was the Revolution itself, but the way in which the Revolution was carried out, that is, the disarming of the German people. By this act the young socialist state was, from the standpoint of foreign policy, surrendered to the captalistic world. The fortification of this state was thus made impossible.

The fact is that today the German people as a nation no longer represent power, for it does not have an army of any significance beyond its relation to the German people. The problems of German policy cannot be solved if the instrument of their solution (a powerful army) is not established. (Munich, Sept. 22, 1928; *Voelkischer Beobachter,* Sept. 23–24, 1928.)

MAN MUST KILL

If men wish to live, then they are forced to kill others. The entire struggle for survival is a conquest of the means of existence which in turn results in the elimination of others from these same sources of subsistence. As long as there are peoples on this earth, there will be nations against nations and they will be forced to protect their vital rights in the same way as the individual is forced to protect his rights.

There is in reality no distinction between peace and war. Life, no matter in what form, is a process which always leads to the same result. Self-preservation will always be the goal of every individual. Struggle is ever-present and will remain. This signifies a constant willingness on the part of man to sacrifice to the utmost. Weapons, methods, instruments, formations, these may change, but in the end the struggle for survival remains. . . .

One is either the hammer or the anvil. We confess that it is our purpose to prepare the German people again for the role of the hammer. For ten years we have preached, and our deepest concern is: How can we again achieve power? We admit freely and openly that, if our Movement is victorious, we will be concerned day and night with the question of how to produce the armed forces which are forbidden us by the peace treaty. We solemnly confess that we consider everyone a scoundrel who does not try day and night to figure out a way to violate this treaty, for we have never recognized this treaty.

We admit, therefore, that as far as we are concerned the German army in its present form is not permanent. For us it will serve only as a great cadre army, that is, as a source of sergeants and officers. And in the meantime we will be continuously at work filling in the ranks. We will take every step which strengthens our arms, which augments the number of our forces, and which increases the strength of our people.

We confess further that we will dash anyone to pieces who should dare to hinder us in this undertaking. . . . Our rights will never be represented by others. Our rights will be protected only when the German Reich is again supported by the point of the German dagger. (Munich, March 15, 1929; *Voelkischer Beobachter,* March 17, 1929.)

THE FATE OF NATIONS

Science must teach the individual the great primitive and fundamental laws, the laws of life. If these laws are disregarded, there can be no development. These fundamental laws alone explain the rise of man. They also account for the growth of our own people. These fundamental laws are from the very outset simple, as the law, for example, that as long as the world has existed, weakness has never been victorious but always strength, the molder of all life.

Life manifests itself only in the play of forces which in turn come to the fore and contribute to the further development of the whole world no matter whether we are dealing with solar systems or with individual persons. Always and everywhere strength is the fundamental factor, never quantity alone.

Never has cowardice directed the destiny of mankind to any good. The picture mankind presents today is the outcome of our ancestral struggles. In comparison with the eighteen hundred million human beings that are in the world today, there are countless billions who, as yet scarcely born, have already died. There are countless billions who later will not be equal to the struggle of life. That which we see today is selection in terms of strength.

The domination of the white race is not the result of mutual understanding among nations. The white race has risen slowly out of bloody struggle and has given the world that which we designate as culture. Every achievement on earth has originated in struggle.

Men and nations with the proper *Weltanschauung* climb steadily, and those without it are as chaff in the wind. The decisions of the latter are beyond comprehension. The present-day political parties in Germany serve as the best illustration of what happens to political organizations without a *Weltanschauung*.

Marxism has a *Weltanschauung* which leads rapidly to destruction. We too have a *Weltanschauung,* and we are convinced that it will lead our people upwards. A *Weltanschauung* is justifiable if it leads a nation forward. The justification of this *Weltanschauung* can be ascertained through an investigation of the general laws of all nature, from an examination of all the laws which form the basis of our own life, from a logical testing of the fate of other nations which have perished, from a scientific investigation of definite methods which bring nations to a position of dominance and of the methods which are responsible for the downfall of nations. . . .

We Nazis say that we have formulated a *Weltanschauung* for ourselves. This can be synthesized in a few propositions. What constitutes our importance and the importance of nations in any event is nothing that is academic *per se*. It is nothing which lies in artificial education.

It is something which originally has been an integral part of one's racial heritage. This heritage of blood is our basic value, our specific weight which we, as human beings, possess once for all. . . . The preservation of this heritage is the first and essential factor. Whenever a nation loses its racial heritage, it perishes.

The second factor is that of leadership. We say that among nations it is not the majorities that are decisive but the evaluation attached to the leader. It is not the sum total but genius itself. There is nothing of lasting importance in the world which does not owe its origin to the creative ability of the individual.

Thus a people must organize its constitution and its political life in such a way, that the greatest emphasis is placed upon the value of leadership. Leadership must not be destroyed by an artificial structure; that is, by the system of parliamentary democracy which cultivates little dwarfs—democracy which represents the conspiracy of dwarfs against him who towers head and shoulders above the masses.

The third factor is struggle, without which nothing on earth is created and without which nothing is preserved. Development means struggle. That is the inspiring outlook of the National Socialist *Weltanschauung*. (Munich, Nov. 29, 1929; *Voelkischer Beobachter,* Dec. 3, 1929.)

THE WEAPONS OF STRIFE

The national treasure of a people is its great men. The people with the most geniuses will be the most highly endowed. The people with the most celebrated poets, musicians and architects will be the richest in the field of art. The people with the greatest number of statesmen and generals will not only achieve the most fame but also the greatest good which will be won through the power of these great men. The greatest national treasure of a people lies in the purity of its blood and in the worth of its important men. It is, therefore, logical that the destiny of a nation should be determined by its great men.

But it is not enough that a people is healthy and strong, that it is rich in men of genius. It is also necessary that a people as a whole recognize that everything on this earth is strife and struggle. Work and struggle are two concepts which are in reality one and the same. That people which makes the greatest sacrifices will achieve the most.

The weapons of struggle are varied. One nation may fight with lies, still another with its blood. We Germans were always strong in the latter weapon. At times in our history when we thought we could cheat fate, fate called unto us and said: You do not understand. If you continue to fight as you do (with lies) then you will lose, for you are fighting with weapons that I never gave you. Only when we fight with weapons that are peculiar unto us (weapons of blood) will we achieve greatness. (Weimar, April 12, 1931; *Voelkischer Beobachter,* April 15, 1931.)

THE DESTRUCTION OF DEMOCRACY

We National Socialists know that no election can exclusively decide the fate of a nation. It is not parliamentary majorities that mold the fate of nations. At best they can only ruin the fate of nations. We know, however, that in this election democracy must be defeated with the weapons of democracy. That is why we are entering into this election with all the energy that we possess; that is why in the next few weeks we will fight on from one end of Germany to the other. . . .

Here is a Movement that represents no interests except those of the German nation in its entirety, a Movement that fights for three fundamental principles: for the re-establishment of German national strength and the removal of all influence of a poisonous, pestiferous, or international nature; for the destruction of the principle of the majority, of madness and half-measures, and the restoration of the principle of authority and the genius of leadership; for the destruction of cowardly submission, self-degradation, self-accusation, self-abandonment, and the re-establishment of the will to resist in the entire German people. . . . If this Movement should achieve victory, internationalism, democracy, and pacifism will vanish in Germany and then the German people will rise up. (Munich, July 18, 1930; *Voelkischer Beobachter,* July 20, 1930.)

THE MEDIOCRITY OF NUMBERS

In all ages it was not democracy that created values, it was individuals. However, it was always democracy that ruined and destroyed individuality. It is madness to think and criminal to proclaim that a majority can suddenly replace the accomplishment of a man of genius. . . . Every people must see in its most capable men the greatest national value, for this is the most lasting value there is. One single inventor, one genius, can mean more for a people than hundreds of millions or even a billion in capital.

Nations have always gone to ruin on the principle of democracy. If Germany has declined in the last fourteen years, it is because the advocacy of the principle of democracy had gone so far that its patrons and representatives in Germany were actually subject to the mediocrity of numbers, whose very sovereignty they preached. They themselves had become so inferior, so puny and dwarfish, that they did not even possess the right to lift themselves above the masses. There has never yet been a regime or a government which gave up the ghost in a more dismal, more lamentable, and more inferior manner than the representatives of the recent system. (Berlin, March 2, 1933; *Voelkischer Beobachter,* March 3, 1933.)

PARLIAMENTARY PERVERSION

In that we deny the principle of parliamentary democracy we strike the strongest blow for the right of the nation to the self-determination of its own life. For in the parliamentary system we see no genuine expression of the nation's will—a will which cannot logically be anything else than a will to the maintenance of the nation—but we do see a distortion, if not a perversion, of that will. The will of a nation to the self-determination of its being manifests most clearly and is of most use when its most capable minds are brought forth. They form the representative leaders of a nation, they alone can be the pride of a nation—certainly never the parliamentary politician who is the product of the ballot box and thinks only in terms of votes. The constructive development of the future leadership of the nation through its most able men will take years; the intelligent education of the German people will take decades. (Nuremberg, Sept. 1, 1933; *Voelkischer Beobachter,* Sept. 2, 1933.)

11

MARXISM

The Mission of the Proletariat

The Marxist concept of the "dictatorship of the working class," as a theory of political rulership, involves paradoxical and contradictory implications—both as an ideological concept and in its practical implementation in Soviet politics. Within the Marxist ideological heritage one finds two conflicting interpretations of the nature of political rule.

One interpretation is that the original writings of Karl Marx (1818–1883) and Friedrich Engels (1820–1895), in emphasizing the spontaneous character or revolutionary action by the working class, recognizes the necessity of political democracy as a precondition for the achievement of socialism. According to the *Communist Manifesto* (1848), the oppressions and exploitations of bourgeois society lead naturally and inevitably to the emergence of an increasingly powerful and more numerous proletariat which becomes a self-conscious independent movement of the immense majority of the people. The Communist Party, as the most advanced and resolute section of the working class, has as its aim the formation of the proletariat into a class; the overthrow of the bourgeoisie and the conquest of power by the proletariat. But the Communist Party has no interest apart from the proletariat; and the *Manifesto* explicitly states that the first stage in the revolution by the working classes is to raise the proletariat to the position of a ruling class, "to win the battle of ballots."

In the Leninist adaptation of Marxism, however, one finds emphasized that spontaneous action by the workers leads only to trade-union consciousness and that socialist ideology must be brought to the working classes by a revolutionary leadership or "vanguard" operating through a highly disciplined, centralized party organization. Leninism also involves a strong repudiation of parliamentary democracy as a hypocritical disguise or mask for an exploitive bourgeois class. Lenin was convinced that proletarian revolution could not be successful without the utilization of force and violence against the apparatus of the bourgeois state.

The period of Bolshevik rule under Vladimir Ilyich Lenin (1870–1924) established a monopoly of a single-party system which was seen as necessary to achieve the goals of the revolution and to safeguard the revolution against domestic and foreign foes. With the death of Lenin, the rule of a single party was replaced by the rule of a single personality: the police-state oppression and terrorism of Stalinism.

Nikita Khrushchev's (1894–   ) accession to power and his denunciation of Stalin was a dramatic development in Soviet leadership. However, its actual implications as a departure from Stalinist principles have been a subject of wide speculation and controversy.

Milovan Djilas (1911–   ), former vice-president of Yugoslavia, created a worldwide sensation with his challenging thesis that modern Communism, in betrayal of the classless society it preaches, has given rise to a "new class," built upon a powerful administrative bureaucracy no less oppressive and exploitive than the economic capitalist class it replaced. From this standpoint, the basic substance of Communism has been little affected by the phases in its evolution from Lenin to Khrushchev; nor in present developments under Kosygin and Brezhnev. In viewing the Marxist concept of political rule, then, one is confronted not only with the problem of assessing internal coherence and consistency within its ideological position, but also with the question of the relation between ideological principles and the actual conduct of Communist leadership.

a. MARX AND ENGELS

To Proletarians, the Bourgeoisie and Communists*

The history of all hitherto existing society is the history of class struggles.

Freeman and slave, patrician and plebeian, lord and serf, guildmaster and journeyman, in a word; oppressor and oppressed, stood in constant opposition to one another, carried on an uninterrupted, now hidden, now open fight, a fight that each time ended, either in a revolutionary reconstitution of society at large, or in the common ruin of the contending classes.

In the early epochs of history, we find almost everywhere a complicated arrangement of society into various orders, a manifold

*These selections are taken from the translation by Samuel Moore in collaboration with Friedrich Engels of *The Communist Manifesto.*

graduation of social rank. In ancient Rome we have patricians, knights, plebeians, slaves; in the Middle Ages, feudal lords, vassals, guild-masters, journeymen, apprentices, serfs; in almost all of these classes, again, subordinate gradations.

The modern bourgeois society that has sprouted from the ruins of feudal society, has not done away with class antagonisms. It has but established new classes, new conditions of oppression, new forms of struggle in place of the old ones.

Our epoch, the epoch of the bourgeoisie, possesses, however, this distinctive feature: it has simplified the class antagonisms. Society as a whole is more and more splitting up into two great hostile camps, into two great classes directly facing each other: Bourgeoisie and Proletariat.

From the serfs of the Middle Ages sprang the chartered burghers of the earliest towns. From these burgesses the first elements of the bourgeoisie were developed.

The discovery of America, the rounding of the Cape, opened up fresh ground for the rising bourgeoisie. The East-Indian and Chinese markets, the colonization of America, trade with the colonies, the increase in the means of exchange and in commodities generally, gave to commerce, to navigation, to industry, an impulse never before known, and thereby, to the revolutionary element in the tottering feudal society, a rapid development.

The feudal system of industry, under which industrial production was monopolized by closed guilds, now no longer sufficed for the growing wants of the new markets. The manufacturing system took its place. The guild-masters were pushed on one side by the manufacturing middle-class; division of labor between the different corporate guilds vanished in the face of division of labor in each single workshop.

Meantime the markets kept ever growing, the demand ever rising. Even manufacturing no longer sufficed. Thereupon steam and machinery revolutionized industrial production. The place of manufacture was taken by the giant, Modern Industry, the place of the industrial middle-class, by industrial millionaires, the leaders of the whole industrial armies, the modern bourgeoisie.

Modern industry has established the world-market for which the discovery of America paved the way. This market has given an immense development to commerce, to navigation, to communication by land. This development has, in its turn, reacted on the extension of industry; and in proportion as industry, commerce, navigation, railways extended, in the same proportion the bourgeoisie developed, increased its capital, and pushed into the background every class handed down from the Middle Ages.

We see, therefore, how the modern bourgeoisie is itself the product of a long course of development, of a series of revolutions in the modes of production and of exchange.

Each step in the development of the bourgeoisie was accompanied by a corresponding political advance of that class. An oppressed class under the sway of the feudal nobility, it became an armed and self-governing association in the medieval commune; here independent urban republic (as in Italy and Germany), there taxable "third estate" of the monarchy (as in France), afterwards, in the period of manufacturing proper, serving either the semi-feudal or the absolute monarchy as a counterpoise against the nobility, and in fact, corner stone of the great monarchies in general—the bourgeoisie has at last, since the establishment of Modern Industry and of the world-market, conquered for itself, in the modern representative State, exclusive political sway. The executive of the modern State is but a committee for managing the common affairs of the whole bourgeoisie.

The bourgeoisie, historically, has played a most revolutionary part.

The bourgeoisie, wherever it has got the upper hand, has put an end to all feudal, patriarchal, idyllic relations. It has pitilessly torn asunder the motley feudal ties that bound man to his "natural superiors," and has left remaining no other nexus between man and man than naked self-interest, than callous "cash payment." It has drowned the most heavenly ecstacies of religious fervor, of chivalrous enthusiasm, of philistine sentimentalism, in the icy water of egotistical calculation. It has resolved personal worth into exchange value, and in place of the numberless indefeasible chartered freedoms, has set up that single unconscionable freedom—Free Trade. In one word, for exploitation, veiled by religious and political illusions, it has substituted naked, shameless, direct, brutal exploitation.

The bourgeoisie has stripped of its halo every occupation hitherto honored and looked up to with reverent awe. It has converted the physician, the lawyer, the priest, the poet, the man of science, into its paid wage-laborers.

The bourgeoisie has torn away from the family its sentimental veil, and has reduced the family relation to a mere money relation.

The bourgeoisie has disclosed how it came to pass that the brutal display of vigor in the Middle Ages, which Reactionists so much admire, found its fitting complement in the most slothful indolence. It has been the first to show what man's activity can bring about. It has accomplished wonders far surpassing Egyptian pyramids, Roman aqueducts, and Gothic cathedrals; it has conducted expeditions that put in the shade all former exoduses of nations and crusades.

The bourgeoisie cannot exist without constantly revolutionizing the instruments of production, and thereby the relations of production, and with them the whole relations of society. Conservation of the old modes of production in unaltered form, was, on the contrary, the first condition of existence for all earlier industrial classes. Constant revolutionizing of production, uninterrupted disturbance of all social conditions, everlasting uncertainty and agitation distinguish the bourgeois epoch from all earlier ones. All fixed, fast-frozen relations, with their train of ancient and venerable prejudices and opinions, are swept away, all newly-formed ones become antiquated before they can ossify. All that is solid melts into air, all that is holy is profaned, and man is at last compelled to face with sober senses his real conditions of life, and his relations with his kind.

The need of a constantly expanding market for its products chases the bourgeoisie over the whole surface of the globe. It must nestle everywhere, settle everywhere, establish connections everywhere.

The bourgeoisie has through its exploitation of the world-market given a cosmopolitan character to production and consumption in every country. To the great chagrin of Reactionists, it has drawn from under the feet of industry the national ground on which it stood. All old-established national industries have been destroyed or are daily being destroyed. They are dislodged by new industries, whose introduction becomes a life and death question for all civilized nations, by industries that no longer work up indigenous raw material, but raw material drawn from the remotest zones; industries whose products are consumed, not only at home, but in every quarter of the globe. In place of the old wants, satisfied by the productions of the country, we find new wants, requiring for their satisfaction the products of distant lands and climes. In place of the old local and national seclusions and self-sufficiency, we have intercourse in every direction, universal interdependence of nations. And as in material, so also in intellectual production. The intellectual creations of individual nations become common property. National one-sidedness and narrow-mindedness become more and more impossible, and from the numerous national and local literatures there arises a world-literature.

The bourgeoisie, by the rapid improvement of all instruments of production, by the immensely facilitated means of communication, draws all, even the most barbarian, nations into civilization. The cheap prices of its commodities are the heavy artillery with which it batters down all Chinese walls, with which it forces the barbarians' intensely obstinate hatred of foreigners to capitulate. It compels all nations, on pain of extinction, to adopt the bourgeois mode of production; it compels them to introduce what it calls civilization into their midst, i.e., to become bourgeois themselves. In a word, it creates a world after its own image.

The bourgeoisie has subjected the country to the rule of the towns. It has created enormous cities, has greatly increased the urban population as compared with the rural, and has thus rescued a considerable part of the population from the idiocy of rural life. Just as it has made the country dependent on the towns, so it has made barbarian and semibarbarian countries dependent on the civilized ones, nations of peasants on nations of bourgeois, the East on the West.

The bourgeoisie keeps more and more doing away with the scattered state of the population, of the means of production, and of property. It has agglomerated population, centralized means of production, and has concentrated property in a few hands. The necessary consequence of this was political centralization. Independent, or but loosely connected provinces, with separate interests, laws, governments and systems of taxation, became lumped together in one nation, with one government, one code of laws, one national class-interest, one frontier and one customs-tariff.

The bourgeoisie, during its rule of scarce one hundred years, has created more massive and more colossal productive forces than have all preceding generations together. Subjection of Nature's forces to man, machinery, application of chemistry to industry and agriculture, steam-navigation, railways, electric telegraphs, clearing of whole continents for cultivation, canalization of rivers, whole populations conjured out of the ground—what earlier century had even a presentiment that such productive forces slumbered in the lap of social labor?

We see then: the means of production and of exchange on whose foundations the bourgeoisie built itself up, were generated in feudal society. At a certain stage in the development of these means of production and of exchange, the conditions under which feudal society produced and exchanged the feudal organization of agriculture and manufacturing industry, in one word, the feudal relations of property became no longer compatible with the already developed productive forces; they became so many fetters. They had to be burst asunder; they were burst asunder.

Into their places stepped free competition, accompanied by a social and political constitution adapted to it, and by the economical and political sway of the bourgeois class.

A similar movement is going on before our own eyes. Modern bourgeois society with its relations of production, of exchange and of property, a society that has conjured up such gigantic means of production and of exchange, is like the sorcerer, who is no longer able to control the powers of the nether world whom he has called up by his spells. For many a decade past the history of industry and commerce is but the history of the revolt of modern productive forces against modern conditions of production, against the property relations that are the condition for the existence of the bourgeoisie and of its rule. It is enough to mention the commercial crises that by their periodical return put on trial, each time more threateningly, the existence of the entire bourgeois society. In these crises a great part not only of the existing products, but also of the previously created productive forces, are periodically destroyed. In these crises there breaks out an epidemic that, in all earlier epochs, would have seemed an absurdity—the epidemic of overproduction. Society suddenly finds itself put back into a state of momentary barbarism, it appears as if a famine, a universal war of devastation had cut off the supply of every means of subsistence; industry and commerce seem to be destroyed; and why? Because there is too much civilization, too much means of subsistence, too much industry, too much commerce. The productive forces at the disposal of society no longer tend to further the development of the conditions of bourgeois property; on the contrary, they have become too powerful for these conditions, by which they are fettered, and so soon as they overcome these fetters, they bring disorder into the whole of bourgeois society, endangering the existence of bourgeois property. The conditions of bourgeois society are too narrow to comprise the wealth created by them. And how does the bourgeoisie get over these crises? On the one hand by enforced destruction of a mass of productive forces, on the other, by the conquest of new markets, and by the more thorough exploitation of the old ones. That is to say, by paving the way for more extensive and more destructive crises, and by diminishing the means whereby crises are prevented.

The weapons with which the bourgeoisie felled feudalism to the ground are now turned against the bourgeoisie itself.

But not only has the bourgeoisie forged the weapons that bring death to itself; it has also called into existence the men who are to wield these weapons—the modern working-class—the proletarians.

In proportion as the bourgeoisie, i.e., capital, is developed, in the same proportion is the proletariat, the modern working-class, developed, a class of laborers who live only so long as they find work, and who find work only so long as their labor increases capital. These laborers, who must sell themselves piecemeal, are a commodity, like every other article of commerce, and are consequently exposed to all the vicissitudes of competition, to all the fluctuations of the market.

Owing to the extensive use of machinery and to division of labor, the work of the proletarians has lost all individual character, and, consequently, all charm for the workman. He becomes an appendage of the machine, and it is only the most simple, most monotonous, and most easily acquired knack that is required of him. Hence, the cost of production of a workman is restricted, almost entirely, to the means of subsistence that he requires for his maintenance, and for the propagation of his race. But the price of a commodity, and also of labor, is equal to its cost of production. In proportion, therefore, as the repulsiveness of the work increases, the wage decreases. Nay, more, in proportion as the use of machinery and division of labor increases, in the same proportion the burden of toil also increases, whether by prolongation of the working hours, by increase of the work enacted in a given time, or by increased speed of the machinery, etc.

Modern industry has converted the little workshop of the patriarchal master into the great factory of the industrial capitalist. Masses of laborers, crowded into the factory, are organized like soldiers. As privates of the industrial army they are placed under the command of a perfect hierarchy of officers and sergeants. Not only are they the slaves of the bourgeois class, and of the bourgeois State; they are daily and hourly enslaved by the machine, by the over-looker, and, above all, by the individual bourgeois manufacturer himself. The more openly this despotism proclaims gain to be its end and aim, the more petty, the more hateful and the more embittering it is.

The less the skill and exertion or strength implied in manual labor, in other words, the more modern industry becomes developed, the more is the labor of man superseded by that of women. Differences of age and sex have no longer any distinctive social validity for the working class. All are instruments of labor, more or less expensive to use, according to their age and sex.

No sooner is the exploitation of the laborer by the manufacturer so far at an end, that he receives his wages in cash, than he is set upon by the other portions of the bourgeoisie, the landlord, the shopkeeper, the pawnbroker, etc.

The low strata of the middle class—the small tradespeople, shopkeepers, and retired tradesmen generally, the handicraftsmen and peasants—all these sink gradually into the proletariat, partly because their diminutive capital does not suffice for the scale on which Modern Industry is carried on, and is swamped in the competition with the large capitalists, partly because their specialized skill is rendered worthless by new methods of production. Thus the proletariat is recruited from all classes of the population.

The proletariat goes through various stages of development. With its birth begins its struggle with the bourgeoisie. At first the contest is carried on by individual laborers, then by the workpeople of a factory, then by the operatives of one trade, in one locality, against the individual bourgeois who directly exploits them. They direct their attacks not against the bourgeois conditions of production, but against the instruments of production themselves; they destroy imported wares that compete with their labor, they smash to pieces machinery, they set factories ablaze, they seek to restore by force the vanished status of the workman of the Middle Ages.

At this stage the laborers still form an incoherent mass scattered over the whole country, and broken up by their mutual competition. If anywhere they unite to form more compact bodies, this is not yet the consequence of their own active union, but of the union of the bourgeoisie, which class, in order to attain its own political ends, is compelled to set the whole proletariat in motion, and is moreover yet, for a time, able to do so. At this stage, therefore, the proletarians do not fight their enemies, but the enemies of their enemies, the remnants of absolute monarchy, the landowners, the nonindustrial bourgeoisie, the petty bourgeoisie. Thus the whole historical movement is concentrated in the hands of the bourgeoisie; every victory so obtained is a victory for the bourgeoisie.

But with the development of industry the proletariat not only increases in number; it becomes concentrated in great masses, its strength grows, and it feels that strength more. The various interests and conditions of life within the ranks of the proletariat are more and more equalized, in proportion as machinery obliterates all distinction of labor and nearly everywhere reduces wages to the same low level. The growing competition among the bourgeoisie, and the resulting commercial crises, make the wages of the worker ever more fluctuating. The unceasing improvement of machinery, ever more rapidly developing, makes their livelihood more and more precarious; the collisions between individual workmen and individual bourgeois take more and more the character of collision between two classes. Thereupon the workers begin to form combinations (Trade Unions) against the bourgeoisie; they club together in order to keep up the rate of wages; they found permanent associations in order to make provision beforehand for these occasional revolts. Here and there the contest breaks out into riots.

Now and then the workers are victorious, but only for a time. The real fruits of their battles lie, not in the immediate results, but in the ever expanding union of the workers. This union is helped on by the improved means of communication that are created by modern industry, and that place the workers of different localities in contact with one another. It was just this contact that was needed to centralize the numerous local struggles, all of the same character, into one national struggle between classes. But every class struggle is a political struggle. And that union, to attain which the burghers of the Middle Ages, with their miserable highways, required centuries, the modern proletarians, thanks to railways, achieve in a few years.

This organization of the proletarians into a class, and consequently into a political party, is continually being upset again by the competition between the workers themselves. But it ever rises up again stronger, firmer, mightier. It compels legislative recognition of particular interests of the workers, by taking advantage of the divisions among the bourgeoisie itself. Thus, the ten-hour bill in England was carried.

Altogether, collisions between the classes of the old society further, in many ways, the course of development of the proletariat. The bourgeoisie finds itself involved in a constant battle. At first with the aristocracy, later on, with those portions of the bourgeoisie itself, whose interests have become antagonistic to the progress of industry; at all times, with the bourgeoisie of foreign countries. In all these battles it sees itself compelled to appeal to the proletariat, to ask for its help, and thus, to drag it into the political arena. The bourgeoisie itself, therefore, supplies the proletariat with its own elements of political and general education, in other words, it furnishes the proletariat with weapons for fighting the bourgeoisie.

Further, as we have already seen, entire sections of the ruling classes are, by the advance of industry, precipitated into the proletariat, or are at least threatened in their conditions of existence. These also supply the proletariat with fresh elements of enlightenment and progress.

Finally, in times when the class-struggle nears the decisive hour, the process of dissolution going on within the ruling class, in fact, within the whole range of old society, assumes such a violent, glaring character, that a small section of the ruling class cuts itself adrift, and joins the revolutionary class, the class that holds the future in its hands. Just as, therefore, at an earlier period, a section of the nobility went over to the bourgeoisie, so now a portion of the bourgeoisie goes over to the proletariat, and in particular, a portion of the bourgeois ideologists, who have raised themselves to the level of comprehending theoretically the historical movements as a whole.

Of all the classes that stand face to face with the bourgeoisie today, the proletariat alone is a really revolutionary class. The other classes decay and finally disappear in the face of modern industry; the proletariat is its special and essential product.

The lower middle-class, the small manufacturer, the shopkeeper, the artisan, the peasant, all these fight against the bourgeoisie, to save from extinction their existence as fractions of the middle class. They are, therefore, not revolutionary, but conservative. Nay more, they are reactionary, for they try to roll back the wheel of history. If by chance they are revolutionary, they are so only in view of their impending transfer into the proletariat; they thus defend not their present, but their future interests; they desert their own standpoint to place themselves at that of the proletariat.

The "dangerous class," the social scum, that passively rotting mass thrown off by the lowest layers of old society, may, here and there, be swept into the movement by a proletarian revolution; its conditions of life, however, prepare it far more for the part of a bribed tool of reactionary intrigue.

In the conditions of the proletariat, those of old society at large are already virtually swamped. The proletarian is without property; his relation to his wife and children has no longer anything in common with the bourgeois family-relations; modern industrial labor, modern subjugation to capital, the same in England as in France, in America as in Germany, has stripped him of every trace of national character. Law, morality, religion, are to him so many bourgeois prejudices, behind which lurk in ambush just as many bourgeois interests.

All the preceding classes that got the upper hand, sought to fortify their already acquired status by subjecting society at large to their conditions of appropriation. The proletarians cannot become masters of the productive forces of society, except by abolishing their own previous mode of appropriation and thereby also every other previous mode of appropriation. They have nothing of their own to secure and to fortify; their mission is to destroy all previous securities for, and insurances of, individual property.

All previous historical movements were movements of minorities, or in the interests of minorities. The proletarian movement is the self-conscious, independent movement of the immense majority, in the interest of the immense majority. The proletariat, the lowest stratum of our present society, cannot stir, cannot raise itself up, without the whole superincumbent strata of official society being sprung into the air.

Though not in substance, yet in form, the struggle of the proletariat with the bourgeoisie is at first a national struggle. The proletariat of each country must, of course, first of all settle matters with its own bourgeoisie.

In depicting the most general phases of the development of the proletariat, we traced the more or less veiled civil war, raging within existing society, up to the point where the war breaks out into open revolution, and where the violent overthrow of the bourgeoisie lays the foundation for the sway of the proletariat.

Hitherto, every form of society has been based, as we have already seen, on the antagonism of oppressing and oppressed classes. But in order to oppress a class, certain conditions must be assured to it under which it can, at least, continue its slavish existence. The serf, in the period of serfdom, raised himself to membership in the commune, just as the petty bourgeois, under the yoke of feudal absolutism, managed to develop into a bourgeois. The modern laborer, on the contrary, instead of rising with the progress of industry, sinks deeper and deeper below the conditions of existence of his own class. He becomes a pauper, and pauperism develops more rapidly than population and wealth. And here it becomes evident that the bourgeoisie is unfit any longer to be the ruling class in society, and to impose its conditions of existence upon society as an overriding law. It is unfit to rule, because it is incompetent to assure an existence to its slave within his slavery, because it cannot help letting him sink into such a state that it has to feed him, instead of being fed by him. Society can no longer live under this bourgeoisie, in other words, its existence is no longer compatible with society.

The essential condition for the existence, and for the sway of the bourgeois class, is the formation and augmentation of capital; the condition for capital is wage-labor. Wage-labor rests exclusively on competition between the laborers. The advance of industry, whose revolutionary promoter is the bourgeoisie, replaces the isolation of the laborers, due to competition, by their revolutionary combination, due to association. The development of Modern Industry, therefore, cuts from under its feet the very foundation on which the bourgeoisie produces and appropriates products. What the bourgeoisie therefore produces, above all, are its own gravediggers. Its fall and the victory of the proletariat are equally inevitable.

In what relation do the Communists stand to the proletarians as a whole?

The Communists do not form a separate party opposed to other working-class parties.

They have no interest separate and apart from those of the proletariat as a whole.

They do not set up any sectarian principles of their own, by which to shape and mold the proletarian movement.

The Communists are distinguished from the other working-class parties by this only: 1. In the national struggles of the proletarians of the different countries, they point out and bring to the front the common interests of the entire proletariat, independently of all nationality. 2. In the various stages of development which the struggle of the working class against the bourgeoisie has to pass through, they always and everywhere represent the interest of the movement as a whole.

The Communists, therefore, are on the one hand, practically, the most advanced and resolute section of the working-class parties of every country, that section which pushes forward all others; on the other hand, theoretically, they have over the great mass of the proletariat the advantage of clearly understanding the line of march, the conditions, and the ultimate general results of the proletarian movement.

The immediate aim of the Communists is the same as that of all the other proletarian parties: formation of the proletariat into a class, overthrow of the bourgeois supremacy, conquest of political power by the proletariat. . . .

b. LENIN

*The Dictatorship of the Proletariat**

. . . Here we have a formulation of one of the most remarkable and most important ideas of Marxism on the subject of the state, namely, the idea of the "dictatorship of the proletariat" (as Marx and Engels began to call it after the Paris Commune); and also, a highly interesting definition of the state, which is also one of the "forgotten words" of Marxism: "the state, i.e., *the proletariat organized as the ruling class.*"

This definition of the state has never been explained in the prevailing propaganda and agitation literature of the official Social-Democratic parties. More than that, it has been deliberately ignored, for it is absolutely irreconcilable with reformism, and is a slap in the face for the common opportunist prejudices and philistine illusions about the "peaceful development of democracy."

The proletariat needs the state—this is repeated by all the opportunists, social-chauvinists and Kautskyites, who assure us that this is what Marx taught. But they "forget" to add that, in the first place, according to Marx, the proletariat needs only a state which is withering away, i.e., a state so constituted that it begins to wither away immediately, and cannot but wither away. And, secondly, the working people need a "state, i.e., the proletariat organised as the ruling class."

The state is a special organisation of force: it is an organisation of violence for the suppression of some class. What class must the proletariat suppress? Naturally, only the exploiting class, i.e., the bourgeoisie. The working people need the state only to suppress the resistance of the exploiters, and only the proletariat can direct this suppression, can carry it out. For the proletariat is the only class that is consistently revolutionary, the only class that can unite all the working and exploited people in the struggle against the bourgeoisie, in completely removing it.

The exploiting classes need political rule to maintain exploitation,

* From Lenin, *Collected Works*, Vol. 25, trans. and ed. by Stepan Apresyan and Jim Riordan (Moscow: Progress Publishers, 1944), pp. 402–5.

i.e., in the selfish interests of an insignificant minority against the vast majority of the people. The exploited classes need political rule in order to completely abolish all exploitation, i.e., in the interests of the vast majority of the people, and against the insignificant minority consisting of the modern slave-owners—the landowners and capitalists.

The petty-bourgeois democrats, those sham socialists who replaced the class struggle by dreams of class harmony, even pictured the socialist transformation in a dreamy fashion—not as the overthrow of the rule of the exploiting class, but as the peaceful submission of the minority to the majority which has become aware of its aims. This petty-bourgeois utopia, which is inseparable from the idea of the state being above classes, led in practice to the betrayal of the interests of the working classes, as was shown, for example, by the history of the French revolution of 1848 and 1871, and by the experience of "socialist" participation in bourgeois Cabinets in Britain, France, Italy and other countries at the turn of the century.

All his life Marx fought against this petty-bourgeois socialism, now revived in Russia by the Socialist-Revolutionary and Menshevik parties. He developed his theory of the class struggle consistently, down to the theory of political power, of the state.

The overthrow of bourgeois rule can be accomplished only by the proletariat, the particular class whose economic conditions of existence prepare it for this task and provide it with the possibility and the power to perform it. While the bourgeoisie break up and disintegrate the peasantry and all the petty-bourgeois groups, they weld together, unite and organise the proletariat. Only the proletariat—by virtue of the economic role it plays in large-scale production—is capable of being the leader of *all* the working and exploited people, whom the bourgeoisie exploit, oppress and crush, often not less but more than they do the proletarians, but who are incapable of waging an *independent* struggle for their emancipation.

The theory of the class struggle, applied by Marx to the question of the state and the socialist revolution, leads as a matter of course to the recognition of the *political rule* of the proletariat, of its dictatorship, i.e., of undivided power directly backed by the armed force of the people. The overthrow of the bourgeoisie can be achieved only by the proletariat becoming the *ruling class,* capable of crushing the inevitable and desperate resistance of the bourgeoisie, and of organising all the working and exploited people for the new economic system.

The proletariat needs state power, a centralized organisation of force, an organisation of violence, both to crush the resistance of the exploiters and to *lead* the enormous mass of the population—the peasants, the petty bourgeoisie, and semi-proletarians—in the work of organising a socialist economy.

By educating the workers' party, Marxism educates the vanguard of the proletariat, capable of assuming power and *leading the whole people* to socialism, of directing and organising the new system, of being the teacher, the guide, the leader of all the working and exploited people in organising their social life without the bourgeoisie and against the bourgeoisie. By contrast, the opportunism now prevailing trains the members of the workers' party to be the representatives of the better-paid workers, who lose touch with the masses, "get along" fairly well under capitalism, and sell their birthright for a mess of pottage, i.e. renounce their role as revolutionary leaders of the people against the bourgeoisie.

Marx's theory of the "state, i.e., the proletariat organised as the ruling class," is inseparably bound up with the whole of his doctrine of the revolutionary role of the proletariat in history. The culmination of this role is the proletarian dictatorship, the political rule of the proletariat.

But since the proletariat needs the state as a *special* form of organisation of violence *against* the bourgeoisie, the following conclusion suggests itself: is it conceivable that such an organisation can be created without first abolishing, destroying the state machine created by the bourgeoisie *for themselves?* The *Communist Manifesto* leads straight to this conclusion, and it is of this conclusion that Marx speaks when summing up the experience of the revolution of 1848–51.

c. LENIN

*The Transition from Capitalism to Communism**

Marx continued:

> Between capitalist and communist society lies the period of the revolutionary transformation of the one into the other. Corresponding to this is also a political transition period in which the state can be nothing but the *revolutionary dictatorship of the proletariat.*

* From Lenin, *Collected Works,* Vol. 25, pp. 459–64.

Marx bases this conclusion on analysis of the role played by the proletariat in modern capitalist society, on the data concerning the development of this society, and on the irreconcilability of the antagonistic interests of the proletariat and the bourgeoisie.

Previously the question was put as follows: to achieve its emancipation, the proletariat must overthrow the bourgeoisie, win political power and establish its revolutionary dictatorship.

Now the question is put somewhat differently: the transition from capitalist society—which is developing towards communism—to communist society is impossible without a "political transition period," and the state in this period can only be the revolutionary dictatorship of the proletariat.

What, then, is the relation of this dictatorship to democracy?

We have seen that the *Communist Manifesto* simply places side by side the two concepts: "to raise the proletariat to the position of the ruling class" and "to win the battle of democracy." On the basis of all that has been said above, it is possible to determine more precisely how democracy changes in the transition from capitalism to communism.

In capitalist society, providing it develops under the most favourable conditions, we have a more or less complete democracy in the democratic republic. But this democracy is always hemmed in by the narrow limits set by capitalist exploitation, and consequently always remains, in effect, a democracy for the minority, only for the propertied classes, only for the rich. Freedom in capitalist society always remains about the same as it was in the ancient Greek republics: freedom for the slave-owners. Owing to the conditions of capitalist exploitation, the modern wage slaves are so crushed by want and poverty that "they cannot be bothered with democracy," "cannot be bothered with politics"; in the ordinary, peaceful course of events, the majority of the population is debarred from participation in public and political life.

The correctness of this statement is perhaps most clearly confirmed by Germany, because constitutional legality steadily endured there for a remarkably long time—nearly half a century (1871–1914)—and during this period the Social-Democrats were able to achieve far more than in other countries in the way of "utilising legality," and organised a larger proportion of the workers into a political party than anywhere in the world.

What is this largest proportion of politically conscious and active wage slaves that has so far been recorded in capitalist society? One million members of the Social Democratic Party—out of fifteen million wage-workers! Three million organised in trade unions—out of fifteen million!

Democracy for an insignificant minority, democracy for the rich— that is the democracy of capitalist society. If we look more closely into the machinery of capitalist democracy, we see everywhere, in the "petty"—supposedly petty—details of the suffrage (residential qualification, exclusion of women, etc.), in the technique of the representative institutions, in the actual obstacles to the right of assembly (public buildings are not for "paupers"!), in the purely capitalist organisation of the daily press, etc., etc.—we see restriction after restriction upon democracy. These restrictions, exceptions, exclusions, obstacles for the poor seem slight, especially in the eyes of one who has never known want himself and has never been in close contact with the oppressed classes in their mass life (and nine out of ten, if not ninety-nine out of a hundred, bourgeois publicists and politicians come under this category); but in their sum total these restrictions exclude and squeeze out the poor from politics, from active participation in democracy.

Marx grasped this essence of capitalist democracy splendidly when, in analysing the experience of the Commune, he said that the oppressed are allowed once every few years to decide which particular representatives of the oppressing class shall represent and repress them in parliament!

But from this capitalist democracy—that is inevitably narrow and stealthily pushes aside the poor, and is therefore hypocritical and false through and through—forward development does not proceed simply, directly and smoothly, towards "greater and greater democracy," as the liberal professors and petty-bourgeois opportunists would have us believe. No, forward development, i.e., development towards communism, proceeds through the dictatorship of the proletariat, and cannot do otherwise, for the *resistance* of the capitalist exploiters cannot be *broken* by anyone else or in any other way.

And the dictatorship of the proletariat, i.e., the organisation of the vanguard of the oppressed as the ruling class for the purpose of suppressing the oppressors, cannot result merely in an expansion of democracy. *Simultaneously* with an immense expansion of democracy, which *for the first time* becomes democracy for the poor, democracy for the people, and not democracy for the money-bags, the dictatorship of the proletariat imposes a series of restrictions on the freedom of the oppressors, the exploiters, the capitalists. We must suppress them in order to free humanity from wage slavery, their resistance must be crushed by force; it is clear that there is no freedom and no democracy where there is suppression and where there is violence.

Engels expressed this splendidly in his letter to Bebel when he said, as the reader will remember, that "the proletariat needs the state, not in the interests of freedom but in order to hold down its adversaries, and as soon as it becomes possible to speak of freedom the state as such ceases to exist."

Democracy for the vast majority of the people, and suppression by force, i.e., exclusion from democracy, of the exploiters and oppressors of the people—this is the change democracy undergoes during the *transition* from capitalism to communism.

Only in communist society, when the resistance of the capitalists has been completely crushed, when the capitalists have disappeared, when there are no classes (i.e., when there is no distinction between the members of society as regards their relation to the social means of production), *only* then "the state . . . ceases to exist," and "it *becomes possible to speak of freedom.*" Only then will a truly complete democracy become possible and be realized, a democracy without any exceptions whatever. And only then will democracy begin to *wither away,* owing to the simple fact that freed from capitalist slavery, from the untold horrors, savagery, absurdities and infamies of capitalist exploitation, people will gradually *become accustomed* to observing the elementary rules of social intercourse that have been known for centuries and repeated for thousands of years in all copy-book maxims. They will become accustomed to observing them without force, without coercion, without subordination, *without the special apparatus* for coercion called the state.

The expression "the state *withers away*" is very well chosen, for it indicates both the gradual and the spontaneous nature of the process. Only habit can, and undoubtedly will, have such an effect; for we see around us on millions of occasions how readily people become accustomed to observing the necessary rules of social intercourse when there is no exploitation, when there is nothing that arouses indignation, evokes protest and revolt, and creates the need for *suppression.*

And so in capitalist society we have a democracy that is curtailed, wretched, false, a democracy only for the rich, for the minority. The dictatorship of the proletariat, the period of transition to communism, will for the first time create democracy for the people, for the majority, along with the necessary suppression of the exploiters, of the minority. Communism alone is capable of providing really complete democracy, and the more complete it is, the sooner it will become unnecessary and wither away of its own accord.

In other words, under capitalism we have the state in the proper sense of one class by another, and, what is more, of the majority by the minority. Naturally, to be successful, such an undertaking as the systematic suppression of the exploited majority by the exploiting minority calls for the utmost ferocity and savagery in the matter of suppressing, it calls for seas of blood, through which mankind is actually wading its way in slavery, serfdom and wage labor.

Furthermore, during the *transition* from capitalism to communism suppression is still necessary, but it is now the suppression of the exploiting minority by the exploited majority. A special apparatus, a special machine for suppression, the "state," is *still* necessary, but this is now a transitional state. It is no longer a state in the proper sense of the word; for the suppression of the minority of exploiters by the majority of the wage slaves of *yesterday* is comparatively so easy, simple and natural a task that it will entail far less bloodshed than the suppression of the risings of slaves, serfs, or wage-laborers, and it will cost mankind far less. And it is compatible with the extension of democracy to such an overwhelming majority of the population that the need for a *special machine* of suppression will begin to disappear. Naturally, the exploiters are unable to suppress the people without a highly complex machine for performing this task, but *the people* can suppress the exploiters even with a very simple "machine," almost without a "machine," without a special apparatus, by the simple *organisation of the armed people* (such as the Soviets of Workers' and Soldiers' Deputies, we would remark, running ahead).

Lastly, only communism makes the state absolutely unnecessary, for there is *nobody* to be suppressed—"nobody" in the sense of a *class,* of a systematic struggle against a definite section of the population. We are not utopians, and do not in the least deny the possibility and inevitability of excesses on the part of the *individual persons,* or the need to stop *such* excesses. In the first place, however, no special machine, no special apparatus of suppression, is needed for this; this will be done by the armed people themselves, as simply and as readily as any crowd of civilised people, even in modern society, interferes to put a stop to a scuffle or to prevent a woman from being assaulted. And, secondly, we know that the fundamental social cause of excesses, which consist in the violation of the rules of social intercourse, is the exploitation of the people, their want and their poverty. With the removal of this chief cause, excesses will inevitably begin to *"wither away."* We do not know how quickly and in what succession, but we do know they will wither away. With their withering away the state will also *wither away.*

Without building utopias, Marx defined more fully what can be defined *now* regarding this future, namely, the difference between the lower and higher phases (levels, stages) of communist society.

d. LENIN

*The Beginning of the Spontaneous Upsurge**

In the previous chapter we pointed out how *universally* absorbed the educated youth of Russia was in the theories of Marxism in the middle of the nineties. In the same period the strikes that followed the famous St. Petersburg industrial war of 1896 assumed a similar general character. Their spread over the whole of Russia clearly showed the depth of the newly awakening popular movement, and if we are to speak of the "spontaneous element" then, of course, it is this strike movement which, first and foremost, must be regarded as spontaneous. But there is spontaneity and spontaneity. Strikes occurred in Russia in the seventies and sixties (and even in the first half of the nineteenth century), and they were accompanied by the "spontaneous" destruction of machinery, etc. Compared with these "revolts," the strikes of the nineties might even be described as "conscious," to such an extent do they mark the progress which the working class movement made in that period. This shows that the "spontaneous element," in essence, represents nothing more or less than consciousness in an *embryonic form.* Even the primitive revolts expressed the awakening of consciousness to a certain extent. The workers were losing their age-long faith in the permanence of the

* "What Is to Be Done," from Lenin, *Collected Works,* Vol. 5, trans. by Joe Fineberg and George Hanna, Victor Jerome, ed. (Moscow: Foreign Language Publishing House, 1961), pp. 374–76.

system which oppressed them and began ... I shall not say to understand, but to sense the necessity for collective resistance, definitely abandoning their slavish submission to the authorities. But this was, nevertheless, more in the nature of outbursts of desperation and vengeance than of *struggle*. The strikes of the nineties revealed far greater flashes of consciousness; definite demands were advanced, the strike was carefully timed, known cases and instances in other places were discussed, etc. The revolts were simply the resistance of the oppressed, whereas the systematic strikes represented the class struggle in embryo, but only in embryo. Taken by themselves, these strikes were simply trade union struggles, not yet Social-Democratic struggles. They marked the awakening antagonisms between workers and employers; but the workers were not, and could not be, conscious of the irreconcilable antagonism of their interests to the whole of the modern political and social system, i.e., theirs was not yet Social-Democratic consciousness. In this sense, the strikes of the nineties, despite the enormous progress they represented as compared with the "revolts," remained a purely spontaneous movement.

We have said that *there could not have been* Social-Democratic consciousness among the workers. It would have to be brought to them from without. The history of all countries shows that the working class, exclusively by its own effort, is able to develop only trade-union consciousness, i.e., the conviction that it is necessary to combine in unions, fight the employers, and strive to compel the government to pass necessary labor legislation, etc. The theory of socialism, however, grew out of the philosophic, historical and economic theories elaborated by educated representatives of the propertied classes, by intellectuals. By their social status, the founders of modern scientific socialism, Marx and Engels, themselves belonged to the bourgeois intelligentsia. In the same way, in Russia, the theoretical doctrine of Social-Democracy arose altogether independently of the spontaneous growth of the working-class movement; it arose as a natural and inevitable outcome of the development of thought among the revolutionary socialist intelligentsia. In the period under discussion, the middle nineties, this doctrine not only represented the completely formulated program of the Emancipation of Labor group, but had already won over to its side the majority of the revolutionary youth of Russia.

Hence, we had both the spontaneous awakening of the working masses, their awakening to conscious life and conscious struggle, and a revolutionary youth, armed with Social-Democratic theory and straining towards the workers. . . .

Since there can be no talk of an independent ideology formulated by the working masses themselves in the process of their movement, the *only* choice is—either bourgeois or socialist ideology. There is no middle course (for mankind has not created a "third" ideology, and, morever, in a society torn by class antagonisms there can never be a non-class or an above-class ideology). Hence, to belittle the socialist ideology *in any way to turn aside from it in the slightest degree* means to strengthen bourgeois ideology. There is much talk of spontaneity. But the *spontaneous* development of the working-class movement leads to its subordination to bourgeois ideology, to *its development along the lines of the Credo program;* for the spontaneous working-class movement is trade-unionism, is *Nur-Gewerkschaftlerei,* and trade-unionism means the ideological enslavement of the workers by the bourgeoisie. Hence, our task, the task of Social-Democracy, is *to combat spontaneity, to divert* the working-class movement from this spontaneous, trade-unionist striving to come under the wing of the bourgeoisie, and to bring it under the wing of revolutionary Social-Democracy. The sentence employed by the authors of the "Economist" letter published in *Iskra,* No. 12, that the efforts of the most inspired ideologists fail to divert the working-class movement from the path that is determined by the interaction of the material elements and the material environment *is* therefore *tantamount to renouncing socialism.* If these authors were capable of fearlessly, consistently, and thoroughly considering what they say, as everyone who enters the arena of literary and public activity should be, there would be nothing left for them but to "fold their useless arms over their empty breasts" and—surrender the field of action to the Struves and Prokopoviches, who are dragging the working-class movement "along the line of least resistance," i.e., along the line of bourgeois trade-unionism, or to the Zubatovs, who are dragging it along the line of clerical and gendarme "ideology.". . .

But why, the reader will ask, does the spontaneous movement, the movement along the line of least resistance, lead to the domination of bourgeois ideology? For the simple reason that bourgeois ideology is far older in origin than socialist ideology, that it is more fully developed, and that it has at its disposal immeasurably more means of dissemination. And the younger the socialist movement in any given country, the more vigorously it must struggle against all attempts to entrench non-socialist ideology, and the more resolutely the workers must be warned against the bad counsellors who shout against "overrating the conscious element," etc. The authors of the Economist letter, in unison with *Rabocheye Dyelo,* inveigh against the intolerance that is characteristic of the infancy of the movement. To this we reply: Yes, our movement is indeed in its infancy, and in order that it may grow up faster, it must become imbued with intolerance against those who retard its growth by their subservience to spontaneity. Nothing is so ridiculous and harmful as pretending that we are "old hands" who have long ago experienced all the decisive stages of the struggle.

e. KHRUSHCHEV

*The Cult of Personality**

Comrades, the Twenty-Second Congress may in all truth be called the Congress of the Party's monolithic unity, the congress of complete unanimity and cohesion. Our enemies fear the growing unity of our ranks. They are speculating on the fact of our Congress having paid considerable attention to the harmful consequences of the personality cult and also the complete exposure of the anti-Party factionalist group. But the enemies of communism are making these efforts in vain, they have nothing to gain from all this.

The thing that distinguishes the Marxist-Leninist parties from all other political parties is that Communists do not waver, they boldly expose the shortcomings and faults in their work and eliminate them. Criticism, even the severest, helps us make progress. This is a sign of the Communist Party's strength, it is evidence of its unbending faith in its cause.

Many of the comrades who have spoken here have wrathfully condemned the subversive, anti-Party activities of the group of factionalists headed by Molotov, Kaganovich and Malenkov. Our entire Party and the whole people have rejected these renegades who opposed everything new, who strove to re-establish the harmful methods that were dominant at the time of the personality cult. They wanted to go

* From Nikita Khrushchev, *Report of the Central Committee of the CPSU, to the 22nd Congress of the Communist Party of the Soviet Union* (New York: Crosscurrents Press, 1961), pp. 219–30.

back to those difficult times for our Party and our country when nobody was guaranteed against violence and repression. Yes, that is precisely what Molotov and the others wanted.

We resolutely reject such methods of so-called leadership. We stand for the solution of inner-Party affairs on the basis of Leninist standards, by methods of conviction and broad democracy, and we shall remain firm in this respect. The Party's strongest weapon is in its ideology, the great doctrine of Marxism-Leninism, that has brought many splendid victories to our Party, the Soviet people and the international Communist movement.

Is it possible for different opinions to make their appearance within the Party at various periods, especially at turning points in its activities? Yes, it is possible. What should be done with those whose opinions differ from those of the others? We are against repressions in such cases, we stand for Leninist methods of conviction and explanation.

I will remind you of an episode from the history of our Party. On the eve of October, at the decisive moment when the whole question was whether or not there was to be a great socialist revolution, Zinoviev and Kamenev came out in the press against the Party's intention to launch an armed uprising and thus revealed the plans of the Central Committee of the Bolshevik Party to its enemies. This was a betrayal of the cause of the revolution.

Lenin exposed Zinoviev and Kamenev and demanded their expulsion from the Party. The further development of the revolution was a full confirmation of the correctness of Lenin's policy of armed uprising. When Zinoviev and Kamenev later announced that they had been mistaken and admitted their guilt, Lenin displayed great magnanimity toward them and himself raised the question of their return to the Party leadership.

Lenin pursued a firm policy aimed at the development of inner-Party democracy. He relied on the support of the masses of Communists and non-Party people.

In the years that followed Lenin's death, the Leninist standards of Party life were brutally distorted under the influence of the cult of Stalin's person. Stalin elevated curtailments of inner-Party and Soviet democracy to the level of norms for inner-Party life and the life of the state. He grossly violated the Leninist principles of leadership and permitted arbitrariness and abuse of power.

Stalin could look at a comrade sitting at the same table with him and say: "There's something shifty about your eyes today." After that you could rest assured that the comrade whose eyes had supposedly been shifty became a suspect.

Comrade Delegates! I wish to inform the Congress of the reaction of the anti-Party group to the proposal to place the question of the abuse of power in the period of the personality cult on the agenda of the Twentieth Congress.

Molotov, Kaganovich, Malenkov, Voroshilov and others raised categorical objections. In answer to their objections they were told that if they opposed the raising of the question we would let the Congress delegates decide. We did not doubt that the Congress would be in favor of discussing the question. Only then did they agree, and the question of the personality cult was presented to the Twentieth Party Congress. But the factionalists did not cease their struggle even after the Congress; they did everything they could to hamper an investigation of abuses of power, afraid that their role as accomplices in mass repressions would be revealed.

Mass repressions began after the assassination of Kirov. Considerable effort will still be required to discover who was guilty of Kirov's death. The more profoundly we study the material on Kirov's death, the greater the number of unanswered questions. There is the unaccountable fact that Kirov's murderer had before that day been twice taken into custody by security police in the vicinity of Smolny and a weapon had been found in his possession. But someone ordered his release on both occasions. Then it turned out that this armed man was in Smolny and in the very corridor along which Kirov usually passed. And it somehow happened that at the moment of the assassination the commander of Kirov's bodyguard was far behind him, although according to his instructions he had no right to be so far away from the man he was protecting.

And there is another very strange fact. When the commander of Kirov's bodyguard was taken for interrogation—he was to have been interrogated by Stalin, Molotov and Voroshilov—an accident was deliberately staged, as the driver of the car afterwards said, by those who should have taken the guard commander for interrogation. They then reported that the commander of the bodyguard had been killed in an accident although he was actually killed by those escorting him.

That is how the man who guarded Kirov was killed. Afterwards the people who had killed him were shot. This was obviously not fortuitous. It was a planned crime. Who could have perpetrated it? A thorough study of this complicated case is now being made.

It turned out that the man who drove the vehicle in which the commander of S. M. Kirov's bodyguard was taken for interrogation is still alive. He says that on the way to the interrogation an officer of the Commissariat of the Interior sat in the cab with him. The vehicle used was a truck (of course, it is very strange that a man was taken to the interrogation in a truck, as though in that particular case no other vehicle could be found. Apparently all the details had been foreseen). Two other Commissariat of the Interior officers were in the back of the truck with the commander of Kirov's bodyguard.

The driver further relates: as they were driving along the street the man sitting in the cab with him suddenly grabbed the wheel out of his hands and turned the truck straight toward a house. The driver grabbed the wheel back and turned the truck so that only the side struck the wall of the house. He was then told that the commander of Kirov's bodyguard had been killed in that accident.

How was it that he was killed and none of those travelling with him even hurt? Why were the two officers escorting the commander of Kirov's guard themselves later shot? Obviously somebody had to have them killed in order to cover up all traces.

There is still a very great deal that has not been explained concerning the circumstances of this and other cases.

Comrades, it is our duty to make a thorough, all-round examination of cases of this sort, resulting from abuse of power. The time will come when we shall die, for we are all mortal, but as long as we continue working we can and must find out a great deal and tell the truth to the Party and the people. It is cur duty to do all in our power to establish the truth now, because the more time is allowed to pass after these events, the more difficult to re-establish the truth. You cannot bring back the dead now, but the true facts must be recorded in the history of the Party. And this must be done so that similar cases can never be repeated in the future.

You may imagine how difficult it was to solve such problems when there were people in the Presidium of the Central Committee who had themselves been guilty of abusing power, of mass repressions. They stubbornly opposed all measures for the exposure of the personality cult and then developed a struggle against the Central Committee. They wanted to change the composition of its leading body and change the Leninist policy of that party, the course mapped out by the Twentieth Congress.

Naturally, they did not want to look into such matters. You have heard Comrade Shelepin's speech. He said a lot at the Congress but it stands to reason he did not tell you everything that has now been revealed. Thousands of absolutely innocent people perished, and, remember, every one of them is a separate story. Many leading Party, government and army people were killed.

Of course, those people in the Presidium of the Central Committee who were responsible for the breaches of legality, for the mass repressions, did everything they could to prevent the exposure of these arbitrary acts perpetrated in the period of the personality cult; then they launched an anti-Party factionalist struggle against the Central Committee leadership, concentrating their fire mainly against me, as First Secretary of the Central Committee, since I, in the course of my duty, was the one who had to raise those questions. I had to take their blows and reply to them.

The members of the anti-Party factionalist group wanted to seize the leadership in the Party and the country, and remove those comrades who had made exposures of the criminal acts perpetrated in the period of the personality cult. The anti-Party group wanted to put Molotov in the leadership. If they had done so, there would obviously have been no exposures of those abuses of power.

Even after the Twentieth Congress had been held and had condemned the personality cult, the anti-Party group did everything it could to prevent the exposures from going further. Molotov said that in big matters good and bad things occur. He justified the acts that had taken place at the time of the personality cult and claimed that such actions are possible and that their repetition in the future is also possible. Such was the line taken by the anti-Party group. That was no simple error. It was a calculated, criminal adventurist position. They wanted to divert the Party and the country from the Leninist path, they wanted to return to the policy and methods of leadership of the personality cult period. They miscalculated, however. The Central Committee, our entire Party, the whole Soviet people dealt a severe rebuff to the anti-Party group, exposed and defeated the factionalists.

Delegates have spoken here with pain in their hearts of many innocent victims among prominent Party and government leaders.

Such prominent army leaders as Tukhachevsky, Yakir, Uborevich, Kork, Yegorov, Eidemann and others were victims of the repressions.

These were people who had great services to their credit, especially Tukhachevsky, Yakir and Uborevich, who were outstanding army leaders. Later Blücher and other prominent army leaders suffered from the repressions.

A rather curious report once found its way into the press abroad to the effect that Hitler, when he was preparing his assault on our country, had fabricated a document showing that Comrades Yakir, Tukhachevsky and others were agents of the German General Staff. This "document," allegedly secret, fell into the hands of President Benes of Czechoslovakia and he, presumably guided by good intentions, passed it on to Stalin. Yakir, Tukhachevsky and other comrades were arrested and were then killed.

Many splendid commanders and political officers of the Red Army were killed. Here among the delegates there are comrades—I do not wish to mention their names, in order not to cause them pain—who spent many years in prison. They were "persuaded," persuaded by the use of certain methods, that they were either German, or British, or some other spies. Some of them "confessed." There were even cases when some of these comrades, on being told that the accusation of espionage had been withdrawn, themselves insisted on their previous depositions; they thought it better to stick to false depositions in order the more quickly to put an end to their torment, the more quickly to go to their death.

That is what the personality cult means! That was the meaning of the actions of Molotov and the others who wanted to restore the evil practices of the period of the personality cult. It was this that the anti-Party group wanted to bring the Party back to, and precisely because of that the struggle against them was so acute and so difficult. Everybody realized what it meant.

I knew Comrade Yakir very well. I also knew Tukhachevsky, but not as well as I knew Yakir. During the conference in Alma Ata this year his son, who was working in Kazakhstan, came to me. He asked me about his father. What could I say to him? When we were examining these cases in the Presidium of the Central Committee and were informed that neither Tukhachevsky nor Yakir nor Uborevich had committed any crimes against the Party and the state, we asked Molotov, Kaganovich and Voroshilov:

"Are you in favor of their rehabilitation?"

"Yes, we are," they answered.

"But it was you who executed those people," we said indignantly.

"When were you following the dictates of your conscience, then or now?"

They did not answer that question. They never will. You have heard what kind of notations they wrote on letters addressed to Stalin. So, what can they say?

In his speech to this Congress Comrade Shelepin has told you how these fine representatives of the Communist Party in the Red Army were killed. He also quoted a letter from Comrade Yakir to Stalin, and read you the resolutions on that letter. It should be said that at one time Stalin had a lot of respect for Yakir.

I can add to that: at the moment Yakir was shot he shouted, "Long live the Party, long live Stalin!"

He had so much faith in the party, in Stalin, that it never entered his mind that the lawlessness was deliberate. He thought that enemies had infiltrated the organs of the People's Commissariat of Internal Affairs.

When Stalin was told how Yakir had behaved before his death, he cursed Yakir.

Let us recall Sergo Ordzhonikidze. I was present at Ordzhonikidze's funeral. I believed what I had been told at the time, that he had died suddenly, because we knew that he had a heart disease. Much later, after the war, I learned quite by accident that he had committed suicide. Sergo's brother had been arrested and shot. Comrade Ordzhonikidze realized that he could no longer work with Stalin, although he had formerly been one of his closest friends. Ordzhonikidze held a leading post in the Party. Lenin had known and valued him, but a situation developed in which he could no longer work normally, and in order to avoid a clash with Stalin and not share responsibility for his abuse of power, he decided to commit suicide.

The fate of the brother of Stalin's first wife, Alyosha Svanidze, who was less known to the rank and file of our Party, was also a tragic one. He was a veteran Bolshevik, but Beria, by means of various machinations, made a case to the effect that Svanidze had been placed near Stalin by the German secret service, although he was Stalin's very close friend. And Svanidze was shot. Before he was shot he was told that Stalin had said that if he asked forgiveness he would be pardoned. When Stalin's words were repeated to Svanidze he asked: "Why should I ask forgiveness? I have not committed any crime." He was shot. After Svanidze's death, Stalin said: "See how proud he is, he died but wouldn't ask forgiveness." It never occurred to Stalin that Svanidze was, above all, an honest man.

And that is how many innocent people died.

That is what the personality cult means. That is why we cannot tolerate even the slightest manifestations of abuse of power.

Comrades, letters have been addressed to the presidium of the Congress by veteran Bolsheviks, in which they write that in the period of the personality cult outstanding leaders of the Party and the Government were done to death, such true Leninists as Chubar, Kosior, Rudzutak, Postyshev, Eikhe, Voznesensky, Kuznetsov and others.

The comrades propose perpetuating the memory of those prominent Party and Government leaders who fell victims to the unfounded repressions in the period of the personality cult.

We consider this a fit and proper proposal. It would be advisable to entrust the Central Committee that will be elected by the Twenty-Second Congress to take a positive decision on this question. Perhaps a monument should be erected in Moscow to perpetuate the memory of comrades who fell victims to arbitrary violence.

While the personality cult dominated, the Party was deprived of normal conditions of life. People who usurp power are no longer accountable to the Party, they put themselves beyond its control. That is the chief danger of the personality cult.

There must always be a situation in the Party that keeps every leader responsible to the Party and its organs, a situation in which the Party can replace any leader when it considers it necessary.

Since the Twentieth Congress, Leninist principles of Party life and collective leadership have now been restored in the Party. Propositions that restore Leninist standards of Party life and preclude the possibility of a recurrence of the personality cult are given legal force in the new Program and the Party rules.

f. KHRUSHCHEV

*Need for Collective Leadership**

Comrades, the Twenty-Second Congress has forcefully confirmed that the course of the Twentieth Party Congress, a course to restore and further develop Leninist norms of Party and state life, to raise the guiding role of the Party and promote the creative initiative of the

* From Khrushchev, *Report . . . to the 22nd Congress,* pp. 235–39.

masses, is the only correct course. The Twenty-Second Congress consolidates this constructive course. Further guarantees against recurrences of the cult of the individual are given in the Program and Rules of the Party, and in the decisions of the Congress. The role of the Party as the great inspiring and organizing force in the building of communism is rising still higher.

I should like to say a few words about the following as well. In many of the speeches at the Congress and not infrequently in the press, too, when mention is made of the activities of the Central Committee of our Party some special emphasis is placed on my person and on my role in the implementation of major measures of the Party and the Government.

I appreciate the kind feelings guiding these comrades. But allow me to state emphatically that everything said about me must refer to the Central Committee of our Leninist Party, to the Presidium of the Central Committee, because not a single major measure nor a single responsible speech was undertaken on anybody's personal instructions. They are all the result of collective discussion and collective decision. This concluding speech, too, has been considered and approved by the leading collective. Our great strength, comrades, lies in collective leadership, in a joint decision on all matters of principle.

Whatever abilities one leader or another may possess, no matter how much energy he puts into the work, no real stable success can be achieved without the support of the collective, without the most active participation of the entire Party and broad masses in the implementation of planned measures. That is something all of us must understand well and constantly bear in mind.

Communist leaders owe their strength to the activity of the masses they lead. If they correctly understand and express the interests of the Party, if they struggle for these interests without stinting their strength, energy and even life, if in big and small things they are inseparable from the Party as the Party is inseparable from the people, such leaders will always have the support of the Party and the people. And the cause that such a leader champions will inevitably triumph.

Naturally, one must possess the qualities needed for the struggle for the cause of the Party, for the vital interests of the people. After all, our ideological adversaries, our enemies, concentrate their fire first and foremost against leaders who, by rallying the activists, and through them the entire population, round the central organs, continue along the only true Leninist path.

Here at the Congress much has been said, for example, about the furious energy with which the anti-Party factionalists Molotov, Kaganovich, Malenkov and others attacked the Leninist Central Committee of the Party and me personally. Acting against the Party line mapped out by the Twentieth Congress, the splitters concentrated their main fire against Khrushchev, who did not suit them. Why against Khrushchev? For the simple reason that by the will of the Party Khrushchev was appointed to the post of First Secretary of the Central Committee. The factionalists thoroughly miscalculated. The Party defeated them both ideologically and organizationally.

The Central Committee of our Party displayed exceptionally high political maturity and a truly Leninist understanding of the situation. It is characteristic that virtually not a single member of the Central Committee, not a candidate supported the miserable handful of splitters.

While firmly opposed to the revolting effects of the cult of the individual, Marxists-Leninists have always recognized the authority of leaders, and will continue to do so.

But it would be wrong to single out any leader, to set him apart in any way from the leading collective, to indulge in excessive praise. This is contrary to the principles of Marxism-Leninism. It may be recalled how uncompromisingly Marx, Engels and Lenin spoke out against people who indulged in extolling their merits. Yet it is simply difficult to overrate the big role and the services Marx, Engels and Lenin, the founders of scientific communism, rendered the working class and all mankind.

Any inclination to self-praise and any special accentuation or excessive exaggeration of the role of individual leaders is profoundly alien to true Marxist-Leninists. It is simply insulting when someone importunately tries to set them apart, to isolate them from the guiding nucleus of comrades.

We Communists highly value and support the prestige of correct and mature leadership. We must safeguard the prestige of leaders recognized by the Party and the people. But every leader must bear in mind the other side of the matter—never to preen himself on his position, to remember that by occupying an office he merely performs the will of the Party, the will of the people, who may have invested him with supreme power, but who never lose control over him. The leader who forgets this pays dearly for such mistakes. I would say that he pays during his lifetime, or else the people do not forgive him after his death, as in the case of the condemnation of the cult of Stalin's personality. A man who forgets that it is his duty to carry out the will of the Party, the will of the people, cannot, properly speaking, be called a real leader. There is no room for such "leaders" either in the Party or in the state apparatus.

To be sure, for many reasons a great deal of power is concentrated in the hands of the individual holding a high office. A leader appointed by the Party and the people must not abuse his powers. In the Reports to the Congress mention has already been made of the measures we have effected, and will continue to effect, in order that the ugly phenomena of the personality cult never recur. But there is one thing no clause in the rules can provide for—the collective of leaders must understand well that a situation must not be allowed to arise, where anyone, albeit the most deserving authority, may cease to heed the opinion of those who advanced him.

It is impermissible, inadmissible, comrades, to let a situation develop where the prestige of an individual assumes such forms that he begins to think he may do anything he pleases and no longer needs the collective. In such cases the individual concerned may stop heeding the voice of the other comrades put into high office like himself, and may start to suppress them. Lenin, our great teacher, was firmly opposed to this, and the Party has paid too heavy a price for not having heeded his wise counsel in due time.

So let us be worthy pupils of Lenin in this important matter as well.

g. DJILAS

The New Class *

Everything happened differently in the U.S.S.R. and other Communist countries from what the leaders—even such prominent ones as Lenin, Stalin, Trotsky, and Bukharin—anticipated. They expected that the state would rapidly wither away, that democracy would be strengthened. The reverse happened. They expected a rapid improvement in the standard of living—there has been scarcely any change in this respect and, in the subjugated East European countries, the

* From Milovan Djilas, *The New Class* (New York: Fredrick A. Praeger, 1957), pp. 37–41; 47–54. By permission.

standard has even declined. In every instance, the standard of living
has failed to rise in proportion to the rate of industrialization, which
was much more rapid. It was believed that the differences between
cities and villages, between intellectual and physical labor, would
slowly disappear; instead these differences have increased. Communist
anticipations in other areas—including their expectations for developments in the non-communist world—have also failed to materialize.

The greatest illusion was that industrialization and collectivization
in the U.S.S.R., and destruction of capitalist ownership, would result
in a classless society. In 1936, when the new Constitution was promulgated, Stalin announced that the "exploiting class" had ceased to
exist. The capitalist and other classes of ancient origin had in fact
been destroyed, but a new class, previously unknown to history, had
been formed.

It is understandable that this class, like those before it, should
believe that the establishment of its power would result in happiness
and freedom for all men. The only difference between this and other
classes was that it treated the delay in the realization of its illusions
more crudely. It thus affirmed that its power was more complete than
the power of any other class before in history, and its class illusions
and prejudices were proportionally greater.

This new class, the bureaucracy, or more accurately the political
bureaucracy, has all the characteristics of earlier ones as well as some
new characteristics of its own. Its origin had its special characteristics
also, even though in essence it was similar to the beginnings of other
classes.

Other classes, too, obtained their strength and power by the revolutionary path, destroying the political, social, and other orders they
met in their way. However, almost without exception, these classes
attained power after new economic patterns had taken shape in the
old society. The case was the reverse with new classes in the Communist systems. It did not come to power to complete a new economic
order but to establish its own and, in so doing, to establish its power
over society.

In earlier epochs the coming to power of some class, some part of
a class, or of some party, was the final event resulting from its formation and its development. The reverse was true in the U.S.S.R. There
the new class was definitely formed after it attained power. Its consciousness had to develop before its economic and physical powers,
because the class had not taken root in the life of the nation. This

class viewed its role in relation to the world from an idealistic point of view. Its practical possibilities were not diminished by this. In spite of its illusions, it represented an objective tendency toward industrialization. Its practical bent emanated from this tendency. The promise of an ideal world increased the faith in the ranks of the new class and sowed illusions among the masses. At the same time it inspired gigantic physical undertakings.

Because this new class had not been formed as a part of the economic and social life before it came to power, it could only be created in an organization of a special type, distinguished by a special discipline based on identical philosophic and ideological views of its members. A unity of belief and iron discipline was necessary to overcome its weaknesses.

The roots of the new class were implanted in a special party, of the Bolshevik type. Lenin was right in his view that his party was an exception in the history of human society, although he did not suspect that it would be the beginning of a new class.

To be more precise, the initiators of the new class are not found in the party of the Bolshevik type as a whole but in that stratum of professional revolutionaries who made up its core even before it attained power. It was not by accident that Lenin asserted after the failure of the 1905 revolution that only professional revolutionaries—men whose sole profession was revolutionary work—could build a new party of the Bolshevik type. It was still less accidental that even Stalin, the future creator of a new class, was the most outstanding example of such a professional revolutionary. The new ruling class has been gradually developing from this very narrow stratum of revolutionaries. These revolutionaries composed its core for a long period. Trotsky noted that in prerevolutionary professional revolutionaries was the origin of the future Stalinist bureaucrat. What he did not detect was the beginning of a new class of owners and exploiters.

This is not to say that the new party and the new class are identical. The party, however, is the core of that class, and its base. It is very difficult, perhaps impossible, to define the limits of the new class and to identify its members. The new class may be said to be made up of those who have special privileges and economic preference because of the administrative monopoly they hold.

Since administration is unavoidable in society, necessary administrative functions may be coexistent with parasitic functions in the same person. Not every member of the party is a member of the new class, any more than every artisan or member of a middle-class party is a bourgeois.

In loose terms, as the new class becomes stronger and attains a more perceptible physiognomy, the role of the party diminishes. The core and the basis of the new class is created in the party and at its top, as well as in the state political organs. The once live, compact party, full of initiative, is disappearing to become transformed into the traditional oligarchy of the new class, irresistibly drawing into its ranks those who aspire to join the new class and repressing those who have any ideals.

The party makes the class, but the class grows as a result and uses the party as a basis. The class grows stronger, while the party grows weaker; this is the inescapable fate of every Communist party in power.

If it were not materially interested in production or if it did not have within itself the potentialities for the creation of a new class, no party could act in so morally and ideologically foolhardy a fashion, let alone stay in power for long. Stalin declared, after the end of the First Five-Year Plan: "If we had not created the apparatus, we would have failed!" He should have substituted "new class" for the word "apparatus," and everything would have been clearer.

It seems unusual that a political party could be the beginning of a new class. Parties are generally the product of classes and strata which have become intellectually and economically strong. However, if one grasps the actual conditions in prerevolutionary Russia and in other countries in which Communism prevailed over national forces, it will be clear that a party of this type is the product of specific opportunities and that there is nothing unusual or accidental in this being so. Although the roots of Bolshevism reach far back into Russian history, the party is partly the product of the unique pattern of international relationships in which Russia found itself at the end of the nineteenth and the beginning of the twentieth century. Russia was no longer able to live in the modern world as an absolute monarchy, and Russia's capitalism was too weak and too dependent on the interests of foreign powers to make it possible to have an industrial revolution. This revolution could only be implemented by a new class, or by a change in the social order. As yet, there was no such class.

In history, it is not important who implements a process, it is only important that the process be implemented. Such was the case in Russia and other countries in which Communist revolutions took place. The revolution created forces, leaders, organizations, and ideas which were necessary to it. The new class came into existence for objective reasons, and by the wish, wits, and actions of its leaders. . . .

The development of modern Communism, and the emergence of the new class, is evident in the character and roles of those who inspired it.

The leaders and their methods, from Marx to Khrushchev, have been varied and changing. It never occurred to Marx to prevent others from voicing their ideas. Lenin tolerated free discussion in his party and did not think that party forums, let alone the party head, should regulate the expression of "proper" or "improper" ideas. Stalin abolished every type of intra-party discussion, and made the expression of ideology solely the right of the central forum—or of himself. Other Communist movements were different. For instance, Marx's International Workers' Union (the so-called First International) was not Marxist in ideology, but a union of varied groups which adopted only the resolutions on which its members agreed. Lenin's party was an *avant-garde* group combining an internal revolutionary morality and ideological monolithic structure with democracy of a kind. Under Stalin the party became a mass of ideologically disinterested men, who got their ideas from above, but were wholehearted and unanimous in the defense of a system that assured them unquestionable privileges. Marx actually never created a party; Lenin destroyed all parties except his own, including the Socialist Party. Stalin relegated even the Bolshevik Party to second rank, transforming its core into the core of the new class, and transforming the party into a privileged impersonal and colorless group.

Marx created a system of the roles of classes, and of class war in society, even though he did not discover them, and he saw that mankind is mostly made up of members of discernible classes, although he was only restating Terence's Stoic philosophy: *"Humani nihil a me alienum puto."* Lenin viewed men as sharing ideas rather than as being members of discernible classes. Stalin saw in men only obedient subjects or enemies. Marx died a poor emigrant in London, but was valued by learned men and valued in the movement; Lenin died as the leader of one of the greatest revolutions, but died as a dictator about whom a cult had already begun to form; when Stalin died, he had already transformed himself into a god.

These changes in personalities are only the reflection of changes which had already taken place and were the very soul of the Communist movement.

Although he did not realize it, Lenin started the organization of the new class. He established the party along Bolshevik lines and developed the theories of its unique and leading role in the building of a new society. This is but one aspect of his many-sided and gigantic work; it is the aspect which came about from his actions rather than his wishes. It is also the aspect which led the new class to revere him.

The real and direct originator of the new class, however, was Stalin. He was a man of quick reflexes and a tendency to coarse humor, not very educated nor a good speaker. But he was a relentless dogmatician and a great administrator, a Georgian who knew better than anyone else whither the new powers of Greater Russia were taking her. He created the new class by the use of the most barbaric means, not even sparing the class itself. It was inevitable that the new class which placed him at the top would later submit to his unbridled and brutal nature. He was the true leader of that class as long as the class was building itself up, and attaining power.

The new class was born in the revolutionary struggle in the Communist Party, but was developed in the industrial revolution. Without the revolution, without industry, the class's position would not have been secure and its power would have been limited.

While the country was being industrialized, Stalin began to introduce considerable variations in wages, at the same time allowing the development toward various privileges to proceed. He thought that industrialization would come to nothing if the new class were not made materially interested in the process, by acquisition of some property for itself. Without industrialization the new class would find it difficult to hold its position, for it would have neither historical justification nor the material resources for its continued existence.

The increase in the membership of the party, or of the bureaucracy, was closely connected with this. In 1927, on the eve of industrialization, the Soviet Communist Party had 887,233 members. In 1934, at the end of the First Five-Year Plan, the membership had increased to 1,874,488. This was a phenomenon obviously connected with industrialization: the prospects for the new class and privileges for its members were improving. What is more, the privileges and the class were expanding more rapidly than industrialization itself. It is difficult to cite any statistics on this point, but the conclusion is self-evident for anyone who bears in mind that the standard of living has not kept pace with industrial production, while the new class actually seized the lion's share of the economic and other progress earned by the sacrifices and efforts of the masses.

The establishment of the new class did not proceed smoothly. It encountered bitter opposition from existing classes and from those revolutionaries who could not reconcile reality with the ideals of their struggle. In the U.S.S.R. the opposition of revolutionaries was most evident in the Trotsky-Stalin conflict. The conflict between Trotsky and Stalin, or between oppositionists in the party and Stalin, as well as the conflict between the regime and the peasantry, became more intense as industrialization advanced and the power and authority of the new class increased.

Trotsky, an excellent speaker, brilliant stylist, and skilled polemicist, a man cultured and of excellent intelligence, was deficient in only one quality: a sense of reality. He wanted to be a revolutionary in a period when life imposed the commonplace. He wished to revive a revolutionary party which was being transformed into something completely different, into a new class unconcerned with great ideals and interested only in the everyday pleasures of life. He expected action from a mass already tired by war, hunger, and death, at a time when the new class already strongly held the reins and has begun to experience the sweetness of privilege. Trotsky's fireworks lit up the distant heavens; but he could not rekindle fires in weary men. He sharply noted the sorry aspect of the new phenomena but he did not grasp their meaning. In addition, he had never been a Bolshevik. This was his vice and his virtue. Attacking the party bureaucracy in the name of the revolution, he attacked the cult of the party and, although he was not conscious of it, the new class.

Stalin looked neither far ahead nor far behind. He had seated himself at the head of the new power which was being born—the new class, the political bureaucracy, and bureaucratism—and became its leader and organizer. He did not preach—he made decisions. He too promised a shining future, but one which bureaucracy could visualize as being real because its life was improving from day to day and its position was being strengthened. He spoke without ardor and color, but the new class was better able to understand this kind of realistic language. Trotsky wished to extend the revolution to Europe; Stalin was not opposed to the idea but this hazardous undertaking did not prevent him from worrying about Mother Russia or, specifically, about ways of strengthening the new system and increasing the power and reputation of the Russian state. Trotsky was a man of the revolution of the past; Stalin was a man of today and, thus, of the future.

In Stalin's victory Trotsky saw the Thermidoric reaction against the revolution, actually the bureaucratic corruption of the Soviet government and the revolutionary cause. Consequently, he understood and was deeply hurt by the amorality of Stalin's methods. Trotsky was the first, although he was not aware of it, who in the attempt to save the Communist movement discovered the essence of contemporary Communism. But he was not capable of seeing it through to the end. He supposed that this was only a momentary cropping up of bureaucracy, corrupting the party and the revolution, and concluded that the solution was in a change at the top, in a "palace revolution." When a palace revolution actually took place after Stalin's death, it could be seen that the essence had not changed; something deeper and more lasting was involved. The Soviet Thermidor of Stalin had not only led to the installation of a government more despotic than the previous one, but also to the installation of a class. This was the continuation of the other side of the coin, the violence of the revolution which had given birth and strength to the new class.

Stalin could, with equal if not greater right, refer to Lenin and all the revolution, just as Trotsky did. For Stalin was the lawful although wicked offspring of Lenin and the revolution.

History has no previous record of a personality like Lenin who, by his versatility and persistence, developed one of the greatest revolutions known to men. It also has no record of a personality like Stalin, who took on the enormous task of strengthening, in terms of power and property, a new class born out of one of the greatest revolutions in one of the largest of the world's countries.

Behind Lenin, who was all passion and thought, stands the dull, gray figure of Joseph Stalin, the symbol of the difficult, cruel, and unscrupulous ascent of the new class to its final power.

After Lenin and Stalin came what had to come; namely, mediocrity in the form of collective leadership. And also there came the apparently sincere, kind-hearted, non-intellectual "man of the people" —Nikita Khrushchev. The new class no longer needs the revolutionaries or dogmatists it once required; it is satisfied with simple personalities, such as Khrushchev, Malenkov, Bulganin, and Shepilov, whose every word reflects the average man. The new class itself is tired of dogmatic purges and training sessions. It would like to live quietly. It must protect itself even from its own authorized leader now that it has been adequately strengthened. Stalin remained the same as he was when the class was weak, when cruel measures were necessary against even those in its own ranks who threatened to deviate. Today this is all unnecessary. Without relinquishing anything it created under Stalin's leadership, the new class appears to be renouncing his authority for the past few years. But it is not really renouncing that authority—only Stalin's methods which, according to Khrushchev, hurt "good Communists."

Lenin's revolutionary epoch was replaced by Stalin's epoch, in which authority and ownership, and industrialization, were strengthened so that the much desired peaceful and good life of the new class could begin. Lenin's *revolutionary* Communism was replaced by Stalin's *dogmatic* Communism, which in turn was replaced by *non-dogmatic* Communism, a so-called collective leadership or a group of oligarchs.

These are the three phases of development of the new class in the U.S.S.R. or of Russian Communism (or of every other type of Communism in one manner or another).

The fate of Yugoslav Communism was to unify these three phases in the single personality of Tito, along with national and personal characteristics. Tito is a great revolutionary, but without original ideas; he has attained personal power, but without Stalin's distrustfulness and dogmatism. Like Khrushchev, Tito is a representative of the people, that is, of the middle-party strata. The road which Yugoslav Communism has traveled—attaining a revolution, copying Stalinism, then renouncing Stalinism and seeking its own form—is seen most fully in the personality of Tito. Yugoslav Communism has been more consistent than other parties in preserving the substance of Communism, yet never renouncing any form which could be of value to it.

The three phases in the development of the new class—Lenin, Stalin, and "collective leadership"—are not completely divorced from each other, in substance or in ideas.

Lenin too was a dogmatist, and Stalin too was a revolutionary, just as collective leadership will resort to dogmatism and to revolutionary methods when necessary. What is more, the non-dogmatism of the collective leadership is applied only to itself, to the heads of the new class. On the other hand, the people must be all the more persistently "educated" in the spirit of the dogma, or of Marxism-Leninism. By relaxing its dogmatic severity and exclusiveness, the new class, becoming strengthened economically, has prospects of attaining greater flexibility.

The heroic era of Communism is past. The epoch of its great leaders has ended. The epoch of practical men has set in. The new class has been created. It is at the height of its power and wealth, but it is without new ideas. It has nothing more to tell the people. The only thing that remains is for it to justify itself.

12

AMERICAN DEMOCRACY
Majority Rule and Minority Rights

American democracy is founded on the principle that legitimate government should be based upon the consent of the governed exercised through the practice of majority rule. But it also embodies an emphasis upon the protection of individual and minority rights against governmental authority and the tyranny of the majority.

Within American political evolution there has been constant tension and conflict between these two principles; among the major spokesmen for American democracy one finds varying degrees of emphasis upon which principle should be given priority. The tradition of popular democracy, stemming from Thomas Jefferson (1743–1826), has embodied a strong affirmation of the principle of majority rule. Acquiescence in decisions of the majority, Jefferson contended, is the vital principle of the Republic from which there is no appeal but to force. Jefferson also believed that the Constitution should not be looked upon with sanctimonious reverence as too sacred to be touched and beyond amendment or replacement. Every generation is independent of the preceding one and has the right to establish its own laws.

Jefferson's confidence in majority rule has not been universally accepted within the American political tradition, and one finds frequent expression of fears of the dangers of majority tyranny—a view widely shared by the authors of the American Constitution. Writing in the *Federalist* papers, James Madison (1751–1836) expressed the view that the chief danger to the Union stems from the harm to the rights of citizens stemming from factions, particularly those that spring from inequalities in the distribution of property. Madison realized that the problems of factions cannot be solved simply by removing the cause, since this would mean the abolition of liberty. The solution must be sought, rather, in controlling the effects of faction. This can be secured through several means. One is through the republican principle of government which permits the delegation of power to a smaller number of individuals whose wisdom can perceive the best interest in the country. Madison also believed that the large territorial area encompassed by the Union would make it difficult for factions to combine together to execute their plans of oppression. Finally, Madison discerned in the principle of separation of powers and the checks and balances of the Constitution an essential means by which rights of citizens can be safeguarded against bureaucratic power. By this means also the excessive power of the majority was to be curbed.

The question, of course, is whether subsequent developments in American democracy have vindicated Madison's hopes and expectations. The omnipotent, and absolute, power of majority rule was a central theme of the famous classic *Democracy in America,* written by a French aristocrat, Alexis de Tocqueville (1805–1859). Viewing America during the early part of the nineteenth century, Tocqueville contended that the main evil of present democratic institutions of the United States does not arise, as is often asserted in Europe, from their weakness, but from their overpowering strength. Tocqueville was not so much alarmed at the excessive liberty which prevails in America as at the inadequate securities which exist against tyranny. Nor does the party wronged have anyone to whom he can appeal for redress; for public opinion, legislative assemblies, executive power, juries, and even judges are subject to majority control. The majority raises formidable barriers to freedom of opinion, and if an author transcends these barriers his political career will be closed forever; he will be subjected to social ostracism, censure and denunciation. Although the nonconformist individual in America will not be subject to actual physical oppression, as in European despotisms of the past, he may suffer a fate worse than death. Tocqueville feared that if ever free institutions in America are destroyed, this will be due to the unlimited power of the majority which may lead minorities to desperation, then to violence, and anarchy will be the result.

The fears of Tocqueville, in light of the general course of American historical development, may perhaps be viewed as exaggerated or unwarranted. But American historical experience does provide ample evidence that popular majorities have, on occasion, threatened and endangered individual freedom and civil liberties. The dilemma of American democracy has been the problem of how to reconcile the conflicting demands of individual freedom and majority power. Approaches to this question have frequently involved stands in which one principle or the other has been elevated to a position of supremacy. The contrast between Madison and Jefferson, however, does not involve radically opposed conceptions of democracy. While Jefferson affirmed majority rule as a basic principle of republican government, he recognized that the majority must be reasonable and that minorities possess equal rights which equal laws must protect and which to violate would be oppression. If Madison put more stress upon the danger of majority tyranny, he recognized that the clash of interests and factional stuggle express the basic essence of liberty and popular government. The mainstream of the American democratic tradition, it may be contended, embodies a concept of democracy which makes neither principle supreme, but would hold that both are mutually interdependent and essentially equal.

a. JEFFERSON

*The Faith in Majority Rule**

Called upon to undertake the duties of the first executive office of our country, I avail myself of the presence of that portion of my fellow citizens which is here assembled, to express my grateful thanks for the favor which they have been pleased to look toward me, to declare a sincere consciousness that the task is above my talents, and that I approach it with those anxious and awful presentiments which the greatness of the charge and the weakness of my powers so justly inspire. A rising nation, spread over a wide and fruitful land, traversing all the seas with the rich productions of their industry, engaged in commerce with nations who feel power and forget right, advancing rapidly to destinies beyond the reach of mortal eye—when I contemplate these transcendent objects, and see the honor, the happiness, and the hopes of this beloved country committed to the issues and the auspices of this day, I shrink from the contemplation, and humble myself before the magnitude of the undertaking. Utterly indeed, should I despair, did not the presence of many whom I here see remind me, that in the other high authorities provided by our Constitution, I shall find resources of wisdom, of virtue, and of zeal, on which to rely under all difficulties. To you, then, gentlemen, who are charged with the sovereign functions of legislation, and to those associated with you, I look with encouragement for that guidance and support which may enable us to steer with safety the vessel in which we are all embarked amid the conflicting elements of a troubled world.

---

* The selection is the "First Inaugural Address," from *The Writings of Thomas Jefferson,* H. A. Washington, ed., Vol. VIII (Washington, D.C.: Taylor and Maury, 1854), pp. 1–5.

During the contest of opinion through which we have passed, the animation of discussion and of exertions has sometimes worn an aspect which might impose on strangers unused to think freely and to speak and to write what they think; but this being now decided by the voice of the nation, announced according to the rules of the Constitution, all will, of course, arrange themselves under the will of the law and unite in common efforts for the common good. All, too, will bear in mind this sacred principle, that though the will of the majority is in all cases to prevail, that will, to be rightful must be reasonable; that the minority possess their equal rights, which equal laws must protect, and to violate which would be oppression. Let us, then, fellow-citizens, unite with one heart and one mind. Let us restore to social intercourse that harmony and affection without which liberty and even life itself are but dreary things. And let us reflect that having banished from our land that religious intolerance under which mankind so long bled and suffered, we have yet gained little if we countenance a political intolerance as despotic, as wicked, and capable of as bitter and bloody persecutions. During the throes and convulsions of the ancient world, during the agonizing spasms of infuriated man, seeking through blood and slaughter his long-lost liberty, it was not wonderful that the agitation of the billows should reach even this distant and peaceful shore; that this should be more felt and feared by some and less by others; that this should divide opinions as to measures of safety. But every difference of opinion is not a difference of principle. We have called by different names brethren of the same principle. We are all republicans—we are federalists. If there be any among us who would wish to dissolve this Union or to change its republican form, let them stand undisturbed as monuments of the safety with which error of opinion may be tolerated where reason is left free to combat it. I know, indeed, that some honest men fear that a republican government cannot be strong; that this government is not strong enough. But would the honest patriot, in the full tide of successful experiment, abandon a government which has so far kept us free and firm, on the theoretic and visionary fear that this government, the world's best hope, may by possibility want energy to preserve itself? I trust not. I believe this, on the contrary, the strongest government on earth. I believe it is the only one where every man, at the call of the laws, would fly to the standard of the law, and would meet invasions of the public order as his own personal concern. Sometimes it is said that man cannot be trusted with the government of himself. Can he, then, be trusted with the government of others? Or have we found angels in the forms of kings to govern him? Let history answer this question.

Let us, then, with courage and confidence pursue our own federal and republican principles, our attachment to our union and representative government. Kindly separated by nature and a wide ocean from the exterminating havoc of one quarter of the globe; too high-minded to endure the degradations of the others; possessing a chosen country, with room enough for the descendants to the hundredth and thousandth generation; entertaining a due sense of our equal right to the use of our own faculties, to the acquisitions of our industry, to honor and confidence from our fellow citizens, resulting not from birth but from our actions and their sense of them; enlightened by a benign religion, professed, indeed, and practiced in various forms, yet all of them including honesty, truth, temperance, gratitude, and the love of man; acknowledging and adoring an overruling Providence, which by all its dispensations proves that it delights in the happiness of man here and his greater happiness hereafter; with all these blessings, what more is necessary to make us a happy and prosperous people? Still one thing more, fellow citizens—a wise and frugal government, which shall restrain men from injuring one another, which shall leave them otherwise free to regulate their own pursuits of industry and improvement, and shall not take from the mouth of labor the bread it has earned. This is the sum of good government, and this is necessary to close the circle of our felicities.

About to enter, fellow citizens, on the exercise of duties which comprehend everything dear and valuable to you, it is proper that you should understand what I deem the essential principles of our government, and consequently those which ought to shape its administration. I will compress them with the narrowest compass they will bear, stating the general principle, but not all its limitations. Equal and exact justice to all men, of whatever state or persuasion, religious or political; peace, commerce, and honest friendship with all nations— entangling alliances with none; the support of the State governments in all their rights, as the most competent administrations for our domestic concerns and the surest bulwarks against anti-republican tendencies; the preservation of the general government in its whole constitutional vigor, as the sheet anchor of our peace at home and safety abroad; a jealous care of the right of election by the people—a

mild and safe corrective of abuses which are lopped by the sword of
the revolution where peaceable remedies are unprovided; absolute
acquiescence in the decisions of the majority—the vital principle of
republics, from which there is no appeal but to force, the vital principle and immediate parent of despotism; a well-disciplined militia—
our best reliance in peace and for the first moments of war, till regu-
lars may relieve them; the supremacy of the civil over the military
authority; economy in the public expense, that labor may be lightly
burdened; the honest payment of our debts and sacred preservation
of the public faith; encouragement of agriculture, and of commerce as
its handmaid; the diffusion of information and the arraignment of all
abuses at the bar of public reason; freedom of religion; freedom of the
press; freedom of person under the protection of the *habeas corpus;*
and trial by juries impartially selected—these principles form the
bright constellation which has gone before us, and guided our steps
through an age of revolution and reformation. The wisdom of our
sages and the blood of our heroes have been devoted to their attainment. They should be the creed of our political faith—the text of civil
instruction—the touchstone by which to try the services of those we
trust; and should we wander from them in moments of error or
alarm, let us hasten to retrace our steps and to regain the road which
alone leads to peace, liberty and safety.

I repair, then, fellow citizens, to the post you have assigned me.
With experience enough in subordinate offices to have seen the difficulties of this, the greatest of all, I have learned to expect that it will
rarely fall to the lot of imperfect man to retire from this station with
the reputation and the favor which bring him into it. Without preten-
sions to that high confidence reposed in our first and great revolutionary character, whose pre-eminent services had entitled him to the
first place in his country's love, and destined for him the fairest page
in the volume of faithful history, I ask so much confidence only as
may give firmness and effect to the legal administration of your
affairs. I shall often go wrong through defect of judgment. When
right, I shall often be thought wrong by those whose positions will
not command a view of the whole ground. I ask your indulgence for
my own errors, which will never be intentional; and your support
against the errors of others, who may condemn what they would not
if seen in all its parts. The approbation implied by your suffrage is a
consolation to me for the past; and my future solicitude will be to
retain the good opinion of those who have bestowed it in advance, to

conciliate that of others by doing them all the good in my power, and to be instrumental to the happiness and freedom of all.

Relying, then, on the patronage of your good will, I advance with obedience to the work, ready to retire from it whenever you become sensible how much better choice it is in your power to make. And may that Infinite Power which rules the destinies of the universe, lead our councils to what is best, and give them a favorable issue for our peace and prosperity.

b. JEFFERSON

*To Samuel Kercheval**

Sir,—I duly received your favor of June the 13th, with the copy of the letters on the calling a convention, on which you are pleased to ask my opinion. I have not been in the habit of mysterious reserve on any subject, nor of buttoning up my opinions within my own doublet. On the contrary, while in public service especially, I thought the public entitled to frankness, and intimately to know whom they employed. But I am now retired: I resign myself, as a passenger, with confidence to those at present at the helm, and ask but for rest, peace and good will. The question you propose, on equal representation, has become a party one, in which I wish to take no public share. Yet, if it be asked for your own satisfaction only, and not to be quoted before the public, I have no motive to withhold it, and the less from you, as it coincides with your own. At the birth of our republic, I committed that opinion to the world, in the draught of a constitution annexed to the *Notes on Virginia,* in which a provision was inserted for a representation permanently equal. The infancy of the subject at that moment, and our inexperience of self-government, occasioned gross departures in that draught from genuine republican canons. In truth, the abuses of monarchy had so much filled all the space of political contemplation, that we imagined everything republic which was not monarchy. We had not yet penetrated to the mother principle, that "governments are republican only in proportion as they embody the will of their people, and execute it." Hence, our first constitutions had really no leading principles in them. But experience and reflection

* *Writings of Thomas Jefferson,* Vol. VII, pp. 9–17.

have but more and more confirmed me in the particular importance
of the equal representation then proposed. On that point, then, I am
entirely in sentiment with your letters; and only lament that a copy-
right of your pamphlet prevents their appearance in the newspapers,
where alone they would be generally read, and produce general effect.
The present vacancy too, of other matter, would give them place in
every paper, and bring the question home to every man's conscience.

But inequality of representation in both Houses of our legislature,
is not the only republican heresy in this first essay of our revolutionary
patriots at forming a constitution. For let it be agreed that a government is republican in proportion as every member composing it has
his equal voice in the direction of its concerns (not indeed in person,
which would be impracticable beyond the limits of a city, or small
township, but) by representatives chosen by himself, and responsible
to him at short periods, and let us bring to the test of this canon every
branch of our constitution.

In the legislature, the House of Representatives is chosen by less
than half the people, and not at all in proportion to those who do
choose. The Senate are still more disproportionate, and for long terms
of irresponsibility. In the Executive, the Governor is entirely independent of the choice of the people, and of their control; his Council
equally so, and at best but a fifth wheel to a wagon. In the Judiciary,
the judges of the highest courts are dependent on none but themselves.

In England, where judges were named and removable at the will of
an hereditary executive, from which branch most misrule was feared,
and has flowed, it was a great point gained, by fixing them for life, to
make them independent of that executive. But in a government
founded on the public will, this principle operates in an opposite
direction, and against that will. There, too, they were still removable
on a concurrence of the executive and legislative branches. But we
have made them independent of the nation itself. They are irremov-
able, but by their own body, for any depravities of conduct, and even
by their own body for the imbecilities of dotage. The justice of the
inferior courts are self-chosen, are for life, and perpetuate their own
body in succession forever, so that a faction once possessing themselves of the bench of a county, can never be broken up, but hold
their county in chains, forever indissoluble. Yet these justices are the
real executive as well as judiciary, in all our minor and most ordinary
concerns. They tax us at will; fill the office of sheriff, the most important of all the executive officers of the county, name nearly all our

military leaders, which leaders, once named, are removable but by themselves. The juries, our judges of all fact, and of law when they choose it, are not selected by the people, nor amenable to them. They are chosen by an officer named by the court and executive. Chosen, did I say? Picked up by the sheriff from the loungings of the court yard, after everything respectable has retired from it. Where then is our republicanism to be found? Not in our constitution certainly, but merely in the spirit of our people. That would oblige even a despot to govern us republicanly. Owing to this spirit, and to nothing in the form of our constitution, all things have gone well. But this fact, so triumphantly misquoted by the enemies of reformation, is not the fruit of our constitution, but has prevailed in spite of it. Our functionaries have done well, because generally honest men. If any were not so, they feared to show it.

But it will be said, it is easier to find faults than to amend them. I do not think their amendment so difficult as is pretended. Only lay down true principles, and adhere to them inflexibly. Do not be frightened into their surrender by the alarms of the timid, or the croakings of wealth against the ascendency of the people. If experience be called for, appeal to that of our fifteen or twenty governments for forty years, and show me where the people have done half the mischief in these forty years, that a single despot would have done in a single year; or show half the riots and rebellions, the crimes and the punishments, which have taken place in any single nation, under kingly government, during the same period. The true foundation of republican government is the equal right of every citizen in his person and property, and in their management. Try by this, as a tally, every provision of our constitution, and see if it hangs directly on the will of the people. Reduce your legislature to a convenient number for full, but orderly discussion. Let every man who fights or pays, exercise his just and equal right in their election. Submit them to approbation or rejection at short intervals. Let the executive be chosen in the same way, and for the same term, by those whose agent he is to be; and leave no screen of a council behind which to skulk from responsibility. It has been thought that the people are not competent electors of judges *learned in the law*. But I do not know that this is true, and, if doubtful, we should follow principle. In this, as in many other elections, they would be guided by reputation, which would not err oftener, perhaps, than the present mode of appointment. In one State of the Union, at least, it has long been tried, and with the most satisfactory success. The judges of Connecticut have been chosen by the people every six months, for nearly two centuries, and I believe there has hardly ever been an instance of change; so powerful is the curb of incessant responsibility. If prejudice, however, derived from a monarchial institution, is still to prevail against the vital elective principle of our own, and if the existing example among ourselves of periodical election of judges by the people be still mistrusted, let us at least not adopt the evil, and reject the good, of the English precedent; let us retain amovability on the concurrence of the executive and legislative branches, and nomination by the executive alone. Nomination to office is an executive function. To give it to the legislature, as we do, is a violation of the principle of the separation of powers. It swerves the members from correctness, by temptations to intrigue for office themselves, and to a corrupt barter of votes; and destroys responsibility by dividing it among a multitude. By leaving nomination in its proper place, among executive functions, the principle of the distribution of power is preserved, and responsibility weighs with its heaviest force on a single head.

The organization of our county administrations may be thought more difficult. But follow principle, and the knot unties itself. Divide the counties into wards of such size as that every citizen can attend, when called cn, and act in person. Ascribe to them the government of their wards in all things relating to themselves exclusively. A justice, chosen by themselves, in each, a constable, a military company, a patrol, a school, the care of their own poor, their own portion of the public roads, the choice of one or more jurors to serve in some court, and the delivery within their own wards of their own votes for all elective officers of higher sphere, will relieve the county administration of nearly all its business, will have it better done, and by making every citizen an acting member of the government, and in the offices nearest and most interesting to him, will attach him by his strongest feelings to the independence of his country, and its republican constitution. The justices thus chosen by every ward, would constitute the county court, would do its judiciary business, direct roads and bridges, levy county and poor rates, and administer all the matters of common interest to the whole country. These wards, called townships in New England, are the vital principle of their governments, and have proved themselves the wisest invention ever devised by the wit of man for the perfect exercise of self-government, and for its preservation. We should thus marshal our government into, 1, the general federal republic, for all concerns foreign and federal; 2, that of the State, for what relates to our own citizens exclusively; 3, the county republics, for the duties and concerns of the county; and 4, the ward republics, for the small, and yet numerous and interesting concerns of the neighborhood; and in government, as well as in every other business of life, it is by division and subdivision of duties alone, that all matters, great and small, can be managed to perfection. And the whole is cemented by giving to every citizen, personally, a part in the administation of the public affairs.

The sum of these amendments is, 1, General Suffrage. 2, Equal representation in the legislature. 3, An executive chosen by the people. 4, Judges elective or amovable. 5, Justices, jurors, and sheriffs elective. 6, Ward divisions. And 7, Periodical amendments of the constitution.

I have thrown out these as loose heads of amendment, for consideration and correction; and their object is to secure self-government by the republicanism of our constitution, as well as by the spirit of the people; and to nourish and perpetuate that spirit. I am not among those who fear the people. They, and not the rich, are our dependence for continued freedom. And to preserve their independence, we must not let our rulers load us with perpetual debt. We must make our election between *economy and liberty,* or *profusion and servitude.* If we run into such debts, as that we must be taxed in our meat and in our drink, in our necessaries and our comforts, in our labors and our amusements, for our callings and our creeds, as the people of England are, our people, like them, must come to labor sixteen hours in the twenty-four, give the earnings of fifteen of these to the government for our debts and daily expenses; and the sixteenth being insufficient to afford us bread, we must live, as they now do, on oatmeal and potatoes; have no time to think, no means of calling the mismanagers to account; but be glad to obtain subsistence by hiring ourselves to rivet their chains on the necks of our fellow-sufferers. Our landholders, too, like theirs, retaining indeed the title and stewardship of estates called theirs, but held really in trust for the treasury, must wander, like theirs, in foreign countries, and be contented with penury, obscurity, exile, and the glory of the nation. This example reads to us the salutory lesson, that private fortunes are destroyed by public as well as by private extravagance. And this is the tendency of all human governments. A departure from principle in one instance becomes a precedent for a second; that second for a third; and so on, till the bulk of the society is reduced to be mere automations of misery, and to have no sensibilities left but for sinning and suffering. Then begins, indeed, the *bellum omnium in omnia,* which some philosophers observing to be so general in this world, have mistaken it for the natural, instead of the abusive state of man. And the fore horse of this frightful team is public debt. Taxation follows that, and in its train wretchedness and oppression.

Some men look at constitutions with sanctimonious reverence, and deem them like the arc of the covenant, too sacred to be touched. They ascribe to the men of the preceding age a wisdom more than human, and suppose what they did to be beyond amendment. I knew that age well; I belonged to it, and labored with it. It deserved well of its country. It was very like the present, but without the experience of the present; and forty years of experience in government is worth a century of book reading; and this they would say themselves, were they to rise from the dead. I am certainly not an advocate for frequent and untried changes in laws and constitutions. I think moderate imperfections had better be borne with; because, when once known, we accommodate ourselves to them, and find practical means of correcting their ill effects. But I know also, that laws and institutions must go hand in hand with the progress of the human mind. As that becomes more developed, more enlightened, as new discoveries are made, new truths disclosed, and manners and opinions change with the change of circumstances, institutions must advance also, and keep pace with the times. We might as well require a man to wear still the coat which fitted him when a boy, as civilized society to remain ever under the regimen of their barbarous ancestors. It is this preposterous idea which has lately deluged Europe in blood. Their monarchs, instead of wisely yielding to the gradual change of circumstances, of favoring progressive accommodation to progressive improvement, have clung to old abuses, entrenched themselves behind steady habits, and obliged their subjects to seek through blood and violence rash and ruinous innovations, which, had they been referred to the peaceful deliberations and collected wisdom of the nation, would have been put into acceptable and salutary forms. Let us follow no such examples, nor weakly believe that one generation is not as capable as another of taking care of itself, and of ordering its own affairs. Let us, as our sister States have done, avail ourselves of our reason and experience, to correct the crude essays of our first and unexperienced, although wise, virtuous, and well-meaning councils. And lastly, let us provide in our constitution for its revision at stated periods. What these periods should be, nature herself indicates. By the European tables of mortality, of the adults living at any one moment of time, a majority will be dead in about nineteen years. At the end of that period, then, a new majority is come into place; or, in other words, a new generation. Each generation is as independent as the one preceding, as that was of all which had gone before. It has then, like them, a right to choose for itself the form of government it believes most promotive of its own happiness; consequently, to accommodate to the circumstances in which it finds itself, that received from its predecessors; and it is for the peace and good of mankind that a solemn opportunity of doing this every nineteen or twenty years, should be provided by the constitution; so that it may be handed on, with periodical repairs, from generation to generation, to the end of time, if anything human can so long endure. It is now forty years since the constitution of Virginia was formed. The same tables inform us, that, within that period, two-thirds of the adults then living are now dead. Have then the remaining third, even if they had the wish, the right to hold in obedience to their will, and to laws heretofore made by them, the other two-thirds, who, with themselves, compose the present mass of adults? If they have not, who has? The dead? But the dead have no rights. They are nothing and nothing cannot own something. Where there is no substance, there can be no accident. This corporeal globe, and everything upon it, belong to its present corporeal inhabitants, during their generation. They alone have a right to direct what is the concern of themselves, alone, and to declare the law of that direction; and this declaration can only be made by their majority. That majority, then, has a right to depute representatives to a convention, and to make the constitution what they think will be the best for themselves. But how collect their voice? This is the real difficulty. If invited by private authority, or county or district meetings, these divisions are so large that few will attend; and their voice will be imperfectly, or falsely pronounced. Here, then, would be one of the advantages of the ward divisions I have proposed. The mayor of every ward, on a question like the present, would call his ward together, take the simple yea or nay of its members, convey these to the county court, who would hand on those of all its wards to the proper general authority; and the voice of the whole people would be thus fairly, fully, and peaceably expressed, discussed, and decided by the common reason of the society. If this avenue be shut to the call of sufferance, it will make itself heard through that of force, and we shall go on, as other nations are doing, in the endless circle of oppression, rebellion, reformation; and oppression, rebellion, reformation, again; and so on forever.

These, Sir, are my opinions of the governments we see among men, and of the principles by which alone we may prevent our own from falling into the same dreadful track. I have given them at greater length than your letter called for. But I cannot say things by halves; and I confide them to your honor, so to use them as to preserve me from the gridiron of the public papers. If you shall approve and enforce them, as you have done that of equal representation, they may do some good. If not, keep them to yourself as the effusions of withered age and useless time. I shall, with not the less truth, assure you of my great respect and consideration.

c. MADISON

The Control of Factions*

Among the numerous advantages promised by a well-constructed Union, none deserves to be more accurately developed than its tendency to break and control the violence of faction. The friend of popular governments never finds himself so much alarmed for their character and fate as when he contemplates their propensity to this dangerous vice. He will not fail, therefore, to set a due value on any plan which, without violating the principles to which he is attached, provides a proper cure for it. The instability, injustice, and confusion introduced into the public councils, have, in truth, been the mortal diseases under which popular governments have everywhere perished; as they continue to be the favorite and fruitful topics from which the adversaries to liberty derive their most specious declamations. The valuable improvements made by the American constitutions on the popular models, both ancient and modern, cannot certainly be too much admired; but it would be unwarrantable partiality, to contend that they have as effectually obviated the danger on this side, as was wished and expected. Complaints are everywhere heard from our most considerate and virtuous citizens, equally the friends of public and private faith, and of public and personal liberty, that our governments are

* From "Federalist No. 10," *The Federalist Papers.*

too unstable, that the public good is disregarded in the conflicts of rival parties, and that measures are too often decided, not according to the rules of justice and the rights of the minor party, but by the superior force of an interested and overbearing majority. However anxiously we may wish that these complaints had no foundation, the evidence of known facts will not permit us to deny that they are in some degree true. It will be found, indeed, on a candid review of our situation, that some of the distresses under which we labor have been erroneously charged on the operation of our governments; but it will be found, at the same time, that other causes will not alone account for many of our heaviest misfortunes; and, particularly, for that prevailing and increasing distrust of public engagements, and alarm for private rights, which are echoed from one end of the continent to the other. These must be chiefly, if not wholly, effects of the unsteadiness and injustice with which a factious spirit has tainted our public administrations.

By a faction, I understand a number of citizens, whether amounting to a majority or minority of the whole, who are united and actuated by some common impulse of passion, or of interest, adverse to the rights of other citizens, or to the permanent and aggregate interest of the community.

There are two methods of curing the mischiefs of faction: the one by removing its causes; the other by controlling its effects.

There are again two methods of removing the causes of faction: the one, by destroying the liberty which is essential to its existence; the other, by giving to every citizen the same opinions, the same passions, and the same interests.

It could never be more truly said than of the first remedy, that it was worse than the disease. Liberty is to faction what air is to fire, an aliment without which it instantly expires. But it could not be less folly to abolish liberty, which is essential to political life, because it nourishes faction, than it would be to wish the annihilation of air, which is essential to animal life, because it imparts to fire its destructive agency.

The second expedient is as impracticable as the first would be unwise. As long as the reason of man continues fallible, and he is at liberty to exercise it, different opinions will be formed. As long as the connection subsists between his reason and his self-love, his opinions and his passions will have a reciprocal influence on each other; and the former will be objects to which the latter will attach themselves.

The diversity in the faculties of men, from which the rights of property originate, is not less an insuperable obstacle to a uniformity of interests. The protection of these faculties is the first object of government. From the protection of different and unequal faculties of acquiring property the possession of different degrees and kinds of property immediately results; and from the influence of these on the sentiments and views of the respective proprietors, ensues a division of the society into different interests and parties.

The latent causes of faction are thus sown in the nature of man; and we see them everywhere brought into different degrees of activity, according to the different circumstances of civil society. A zeal for different opinions concerning religion, concerning government, and many other points, as well of speculation as of practice; an attachment to different leaders ambitiously contending for pre-eminence and power; or to persons of other descriptions whose fortunes have been interesting to the human passions, have, in turn, divided mankind into parties, inflamed them with mutual animosity, and rendered them much more disposed to vex and oppress each other than to co-operate for their common good. So strong is this propensity of mankind to fall into mutual animosities, that where no substantial occasion presents itself, the most frivolous and fanciful distinctions have been sufficient to kindle their unfriendly passions and excite their most violent conflicts. But the most common and durable source of factions has been the various and unequal distribution of property. Those who hold and those who are without property have ever formed distinct interests in society. Those who are creditors, and those who are debtors, fall under a like discrimination. A landed interest, a manufacturing interest, a mercantile interest, a moneyed interest, with many lesser interests, grow up of necessity in civilized nations, and divide them into different classes, actuated by different sentiments and views. The regulation of these various and interfering interests forms the principal task of modern legislation, and involves the spirit of party and faction in the necessary and ordinary operations of the government.

No man is allowed to be a judge in his own cause, because his interest would certainly bias his judgment, and, not improbably, corrupt his integrity. With equal, nay, with greater reason, a body of men are unfit to be both judges and parties at the same time; yet what are many of the most important acts of legislation but so many judicial determinations, not indeed concerning the rights of single persons, but concerning the rights of large bodies of citizens? And what are the different classes of legislators but advocates and parties to the causes which they determine? Is a law proposed concerning private debts? It is a question to which the creditors are parties on one side and the debtors on the other. Justice ought to hold the balance between them. Yet the parties are, and must be, themselves the judges; and the most numerous party, or, in other words, the most powerful faction must be expected to prevail. Shall domestic manufacturers be encouraged, and in what degree, by restrictions on foreign manufacturers? are questions which would be differently decided by the landed and the manufacturing classes, and probably by neither with a sole regard to justice and the public good. The apportionment of taxes on the various descriptions of property is an act which seems to require the most exact impartiality; yet there is, perhaps, no legislative act in which greater opportunity and temptation are given to a predominant party to trample on the rules of justice. Every shilling with which they overburden the inferior number is a shilling saved to their own pockets.

It is in vain to say that enlightened statesmen will be able to adjust these clashing interests, and render them all subservient to the public good. Enlightened statesmen will not always be at the helm. Nor, in many cases, can such an adjustment be made at all without taking into view indirect and remote considerations, which will rarely prevail over the immediate interest which one party may find in disregarding the rights of another or the good of the whole.

The inference to which we are brought is, that the *causes* of faction cannot be removed, and that relief is only to be sought in the means of controlling its *effects*.

If a faction consists of less than a majority, relief is supplied by the republican principle, which enables the majority to defeat its sinister views by regular vote. It may clog the administration, it may convulse the society; but it will be unable to execute and mask its violence under the forms of the Constitution. When a majority is included in a faction, the form of popular government, on the other hand, enables it to sacrifice to its ruling passion or interest both the public good and the right of other citizens. To secure the public good and private rights against the danger of such a faction, and at the same time to preserve the spirit and the form of popular government, is then the great object to which our inquiries are directed. Let me add that it is the great desideratum by which this form of government can be rescued from the opprobrium under which it has so long labored, and be recommended to the esteem and adoption of mankind.

By what means is this object attainable? Evidently by one of two only. Either the existence of the same passion or interest in a majority at the same time must be prevented, or the majority, having such co-existent passion or interest, must be rendered, by their number and local situation, unable to concert and carry into effect schemes of oppression. If the impulse and the opportunity be suffered to coincide, we well know that neither moral nor religious motives can be relied on as an adequate control. They are not found to be such on the injustice and violence of individuals, and lose the efficacy in proportion to the number combined together, that is, in proportion as their efficacy becomes needful.

From this view of the subject it may be concluded that a pure democracy, by which I mean a society consisting of a small number of citizens, who assemble and administer the government in person, can admit of no cure for the mischiefs of faction. A common passion or interest will, in almost every case, be felt by a majority of the whole; a communication and concert result from the form of government itself; and there is nothing to check the inducements to sacrifice the weaker party or an obnoxious individual. Hence it is that such democracies have ever been spectacles of turbulence and contention; have ever been found incompatible with personal security or the rights of property; and have in general been as short in their lives as they have been violent in their deaths. Theoretic politicians, who have patronized this species of government, have erroneously supposed that by reducing mankind to a perfect equality in their political rights, they would, at the same time, be perfectly equalized and assimilated in their possessions, their opinions, and their passions.

A republic, by which I mean a government in which the scheme of representation takes place, opens a different prospect, and promises the cure for which we are seeking. Let us examine the points in which it varies from pure democracy, and we shall comprehend both the nature of the cure and the efficacy which it must derive from the Union.

The two great points of difference between a democracy and a republic are: first, the delegation of the government, in the latter, to a small number of citizens elected by the rest; secondly, the greater number of citizens, and greater sphere of country, over which the latter may be extended.

The effect of the first difference is, on the one hand, to refine and enlarge the public views, by passing them through the medium of a chosen body of citizens, whose wisdom may best discern the true interest of their country, and whose patriotism and love of justice will be least likely to sacrifice it to temporary or partial considerations. Under such a regulation, it may well happen that the public voice, pronounced by the representatives of the people, will be more consonant to the public good than if pronounced by the people themselves, convened for the purpose. On the other hand, the effect may be inverted. Men of factious tempers, of local prejudices, or of sinister designs, may, by intrigue, by corruption, or by other means, first obtain the suffrages, and then betray the interests, of the people. The question resulting is, whether small or extensive republics are more favorable to the election of proper guardians of the public weal; and it is clearly decided in favor of the latter by two obvious considerations:

In the first place, it is to be remarked that, however small the republic may be, the representatives must be raised to a certain number, in order to guard against the cabals of a few; and that, however large it may be, they must be limited to a certain number, in order to guard against the confusion of a multitude. Hence, the number of representatives in the two cases not being in proportion to that of the two constituents, and being proportionally greater in the small republic, it follows that, if the proportion of fit characters be not less in the large than in the small republic, the former will present a greater option, and consequently a greater probability of a fit choice.

In the next place, as each representative will be chosen by a greater number of citizens in the large than in the small republic, it will be more difficult for unworthy candidates to practice with success the vicious arts by which elections are too often carried; and the suffrages of the people being more free, will be more likely to center in men who possess the most attractive merit and the most diffusive and established characters.

It must be confessed that in this, as in most other cases, there is a mean, on both sides of which inconveniences will be found to lie. By enlarging too much the number of electors, you render the representative too little acquainted with all their local circumstances and lesser interests; as by reducing it too much, you render him unduly attached to these, and too little fit to comprehend and pursue great and national objects. The federal Constitution forms a happy combination in this respect; the great and aggregate interests being referred to the national, the local and particular to the State legislatures.

The other point of difference is, the greater number of citizens and extent of territory which may be brought within the compass of republican than of democratic government; and it is this circumstance principally which renders factious combinations less to be dreaded in the former than in the latter. The smaller the society, the fewer probably will be the distinct parties and interests composing it; the fewer the distinct parties and interests the more frequently will a majority be found of the same party; and the smaller the number of individuals composing a majority, and the smaller the compass within which they are placed, the more easily will they concert and execute their plans of oppression. Extend the sphere and you take in a greater variety of parties and interests; you make it less probable that a majority of the whole will have a common motive to invade the rights of other citizens; or if such a common motive exists, it will be more difficult for all who feel it to discover their own strength, and to act in unison with each other. Besides other impediments, it may be remarked that, where there is a consciousness of unjust or dishonorable purposes, communication is always checked by distrust in proportion to the number whose concurrence is necessary.

Hence, it clearly appears, that the same advantage which a republic has over a democracy in controlling the effects of faction, is enjoyed by a large over a small republic—is enjoyed by the Union over the States composing it. Does the advantage consist in the substitution of representatives whose enlightened views and virtuous sentiments render them superior to local prejudices and to schemes of injustice? It will not be denied that the representation of the Union will be most likely to possess these requisite endowments. Does it consist in the greater security afforded by a greater variety of parties, against the event of any one party being able to outnumber and oppress the rest? In an equal degree does the increased variety of parties comprised within the Union increase this security? Does it, in fine, consist in the greater obstacles opposed to the concert and accomplishment of the secret wishes of an unjust and interested majority? Here, again, the extent of the Union gives it the most palpable advantage.

The influence of factious leaders may kindle a flame within their particular States, but will be unable to spread a general conflagration through the other States. A religious sect may degenerate into a political faction in a part of the Confederacy; but the variety of sects dispersed over the entire face of it must secure the national councils against any danger from that source. A rage for paper money, for an abolition of debts, for an equal division of property, or for any other improper or wicked project, will be less apt to pervade the whole body of the Union than a particular member of it; in the same proportion as such a malady is more likely to taint a particular county or district, than an entire State.

In the extent and proper structure of the Union, therefore, we behold a republican remedy for the diseases most incident to republican government. And according to the degree of pleasure and pride we feel in being republicans, ought to be our zeal in cherishing the spirit and supporting the character of Federalists.

d. MADISON

*Separation of Powers**

Having reviewed the general form of the proposed government and the general mass of power allotted to it, I proceed to examine the particular structure of this government, and the distribution of this mass of power among its constituent parts.

One of the principal objections inculcated by the more respectable adversaries to the Constitution, is its supposed violation of the political maxim, that the legislative, executive, and judiciary departments ought to be separate and distinct. In the structure of the federal government, no regard, it is said, seems to have been paid to this essential precaution in favor of liberty. The several departments of power are distributed and blended in such a manner as at once to destroy all symmetry and beauty of form, and to expose some of the essential parts of the edifice to the danger of being crushed by the disproportionate weight of other parts.

No political truth is certainly of greater intrinsic value, or is stamped with the authority of more enlightened patrons of liberty, than that on which the objection is founded. The accumulation of all powers, legislative, executive, and judiciary, in the same hands, whether of one, a few, or many, and whether hereditary, self-appointed, or elective, may justly be pronounced the very definition of tyranny. Were the federal Constitution, therefore, really chargeable with the accumulation of power, or with a mixture of powers, having

* From "Federalist No. 47," *The Federalist Papers.*

a dangerous tendency to such an accumulation, no further arguments would be necessary to inspire a universal reprobation of the system. I persuade myself, however, that it will be made apparent to every one, that the charge cannot be supported, and that the maxim on which it relies has been totally misconceived and misapplied. In order to form correct ideas on this important subject, it will be proper to investigate the sense in which the preservation of liberty requires that the three great departments of power should be separate and distinct.

The oracle who is always consulted and cited on this subject is the celebrated Montesquieu. If he be not the author of this invaluable precept in the science of politics, he has the merit at least of displaying and recommending it most effectually to the attention of mankind. Let us endeavour, in the first place, to ascertain his meaning on this point.

The British Constitution was to Montesquieu what Homer had been to the didactic writers on epic poetry. As the latter have considered the work of the immortal bard as the perfect model from which the principles and rules of the epic art were to be drawn, and by which all similar works were to be judged, so this great political critic appears to have viewed the Constitution of England as the standard, or to use his own expression, as the mirror of political liberty; and to have delivered, in the form of elementary truths, the several characteristic principles of that particular system. That we may be sure, then, not to mistake his meaning in this case, let us recur to the source from which the maxim was drawn.

On the slightest view of the British Constitution, we must perceive that the legislative, executive, and judiciary departments are by no means totally separate and distinct from each other. The executive magistrate forms an integral part of the legislative authority. He alone has the prerogative of making treaties with foreign sovereigns, which, when made, have, under certain limitations, the force of legislative acts. All the members of the judiciary department are appointed by him, can be removed by him on the address of the two Houses of Parliament, and form, when he pleases to consult them, one of his constitutional councils. One branch of the legislative department forms also a great constitutional council to the executive chief, as, on another hand, it is the sole depository of judicial power in cases of impeachment, and is invested with the supreme appellate jurisdiction in all other cases. The judges, again, are so far connected with the legislative department as often to attend and participate in its deliberations, though not admitted to a legislative vote.

From these facts, by which Montesquieu was guided, it may clearly be inferred that, in saying, "There can be no liberty where the legislative and executive powers are united in the same person, or body of magistrates," or, "if the power of judging be not separated from the legislative and executive powers," he did not mean that these departments ought to have no *partial agency* in, or no *control* over, the acts of each other. His meaning, as his own words import, and still more conclusively as illustrated by the example in his eye, can amount to no more than this, that where the *whole* power of one department is exercised by the same hands which possess the *whole* power of another department, the fundamental principles of a free constitution are subverted. This would have been the case in the constitution examined by him, if the King, who is the sole executive magistrate, had possessed also the complete legislative power, or the supreme administration of justice; or if the entire legislative body had possessed the supreme judiciary, or the supreme executive authority. This, however, is not among the vices of that constitution. The magistrate in whom the whole executive power resides cannot of himself make a law, though he can put a negative on every law; nor administer justice in person, though he has the appointment of those who do administer it. The judges can exercise no executive prerogative, though they are shoots from the executive stock; nor any legislative function, though they may be advised with by the legislative councils. The entire legislature can perform no judiciary act, though by the joint act of two of its branches the judges may be removed from their offices, and though one of its branches is possessed of the judicial power in the last resort. The entire legislature, again, can exercise no executive prerogative, though one of its branches constitutes the supreme executive magistracy, and another, on the impeachment of a third, can try and condemn all the subordinate officers in the executive department.

The reasons on which Montesquieu grounds his maxim are a further demonstration of his meaning. "When the legislative and executive powers are united in the same person or body," says he, "there can be no liberty, because apprehension may arise lest *the same* monarch or senate should *enact* tyrannical laws to *execute* them in a *tyrannical* manner." Again: "Were the power of judging joined with the legislative, the life and liberty of the subject would be exposed to arbitrary control, for *the judge* would then be *the legislator*. Were it joined to the executive power, *the judge* might behave with all the violence of *an oppressor*." Some of these reasons are more fully explained in the

other passages; but briefly stated as they are here, they sufficiently
establish the meaning which we have put on this celebrated maxim of
this celebrated author.

e. MADISON

Checks and Balances*

To what expedient, then, shall we finally resort for maintaining in
practice the necessary partition of power among the several departments, as laid down in the Constitution? The only answer that can be
given is, that as all these exterior provisions are found to be inadequate, the defect must be supplied, by so contriving the interior structure of the government as that its several constituent parts may, by
their mutual relations, be the means of keeping each other in their
proper places. Without presuming to undertake a full development on
this important idea, I will hazard a few general observations, which
may perhaps place it in a clearer light, and enable us to form a more
correct judgment of the principles and structure of the government
planned by the convention.

In order to lay a due foundation for the separate and distinct exercise of the different powers of government, which to a certain extent
is admitted on all hands to be essential to the preservation of liberty,
it is evident that each department should have a will of its own; one
consequently should be so constituted that the numbers of each should
have as little agency as possible in the appointment of the members of
the others. Were this principle rigorously adhered to, it would require
that all the appointments for the supreme executive, legislative, and
judiciary magistracies should be drawn from the same fountain of
authority, the people, through channels having no communication
whatever with one another. Perhaps such a plan of constructing the
several departments would be less difficult in practice than it may in
contemplation appear. Some difficulties, however, and some addi-
tional expense would attend the execution of it. Some deviations,
therefore, from the principle must be admitted. In the constitution of
the judiciary department in particular, it might be inexpedient to insist
rigorously on the principle: first, because peculiar qualifications being

* From "Federalist No. 51," *The Federalist Papers.*

essential in the members, the primary consideration ought to be to select that mode of choice which best secures these qualifications; secondly, because the permanent tenure by which the appointments are held in that department, must soon destroy all sense of dependence on the authority conferring them.

It is equally evident, that the members of each department should be as little dependent as possible on those of the others, for the emoluments annexed to their offices. Were the executive magistrate, or the judges not independent of the legislature in this particular, their independence in every other would be merely nominal.

But the great security against a gradual concentration of the several powers in the same department, consists in giving to those who administer each department the necessary constitutional means and personal motive to resist encroachments of the others. The provision for defence must in this, as in all other cases, be made commensurate to the danger of attack. Ambition must be made to counteract ambition. The interest of the man must be connected with the constitutional rights of the place. It may be a reflection on human nature, that such devices should be necessary to control the abuses of government, but what is government itself, but the greatest of all reflections on human nature? If men were angels, no government would be necessary. If angels were to govern men, neither external nor internal controls on government would be necessary. In framing a government which is to be administered by men over men, the great difficulty lies in this: you must first enable the government to control the governed; and in the next place oblige it to control itself. A dependence on the people is, no doubt, the primary control on the government; but experience has taught mankind the necessity of auxiliary precautions.

This policy of supplying, by opposite and rival interests, the defect of better motives, might be traced through the whole system of human affairs, private as well as public. We see it particularly displayed in all the subordinate distributions of power, where the constant aim is to divide and arrange the several offices in such a manner as that each may be a check on the other—that the private interest of every individual may be a sentinel over the public rights. These inventions of prudence cannot be less requisite in the distribution of the supreme powers of the State.

But it is not possible to give to each department an equal power of self-defence. In republican government, the legislative authority necessarily predominates. The remedy for this inconveniency is to divide the legislature into different branches; and to render them, by different modes of election and different principles of action, as little connected with each other as the nature of their common functions and their common dependence on the society will admit. It may even be necessary to guard against dangerous encroachments by still further precautions. As the weight of the legislative authority requires that it should be thus divided, the weakness of the executive may require, on the other hand, that it should be fortified. An absolute negative on the legislature appears, at first view, to be the natural defence with which the executive magistrate should be armed. But perhaps it would be neither altogether safe nor alone sufficient. On ordinary occasions it might not be exerted with the requisite firmness, and on extraordinary occasions it might be perfidiously abused. May not this defect of an absolute negative be supplied by some qualified connection between this weaker department and the weaker branch of the stronger department, by which the latter may be led to support the constitutional rights of the former, without being too much detached from the rights of its own department?

If the principles on which these observations are founded be just, as I persuade myself they are, and they be applied as a criterion to the several State constitutions, and to the federal Constitution, it will be found that if the latter does not perfectly correspond with them, the former are infinitely less able to bear such a test.

There are, moreover, two considerations particularly applicable to the federal system of America, which place that system in a very interesting point of view.

First. In a single republic, all the power surrendered by the people is submitted to the administration of a single government; and the usurpations are guarded against by a division of the government into distinct and separate departments. In the compound republic of America, the power surrendered by the people is first divided between two distinct governments, and then the portion allotted to each subdivided among distinct and separate departments. Hence a double security arises to the rights of the people. The different governments will control each other, at the same time that each will be controlled by itself.

Second. It is of great importance in a republic not only to guard the society against the oppression of its rulers, but to guard one part of the society against the injustice of the other part. Different interests necessarily exist in different classes of citizens. If a majority be united by a common interest, the rights of the minority will be insecure. There are but two methods of providing against this evil; the one by creating a will in the community independent of the majority —that is, of the society itself; the other, by comprehending in the society so many separate descriptions of citizens as will render an unjust combination of a majority of the whole very improbable, if not impracticable. The first method prevails in all governments possessing an hereditary or self-appointed authority. This, at best, is but a precarious security; because a power independent of the society may as well espouse the unjust views of the major, as the rightful interests of the minor party, and may possibly be turned against both parties. The second method will be exemplified in the federal republic of the United States. Whilst all authority in it will be derived from and dependent on the society, the society itself will be broken into so many parts, interests and classes of citizens, that the rights of individuals, or of the minority, will be in little danger from interested combinations of the majority. In a free government the security for civil rights must be the same as that for religious rights. It consists in the one case in the multiplicity of interests, and in the other in the multiplicity of sects. The degree of security in both cases will depend on the number of interests and sects; and this may be presumed to depend on the extent of country and number of people comprehended under the same government. This view of the subject must particularly recommend a proper federal system to all the sincere and considerate friends of republican government, since it shows that in exact proportions as the territory of the Union may be formed into more circumscribed Confederacies, or States, oppressive combinations of a majority will be facilitated; the best security, under the republican forms, for the rights of every class of citizens, will be diminished; and consequently the stability and independence of some member of the government, the only other security, must be proportionally increased. Justice is the end of government. It is the end of civil society. It ever has been and ever will be pursued until it be obtained, or until liberty be lost in the pursuit. In a society under the forms of which the stronger faction can readily unite and oppress the weaker, anarchy may as truly be said to reign as in a state of nature, where the weaker individual is not secured against the violence of the stronger; and as, in the latter state, even the stronger individuals are prompted, by the uncertainty of the condition, to submit to a government which may protect the weak as well as themselves; so, in the former state, will the more powerful factions or parties be gradually induced, by a like motive, to wish for a government which will protect all parties, the weaker as well as the more powerful. It can be little doubted that if the State of Rhode Island was separated from the Confederacy and left to itself, the insecurity of rights under the popular form of government within such narrow limits would be displayed by such reiterated oppressions of factious majorities that some power altogether independent of the people would soon be called for by the voice of the very factions whose misrule had proved the necessity of it. In the extended republic of the United States, and among the great variety of interests, parties, and sects which it embraces, a coalition of a majority of the whole society could seldom take place on any other principles than those of justice and the general good; whilst there being thus less danger to a minor from the will of a major party, there must be less pretext, also, to provide for the security of the former, by introducing into the government a will not dependent on the latter, or, in other words, a will independent of the society itself. It is no less certain than it is important, notwithstanding the contrary opinions which have been entertained, that the larger the society, provided it lie within a practical sphere, the more duly capable it will be of self-government. And happily for the *republican cause,* the practicable sphere may be carried to a very great extent, by a judicious modification and a mixture of the *federal principle.*

f. TOCQUEVILLE

*The Tyranny of the Majority**

The very essence of democratic government consists in the absolute sovereignty of the majority; for there is nothing in democratic States which is capable of resisting it. Most of the American Constitutions have sought to increase this natural strength of the majority by artificial means.

The legislature is, of all political institutions, the one which is most

* From "Unlimited Power of the Majority in the United States, and Its Consequences," from Alexis de Tocqueville, *Democracy in America,* trans. by Henry Reeve, Henry Steele Commager. ed. (New York: Oxford University Press, 1947), pp. 156–69. Used by permission.

easily swayed by the wishes of the majority. The Americans determined that the members of this legislature should be elected by the people immediately, and for a very brief term, in order to subject them, not only to the general convictions, but even to the daily passions, of their constituents. The members of both Houses are taken from the same class in society, and are nominated in the same manner; so that the modifications of the legislative bodies are almost as rapid and quite as irresistible as those of a single assembly. It is to a legislature thus constituted that almost all the authority of the government has been entrusted.

But while the law increased the strength of those authorities which of themselves were strong, it enfeebled more and more those which were naturally weak. It deprived the representatives of the executive of all stability and independence, and by subjecting them completely to the caprices of the legislature, it robbed them of the slender influence which the nature of a democratic government might have allowed them to retain. In several States the judicial power was also submitted to the elective discretion of the majority, and in all of them its existence was made to depend on the pleasure of the legislative authority, since the representatives were empowered annually to regulate the stipend of the judges.

Custom, however, has done even more than law. A proceeding which will in the end set all the guarantees of representative government at naught is becoming more and more general in the United States; it frequently happens that the electors, who choose a delegate, point out a certain line of conduct to him, and impose upon him a certain number of positive obligations which he is pledged to fulfil. With the exception of the tumult, this comes to the same thing as if the majority of the populace held its deliberations in the market place.

Several other circumstances concur in rendering the power of the majority in America not only preponderant, but irresistible. The moral authority of the majority is partly based upon the notion that there is more intelligence and more wisdom in a great number of men collected together than in a single individual, and that the number of legislators is more important than their quality. The theory of equality is, in fact, applied to the intellect of man; and human pride is thus assailed in its last retreat by a doctrine which the minority hesitate to admit, and in which they very slowly concur. Like all other powers, and perhaps more than all other powers, the authority of the many requires the sanction of time; at first it enforces obedience by constraint, but its laws are not respected until they have long been maintained.

The right of governing society, which the majority supposes itself to derive from its superior intelligence, was introduced into the United States by the first settlers, and this idea, which would be sufficient of itself to create a free nation, has now been amalgamated with the manners of the people and the minor incidents of social intercourse.

The French, under the old monarchy, held it for a maxim (which is still a fundamental principle of the English Constitution) that the king could do no wrong; and if he did do wrong, the blame was imputed to his advisers. This notion was highly favorable to habits of obedience, and it enabled the subject to complain of the law without ceasing to love and honor the lawgiver. The Americans entertain the same opinion with respect to the majority.

The moral power of the majority is founded upon yet another principle, which is, that the interests of the many are to be preferred to those of the few. It readily will be perceived that the respect here professed for the rights of the majority must naturally increase or diminish according to the state of parties. When a nation is divided into several irreconcilable factions, the privilege of the majority is often overlooked, because it is intolerable to comply with its demands.

If there existed in America a class of citizens whom the legislating majority sought to deprive of exclusive privileges which they had possessed for ages, and to bring down from an elevated station to the level of the ranks of the multitude, it is probable that the minority would be less ready to comply with its laws. But as the United States were colonized by men holding equal rank among themselves, there is as yet no natural or permanent source of dissension between the interests of its different inhabitants.

There are certain communities in which the persons who constitute the minority can never hope to draw over the majority to their side, because they must then give up the very point which is at issue between them. Thus, an aristocracy can never become a majority while it retains its exclusive privileges, and it cannot cede its privileges without ceasing to be an aristocracy.

In the United States political questions cannot be taken up in so general and absolute a manner, and all parties are willing to recognize the rights of the majority, because they all hope to turn those rights to their own advantage at some future time. The majority therefore in that country exercises a prodigious actual authority, and a moral influence which is scarcely less preponderant; no obstacles exist which can impede or so much as retard its progress, or which can induce it to heed the complaints of those whom it crushes upon its path. This state of things is fatal in itself and dangerous for the future.

I have already spoken of the natural defects of democratic institutions, and they all of them increase in the exact ratio of the power of the majority. To begin with the most evident: the mutability of the laws is an evil inherent in democratic government, because it is natural to democracies to raise men to power in very rapid succession. But this evil is more or less sensible in proportion to the authority and the means of action which the legislature possesses.

In America the authority exercised by the legislative bodies is supreme, nothing prevents them from accomplishing their wishes with celerity, and with irresistible power, while they are supplied by new representatives every year. That is to say, the circumstances which contribute most powerfully to democratic instability, and which admit of the free application of caprice to every object in the State, are here in full operation. In conformity with this principle, America is, at the present day, the country in the world where laws last the shortest time. Almost all the American constitutions have been amended within the course of thirty years; there is therefore, not a single American State which has not modified the principles of its legislation in that lapse of time. As for the laws themselves, a single glance upon the archives of the different States of the Union suffices to convince one that in America the activity of the legislator never slackens. Not that the American democracy is naturally less stable than any other, but that it is allowed to follow its capricious propensities in the formation of the laws.

The omnipotence of the majority and the rapid as well as absolute manner in which its decisions are executed in the United States has not only the effect of rendering the law unstable, but it exercises the same influence upon the execution of the law and the conduct of the public administration. As the majority is the only power which it is important to court, all its projects are taken up with the greatest ardor, but no sooner is its attention distracted than all this ardor ceases; while in the free States of Europe the administration is at once independent and secure, so that the projects of the legislature are put into execution, although its immediate attention may be directed to other objects.

In America certain ameliorations are undertaken with much more

zeal and activity than elsewhere; in Europe the same ends are promoted by much less effort, more continuously applied.

Some years ago several pious individuals undertook to ameliorate
the condition of the prisons. The public was excited by the statements
which they put forward, and the regeneration of criminals became a
very popular undertaking. New prisons were built, and for the first
time the idea of reforming as well as of punishing the delinquent
formed a part of prison discipline. But this happy alteration, in which
the public had taken so hearty an interest, and which the exertions of
the citizens had irresistibly accelerated, could not be completed in a
moment. While the new penitentiaries were being erected (and it was
the pleasure of the majority that they should be terminated with all
possible celerity), the old prisons existed, which still contained a great
number of offenders. These jails became more unwholesome and more
corrupt in proportion as the new establishments were beautified and
improved, forming a contrast which may readily be understood. The
majority was so eagerly employed in founding the new prisons that
those which already existed were forgotten; and as the general attention was diverted to a novel object, the care which hitherto had been
bestowed upon the others ceased. The salutary regulations of discipline were first relaxed, and afterward broken; so that in the immediate neighborhood of a prison which bore witness to the mild and
enlightened spirit of our time, dungeons might be met with which
reminded the visitor of the barbarity of the Middle Ages.

I hold it to be an impious and an execrable maxim that politically
speaking, a people has a right to do whatsoever it pleases, and yet I
have asserted that all authority originates in the will of the majority.
Am I, then, in contradiction with myself?

A general law—which bears the name of Justice—has been made
and sanctioned, not only by a majority of this or that people, but by
a majority of mankind. The rights of every people are consequently
confined within the limits of what is just. A nation may be considered
in the light of a jury which is empowered to represent society at large,
and to apply the great and general law of justice. Ought such a jury
which represents society, to have more power than the society in
which the law it applies originate?

When I refuse to obey an unjust law, I do not contest the right
which the majority has of commanding, but I simply appeal from the
sovereignty of the people to the sovereignty of mankind. It has been
asserted that a people can never entirely outstep the boundaries of

justice and of reason in those affairs which are more peculiarly its own, and that consequently full power may fearlessly be given to the majority by which it is represented. But this language is that of a slave.

A majority taken collectively may be regarded as a being whose opinions, and most frequently whose interests are opposed to those of another being, which is styled a minority. If it be admitted that a man, possessing absolute power, may misuse that power by wronging his adversaries, why should a majority not be liable to the same reproach? Men are not apt to change their characters by agglomeration; nor does their patience in the presence of obstacles increase with the consciousness of their strength. And for these reasons I can never willingly invest any number of my fellow creatures with that unlimited authority which I should refuse to any one of them.

I do not think that it is possible to combine several principles in the same government, so as at the same time to maintain freedom, and really to oppose them to one another. The form of government which is usually termed mixed has always appeared to me to be a mere chimera. Accurately speaking, there is no such thing as a mixed government (with the meaning usually given to that word), because in all communities some one principle of action may be discovered which preponderates over the others.

I am of the opinion that some one social power must always be made to predominate over the others; but I think that liberty is endangered when this power is checked by no obstacles which may retard its course, and force it to moderate its own vehemence.

Unlimited power is in itself a bad and dangerous thing; human beings are not competent to exercise it with discretion, and God alone can be omnipotent, because his wisdom and his justice are always equal to his power. But no power upon earth is so worthy of honor for itself, or of reverential obedience to the rights which it represents, that I would consent to admit its uncontrolled and all-predominant authority. When I see that the right and the means of absolute command are conferred on a people or upon a king, upon an artistocracy or a democracy, a monarchy or a republic, I recognize the germ of tyranny, and I journey onward to a land of more hopeful institutions.

In my opinion the main evil of the present democratic institutions of the United States does not arise, as is often asserted in Europe, from their weakness, but from their overpowering strength; and I am not so much alarmed at the excessive liberty which reigns in that country as at the very inadequate securities which exist against tyranny.

When an individual or a party is wronged in the United States, to whom can he apply for redress? If to public opinion, public opinion constitutes the majority; if to the legislature, it represents the majority, and implicitly obeys its injunctions; if to the executive power, it is appointed by the majority, and remains a passive tool in its hands; the public troops consist of the majority under arms; the jury is the majority invested with the right of hearing judicial cases; and in certain States even the judges are elected by the majority. However iniquitous or absurd the evil of which you complain may be, you must submit to it as well as you can.

If, on the other hand, a legislative power could be so constituted as to represent the majority without necessarily being the slave of its passions; an executive, so as to retain a certain degree of uncontrolled authority; and a judiciary, so as to remain independent of the two other powers; a government would be formed which would still be democratic without incurring any risk of tyrannical abuse.

I do not say that tyrannical abuses frequently occur in America at the present day, but I maintain that no sure barrier is established against them, and that the causes which mitigate the government are to be found in the circumstances and the manners of the country more than in its laws.

A distinction must be drawn between tyranny and arbitrary power. Tyranny may be exercised by means of the law, and in that case it is not arbitrary; arbitrary power may be exercised for the good of the community at large, in which case it is not tyrannical. Tyranny usually employs arbitrary means, but, if necessary, it can rule without them.

In the United States the unbounded power of the majority, which is favorable to the legal despotism of the legislature, is likewise favorable to the arbitrary authority of the magistrate. The majority has an entire control over the law when it is made and when it is executed; and as it possesses an equal authority over those who are in power and the community at large, it considers public officers as its passive agents, and readily confides the task of serving its designs to their vigilance. The details of their office and the privileges which they are to enjoy are rarely defined beforehand; but the majority treats them as a master does his servants when they are always at work in his sight, and he has the power of directing or reprimanding them at every instant.

In general, the American functionaries are far more independent than the French civil officers within the sphere which is prescribed to them. Sometimes, even, they are allowed by the popular authority to exceed those bounds; and as they are protected by the opinion, and backed by the co-operation, of the majority, they venture upon such manifestations of their power as astonish a European. By this means habits are formed in the heart of a free country which may some day prove fatal to its liberties.

It is in the examination of the display of public opinion in the United States that we clearly perceive how far the power of the majority surpasses all the powers with which we are acquainted in Europe. Intellectual principles exercise an influence which is so invisible, and often so inappreciable, that they baffle the toils of oppression. At the present time the most absolute monarchs in Europe are unable to prevent certain notions, which are opposed to their authority, from circulating in secret throughout their dominions, and even in their courts. Such is not the case in America; as long as the majority is still undecided, discussion is carried on; but as soon as its decision is irrevocably pronounced, a submissive silence is observed, and the friends, as well as the opponents, of the measure unite in assenting to its propriety. The reason of this is perfectly clear: no monarch is so absolute as to combine all the powers of society in his own hands, and to conquer all opposition with the energy of a majority which is invested with the right of making and of executing the laws.

The authority of a king is purely physical, and it controls the actions of the subject without subduing his private will; but the majority possesses a power which is physical and moral at the same time; it acts upon the will as well as upon the actions of men, and it represses not only all contest, but all controversy.

I know no country in which there is so little true independence of mind and freedom of discussion as in America. In any constitutional state in Europe every sort of religious and political theory may be advocated and propagated abroad; for there is no country in Europe so subdued by any single authority as not to contain citizens who are ready to protect the man who raises his voice in the cause of truth from the consequences of his hardihood. If he is unfortunate enough to live under an absolute government, the people is upon his side; if he inhabits a free country, he may find a shelter behind the authority of the throne, if he requires one. The aristocratic part of society

supports him in some countries, and the democracy in others. But in a
nation where democratic institutions exist, organized like those of the
United States, there is but one sole authority, one single element of
strength and of success, with nothing beyond it.

In America, the minority raises very formidable barriers to the
liberty of opinion: within these barriers an author may write whatever
he pleases, but he will repent it if he ever step beyond them. Not that
he is exposed to the terrors of an *auto-da-fé*, but he is tormented by
the slights and persecution of daily obloquy. His political career is
closed forever, since he has offended the only authority which is able
to promote his success. Every sort of compensation, even that of cele-
brity, is refused to him. Before he published his opinions he imagined
that he held them in common with many others; but no sooner has he
declared them openly than he is loudly censured by his overbearing
opponents, while those who think like him, without having the courage
to speak, abandon him in silence. He yields at length, oppressed by
the daily efforts he has been making, and he subsides into silence, as
if he was tormented by remorse for having spoken the truth.

Fetters and headsmen were the coarse instruments which tyranny
formerly employed, but the civilization of our age has refined the arts
of despotism, which seemed, however, to have been sufficiently perfected before. The excesses of monarchical power had devised a
variety of physical means of oppression: the democratic republics of
the present day have rendered it as entirely an affair of the mind as
that will which it is intended to coerce. Under the absolute sway of
an individual despot the body was attacked in order to subdue the
soul, and the soul escaped the blows which were directed against it
and rose superior to the attempt; but such is not the course adopted
by tyranny in democratic republics; there the body is left free, and
the soul is enslaved. The sovereign can no longer say, "You shall
think as I do on pain of death," but he says, "You are free to think
differently from me, and to retain your life, your property, and all that
you possess; but if such be your determination, you are henceforth an
alien among your people. You may retain your civil rights, but they
will be useless to you, for you will never be chosen by your fellow
citizens if you solicit their suffrage, and they will affect to scorn you
if you solicit their esteem. You will remain among men, but you will
be deprived of the rights of mankind. Your fellow creatures will shun
you like an impure being, and those who are most persuaded of your
innocence will abandon you too, lest they should be shunned in their

turn. Go in peace! I have given you your life, but it is existence incomparably worse than death."

Monarchial institutions have thrown an odium upon despotism; let us beware lest democratic republics should restore oppression, and should render it less odious and less degrading in the eyes of the many by making it still more onerous to the few. . . .

The tendencies to which I have just alluded are as yet very slightly perceptible in political society, but they already begin to exercise an unfavorable influence upon the national character of the Americans. I am inclined to attribute the singular paucity of distinguished political characters to the ever-increasing activity of the despotism of the majority in the United States. When the American Revolution broke out they arose in great numbers, for public opinion then served not to tyrannize over, but to direct the exertions of individuals. Those celebrated men took a full part in the general agitation of mind common at that period, and they attained a high degree of personal fame, which was reflected back upon the nation, but which was by no means borrowed from it. . . .

In free countries, where everyone is more or less called upon to give his opinion in the affairs of state; in democratic republics, where public life is incessantly commingled with domestic affairs, where the sovereign authority is accessible on every side, and where its attention can almost always be attracted by vociferation, more persons are to be met with who speculate upon its foibles and live at the cost of its passions than in absolute monarchies. Not because men are naturally worse in these States than elsewhere, but the temptation is stronger, and of easier access at the same time. The result is a far more extensive debasement of the characters of citizens.

Democratic republics extend the practice of currying favor with the many, and they introduce it into a greater number of classes at once: this is one of the most serious reproaches that can be addressed to them. In democratic States organized on the principles of the American republics, this is more especially the case, where the authority of the majority is so absolute and so irresistible that a man must give up his rights as a citizen, and almost abjure his quality as a human being, if he intends to stray from the track which it lays down.

In that immense crowd which throngs the avenues to power in the United States I found very few men who displayed any of that manly candor and that masculine independence of opinion which frequently distinguished the Americans in former times, and which constitutes

the leading feature in distinguished characters, wheresoever they may
be found. It seems, at first sight, as if all the minds of the Americans
were formed upon one model, so accurately do they correspond in
their manner of judging. A stranger does, indeed, sometimes meet
with Americans who dissent from these rigorous formularies; with
men who deplore the defects of the laws, the mutability and the
ignorance of democracy; who even go so far as to observe the evil
tendencies which impair the national character, and to point out such
remedies as it might be possible to apply; but no one is there to hear
these things besides yourself, and you, to whom these secret reflections
are confided, are a stranger and a bird of passage. They are very ready
to communicate truths which are useless to you, but they continue to
hold a different language in public.

Despotism debases the oppressed much more than the oppressor: in
absolute monarchies the king has often great virtues, but the courtiers
are invariably servile. It is true that the American courtiers do not say
"Sire," or "Your Majesty"—a distinction without a difference. They
are forever talking of the natural intelligence of the populace they
serve; they do not debate the question as to which of the virtues of
their master is pre-eminently worthy of admiration, for they assure
him that he possesses all the virtues under heaven without having
acquired them, or without caring to acquire them; they do not give
him their daughters and their wives to be raised at his pleasure to the
rank of his concubines, but by sacrificing their opinions, they prosti-
tute themselves. Moralists and philosophers in America are not
obliged to conceal their opinions under the veil of allegory; but, before they venture upon a harsh truth, they say: "We are aware that
the people which we are addressing is too superior to all the weaknesses of human nature to lose the command of its temper for an
instant; and we should not hold this language if we were not speaking
to men whom their virtues and their intelligence render more worthy
of freedom than all the rest of the world." It would have been impossible for the sycophants of Louis XIV to flatter more dexterously. For
my part, I am persuaded that in all governments, whatever their
nature may be, servility will cower to force, and adulation will cling
to power. The only means of preventing men from degrading themselves is to invest no one with that unlimited authority which is the
surest method of debasing them.

Governments usually fall a sacrifice to impotence or to tyranny. In
the former case their power escapes from them; it is wrested from

their grasp in the latter. Many observers who have witnessed the anarchy of democratic States, have imagined that the government of those States was naturally weak and impotent. The truth is that when once hostilities are begun between parties, the government loses its control over society. But I do not think that a democratic power is naturally without force or without resources: say, rather, that it is almost always by the abuse of its force and the misemployment of its resources that a democratic government fails. Anarchy is almost always produced by its tyranny or its mistakes, but not by its want of strength.

It is important not to confound stability with force, or the greatness of a thing with its duration. In democratic republics, the power which directs society is not stable; for it often changes hands and assumes a new direction. But whichever way it turns, its force is almost irresistible. The governments of the American republics appear to me to be as much centralized as those of the absolute monarchies of Europe, and more energetic than they are. I do not, therefore, imagine that they will perish from weakness.

If ever the free institutions of America are destroyed, that event may be attributed to the unlimited authority of the majority, which may at some future time urge the minorities to desperation, and oblige them to have recourse to physical force. Anarchy will then be the result, but it will have been brought about by despotism. . . .

SUGGESTIONS FOR FURTHER READING

Aristotle. *Politics,* translated by Benjamin Jowett (New York: Modern Library, 1943). This famous classic contains much wisdom and insight that continues to be of relevant value to the problem of defining the nature of politics and political rule. Of particular significance, as a focus upon the problem of legitimacy, is Aristotle's analysis of the question of conflicting claims to power (Book III, Chapters 11, 12, 13).

Lipson, Leslie. *The Great Issues of Politics,* 3rd ed. (Englewood Cliffs, N.J.: Prentice-Hall, 1965). This book provides an excellent introduction to basic concepts and principles of political science: the origins of the state, the nature of power and authority, rival conceptions of political rule. Chapter 8, "The Sources of Authority," is of special interest as an analysis of different concepts of legitimacy associated with both authoritarian and democratic traditions of political rule.

Merriam, Charles. *Political Power* (New York: Collier Books, 1964). This is a pioneer work in modern scientific approaches to the analysis of political power. Chapter 4, "The Credenda and Miranda of Power," is of particular value as an analysis of the different forms of justification of political power in the history of Western political thought.

Dahl, Robert A. *Modern Political Analysis* (Englewood Cliffs, N.J.: Prentice-Hall, 1963). A convenient, concise analysis of basic concepts in political science, bringing to bear the fruits of recent empirical and theoretical studies. Of special value is his analysis of the dynamics of political influence, the acquisition of legitimacy and the role of ideology in the justification of leadership.

Friedrich, Carl. *Man and His Government* (New York: McGraw Hill, 1963). A comprehensive survey of modern political experience combining a searching philosophical insight with a sound grasp of modern empirical studies. Of particular significance are the chapters on "Rule and Rulership" and "Legitimacy and Political Obligations."

Weber, Max. *Theory of Social and Economic Organization* (New York: Oxford University Press, 1947; New York: Free Press, 1957). This is a famous classic in sociology which contains an analysis of the concept of legitimacy that has had wide influence upon political science.

Commager, Henry Steele. *Majority Rule and Minority Rights* (Gloucester, Mass.: Peter Smith, 1950). A lucid, penetrating analysis of a perennial problem in American political thought. Commager endeavors to show that the Jeffersonian concept of majority rule provides the best ideological basis for resolving the conflicting claims of liberty and authority.

MacIver, R. M. *The Web of Government,* rev. ed. (New York: Macmillan, 1965). An excellent analysis of the origins of government, the nature of political authority, and the grounds of legitimacy.